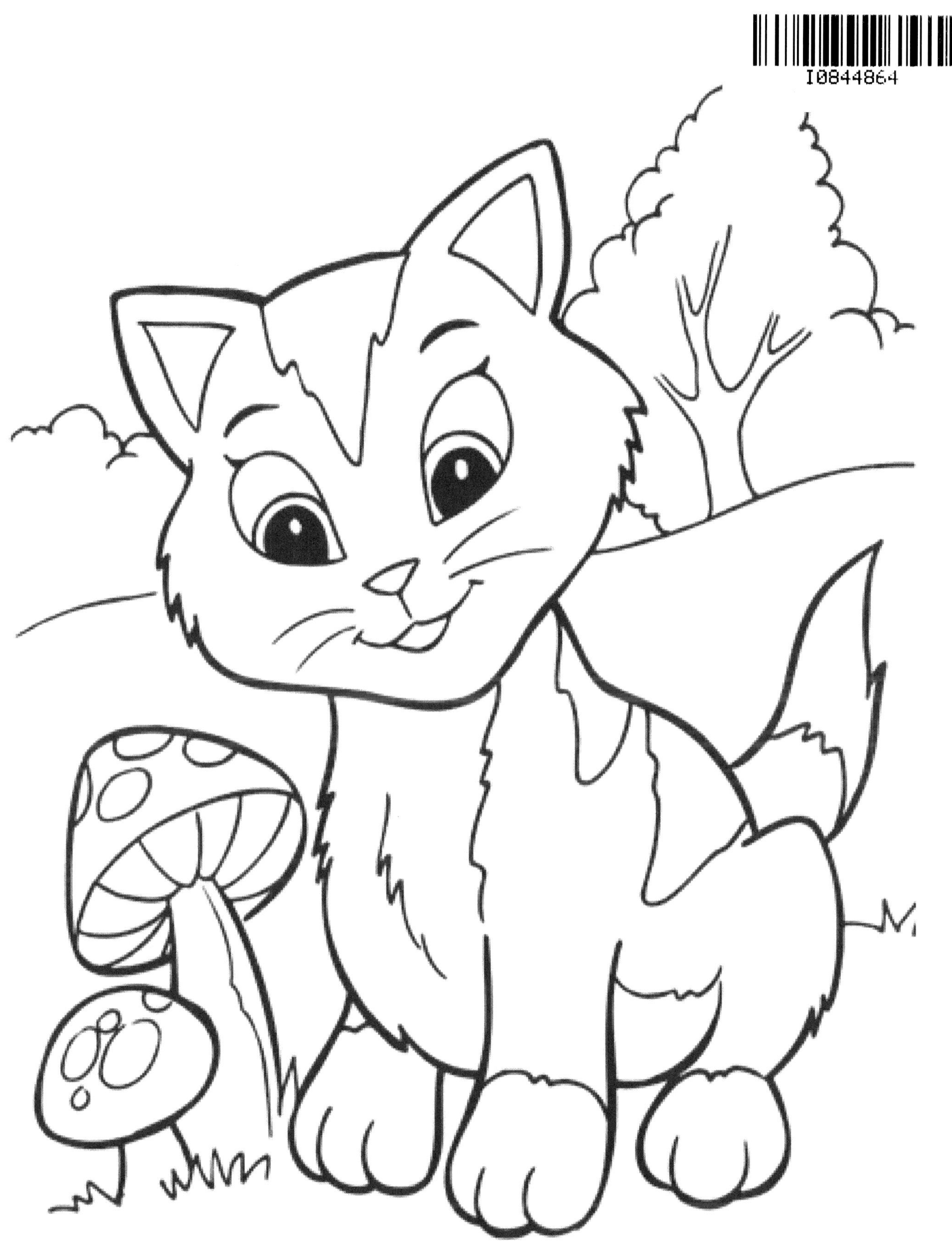

I0844864

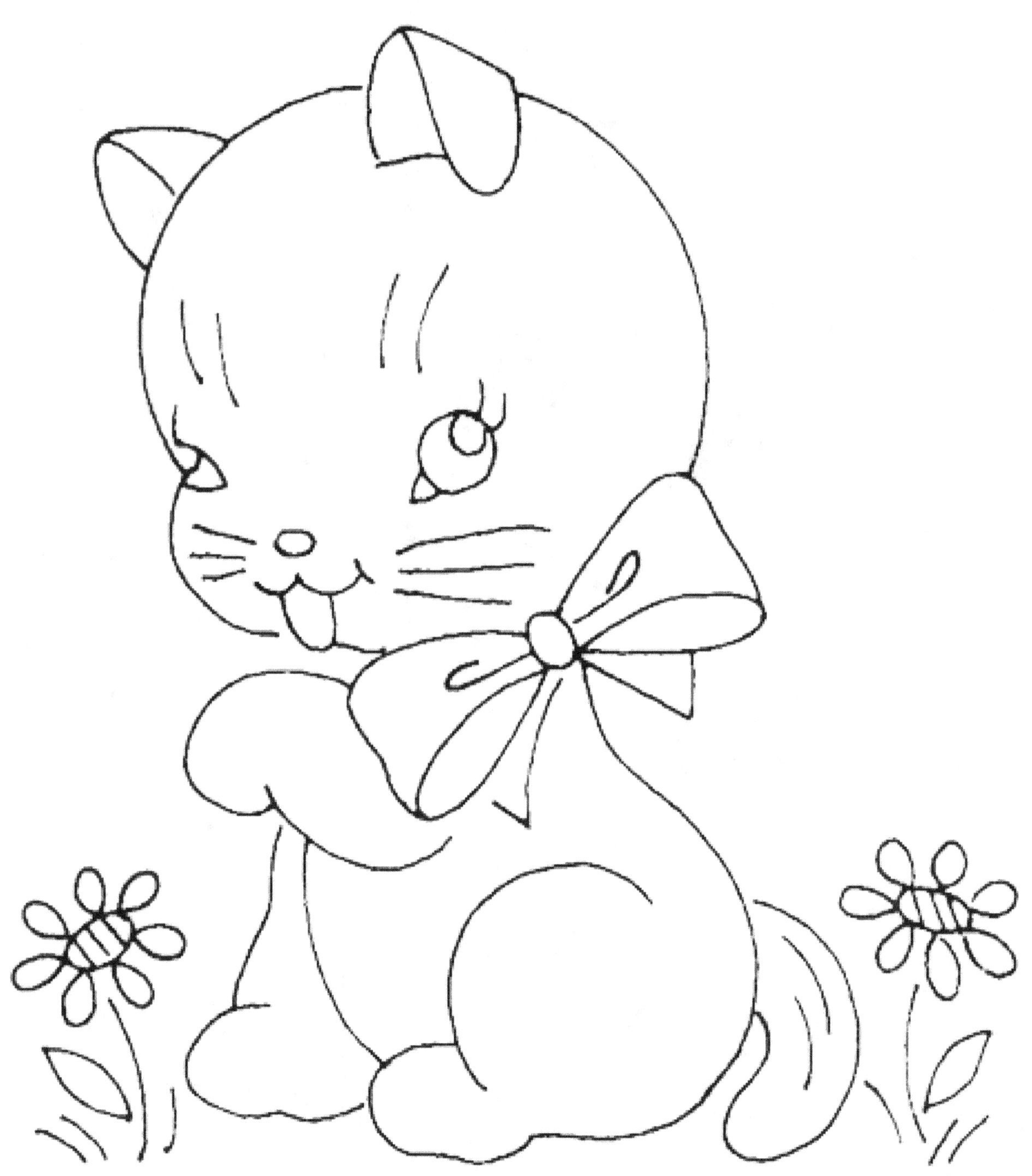

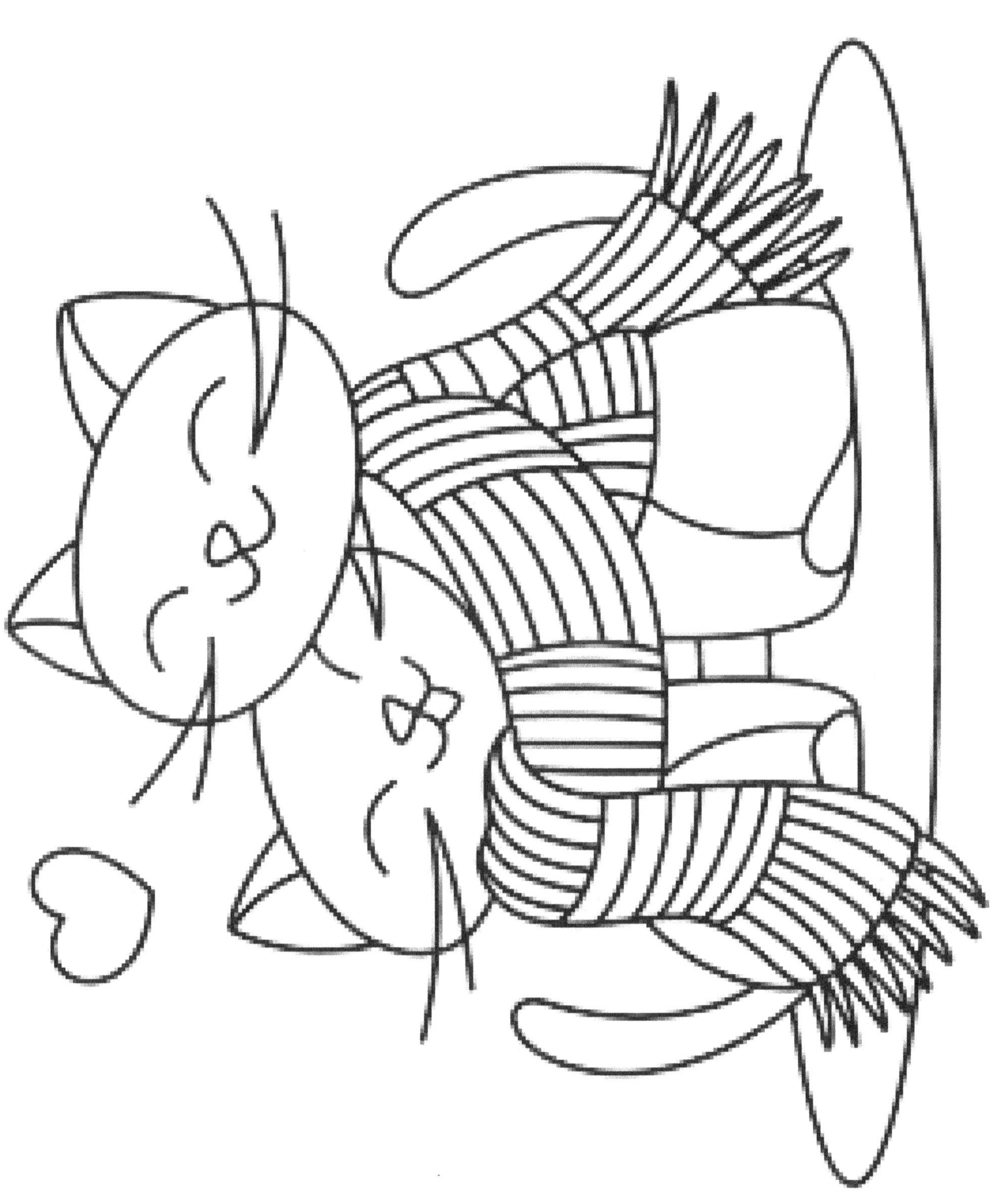

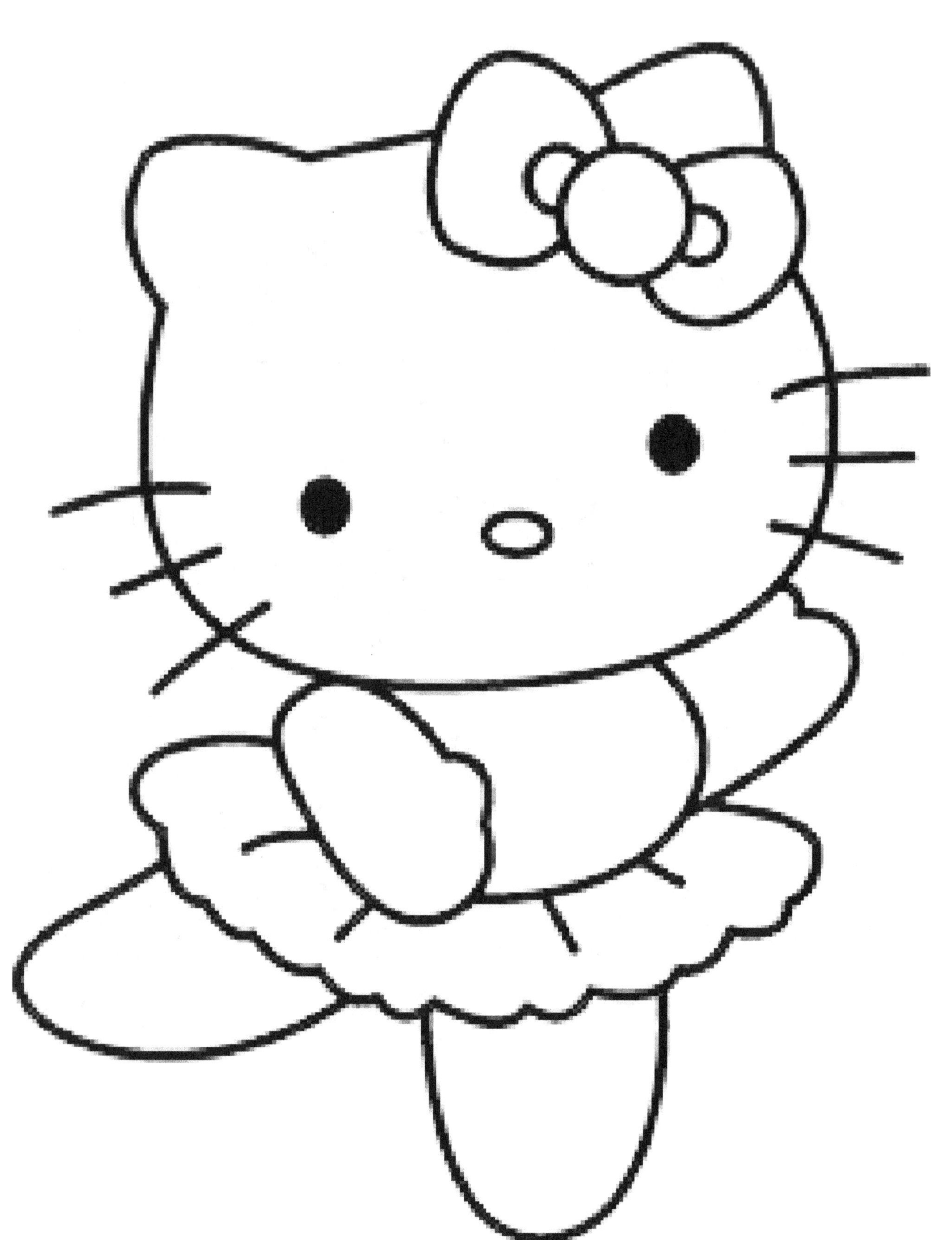

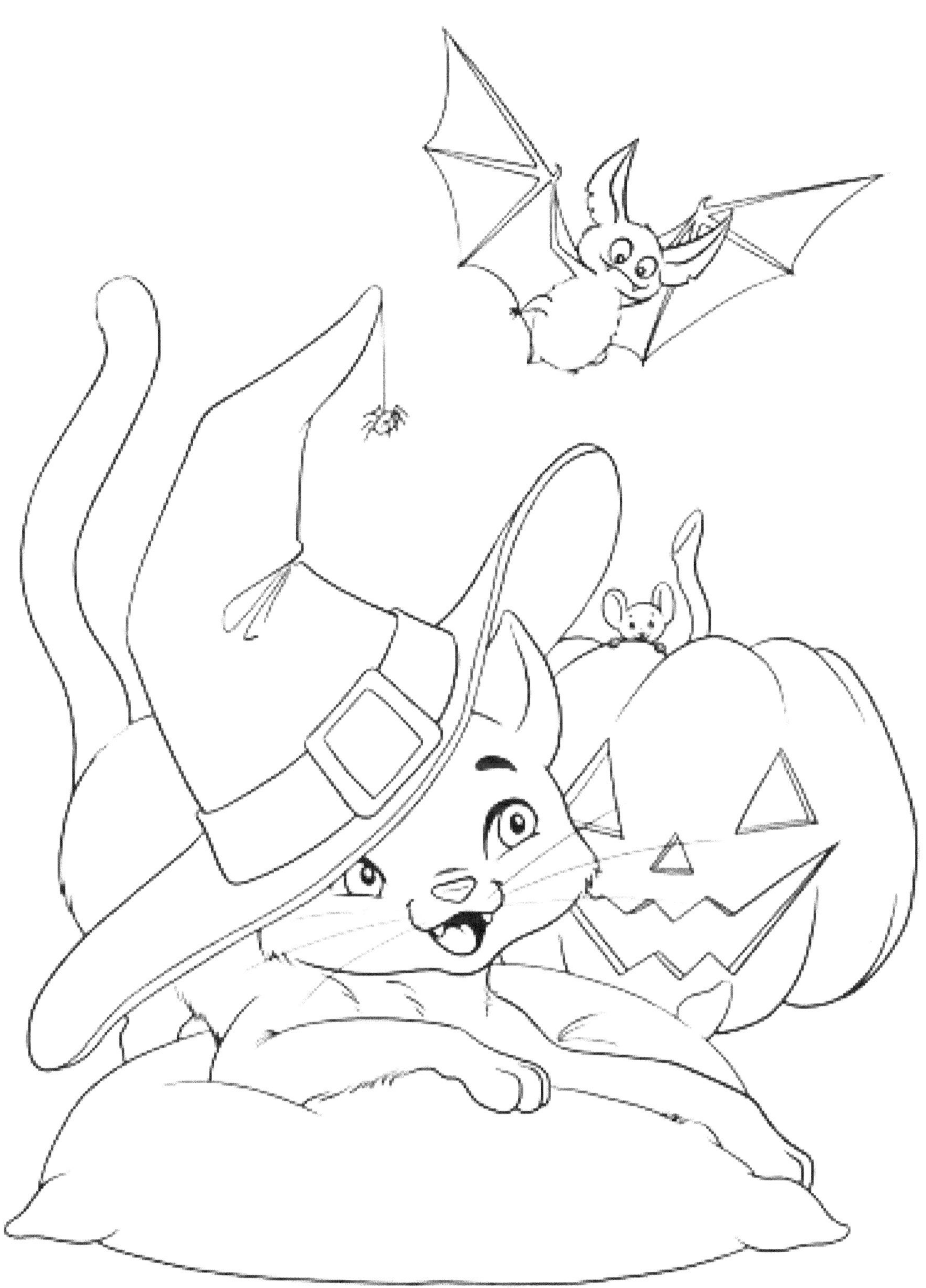

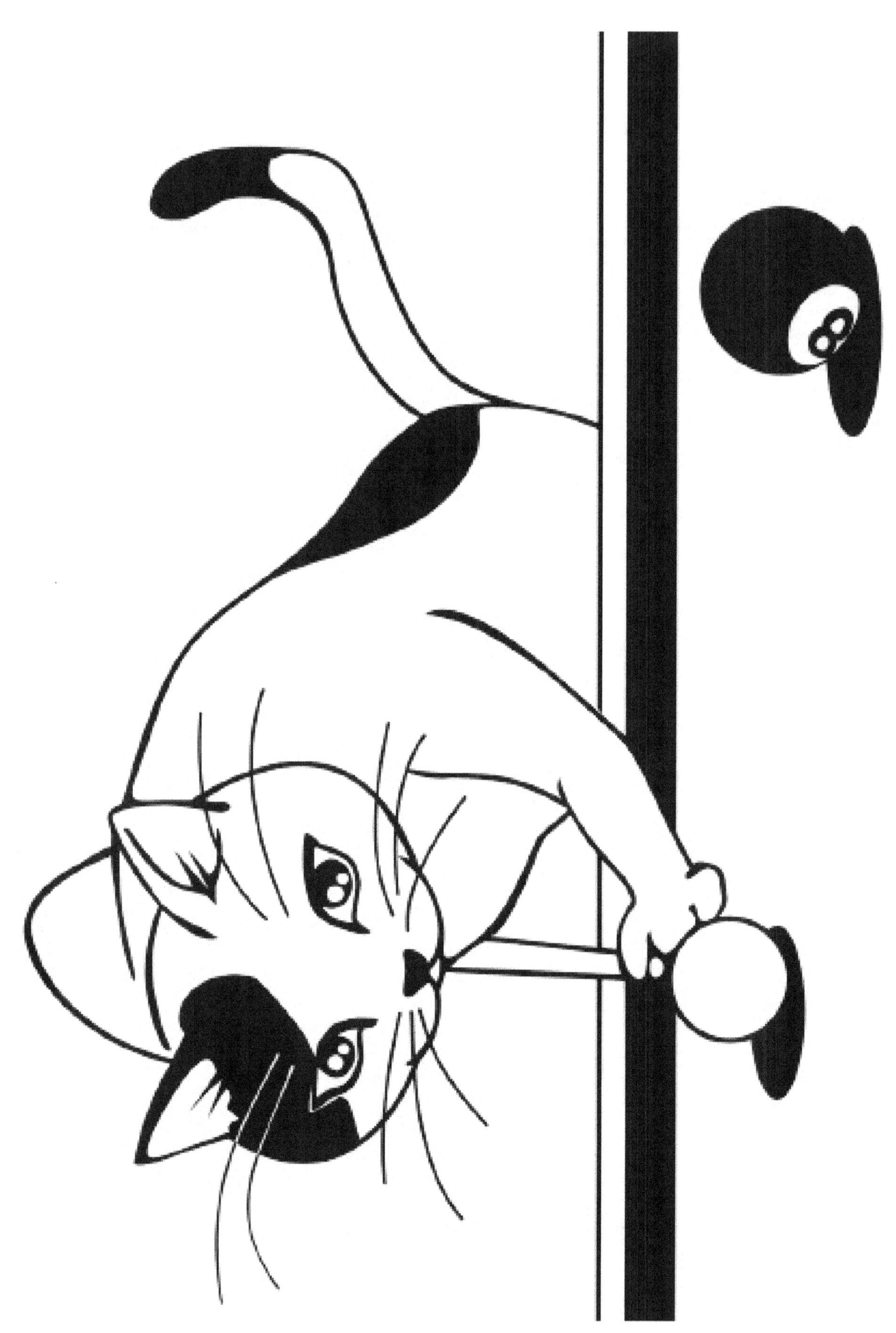

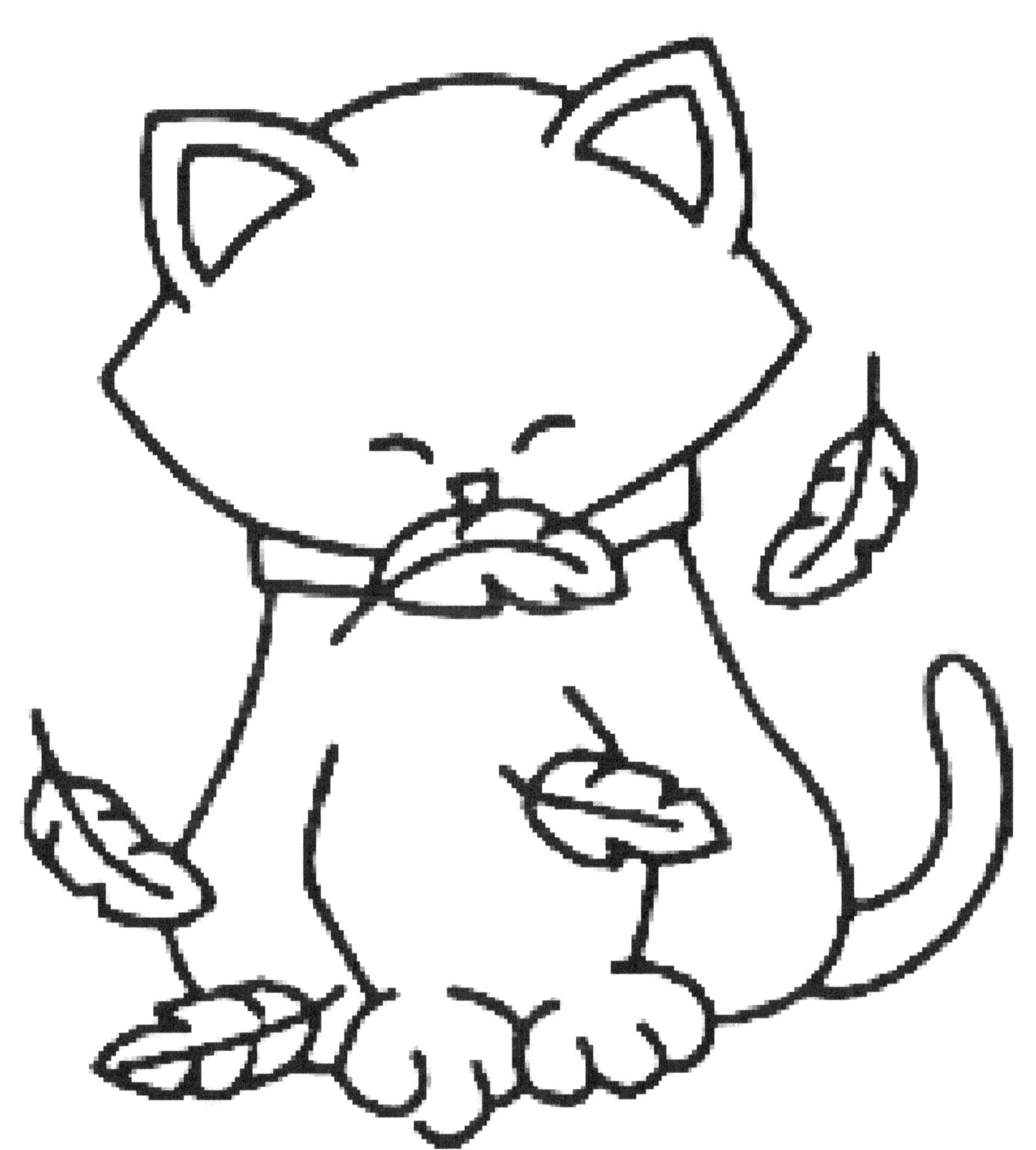

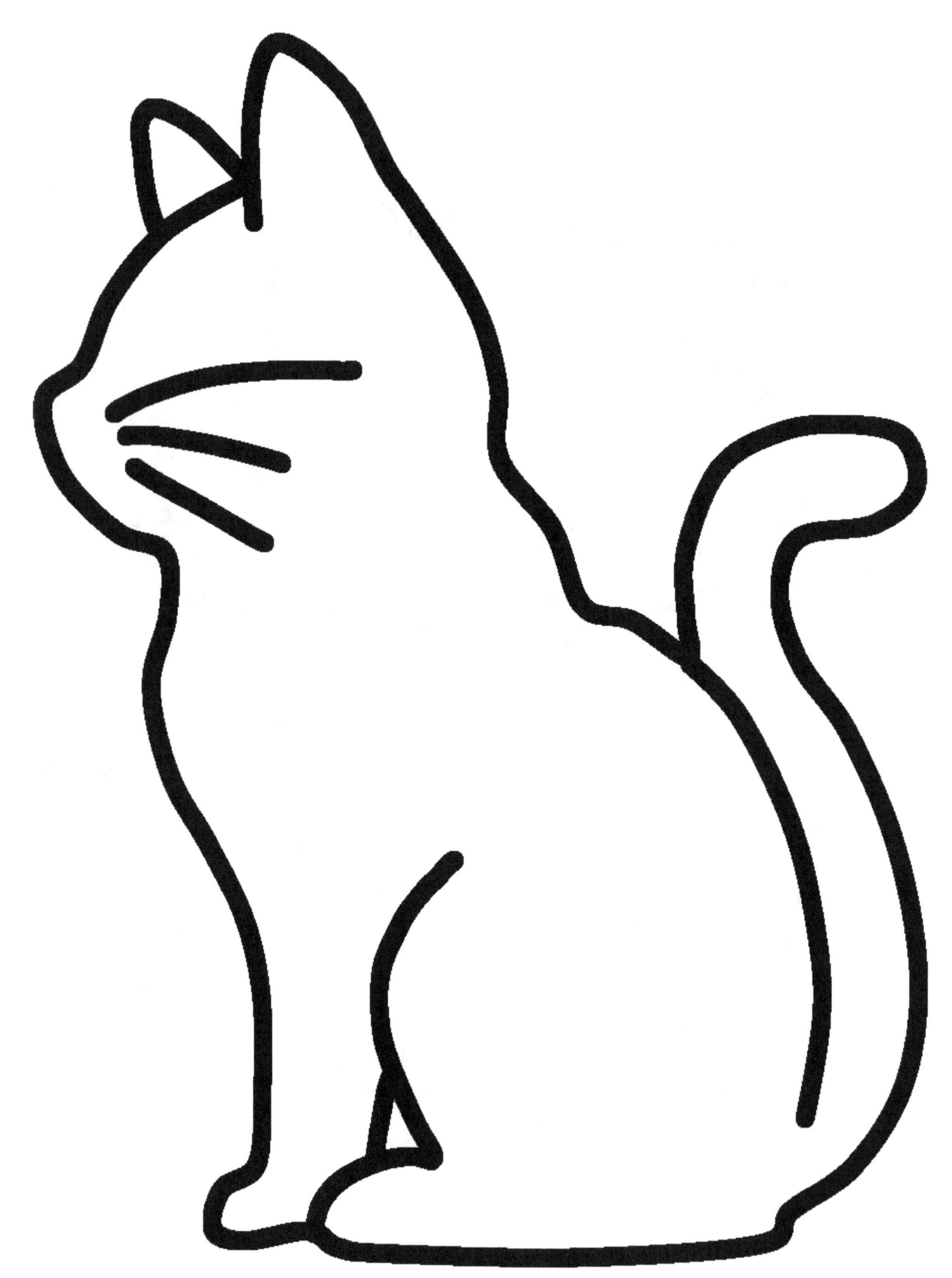

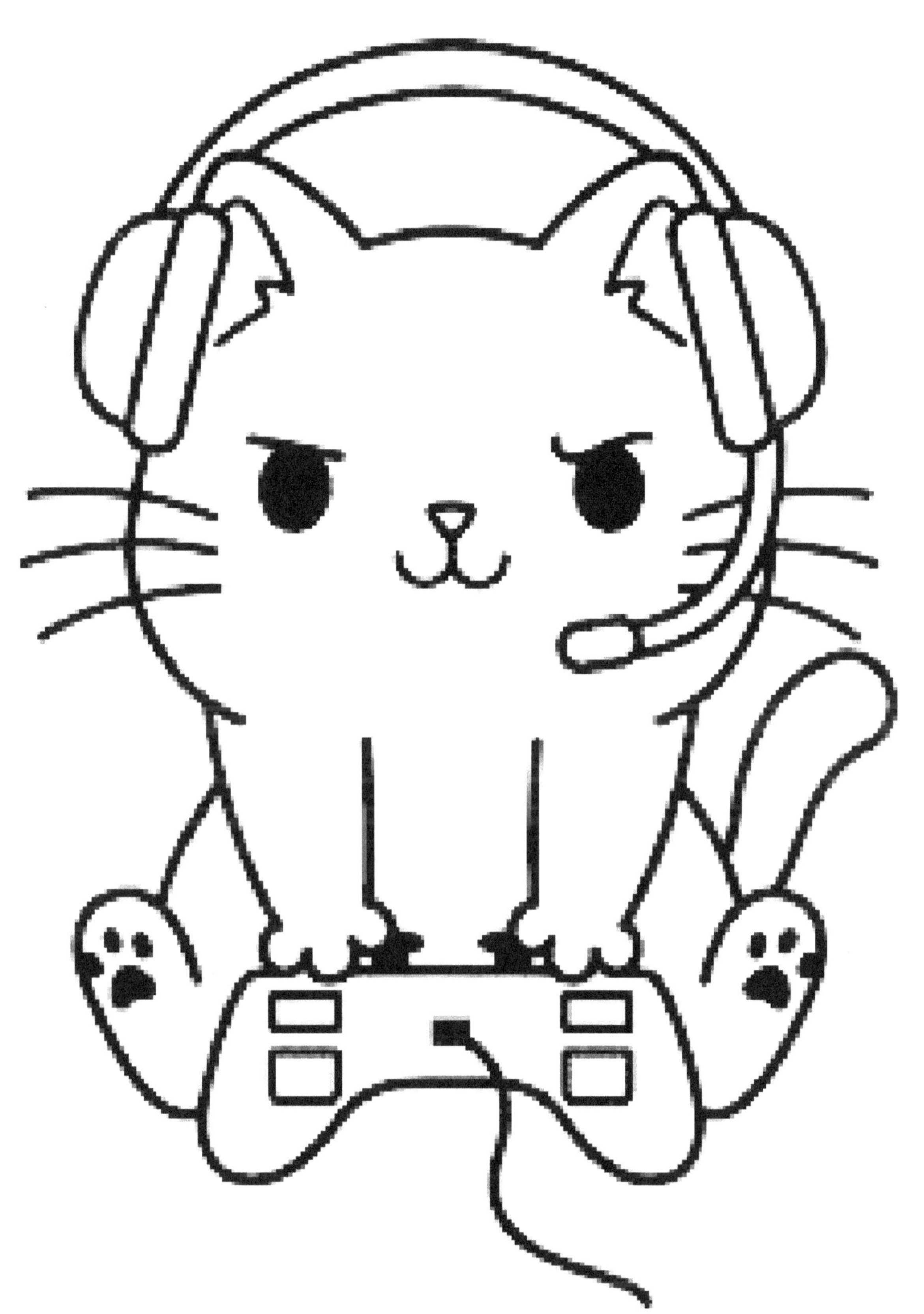

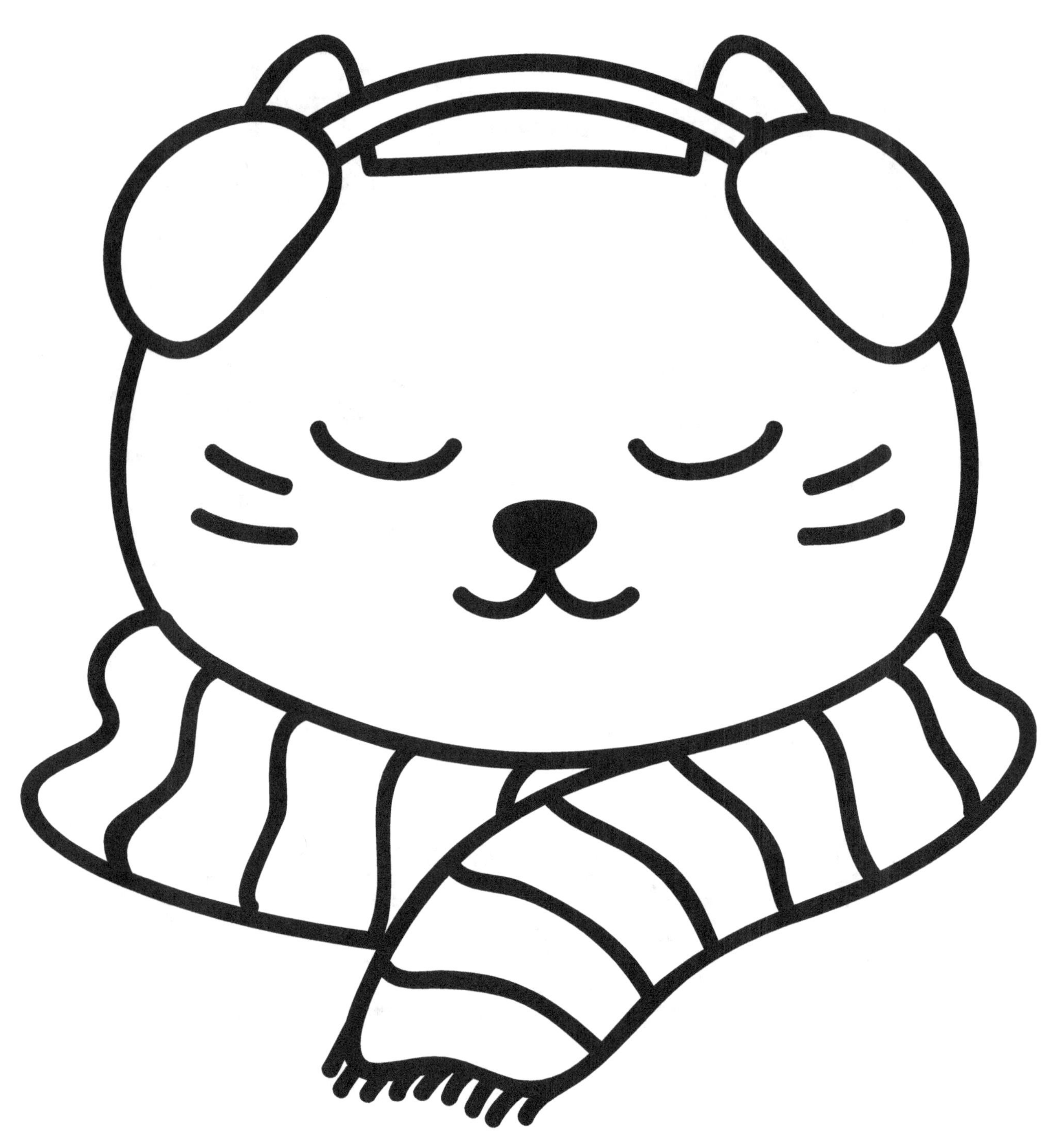

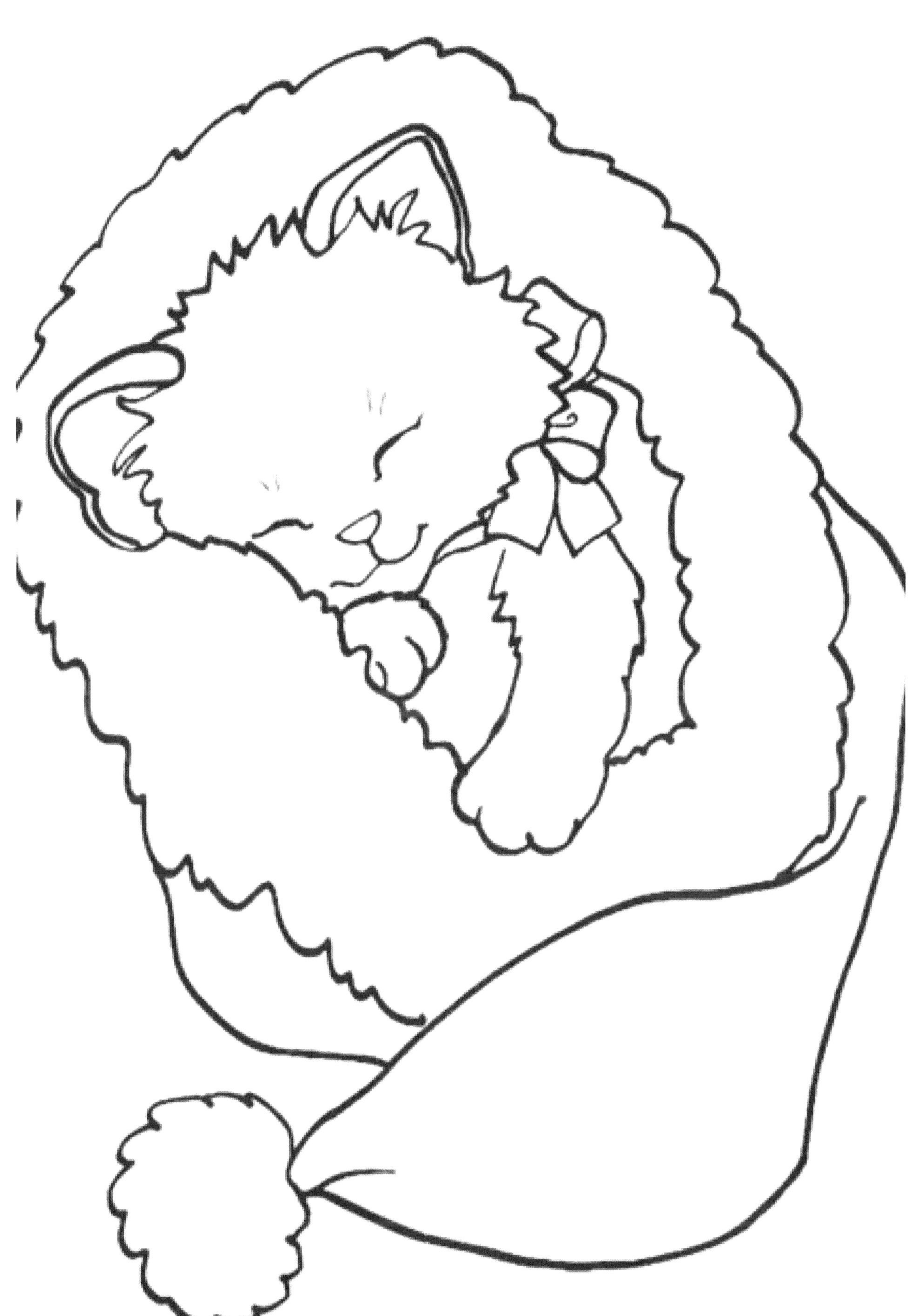

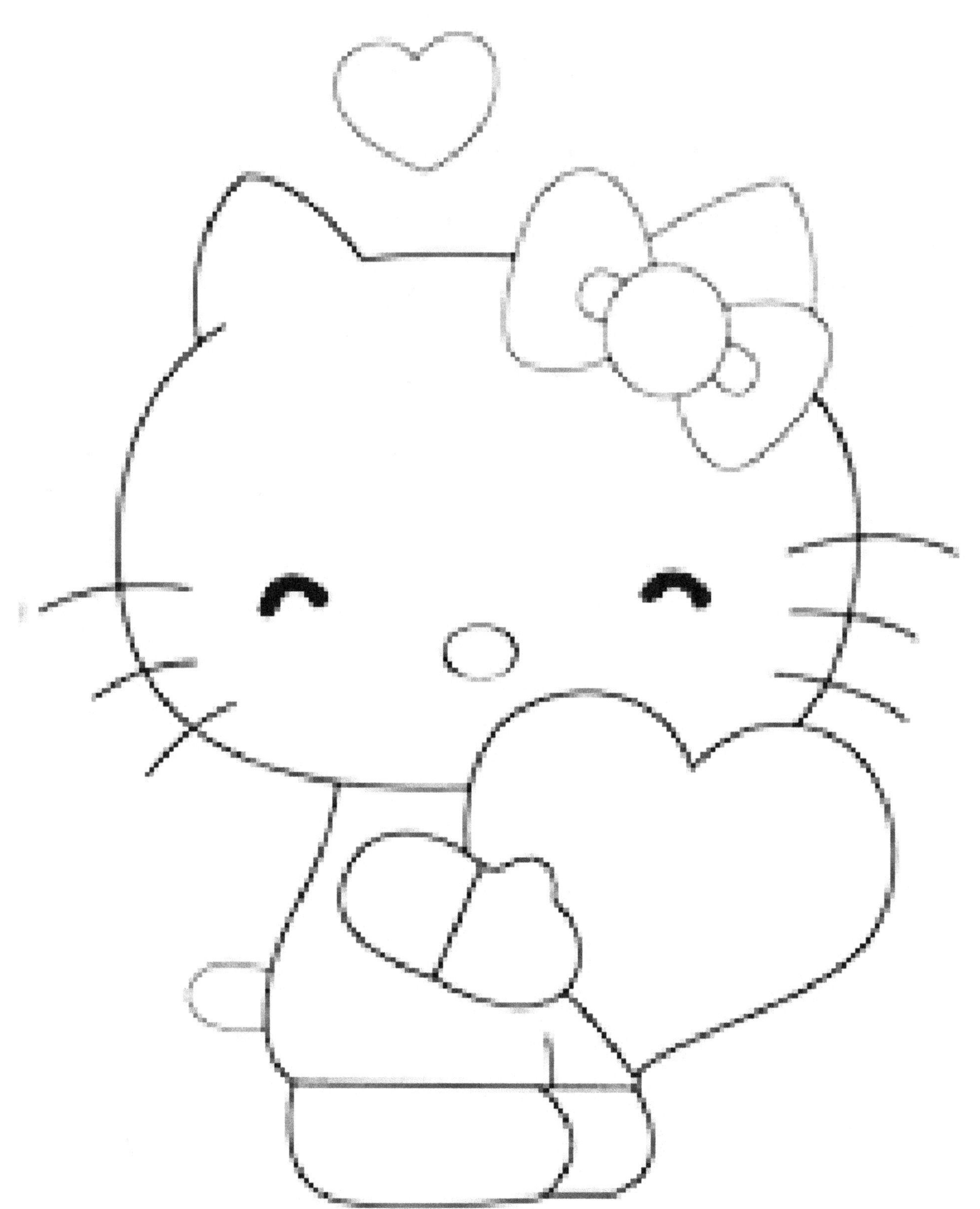

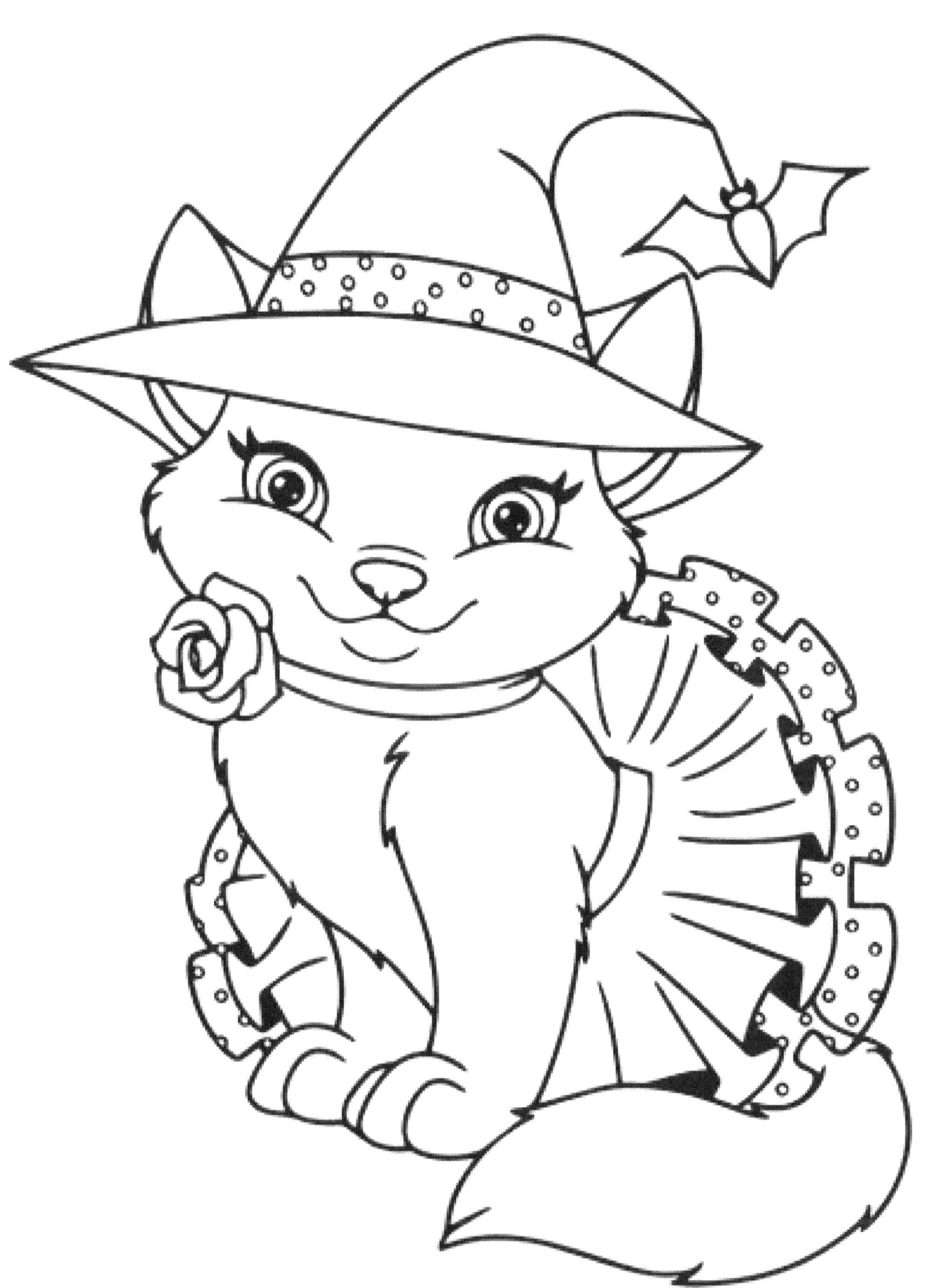

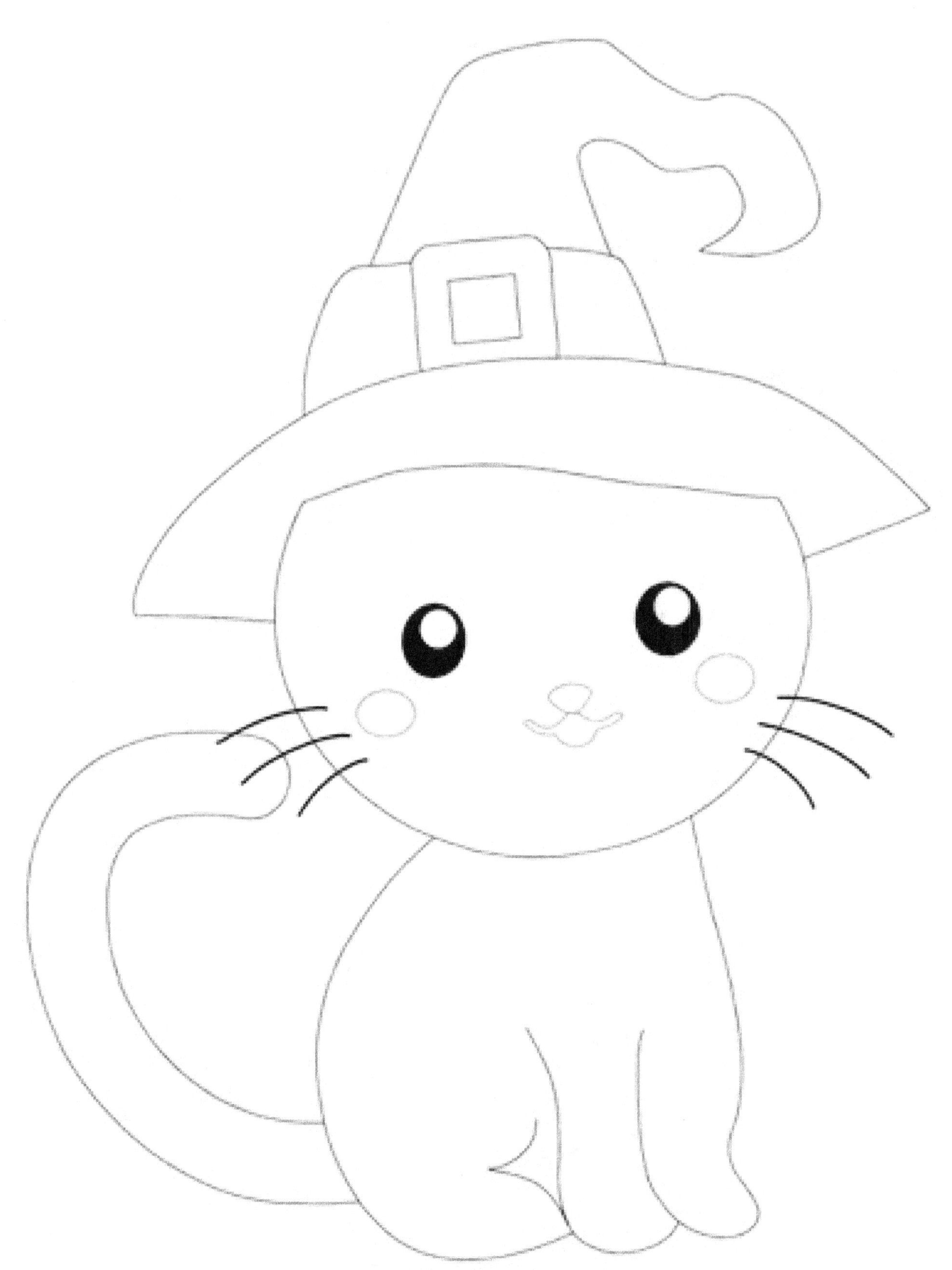

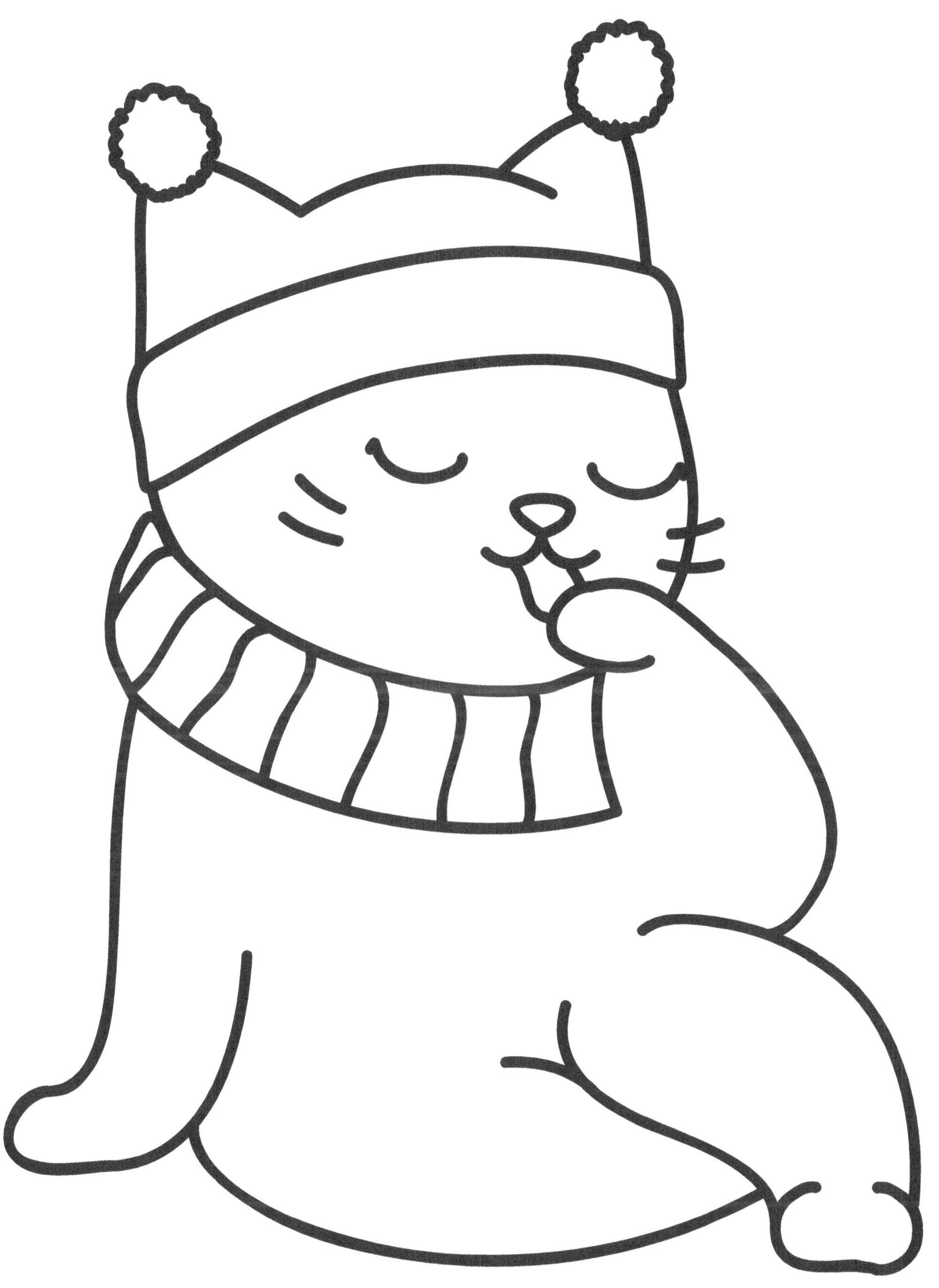

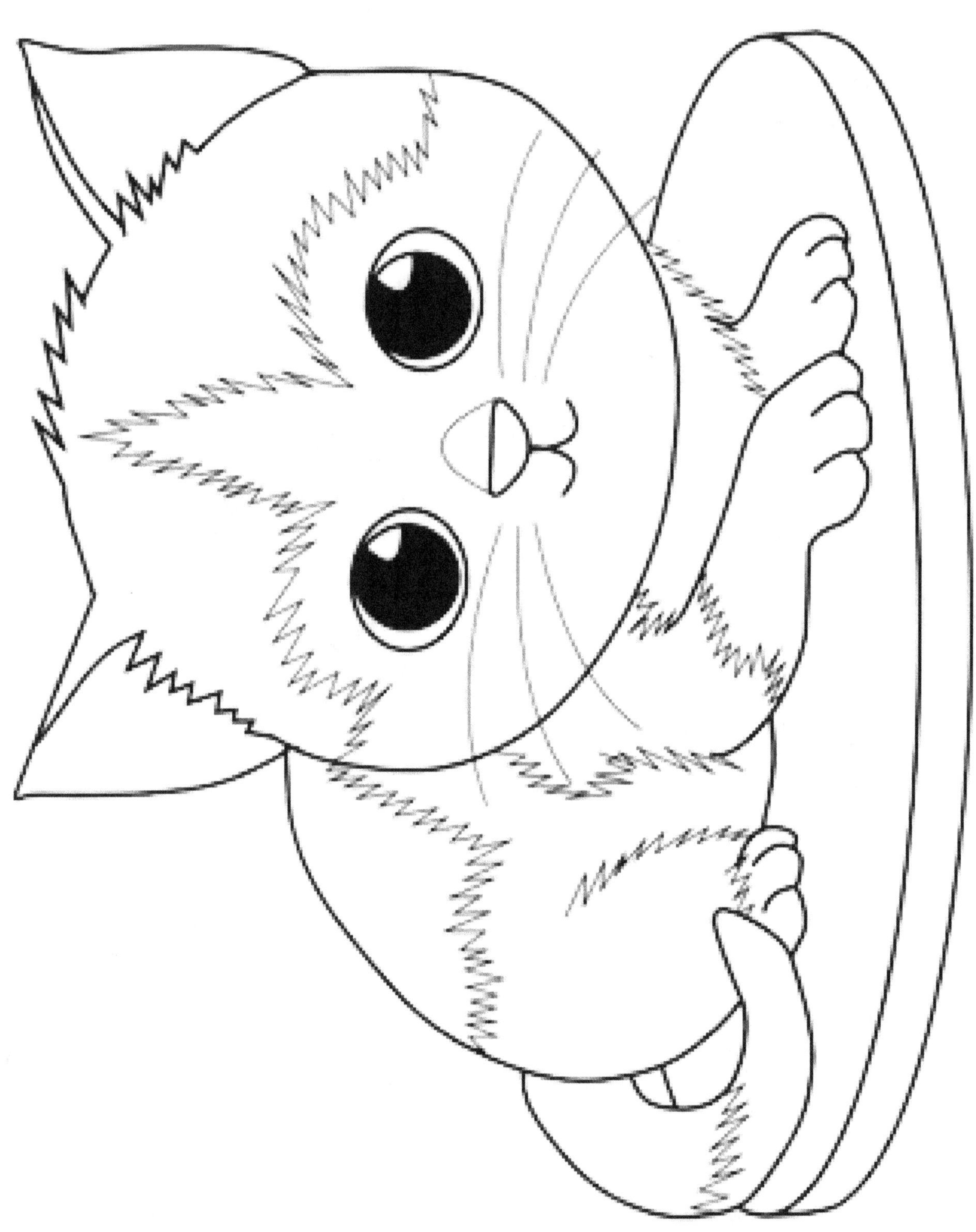

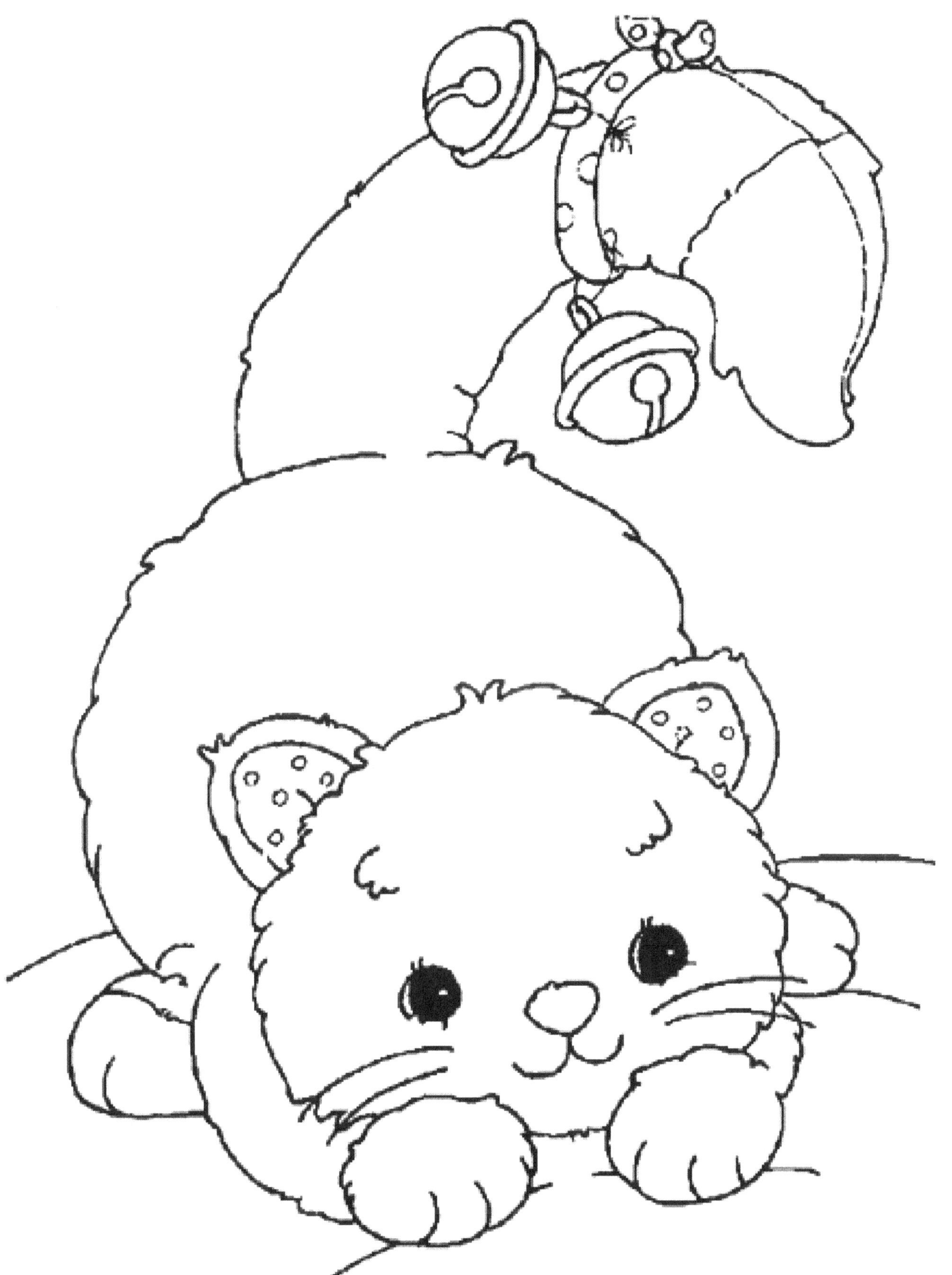

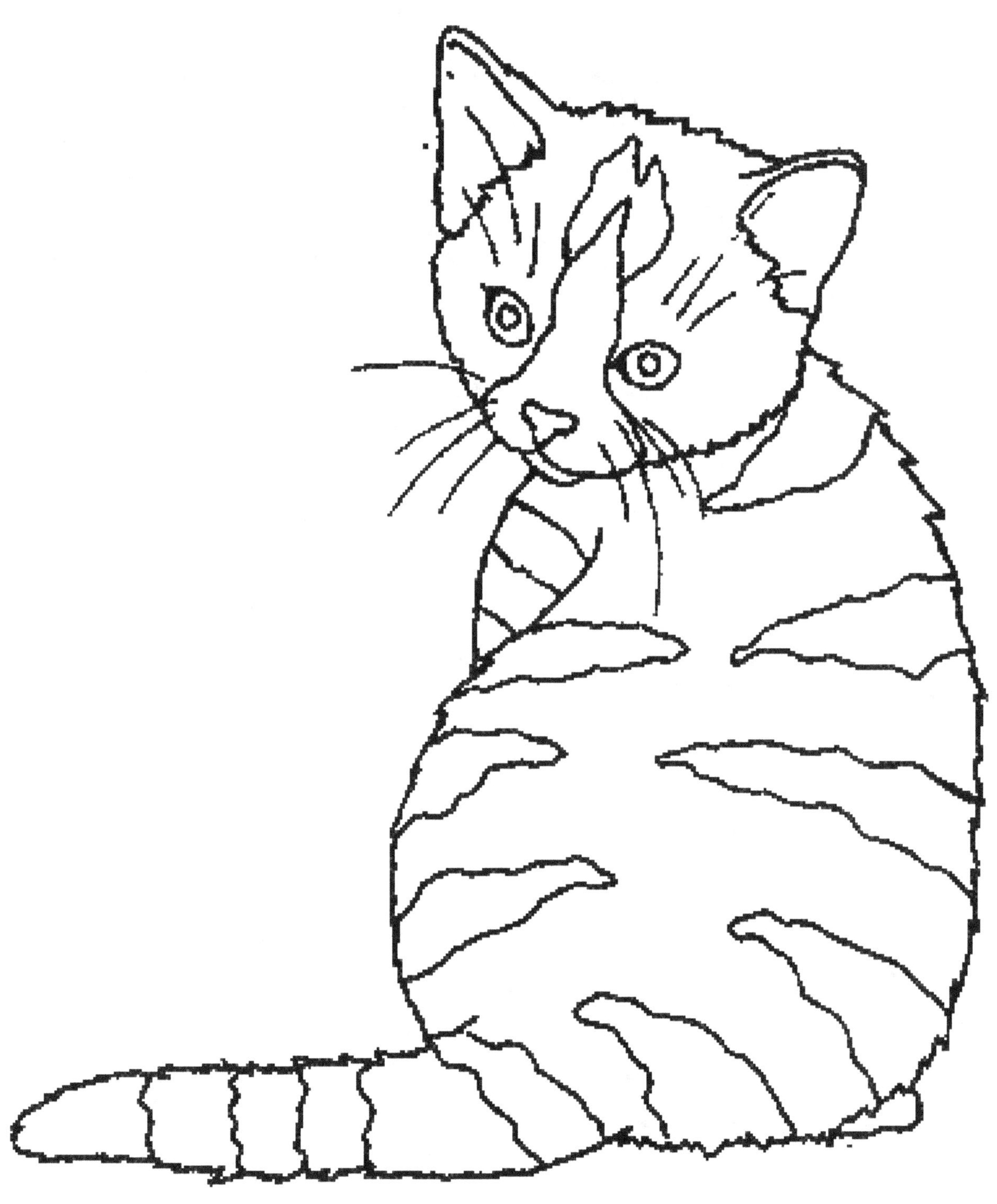

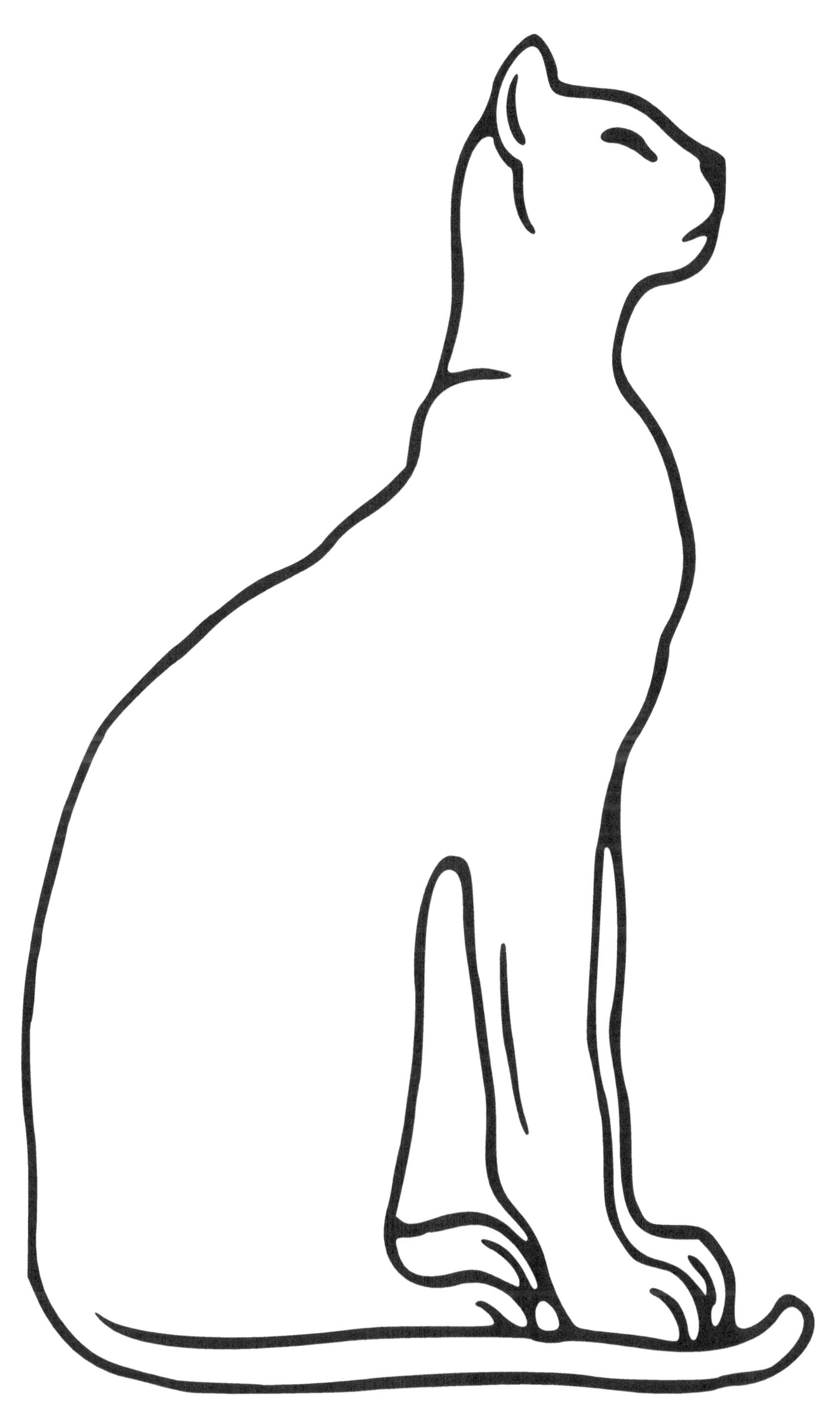

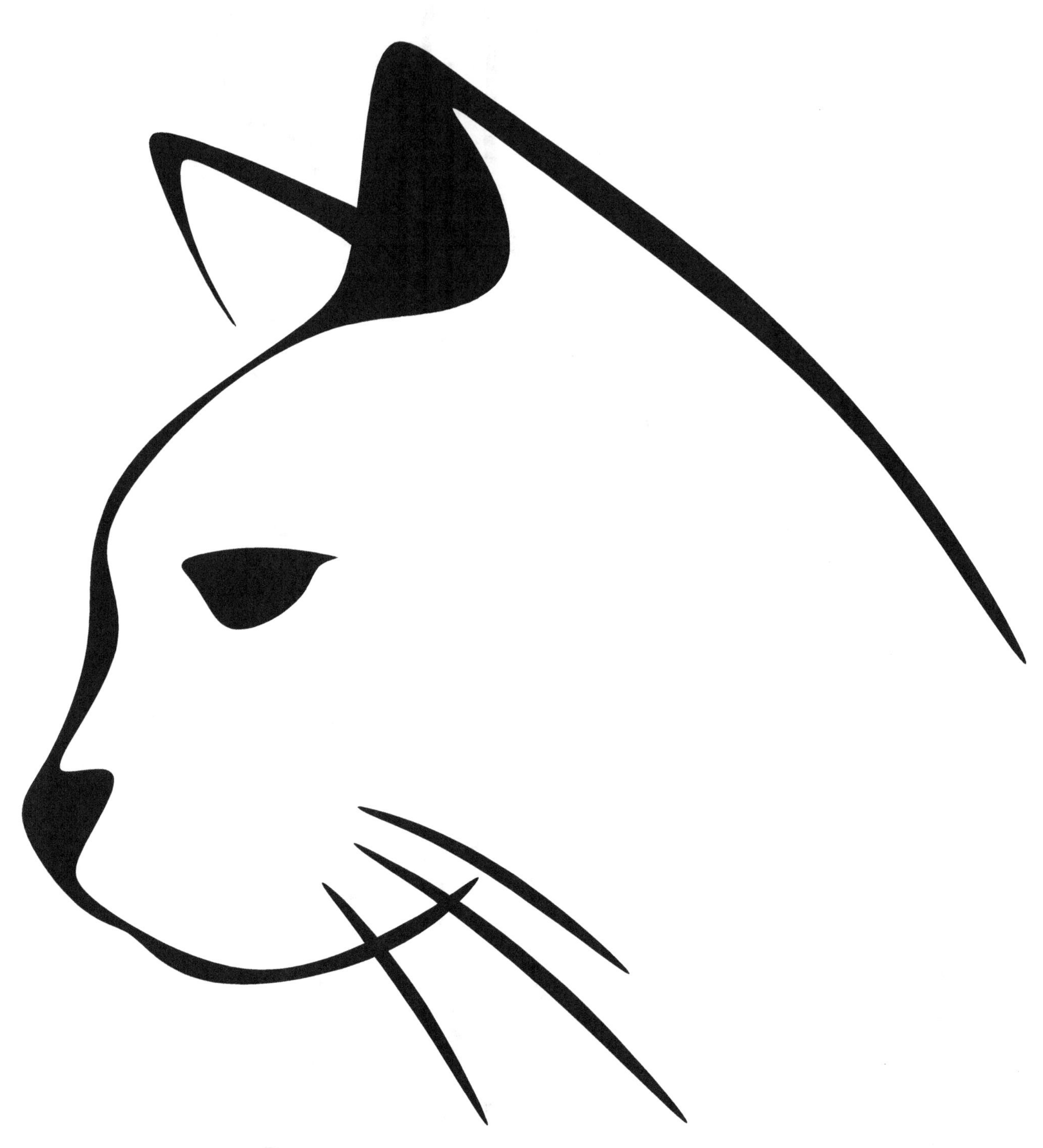

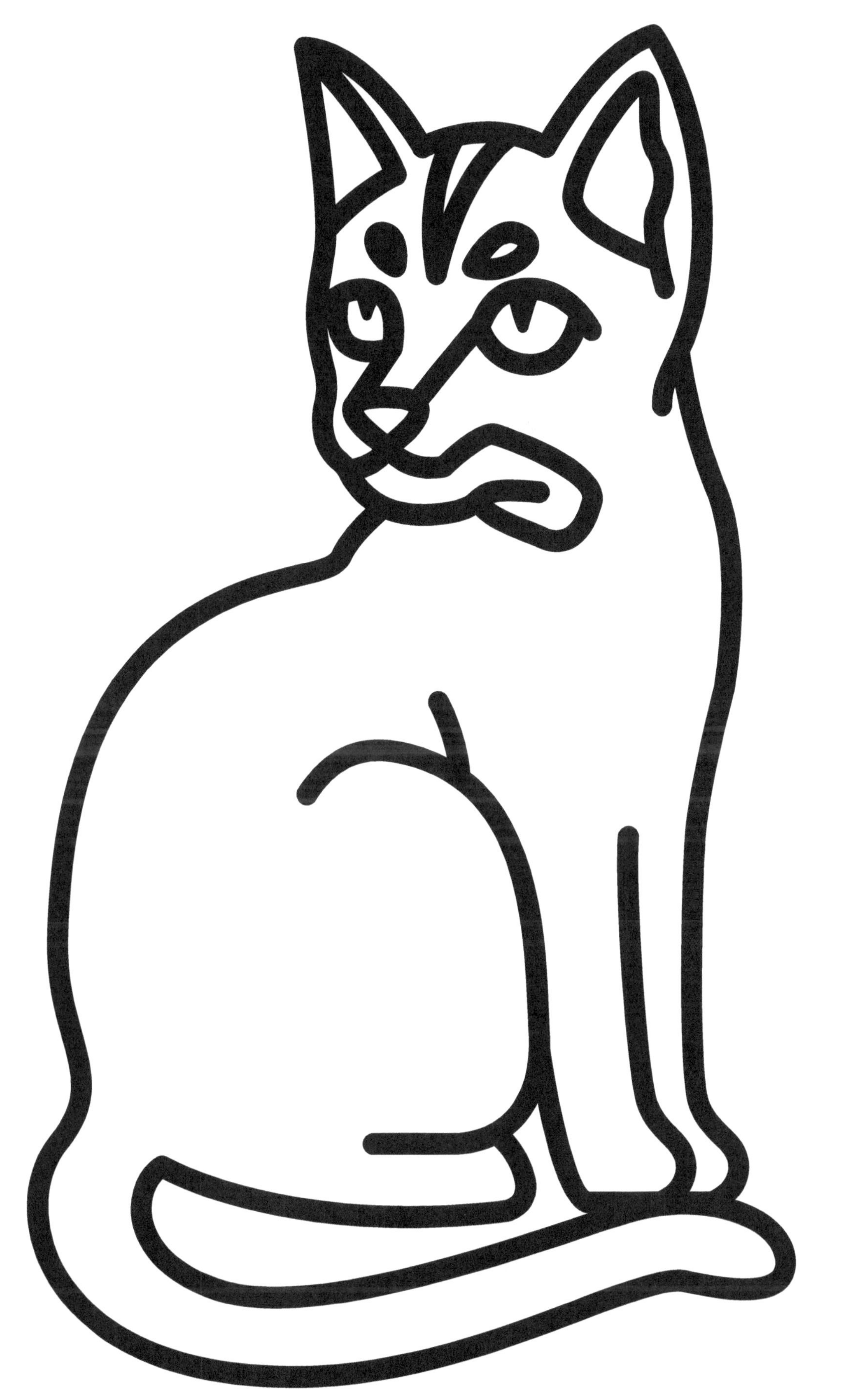

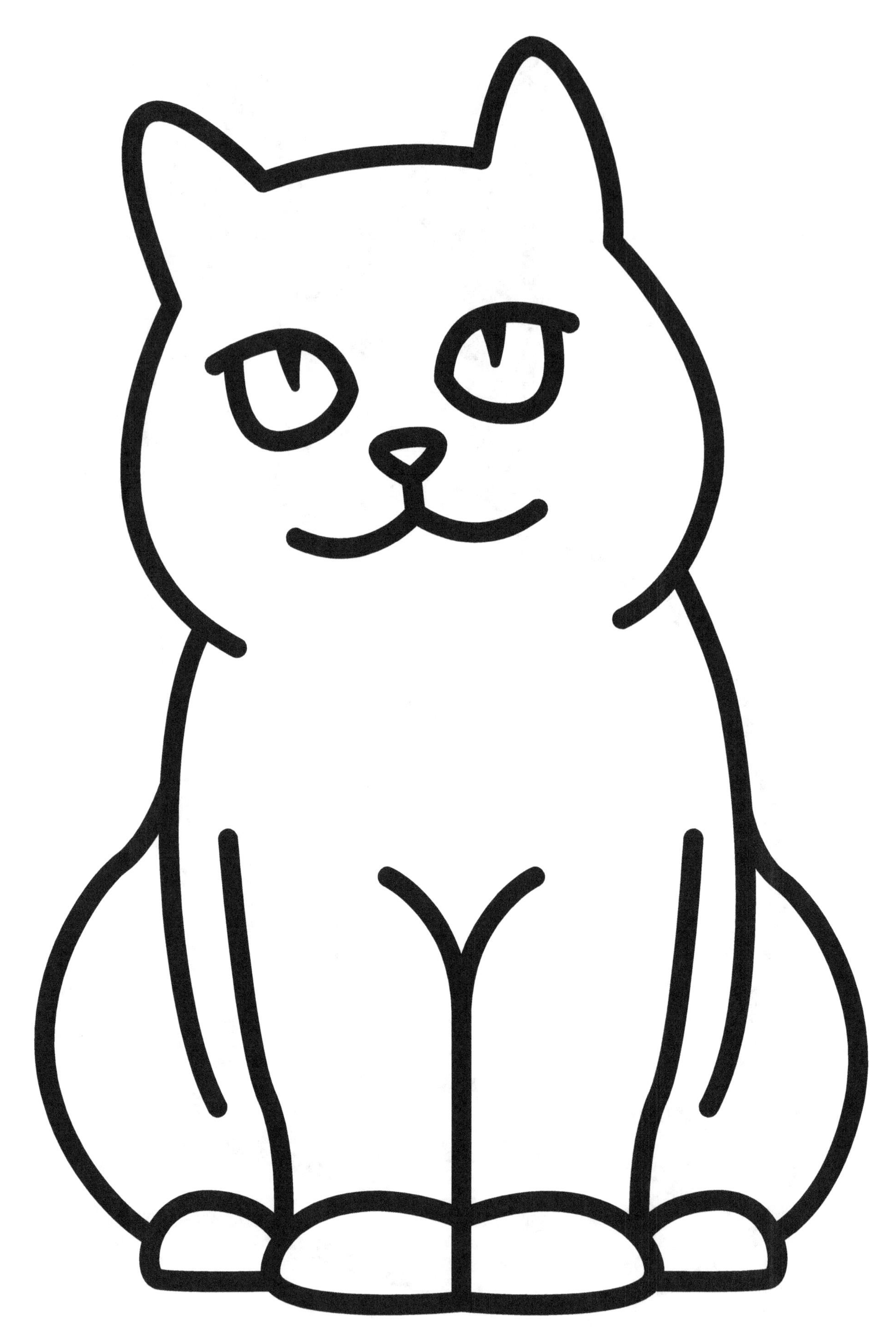

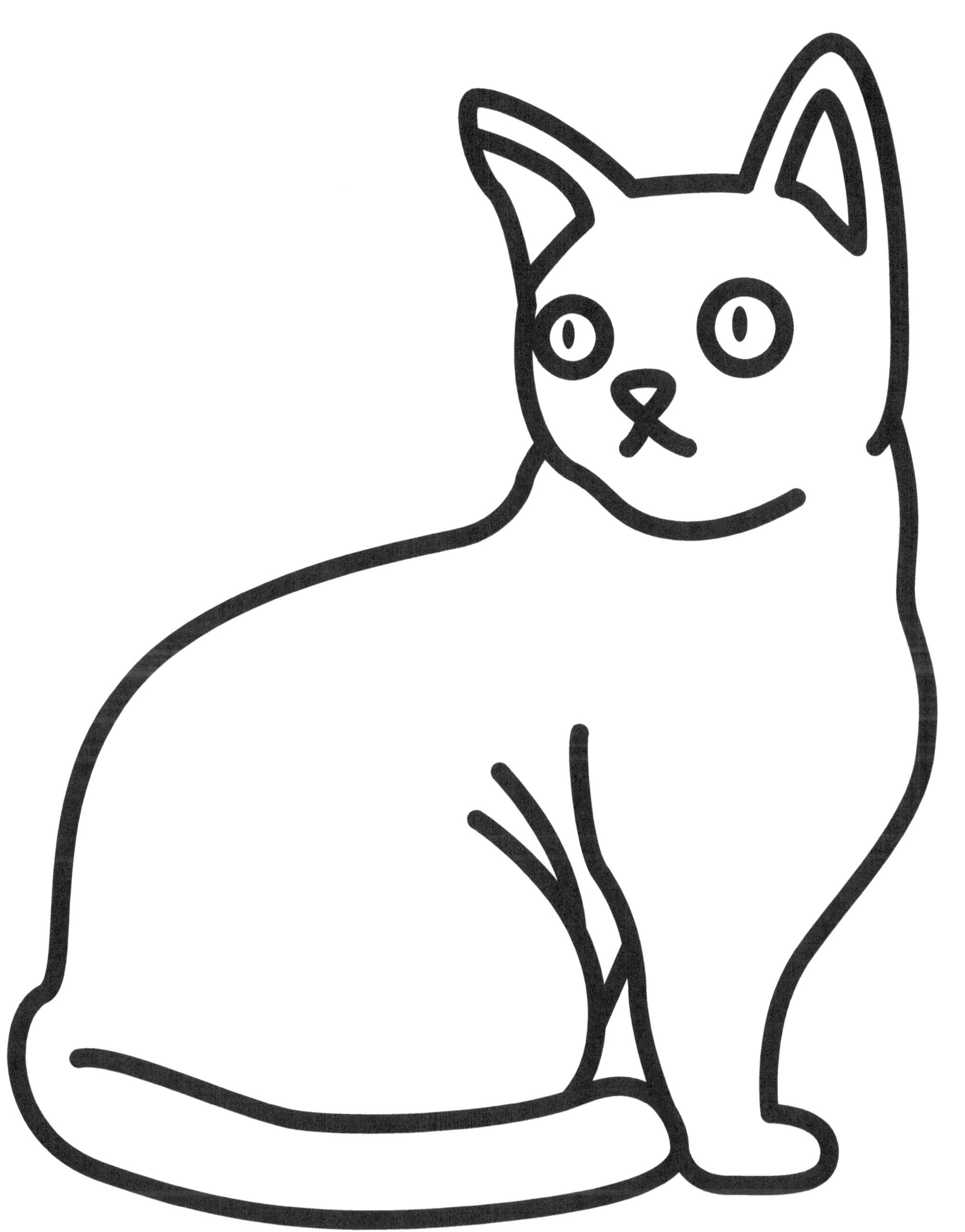

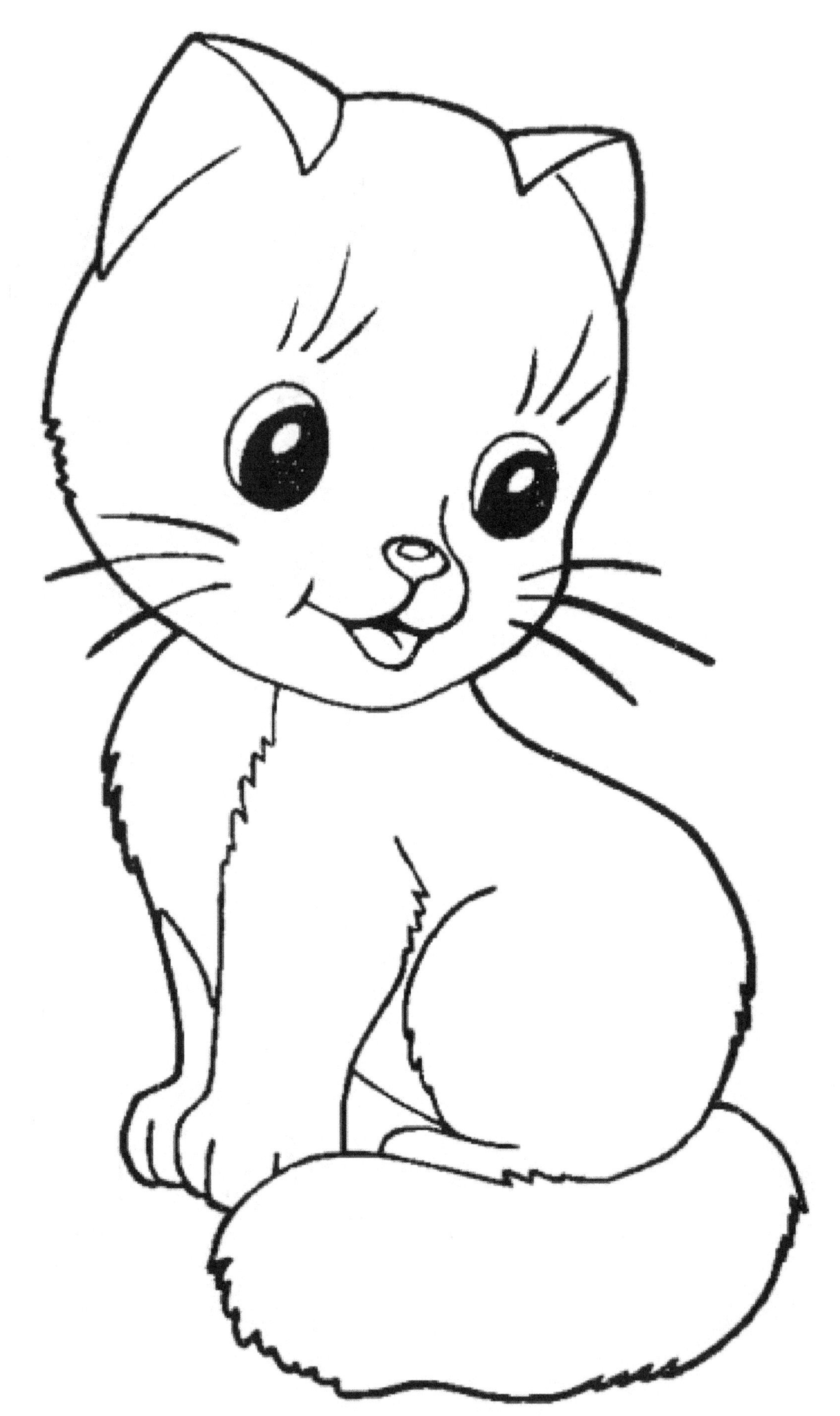

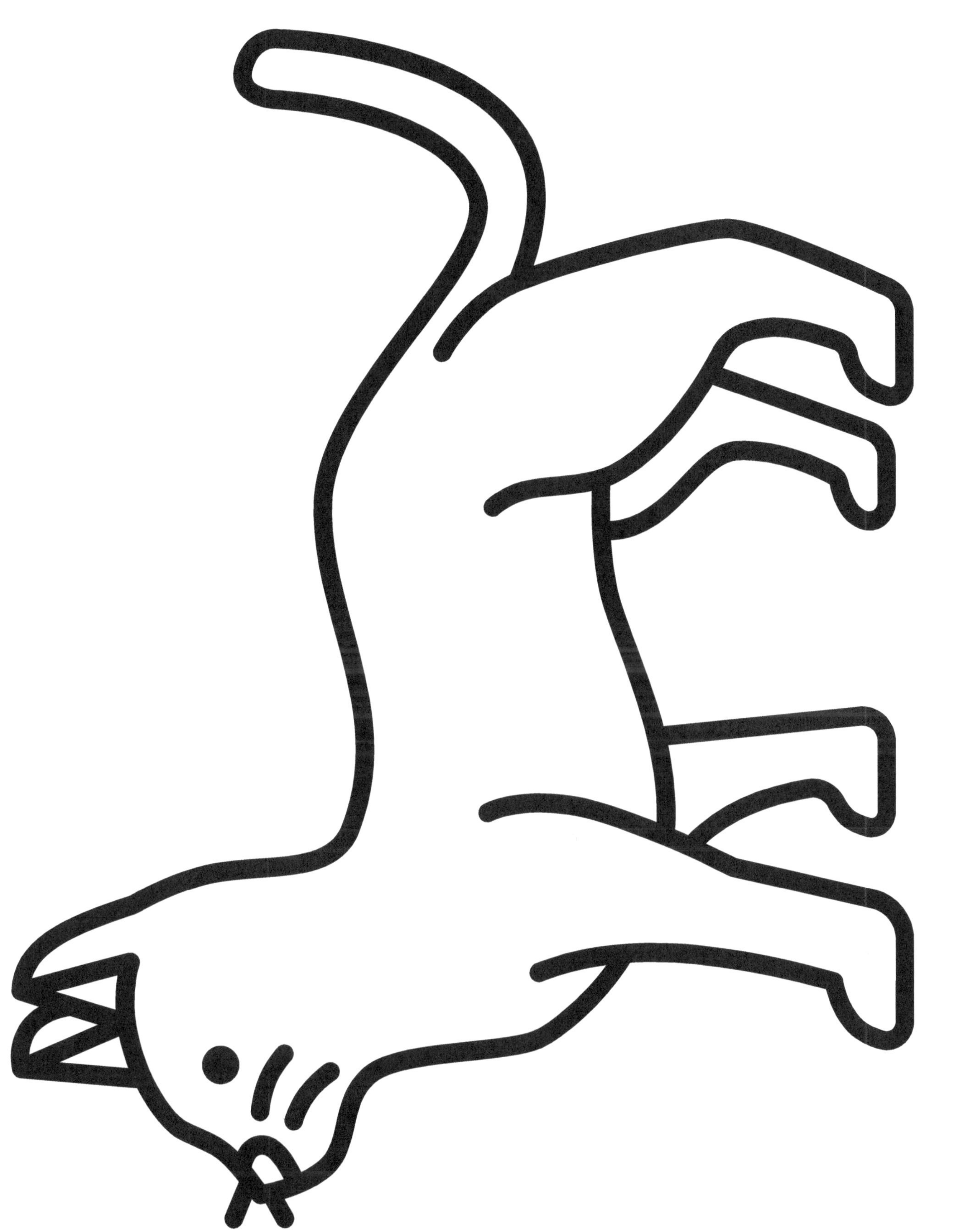

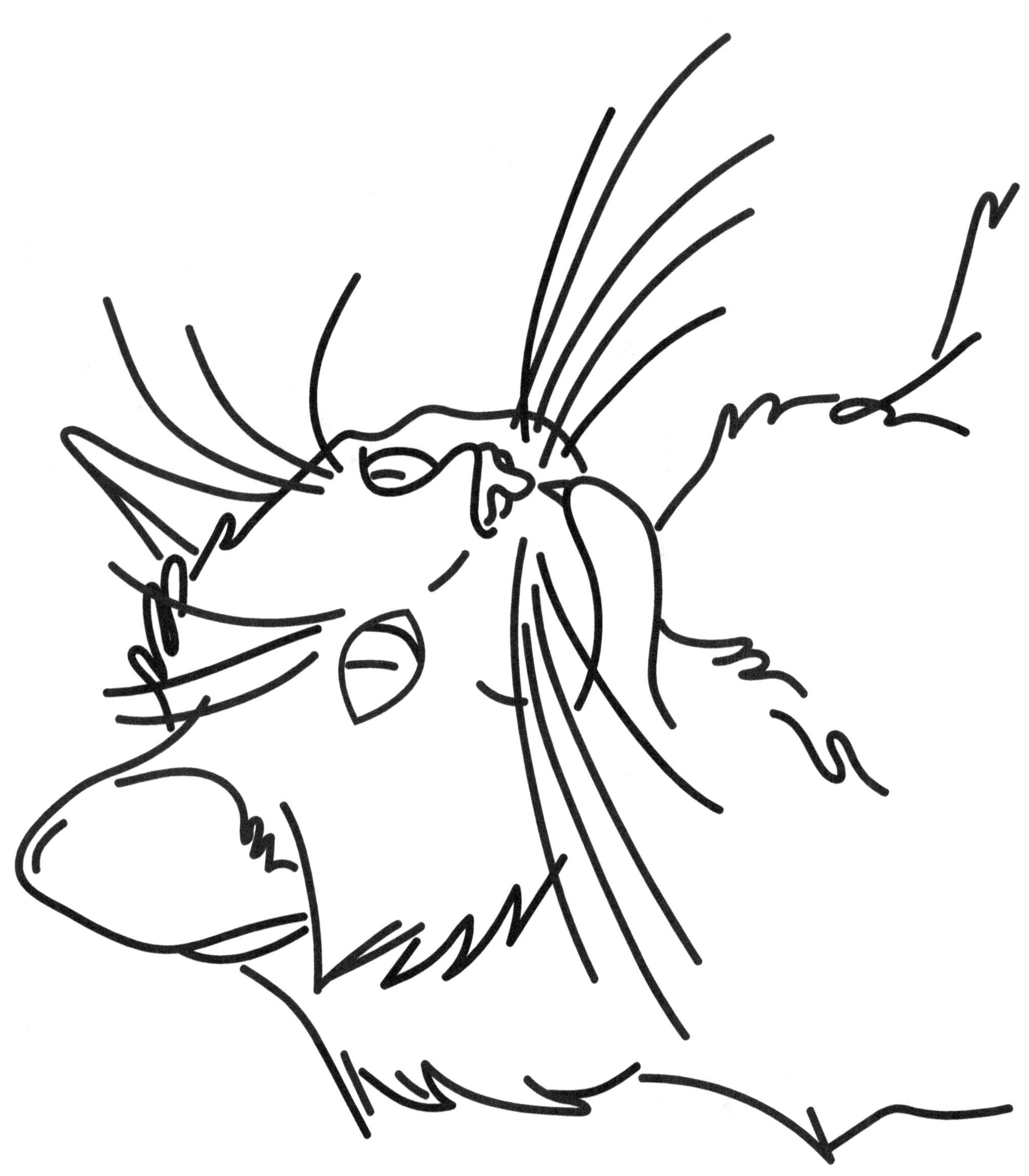

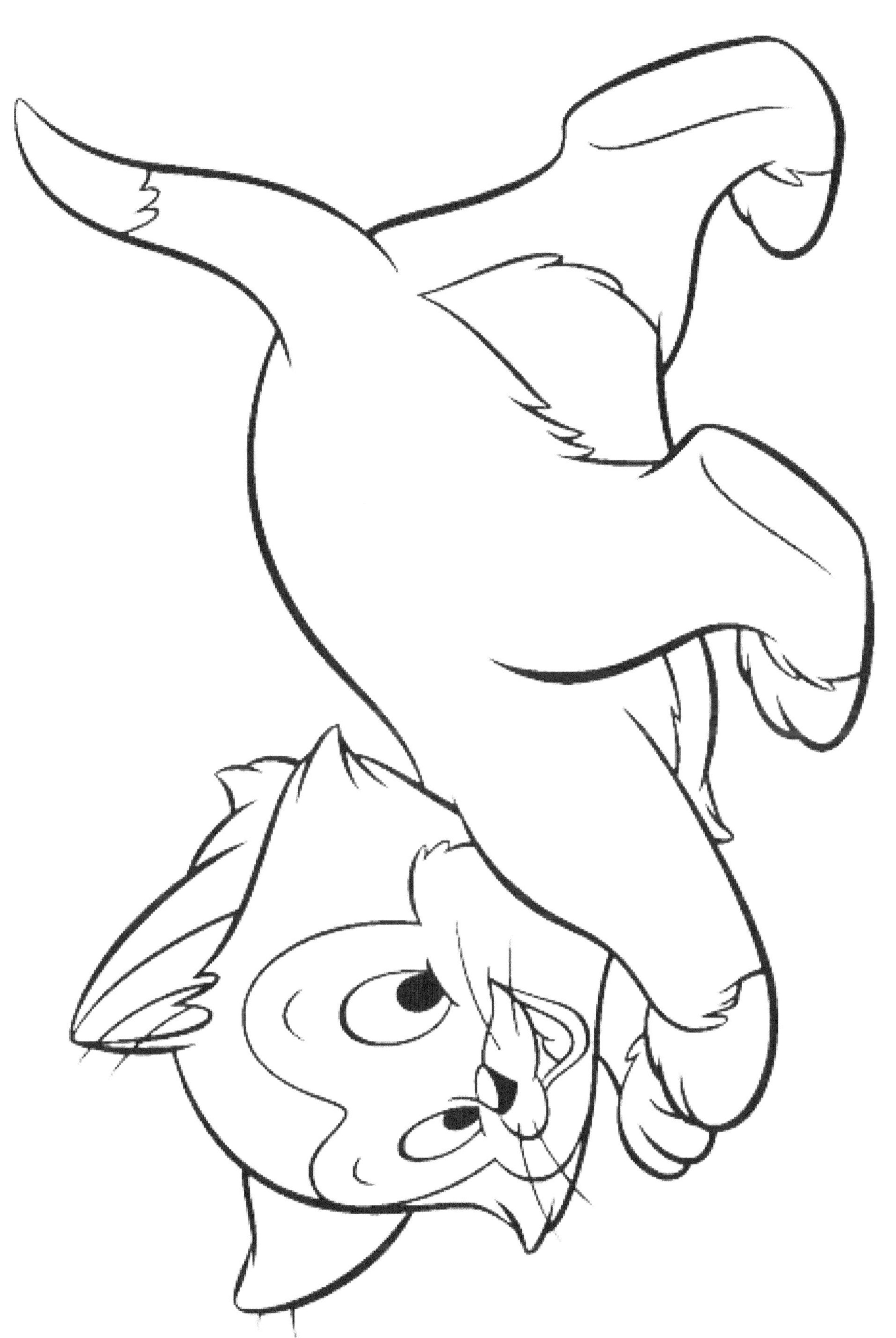

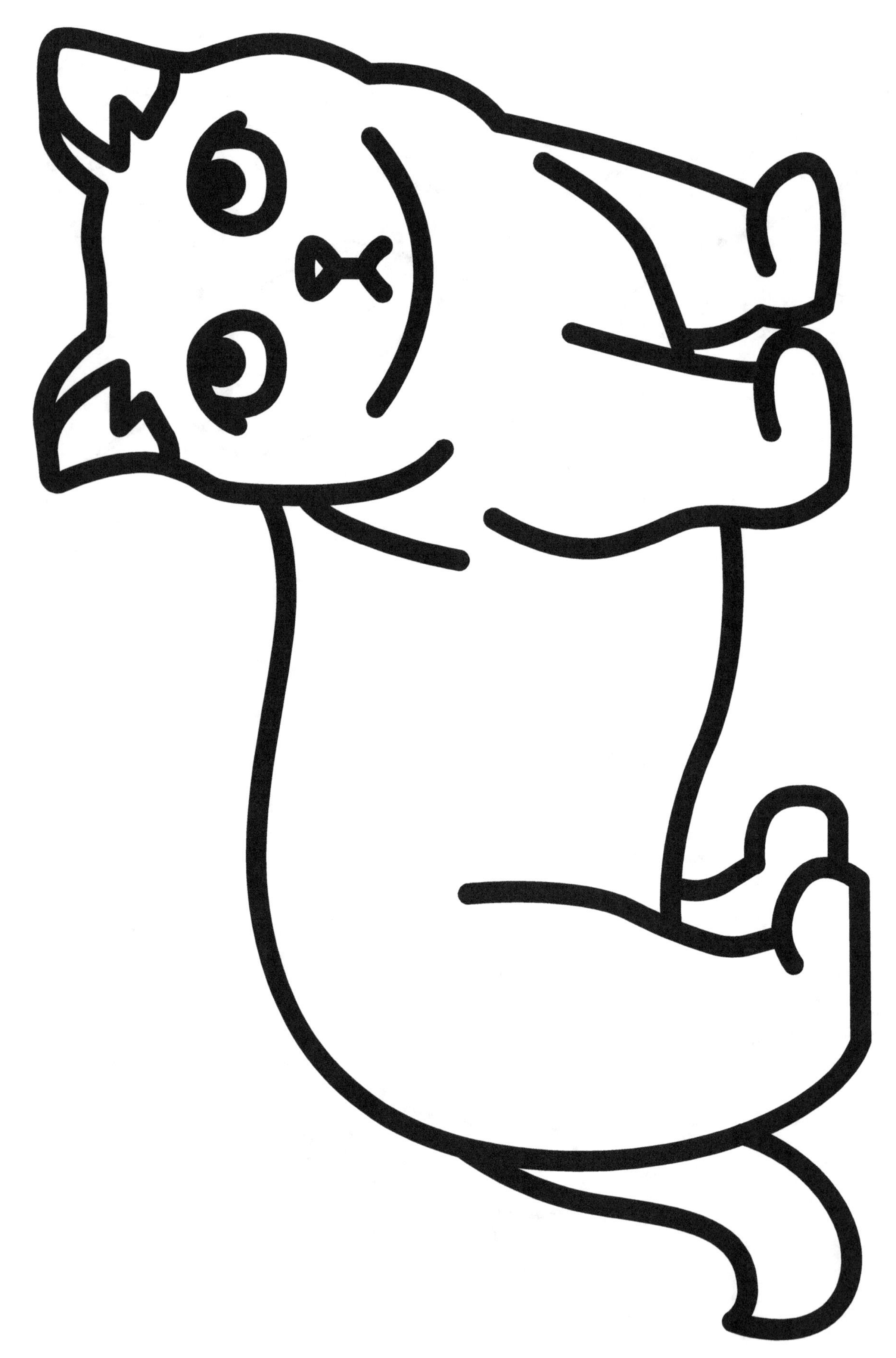

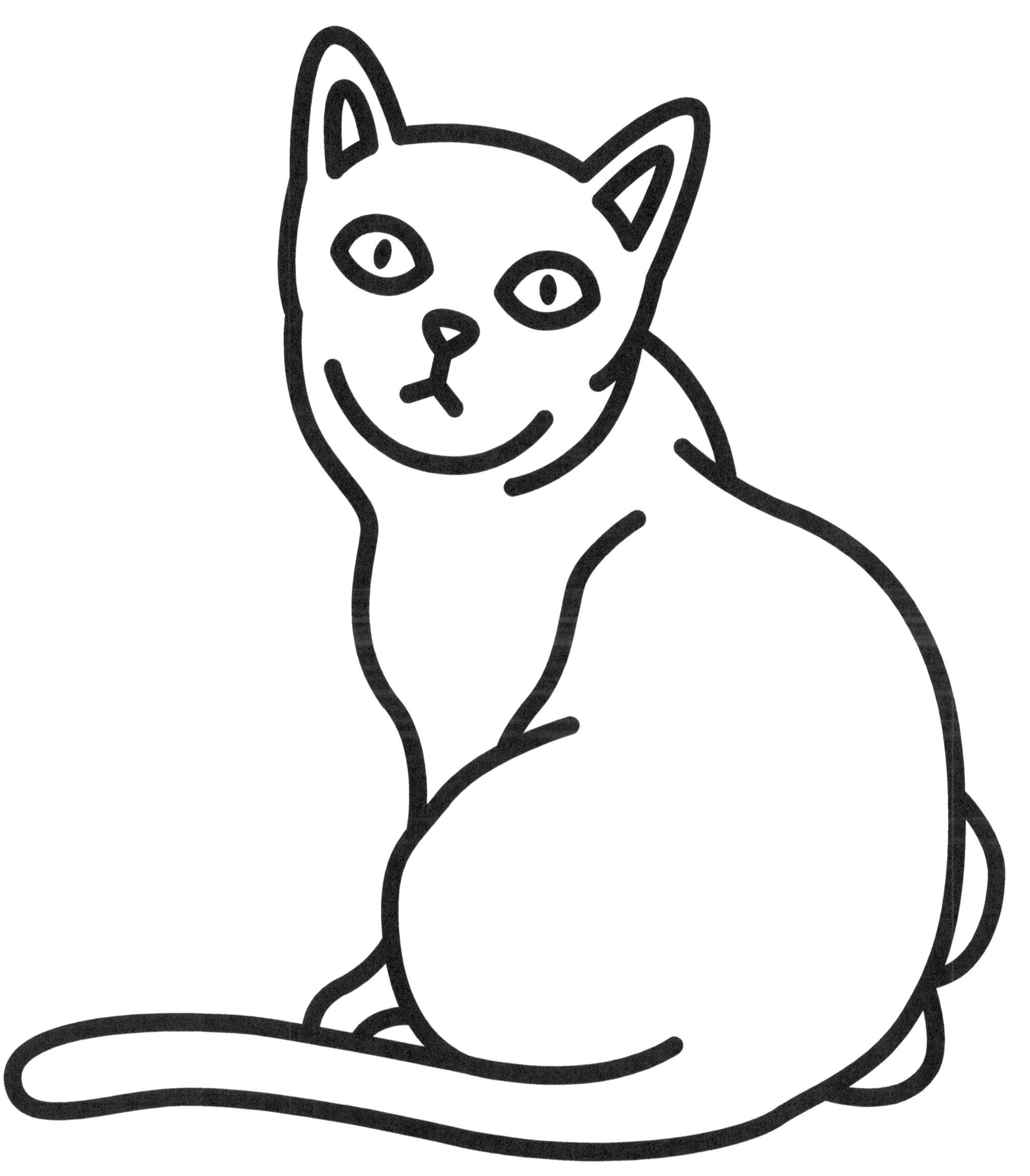

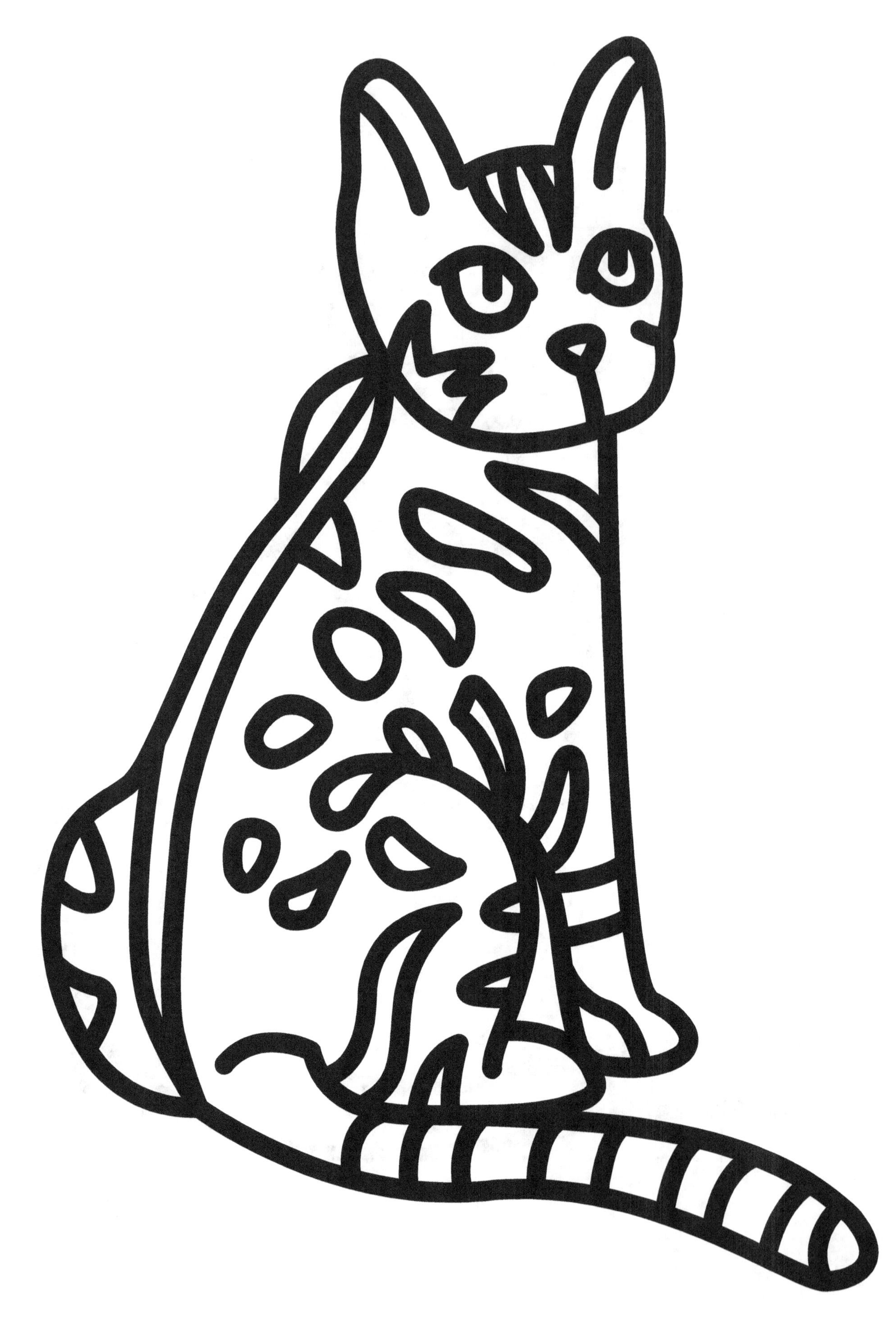

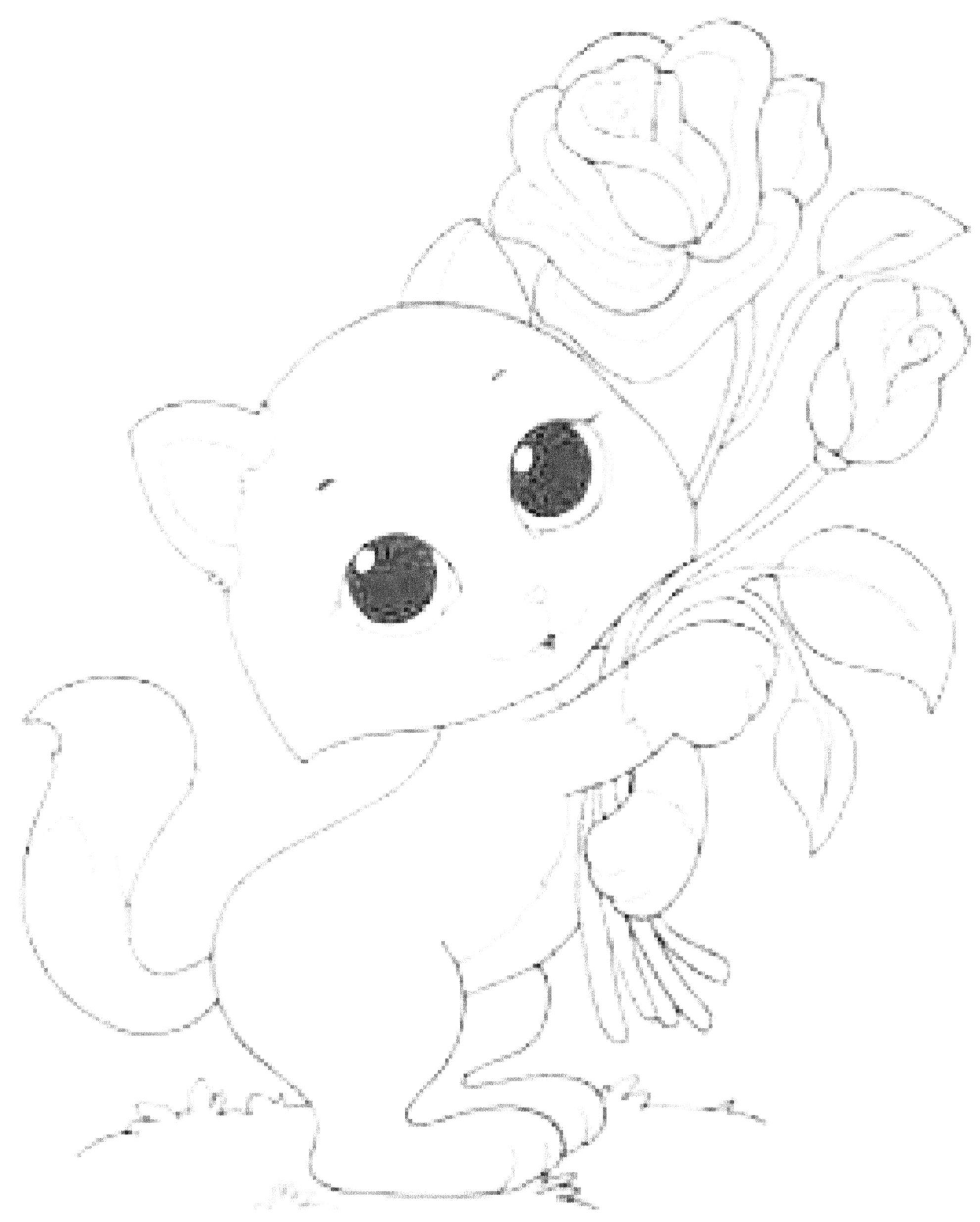

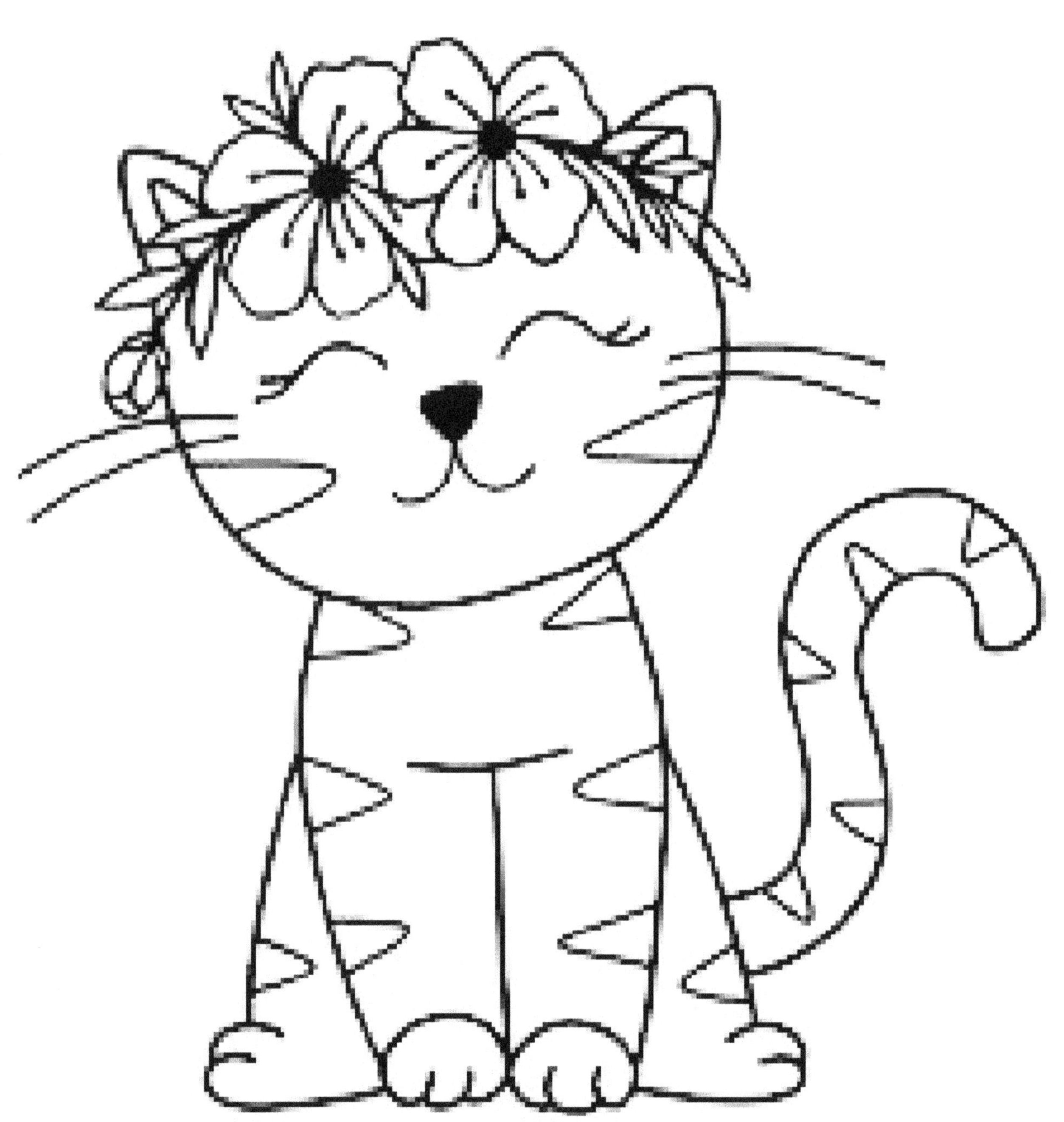

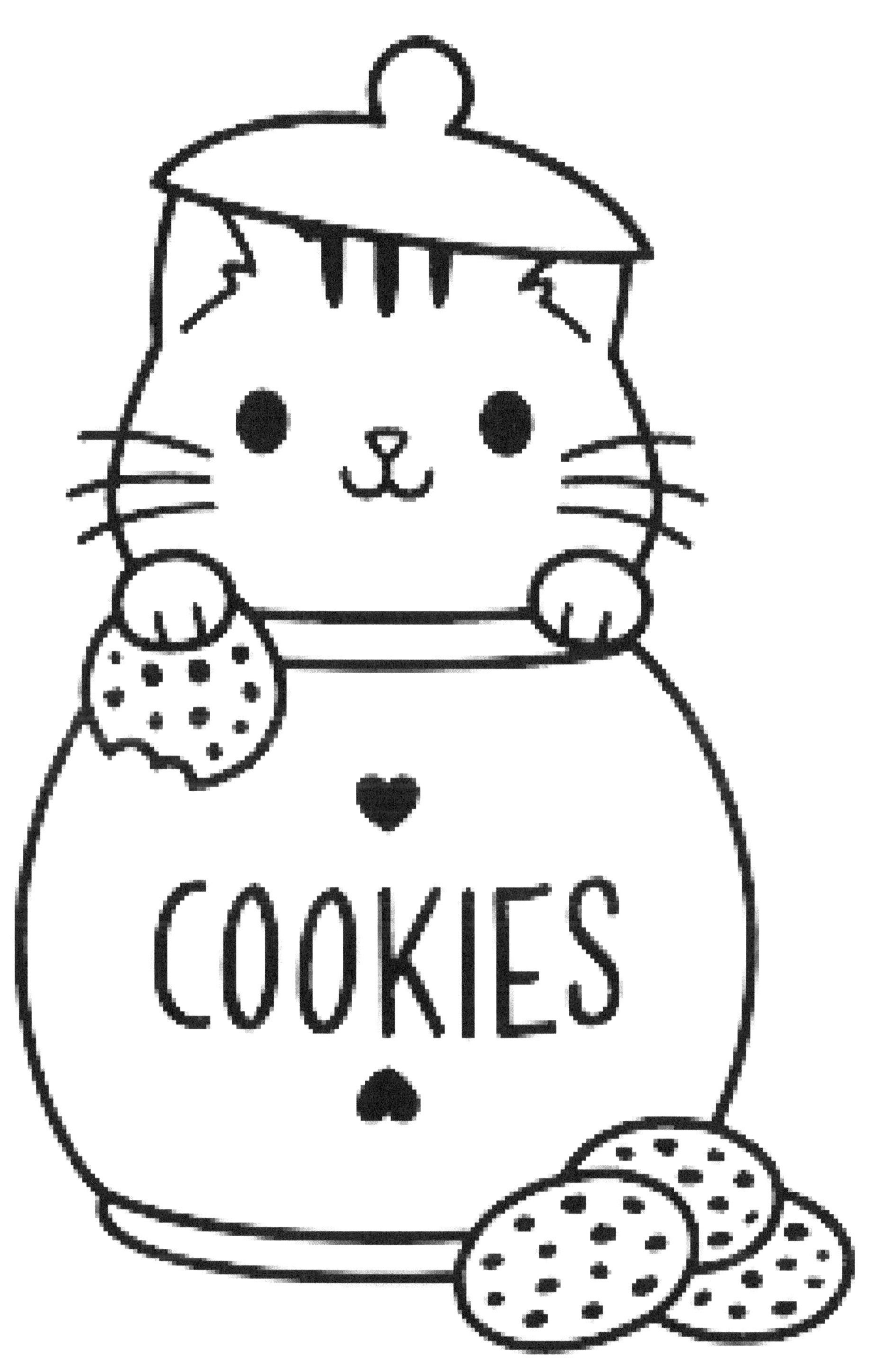

COOKIES

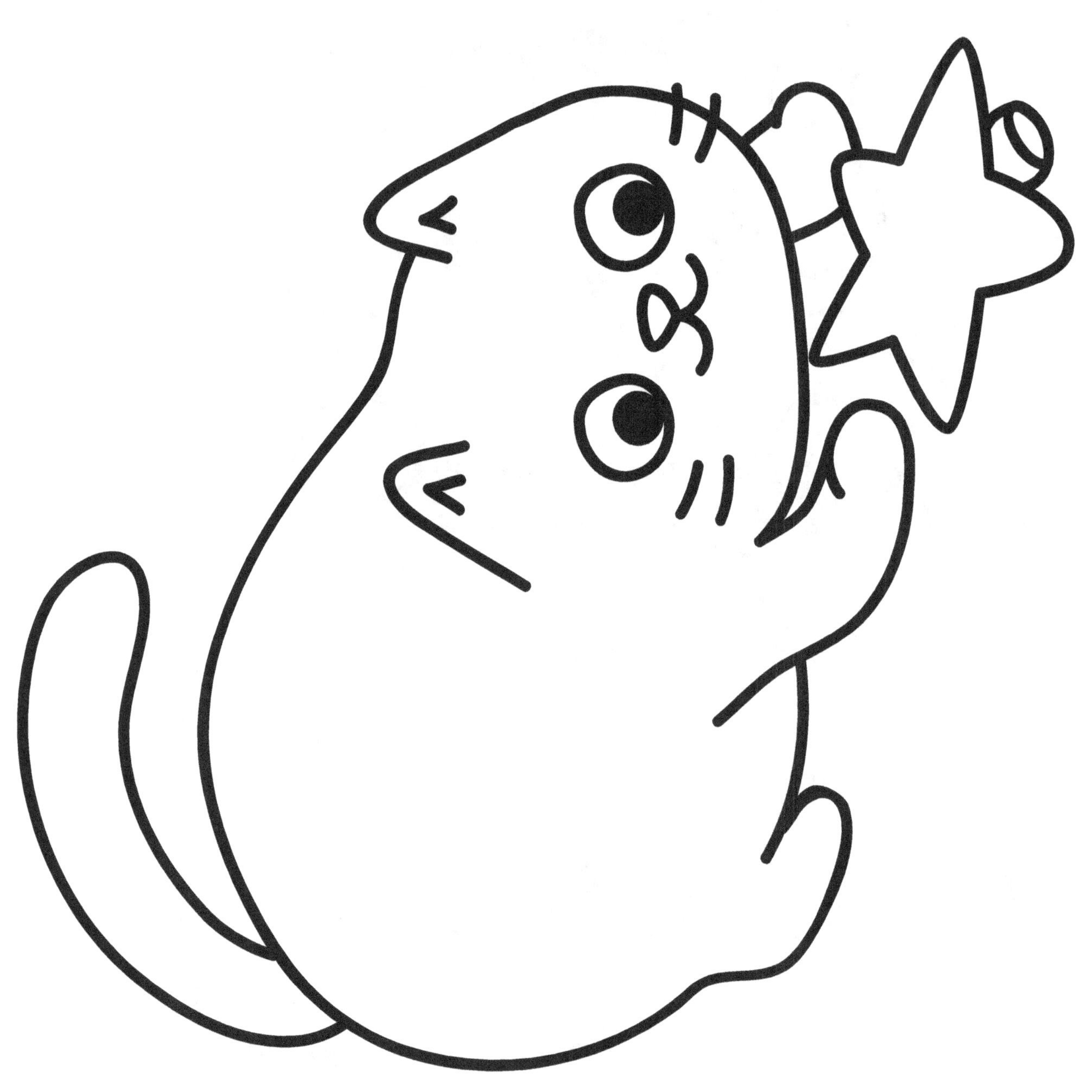

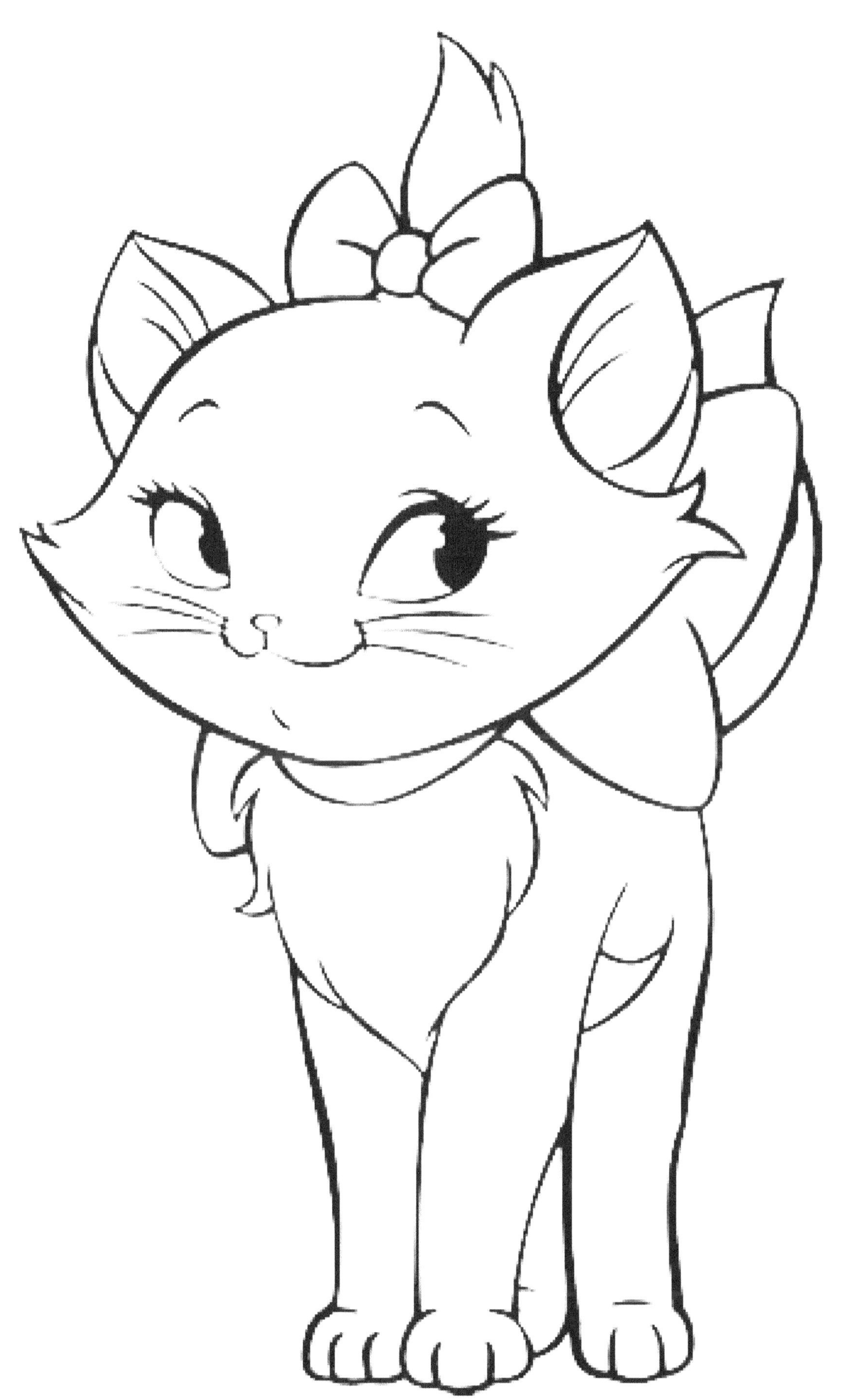

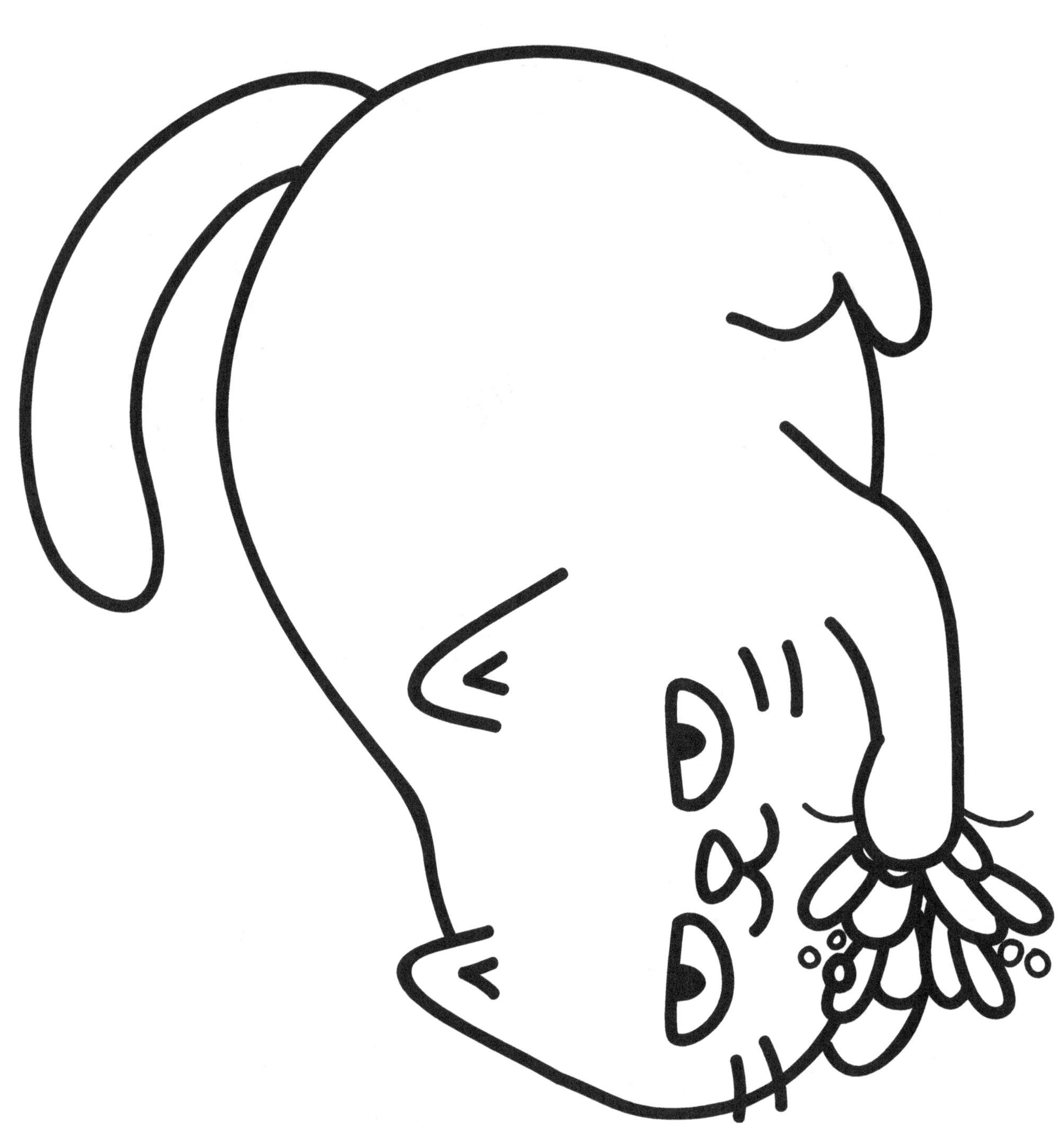

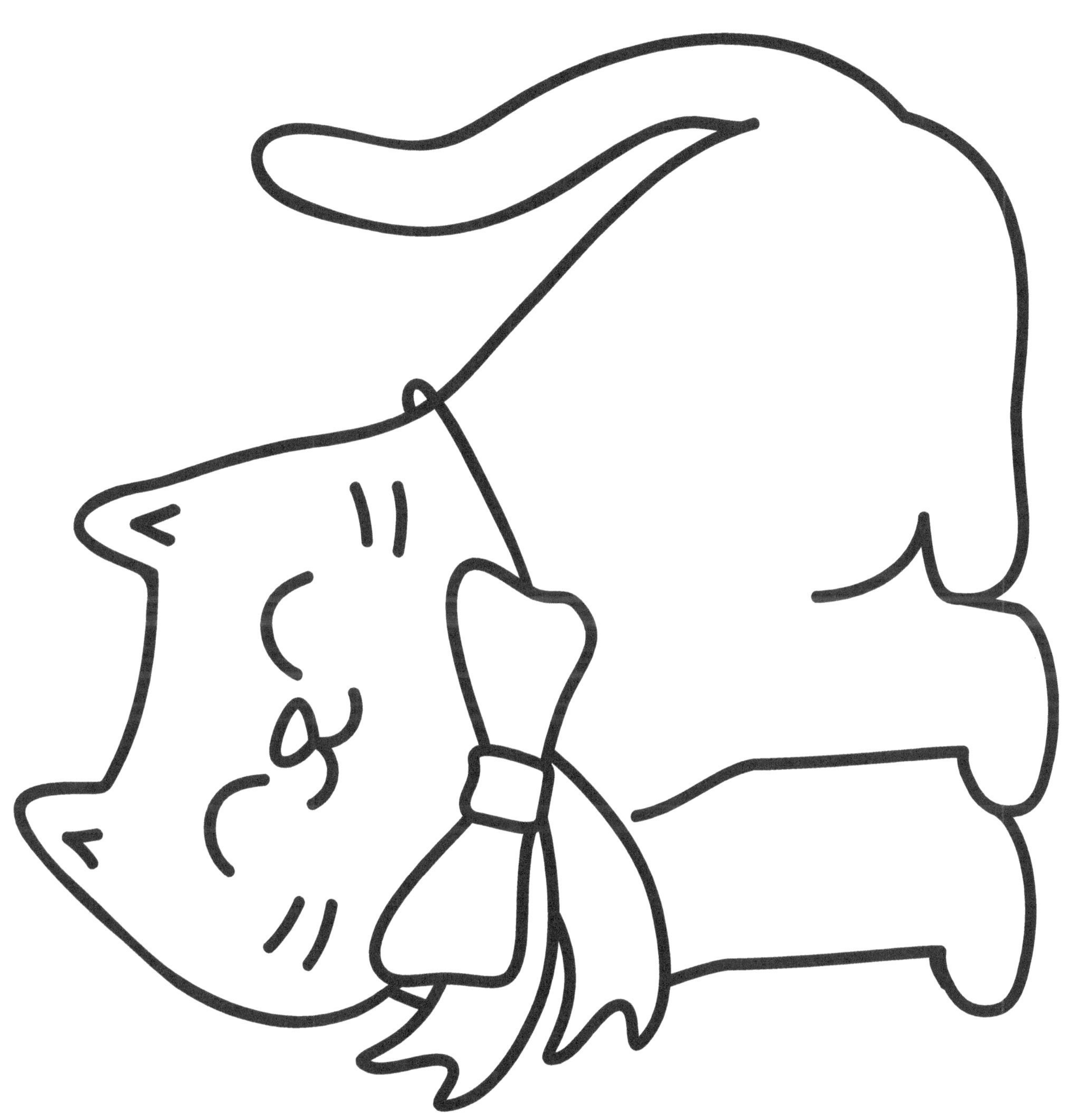

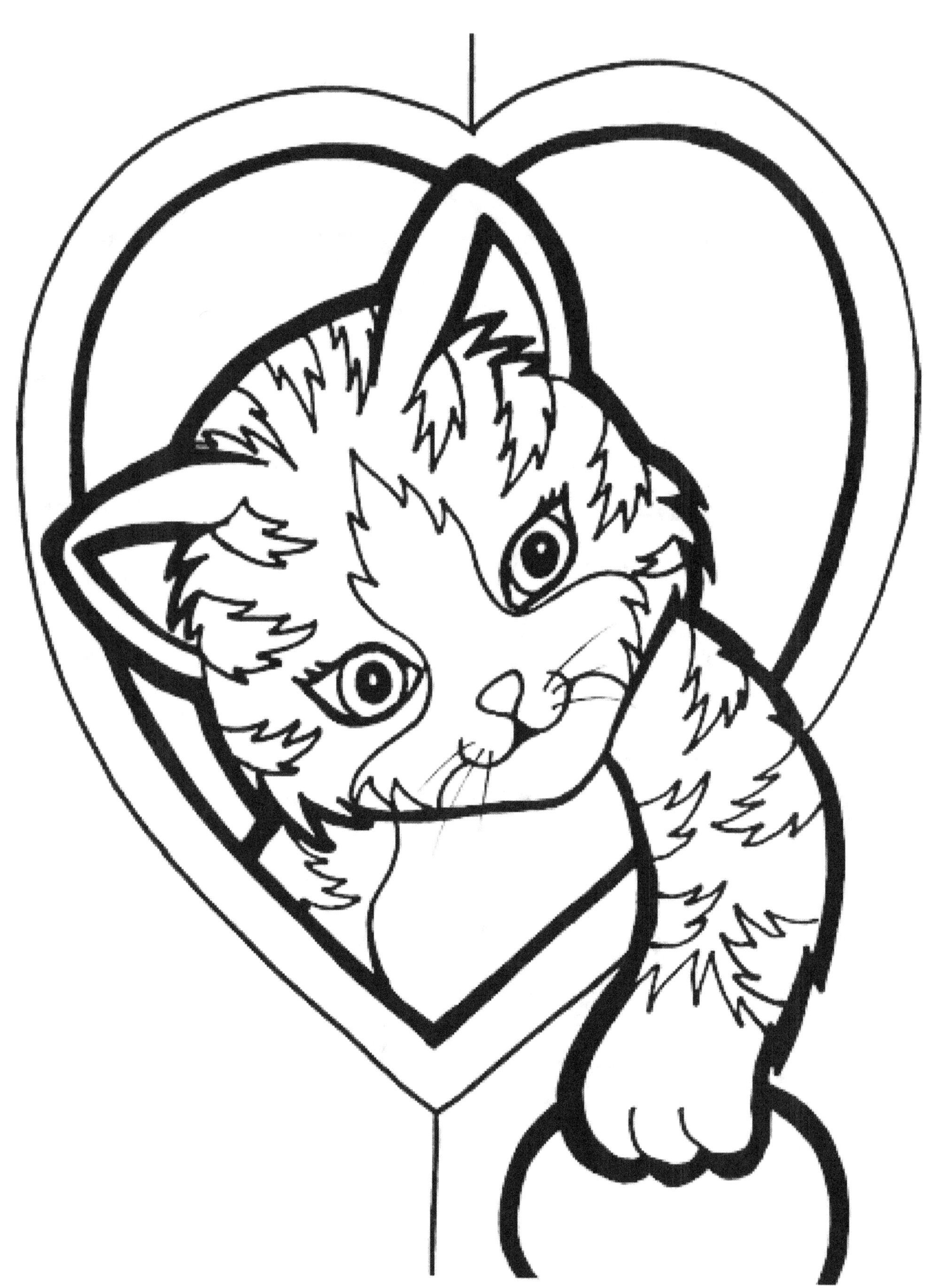

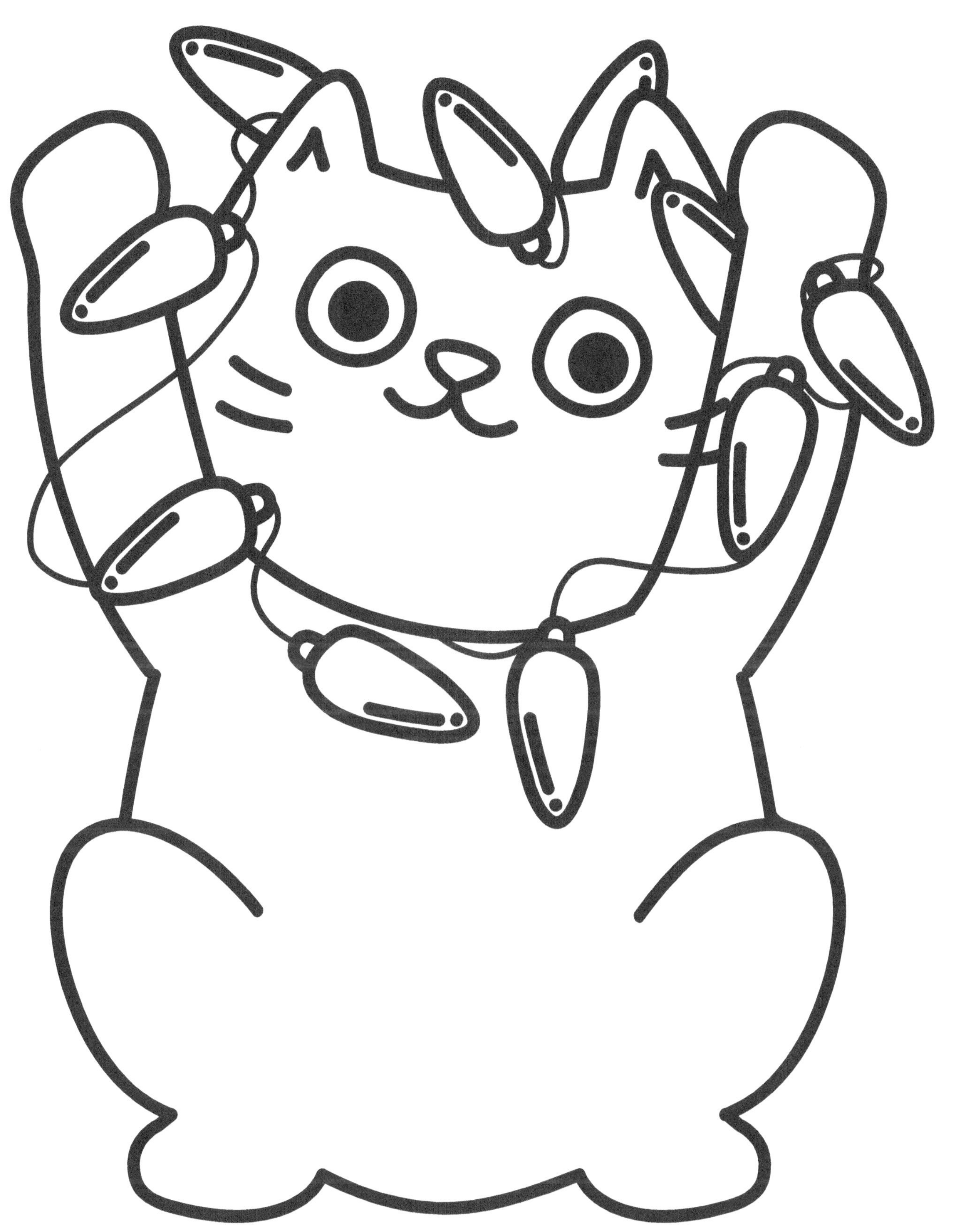

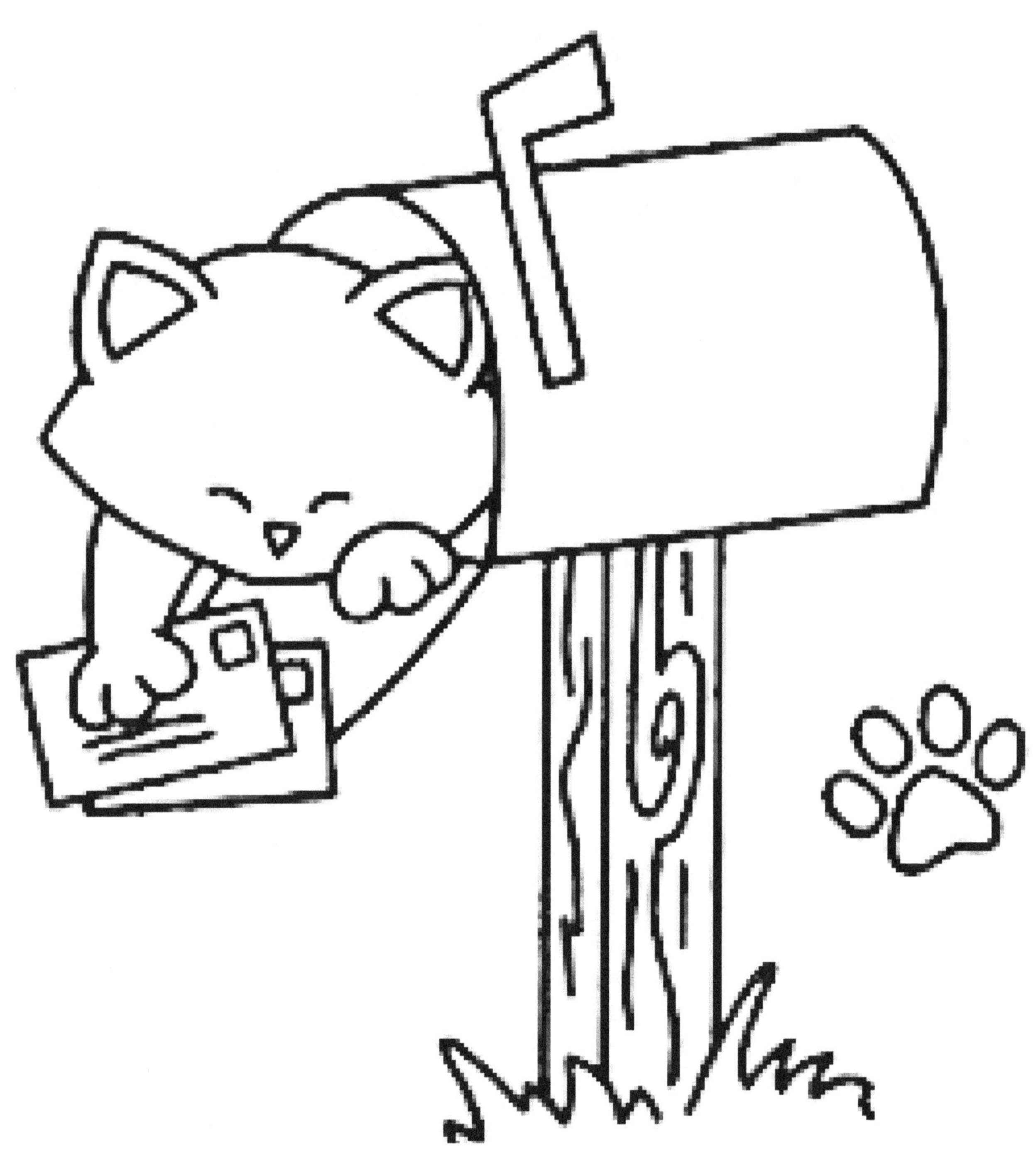

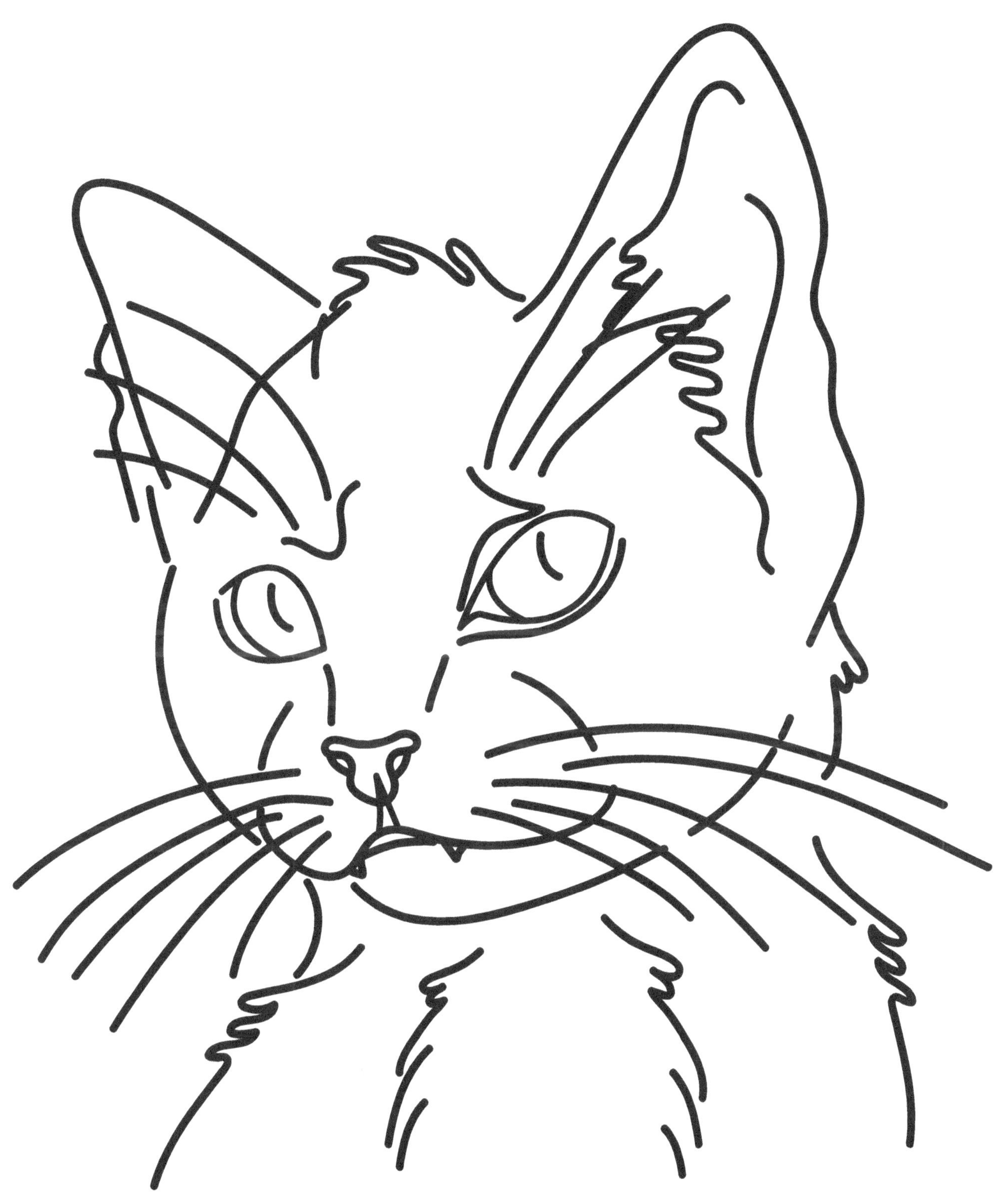

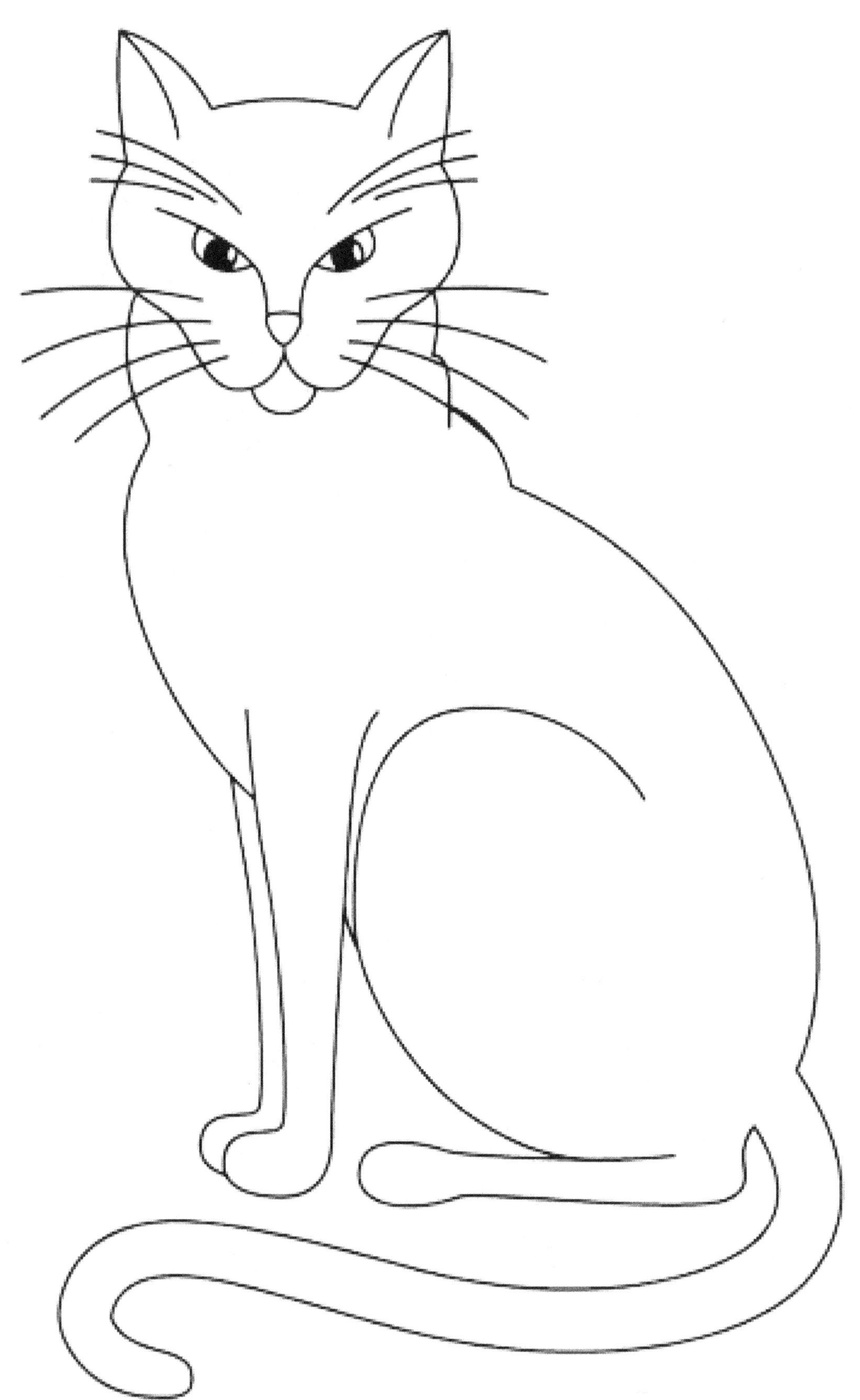

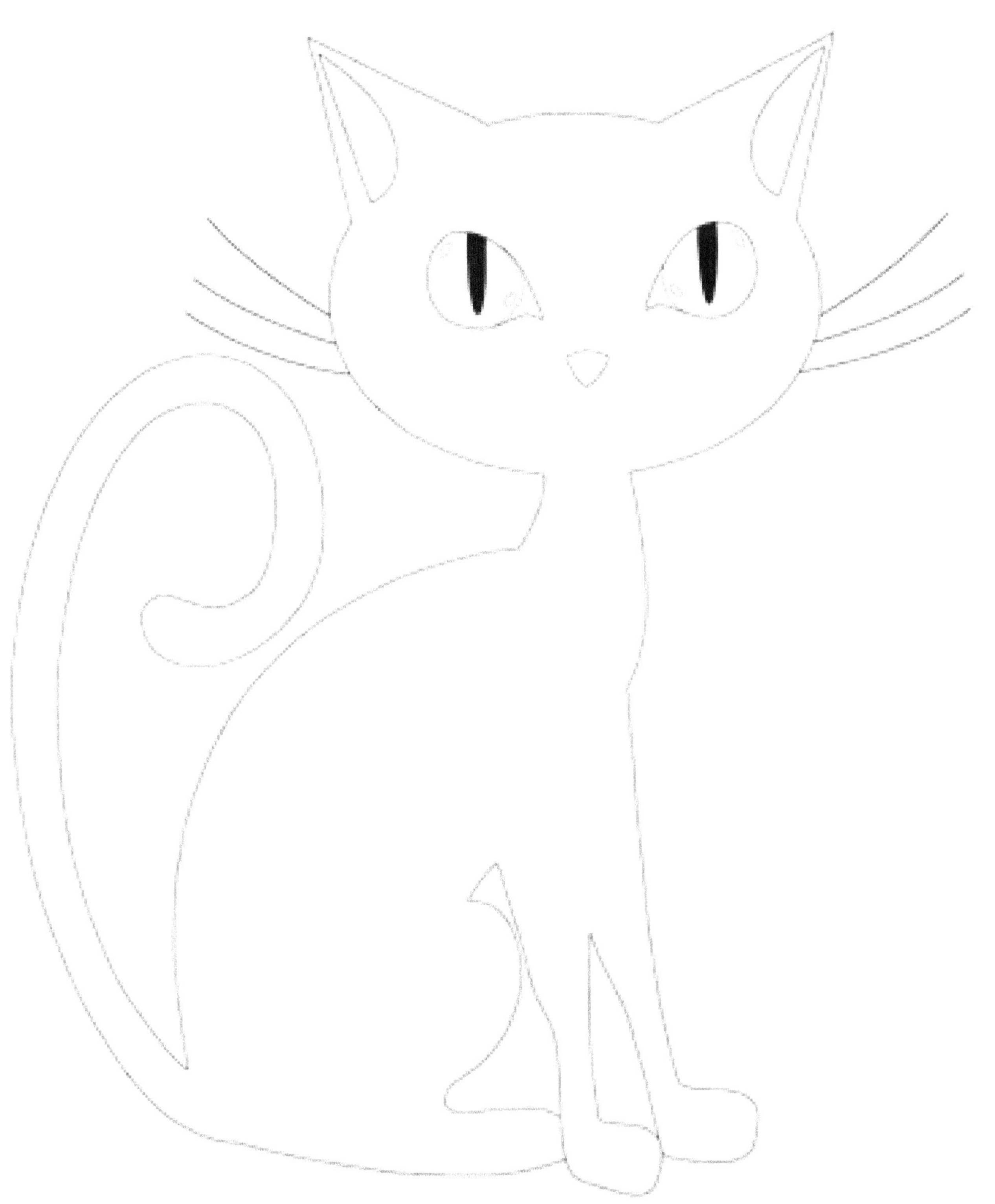

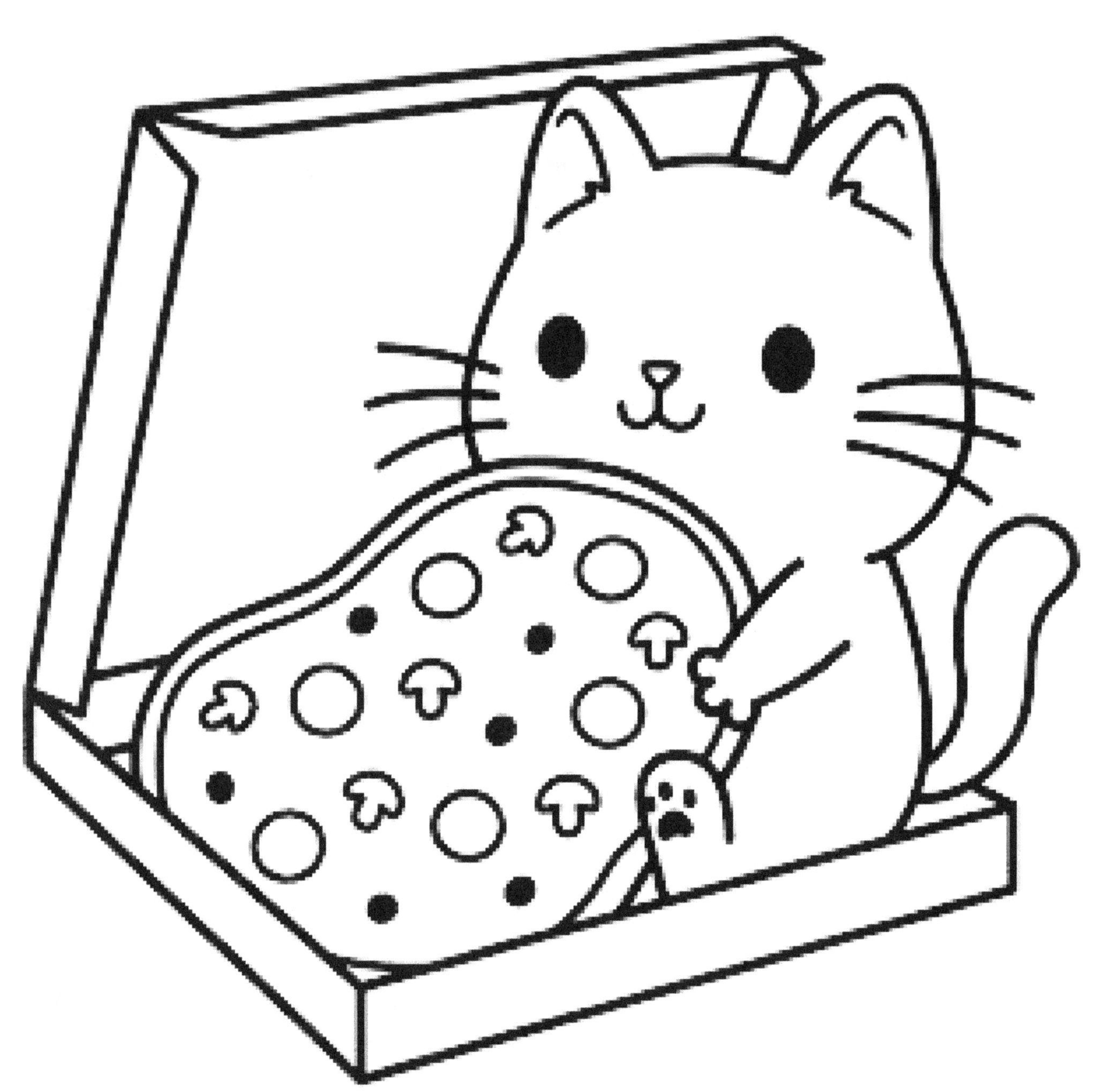

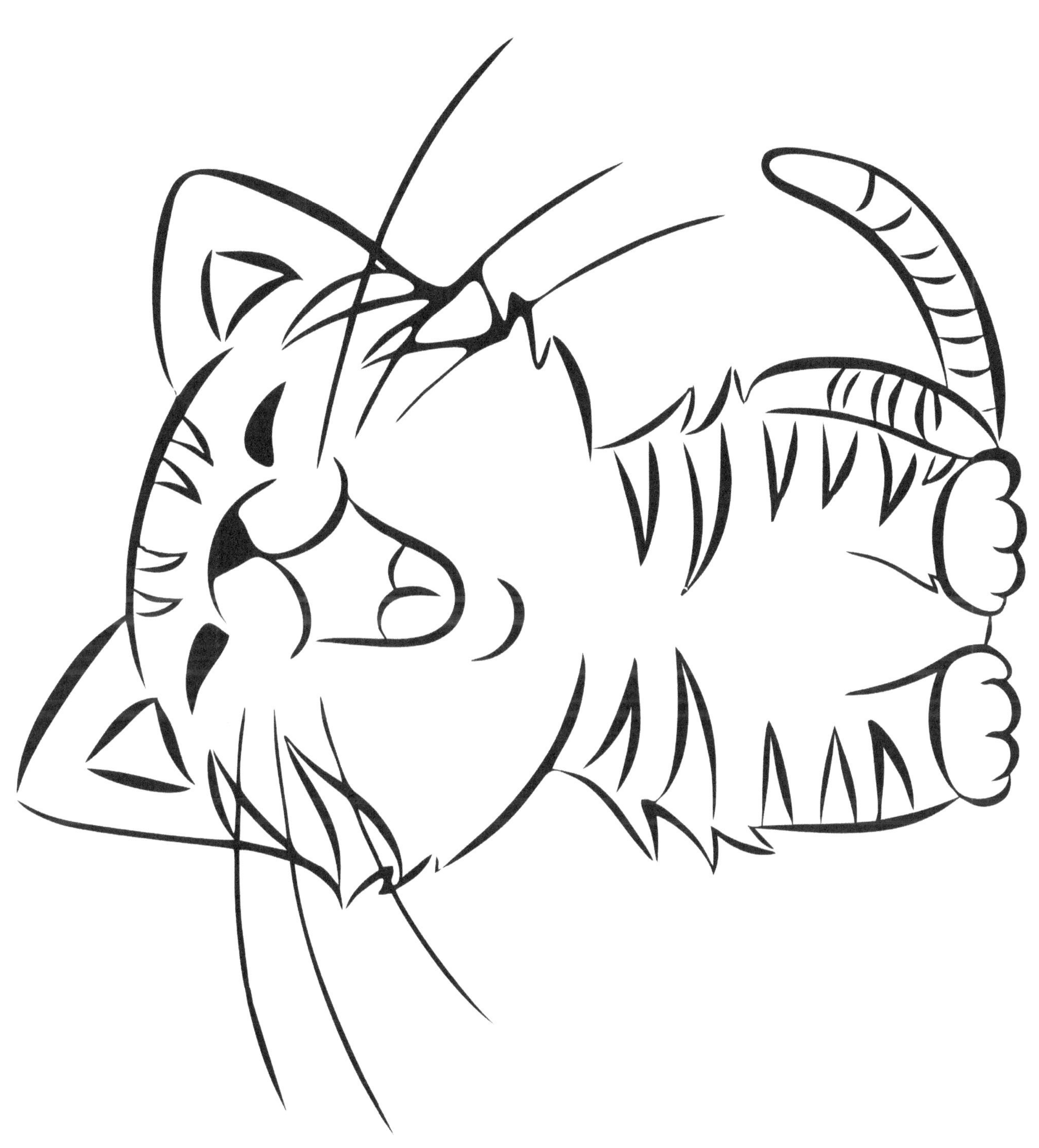

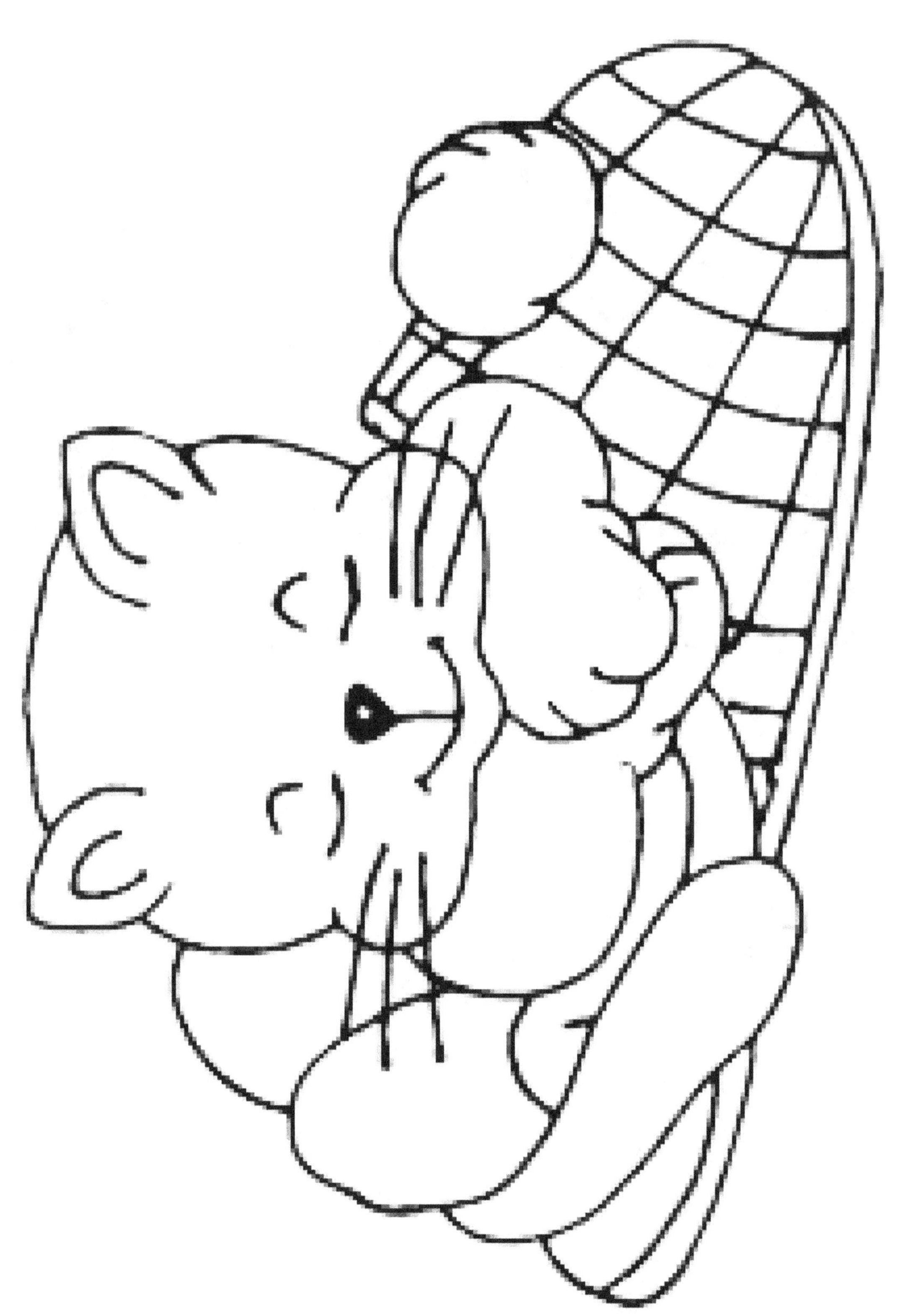

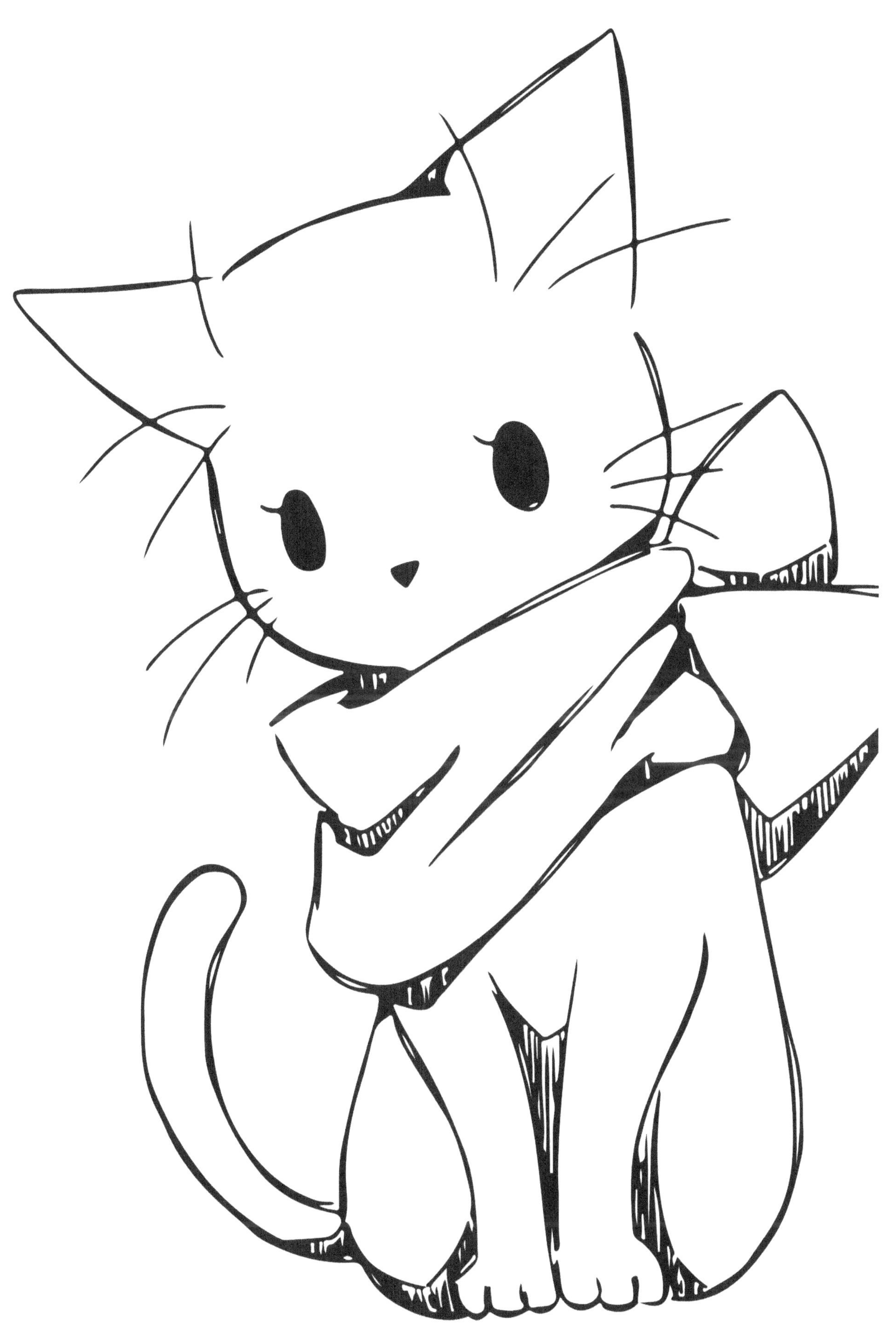

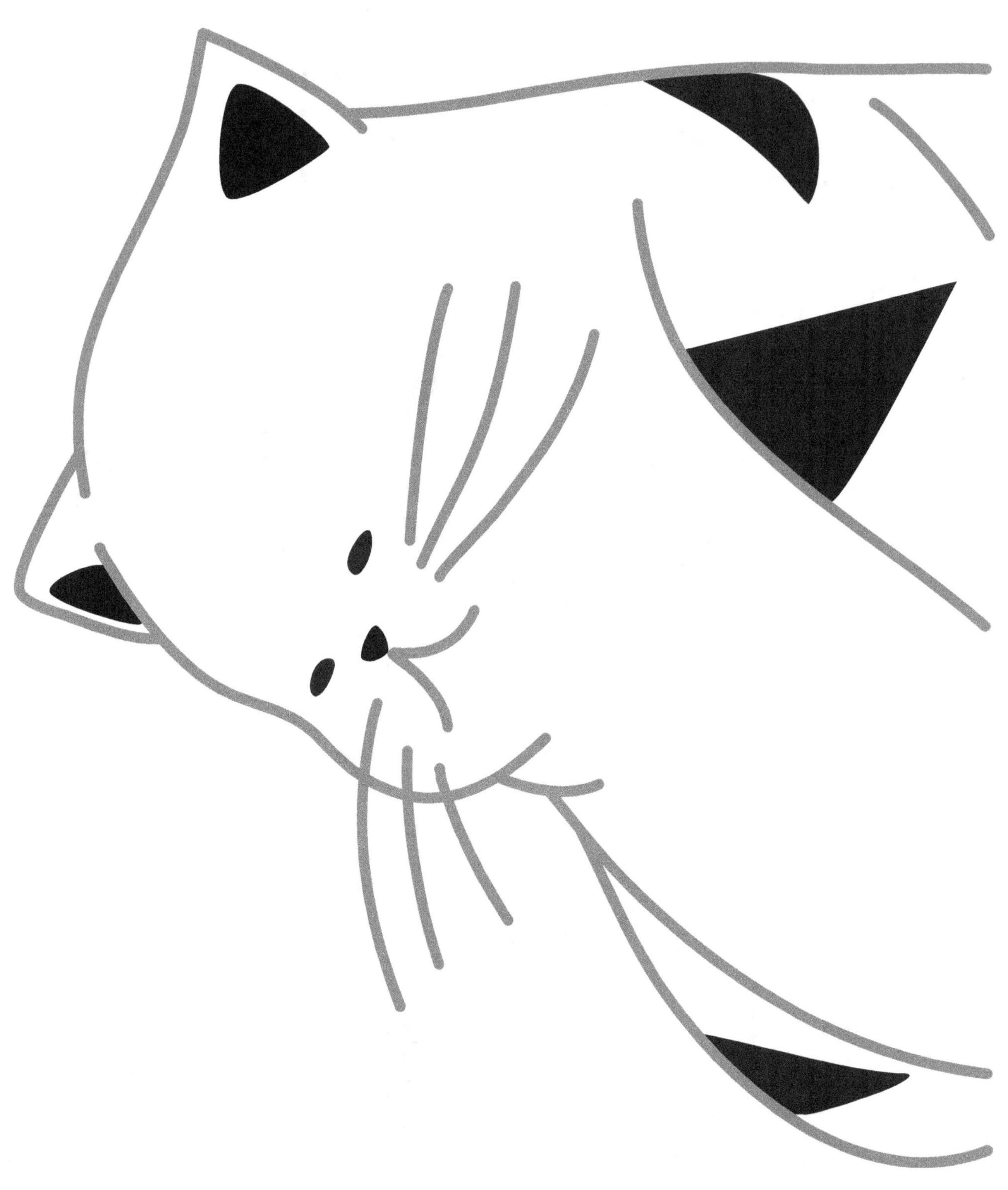

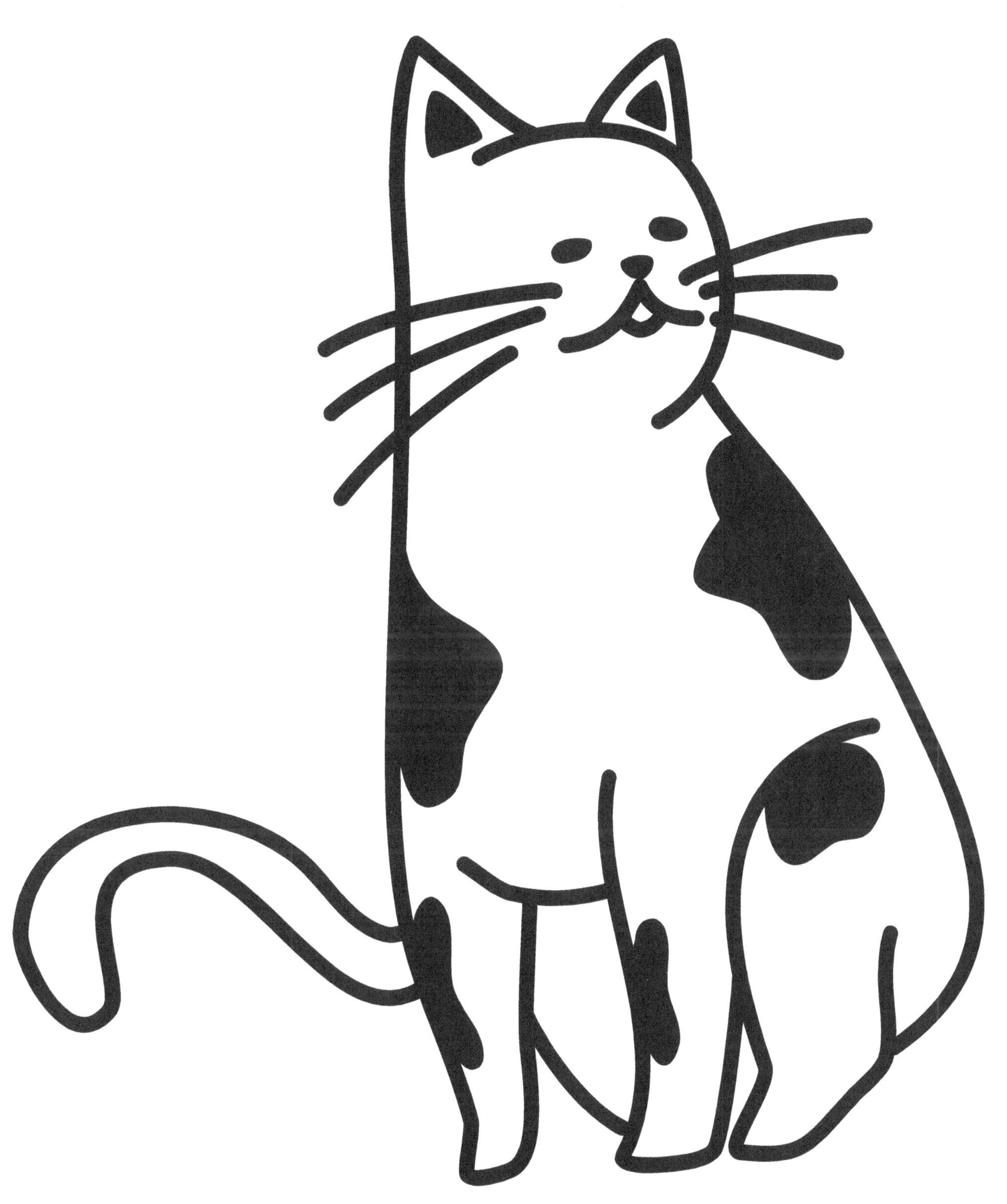

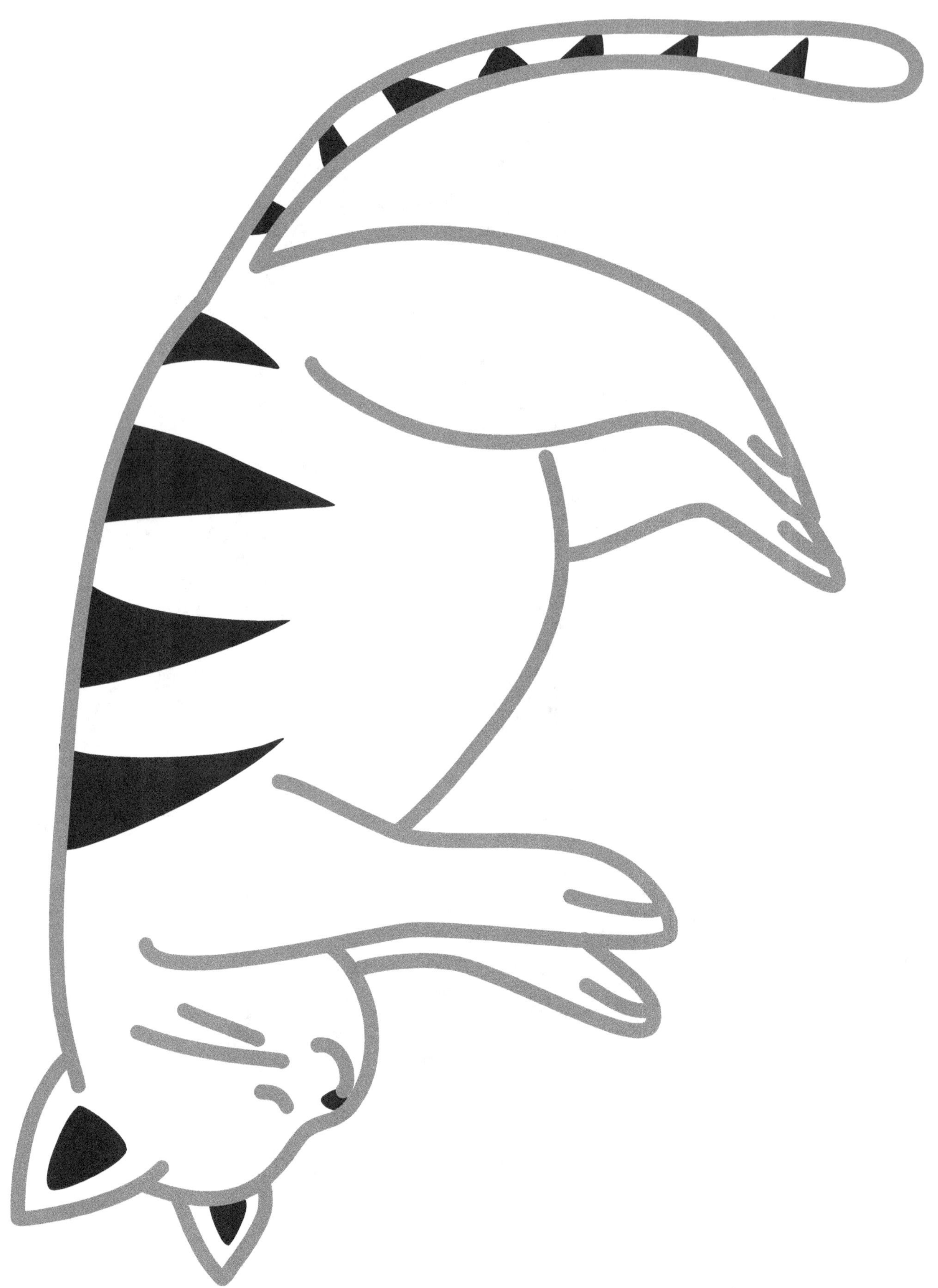

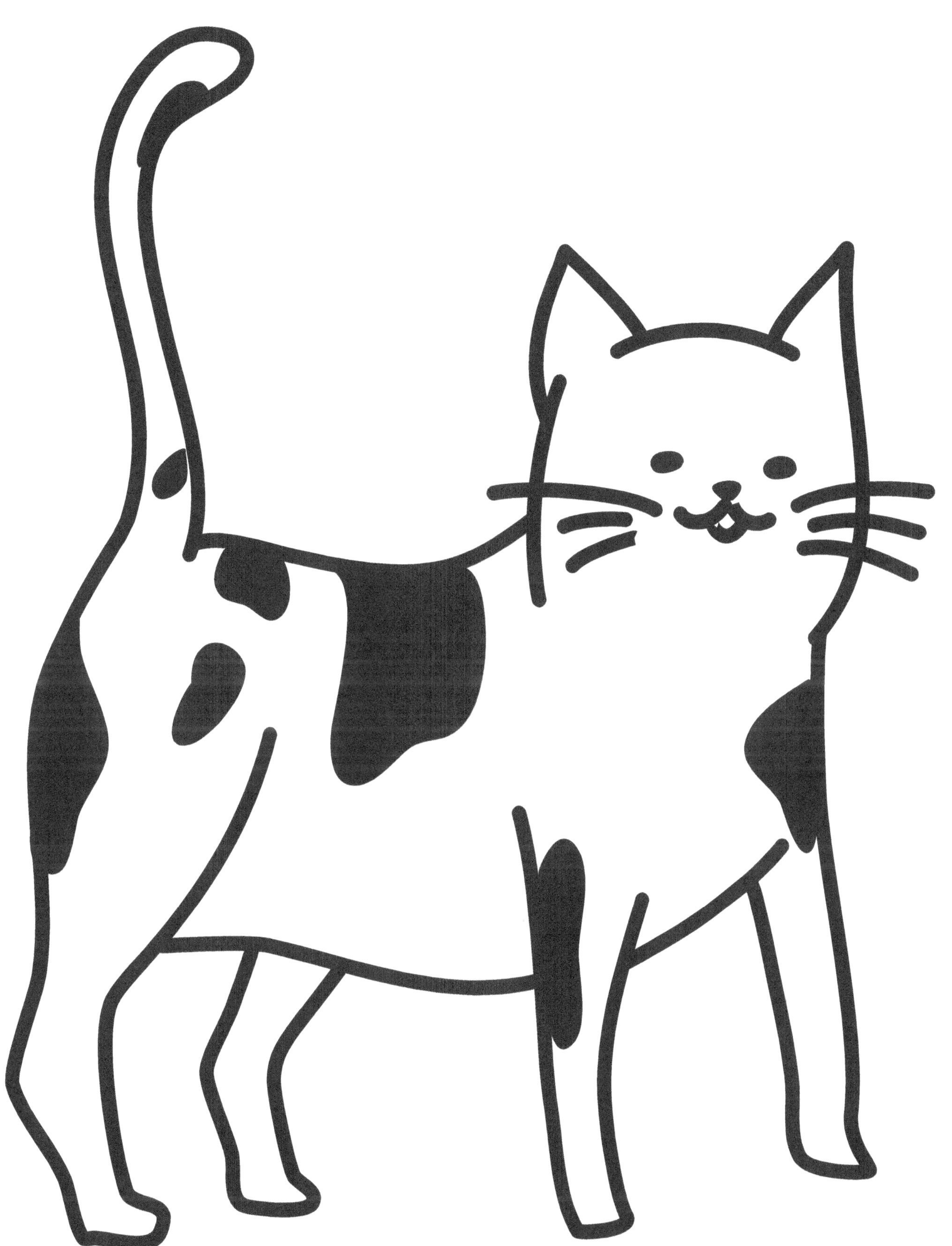

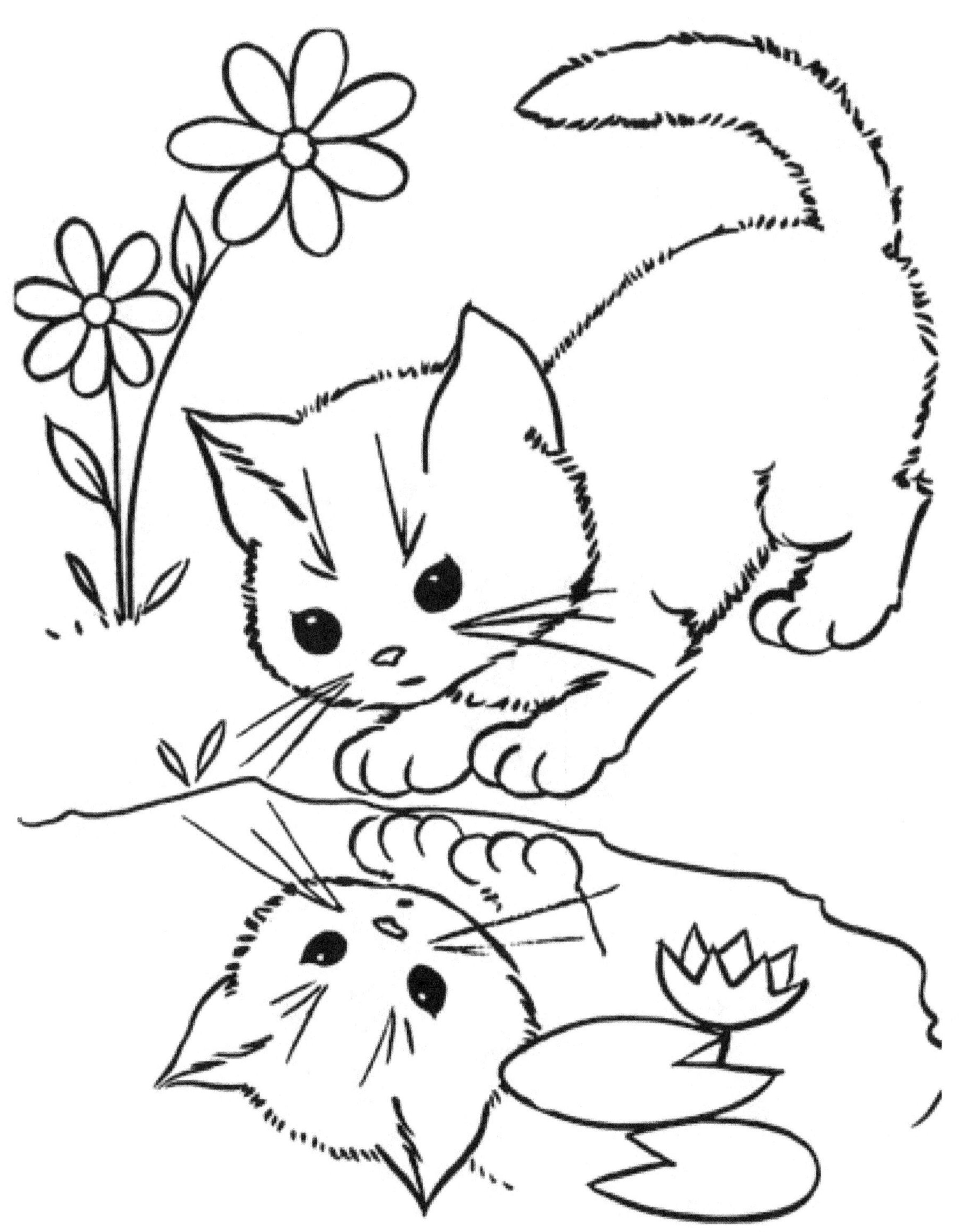

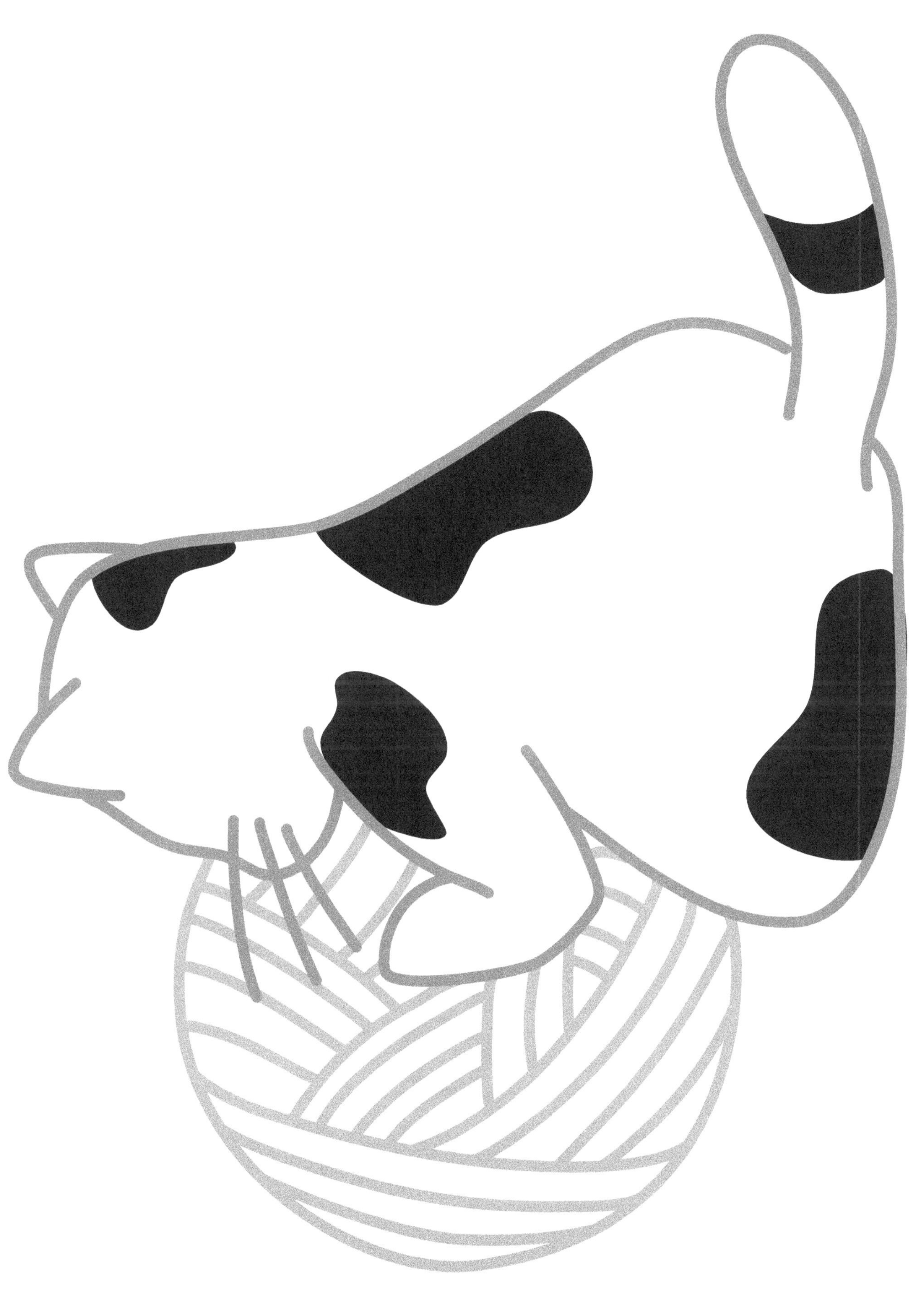

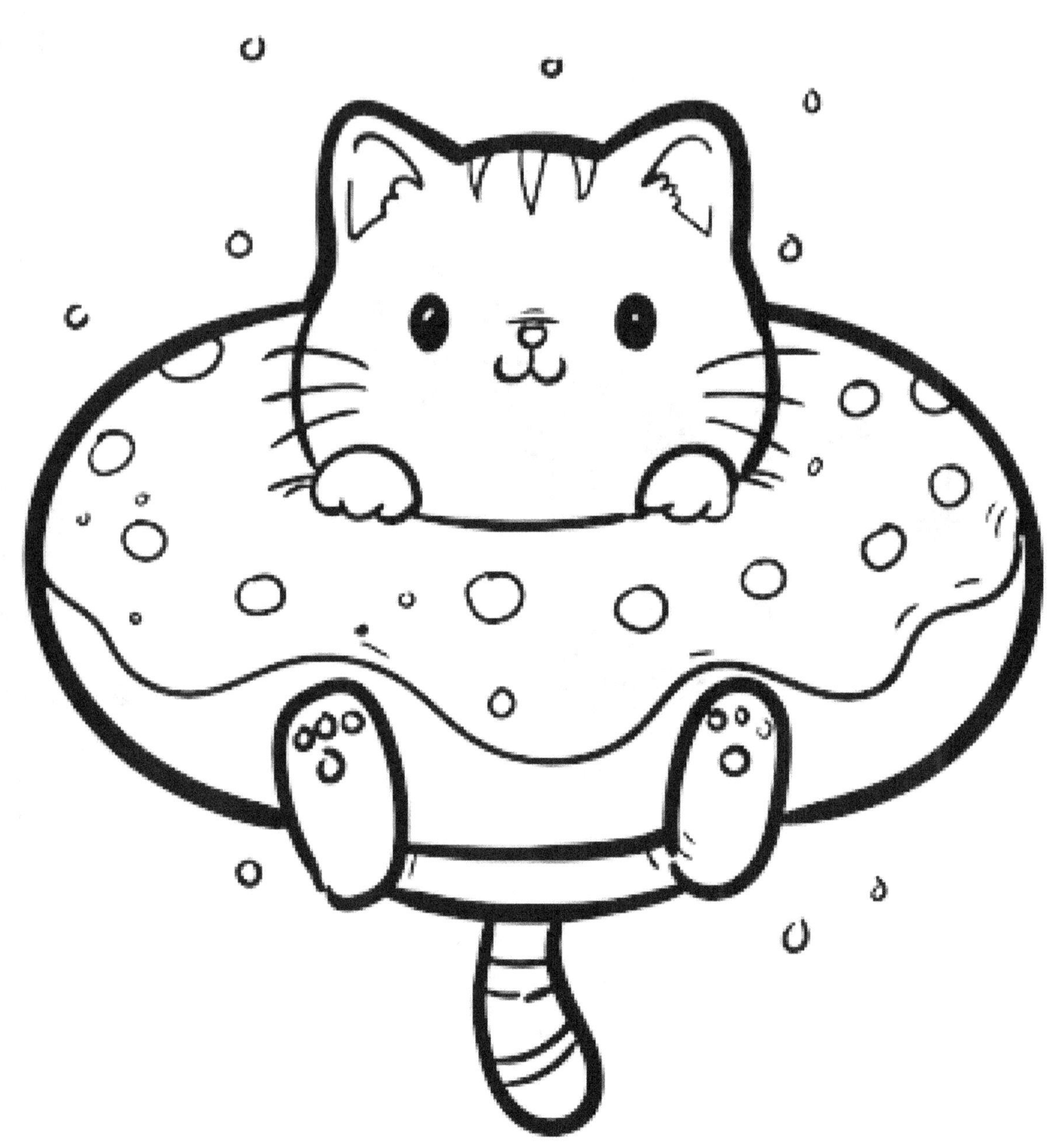

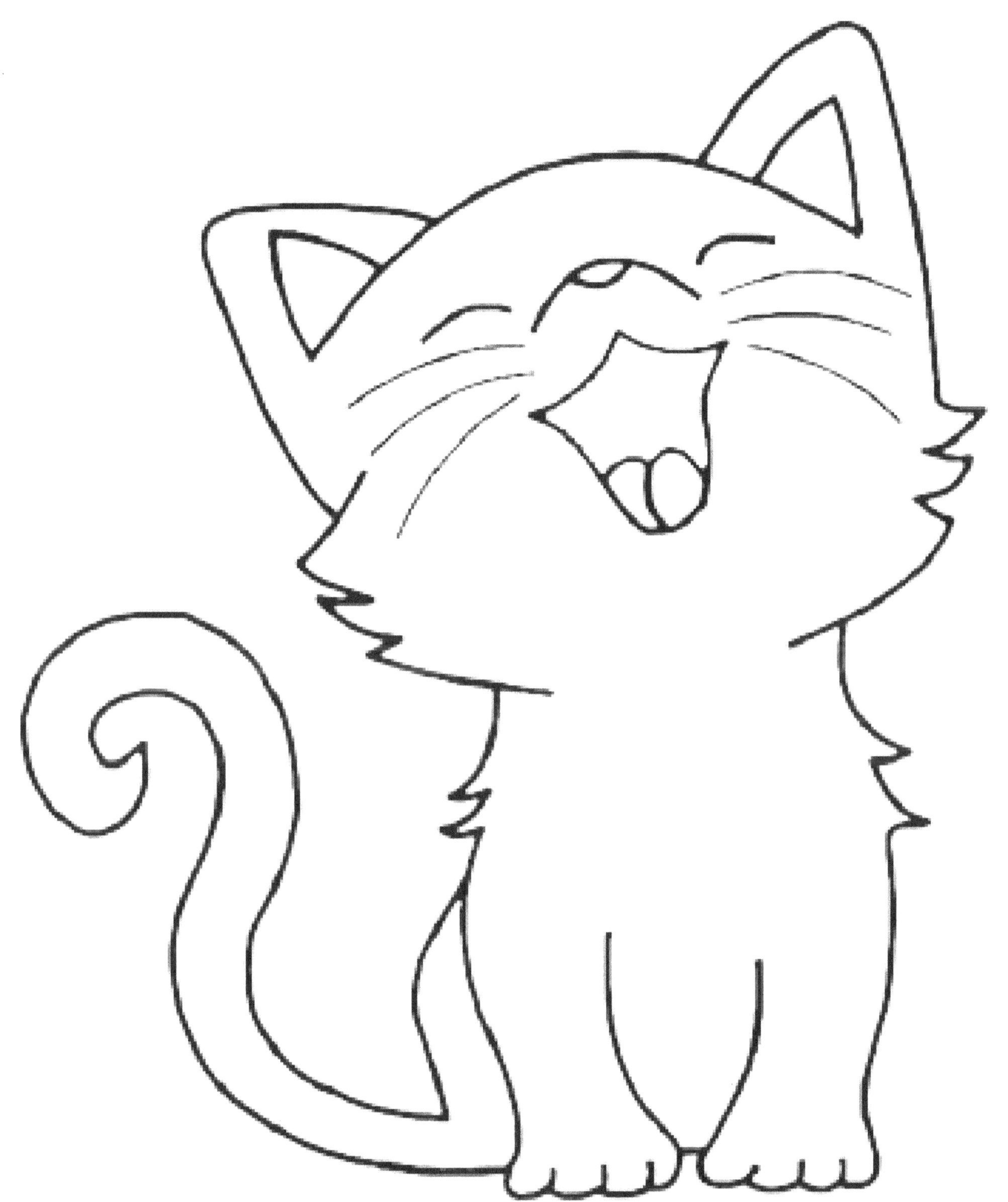

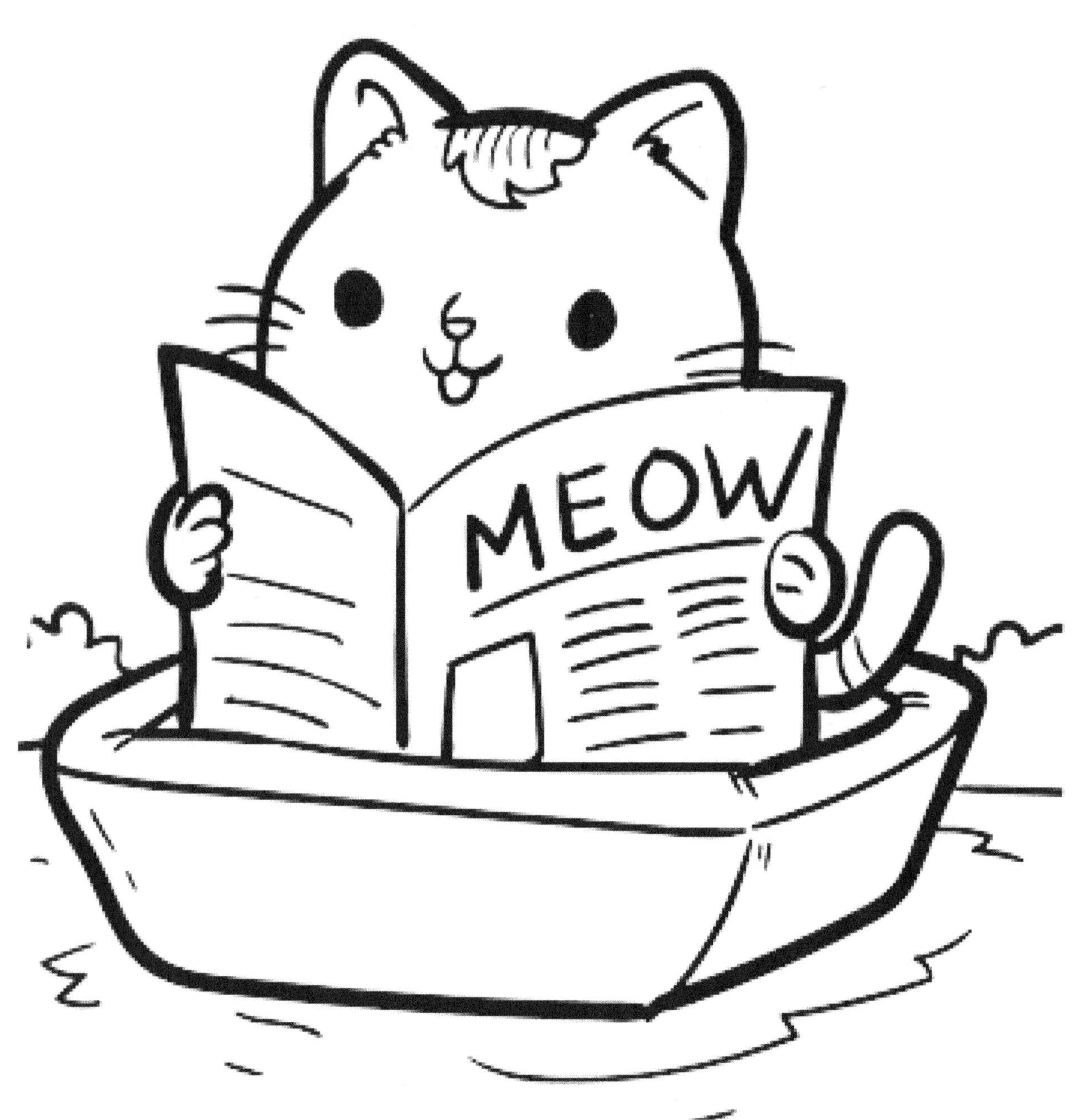
MEOW

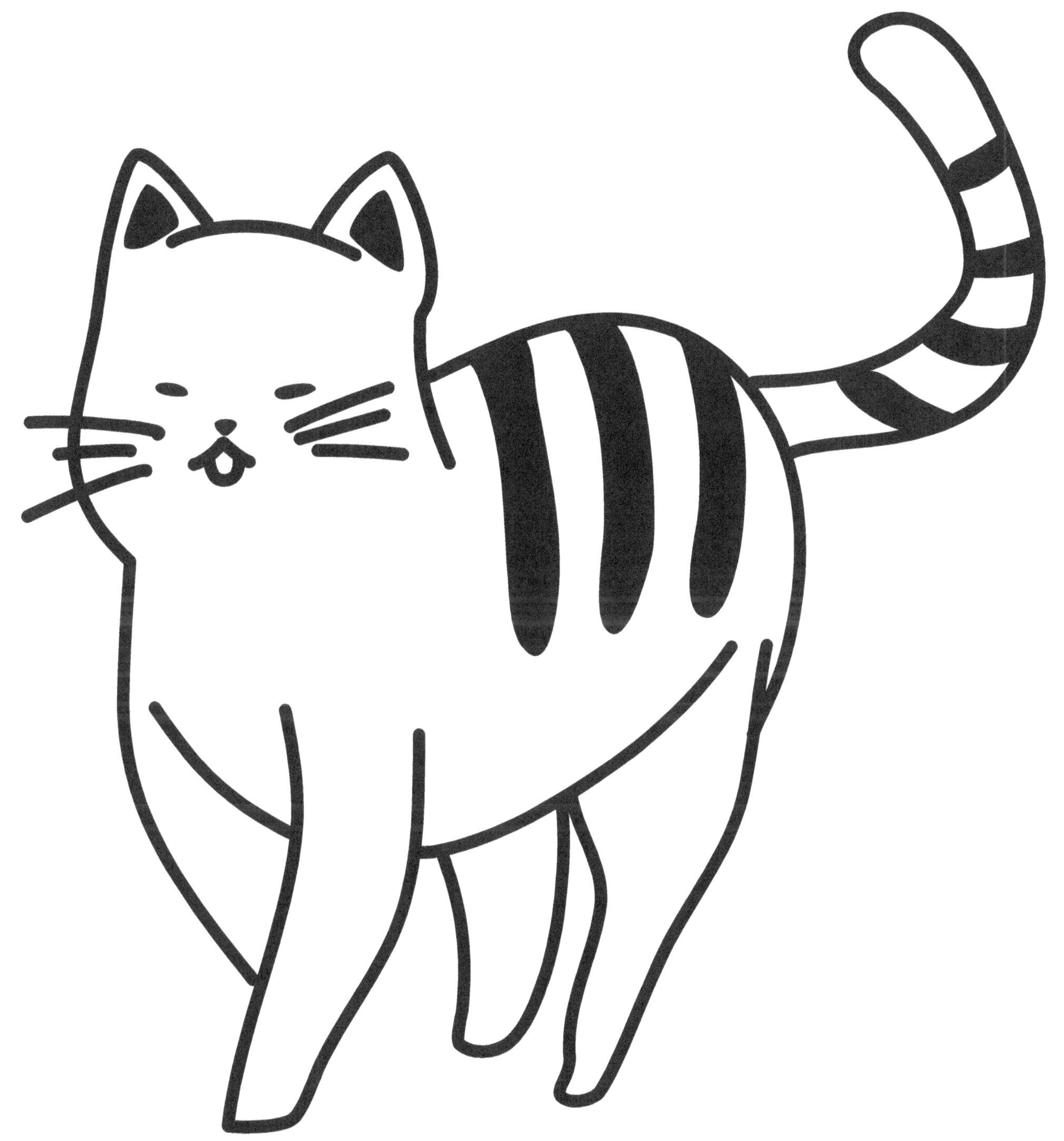

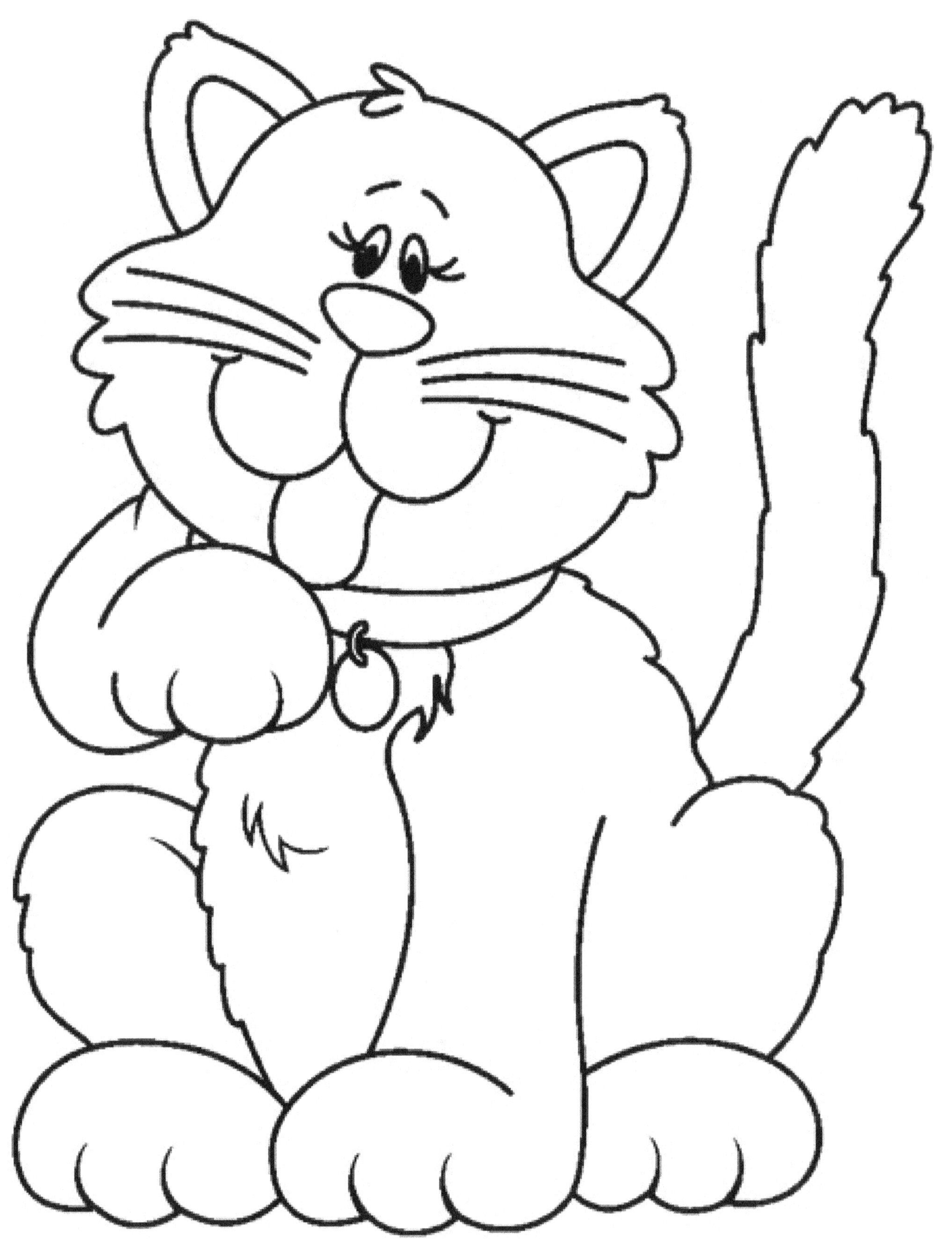

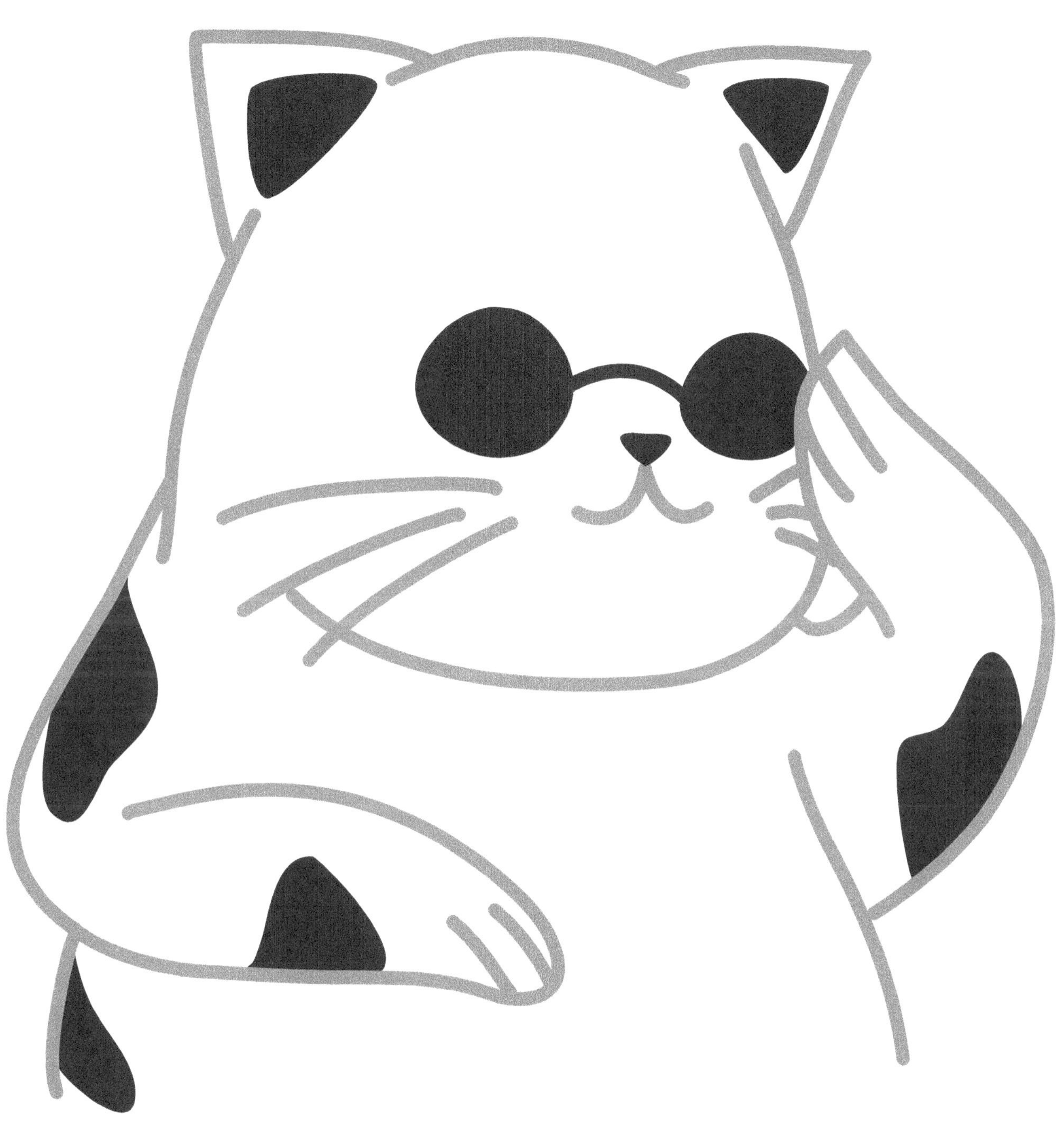

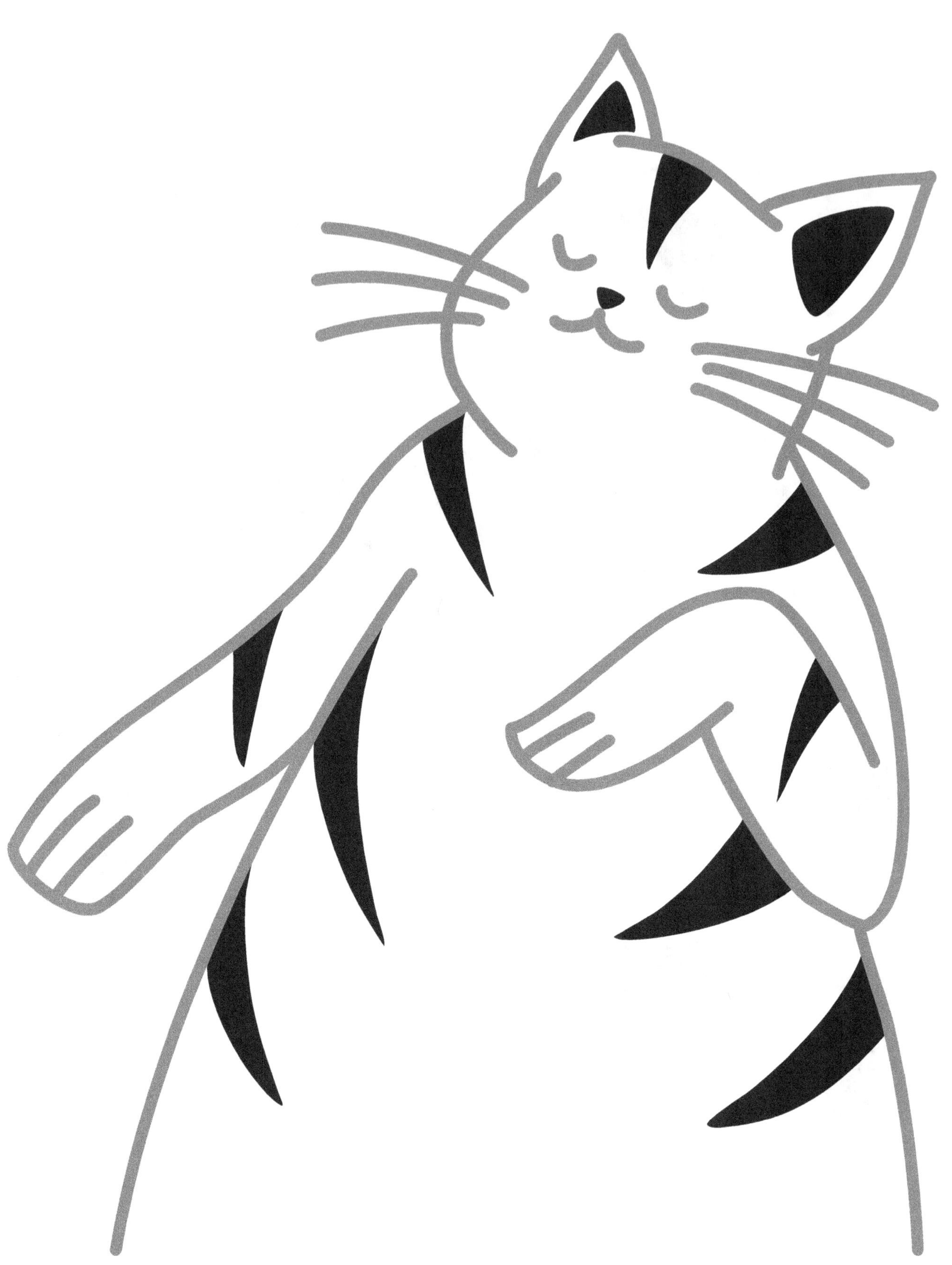

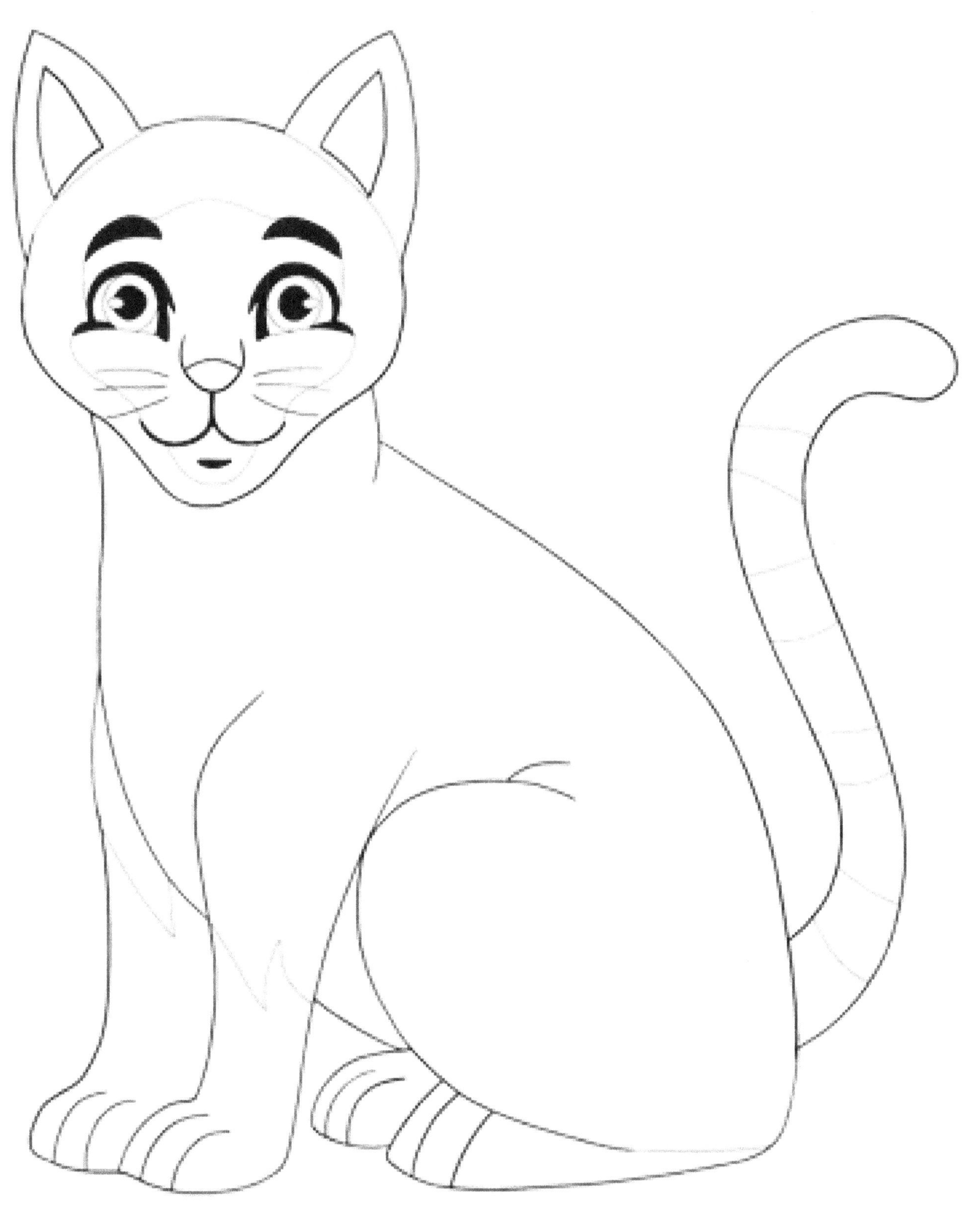

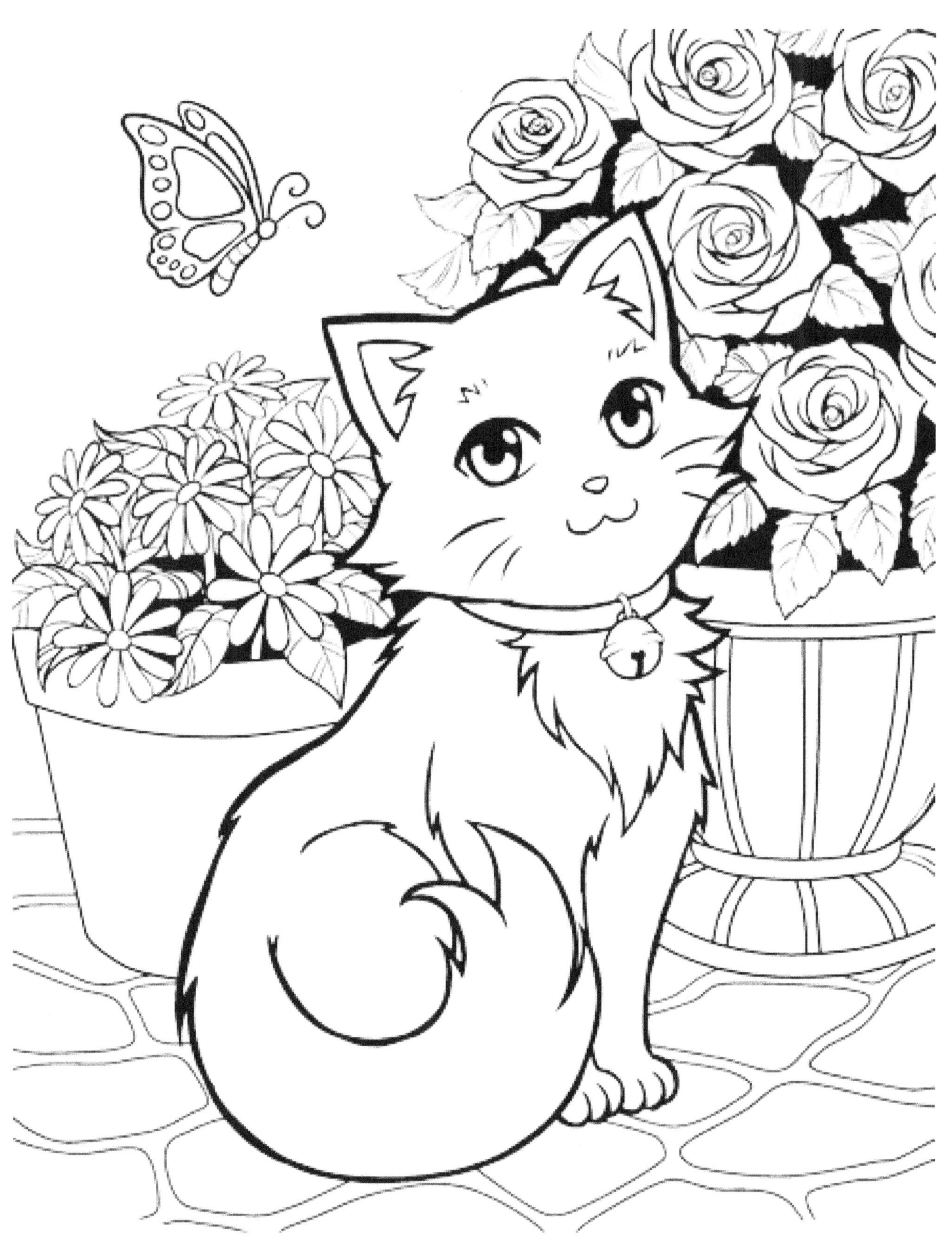

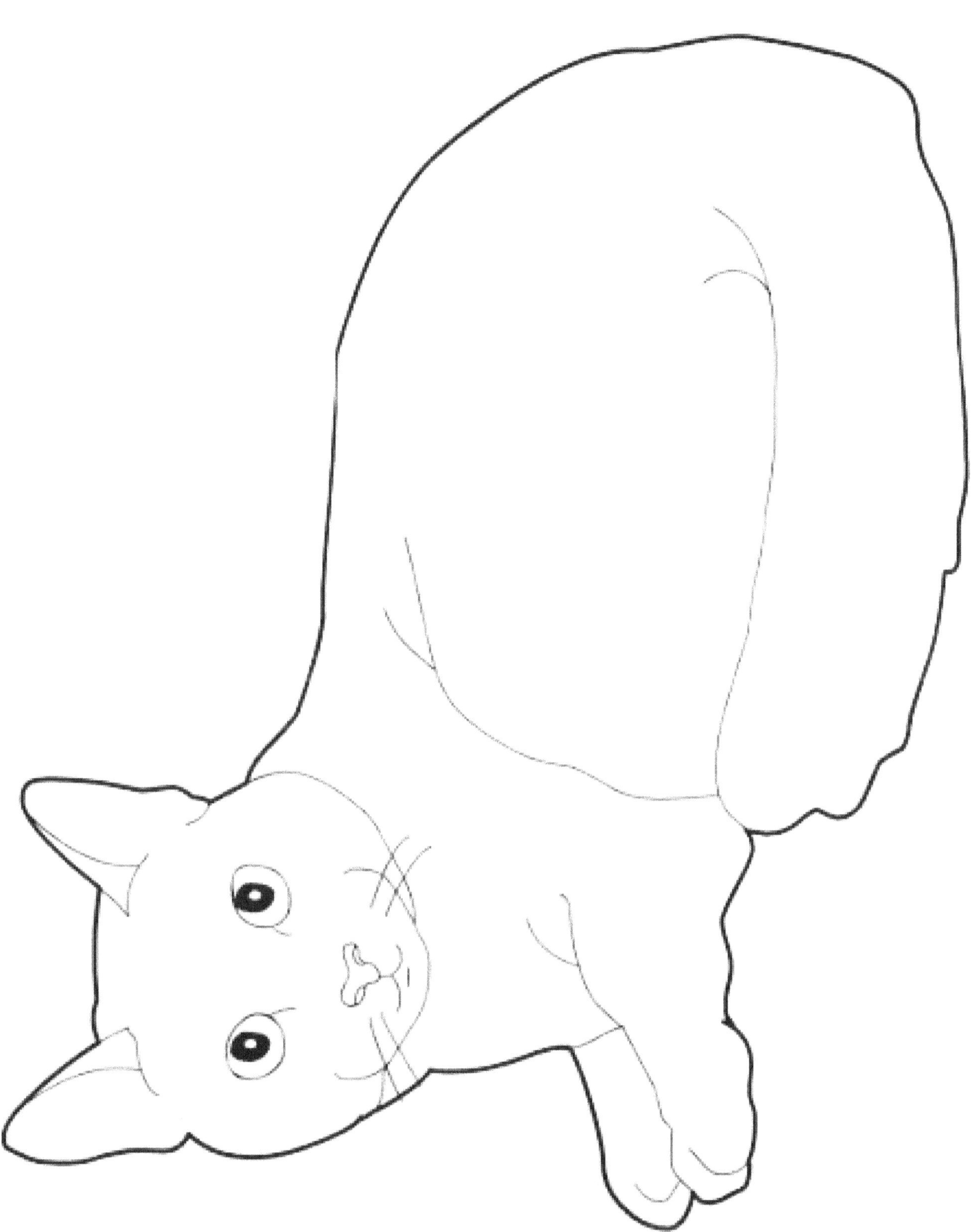

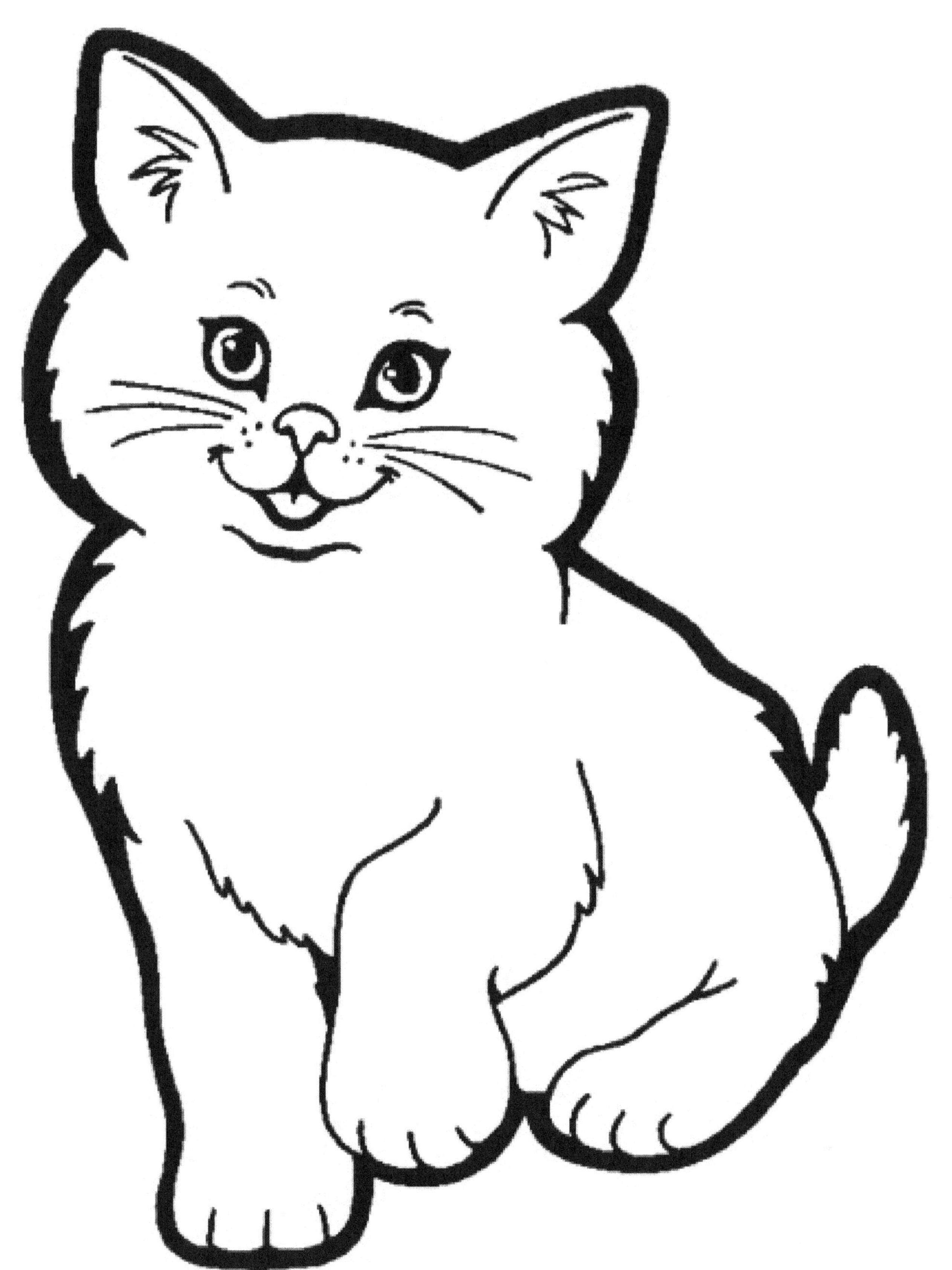

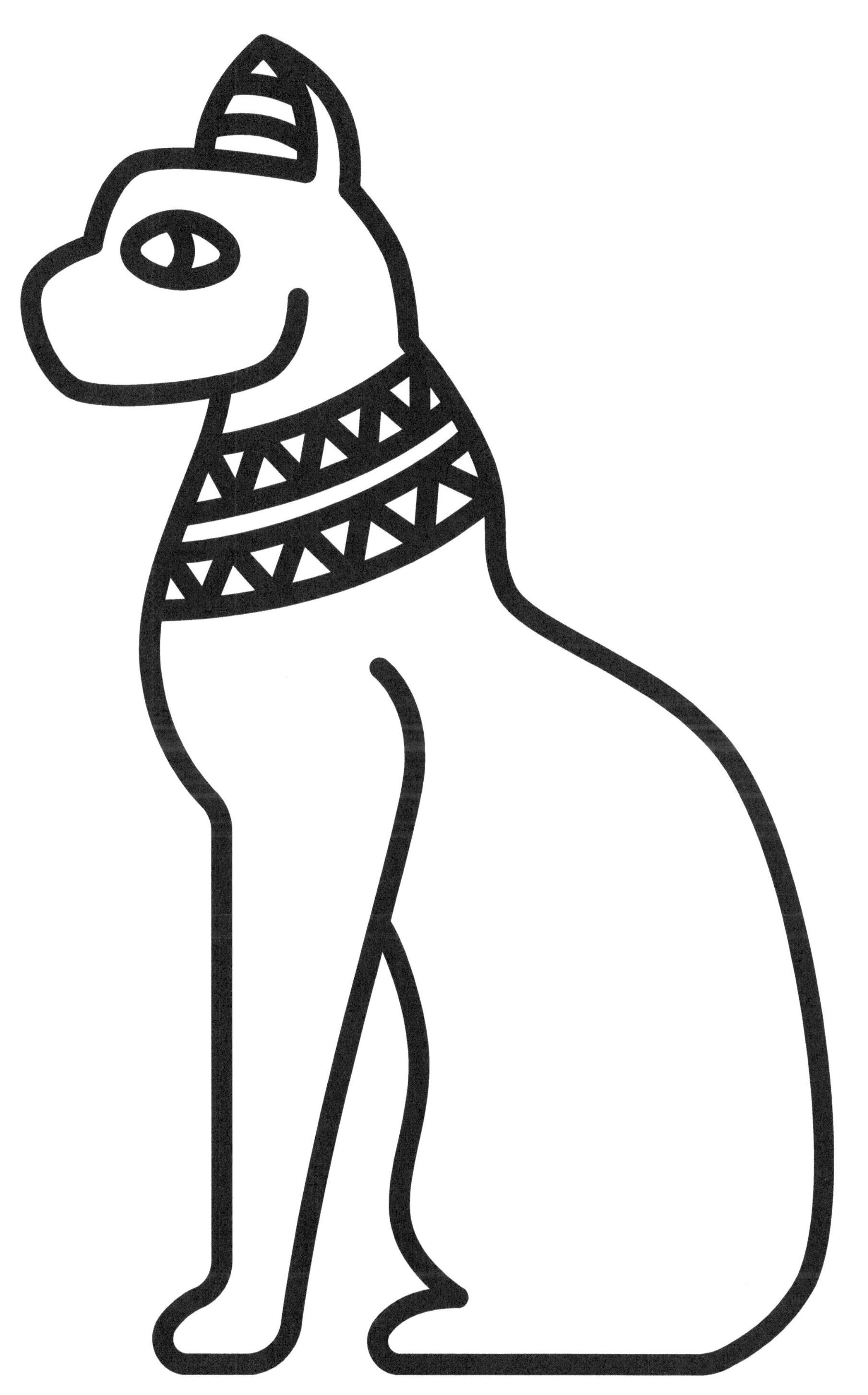

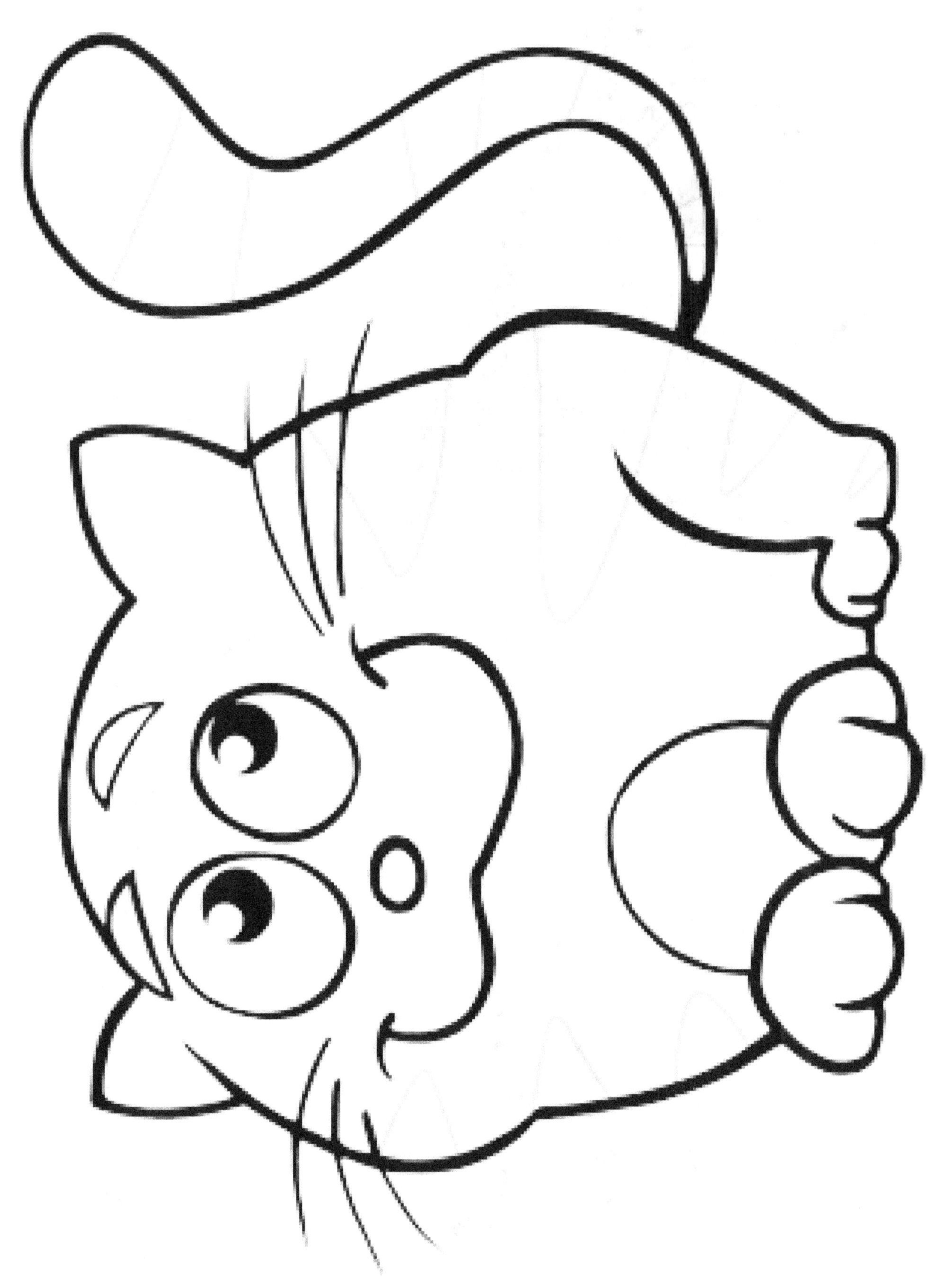

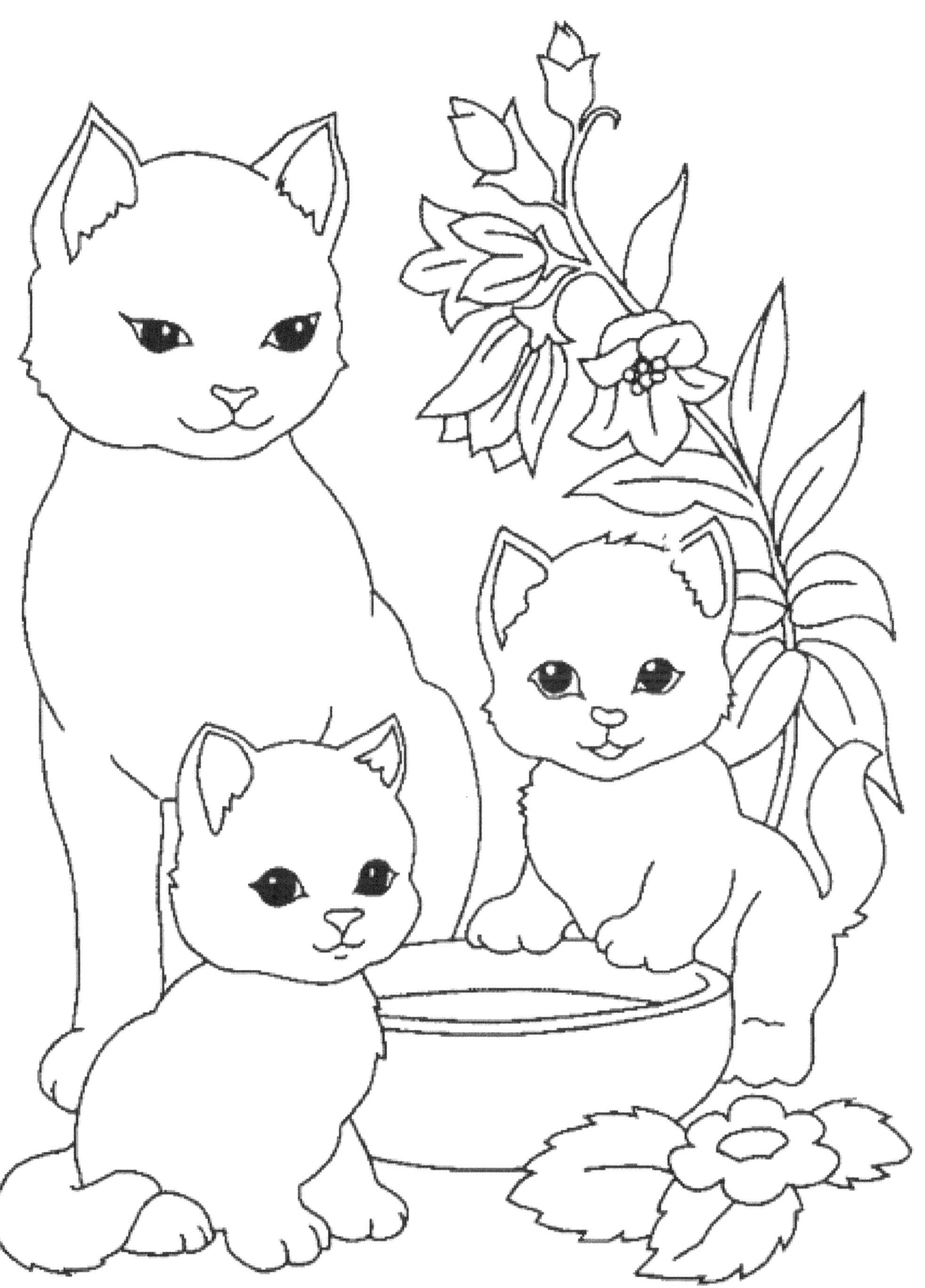

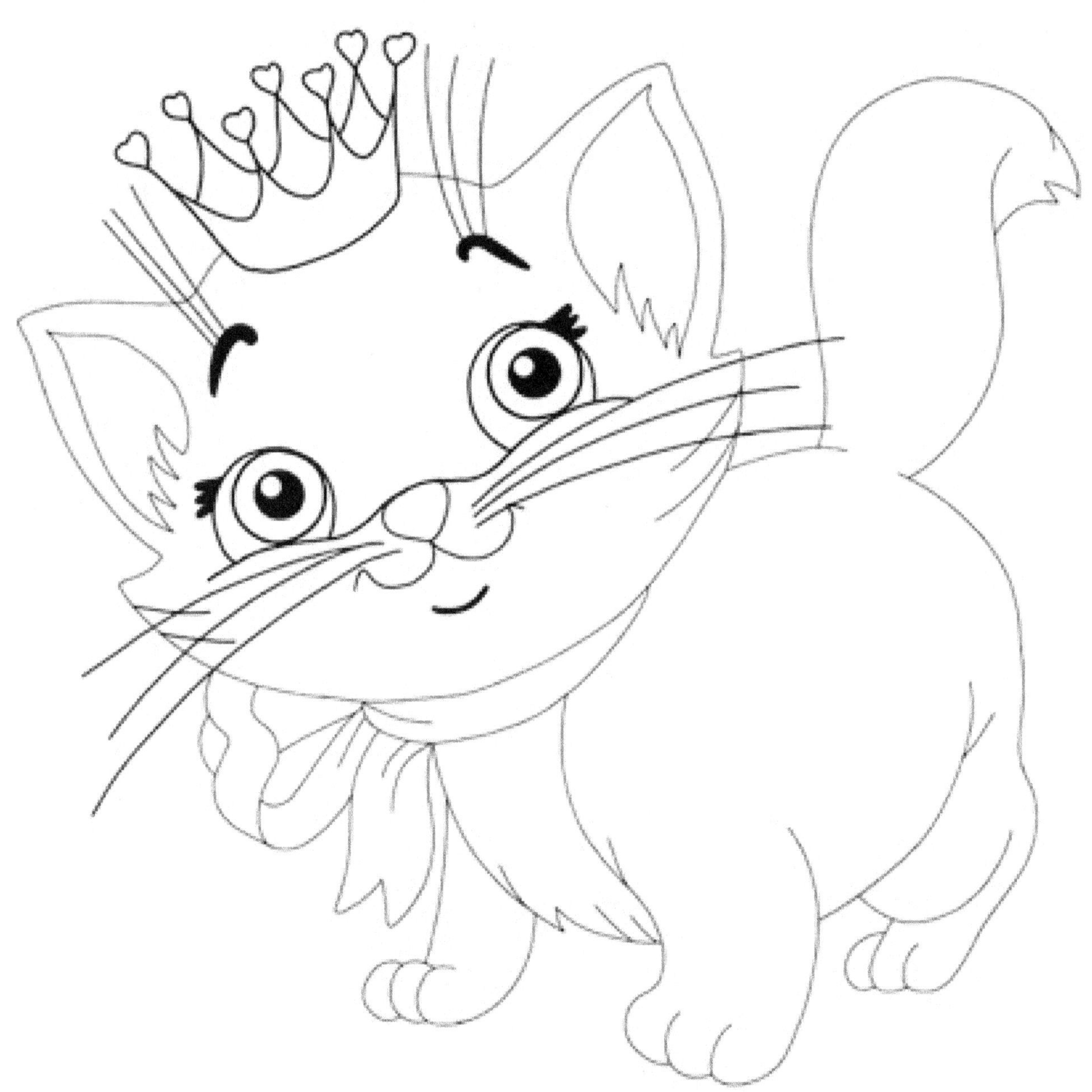

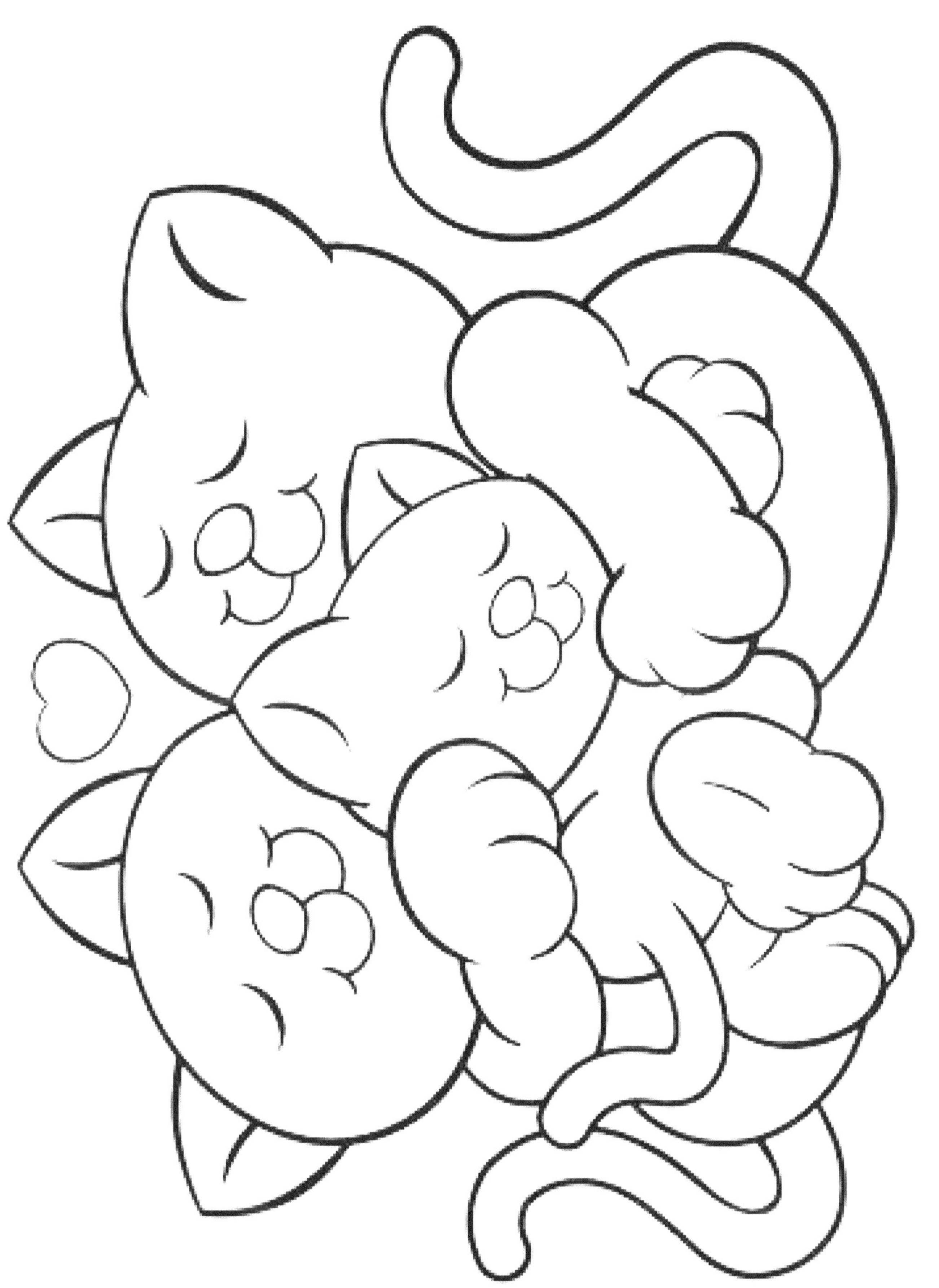

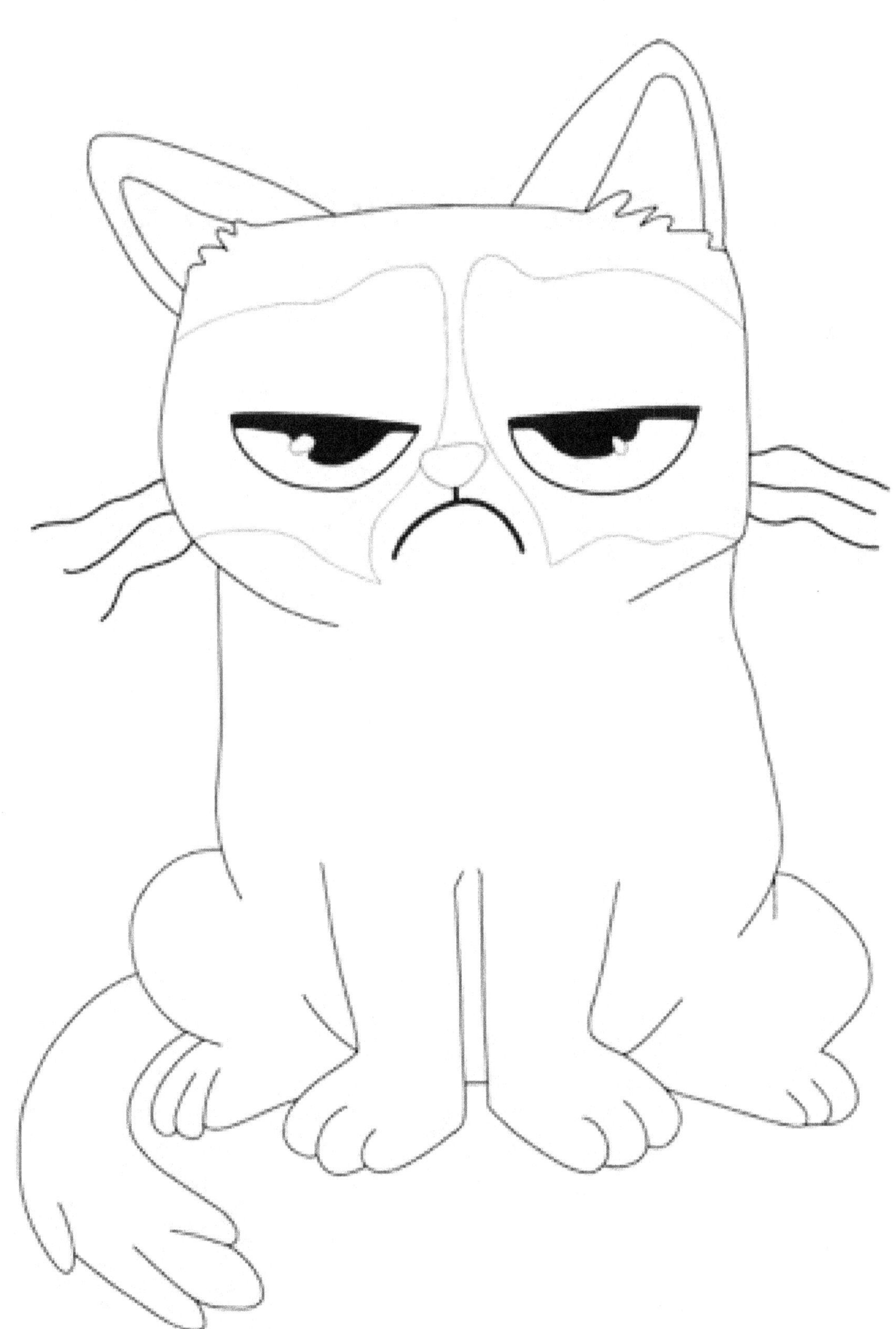

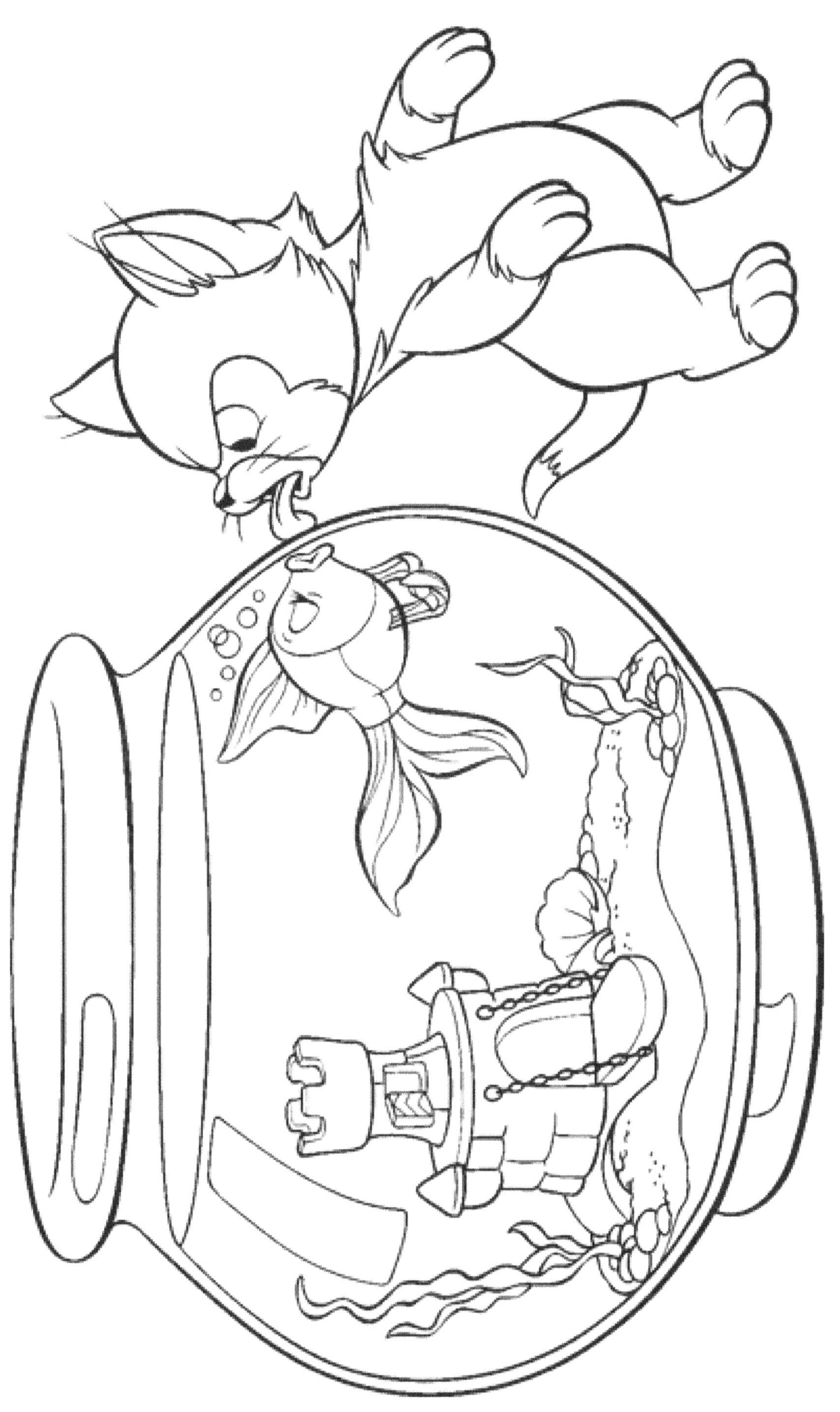

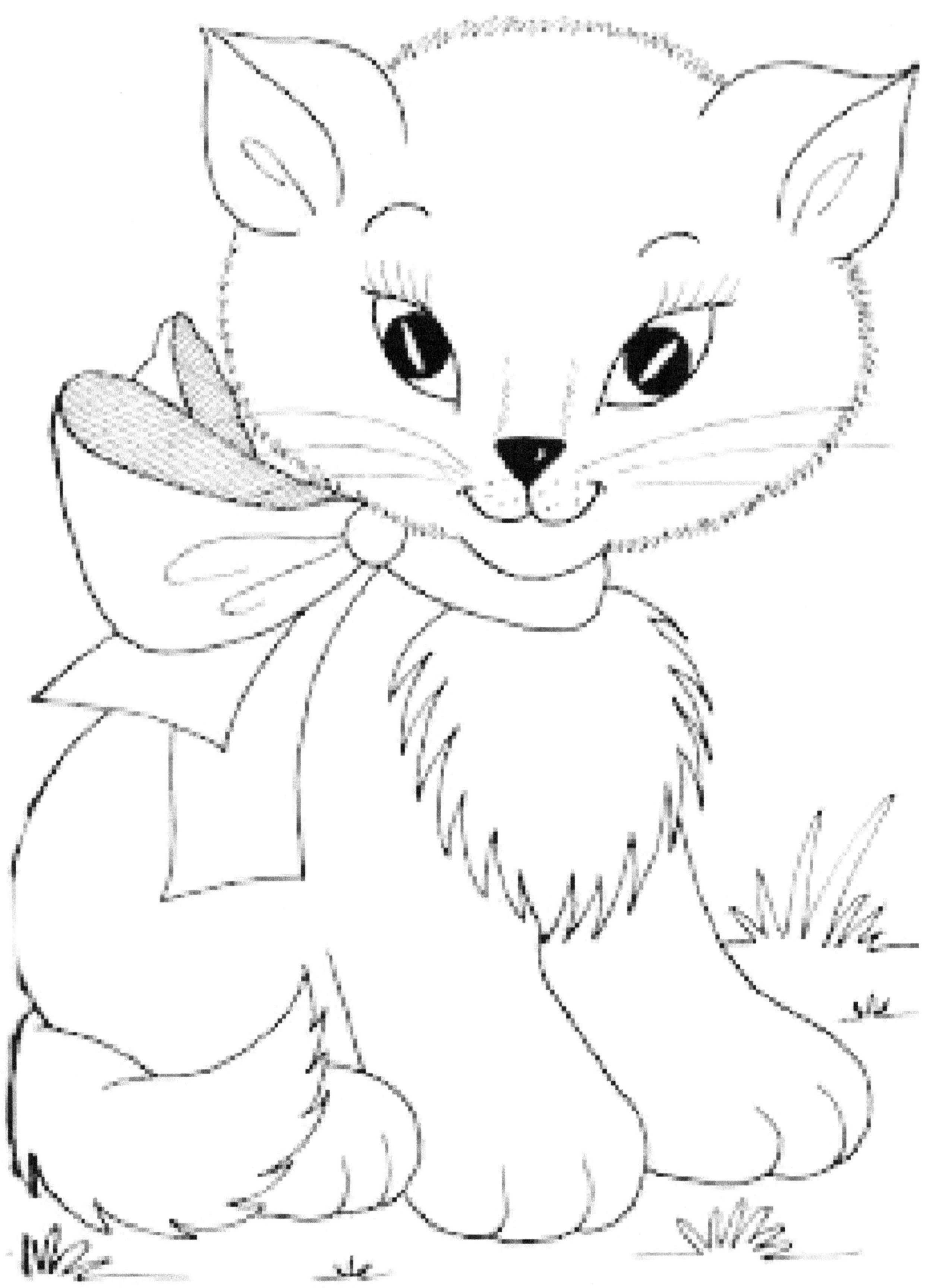

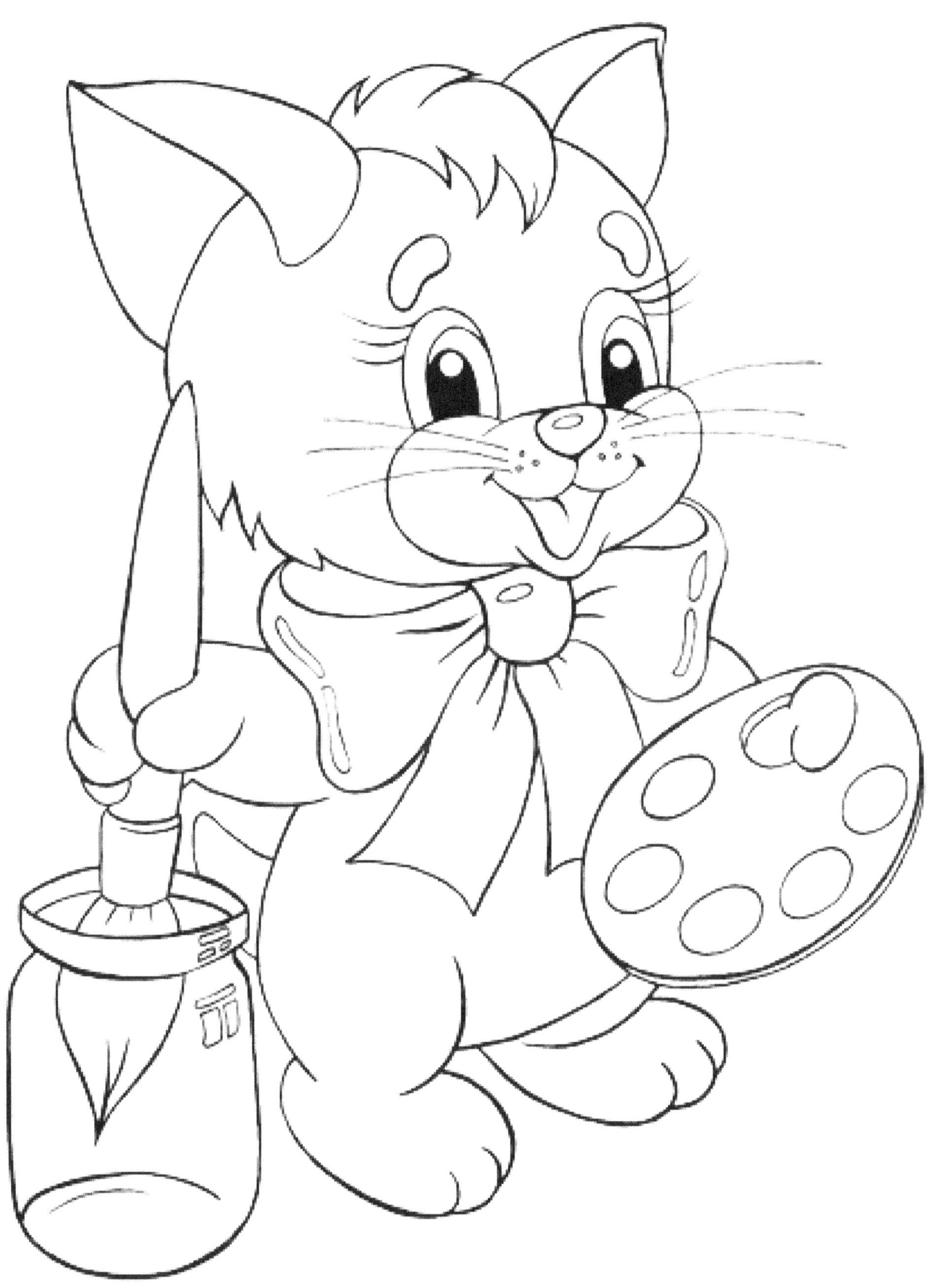

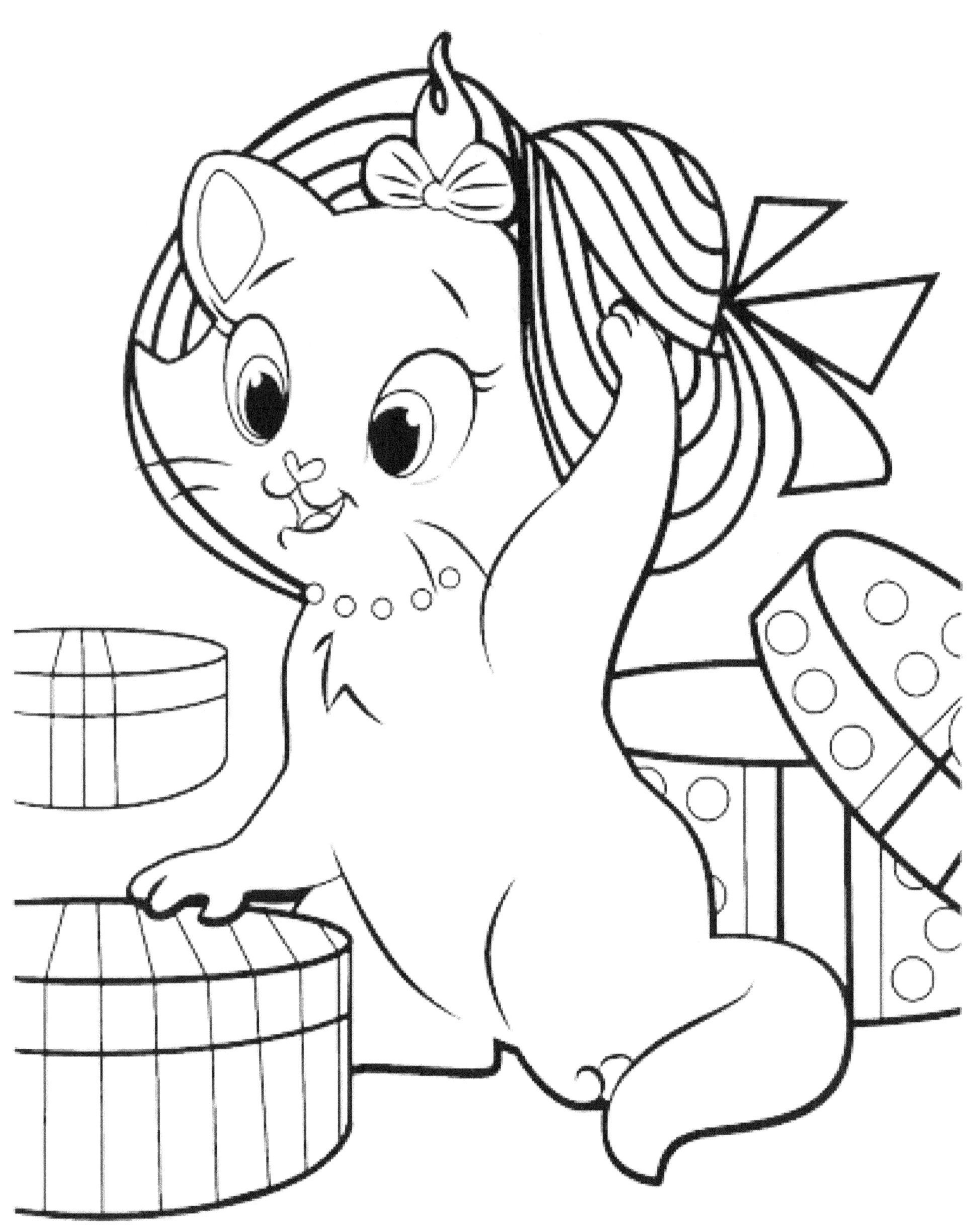

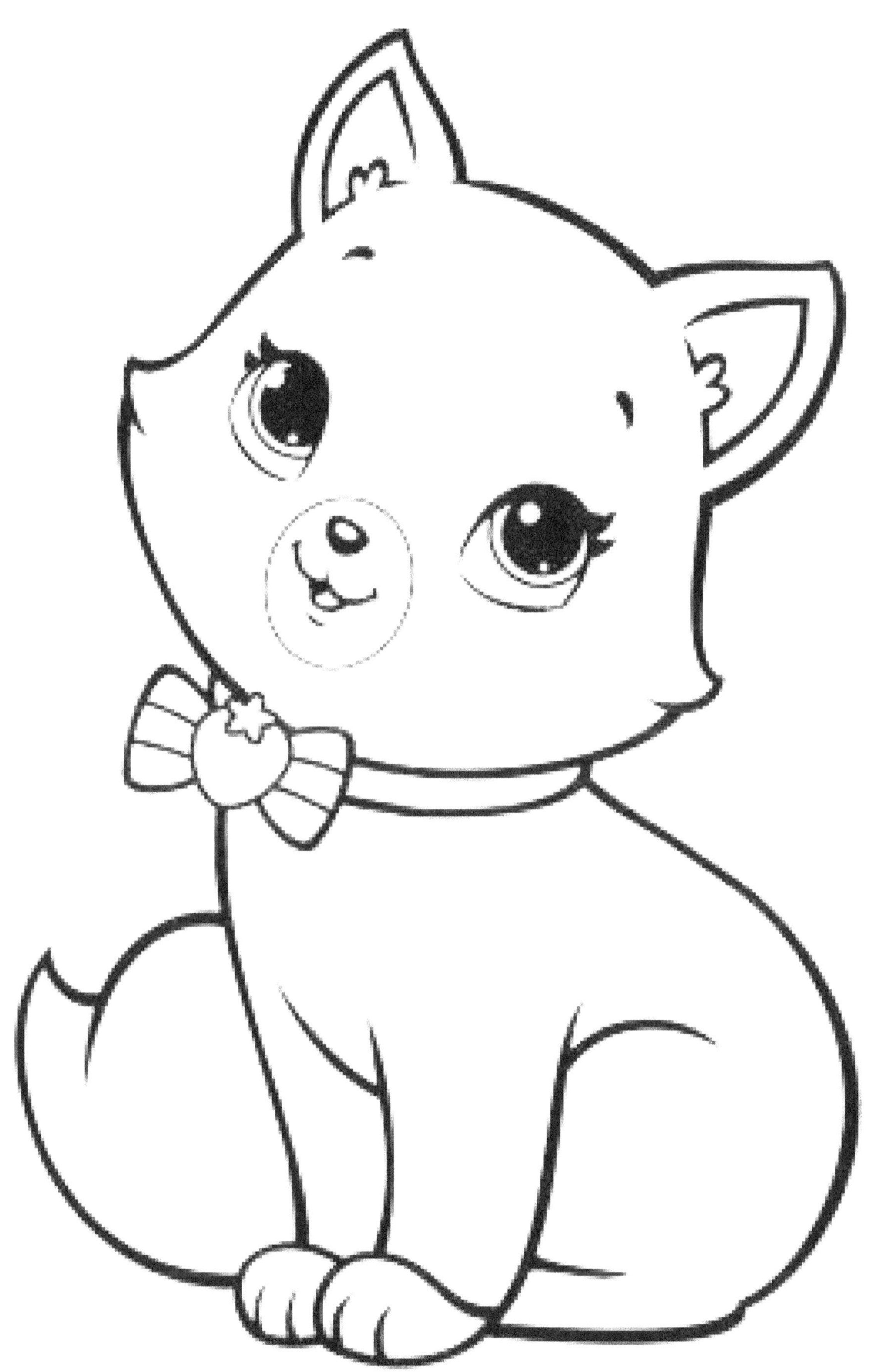

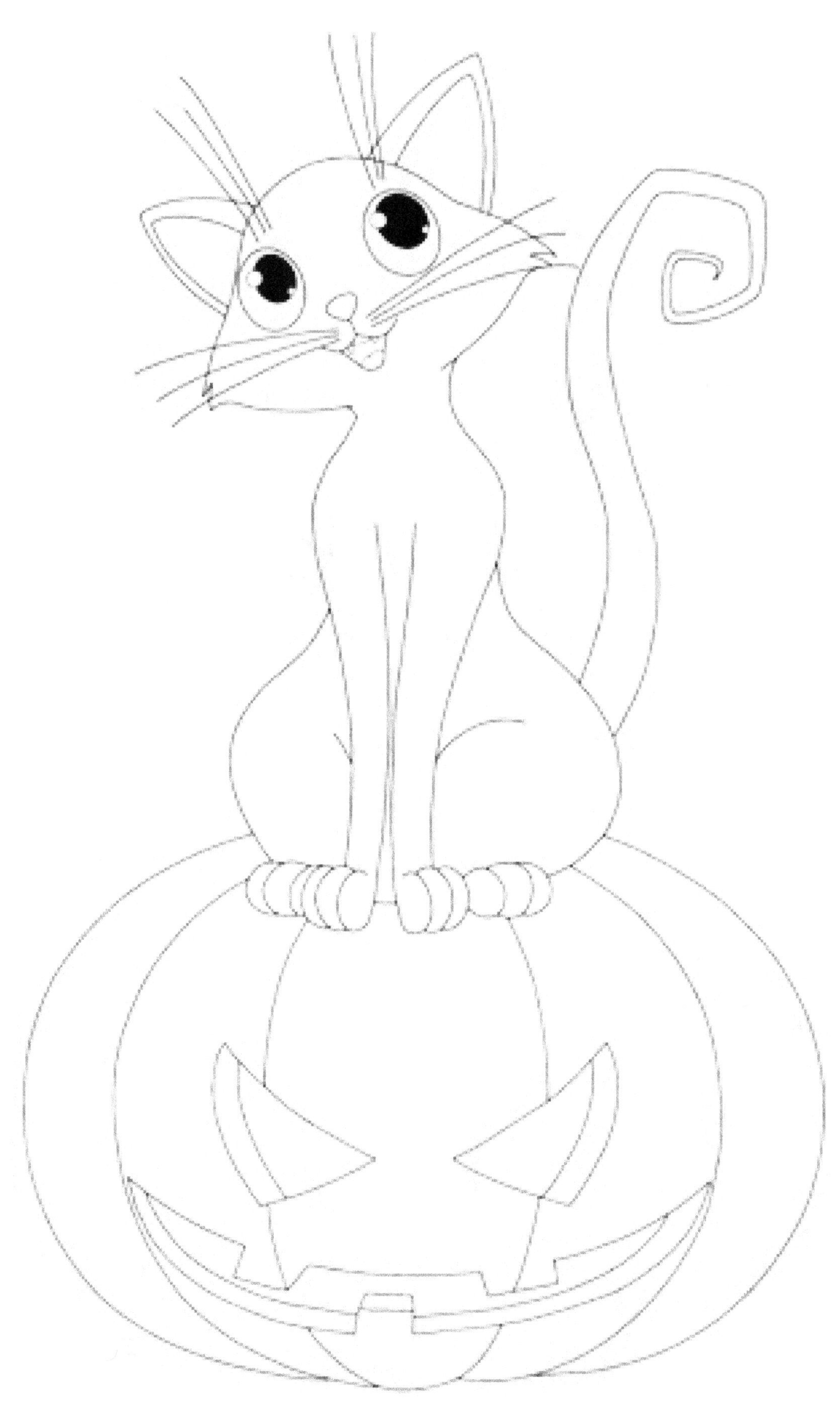

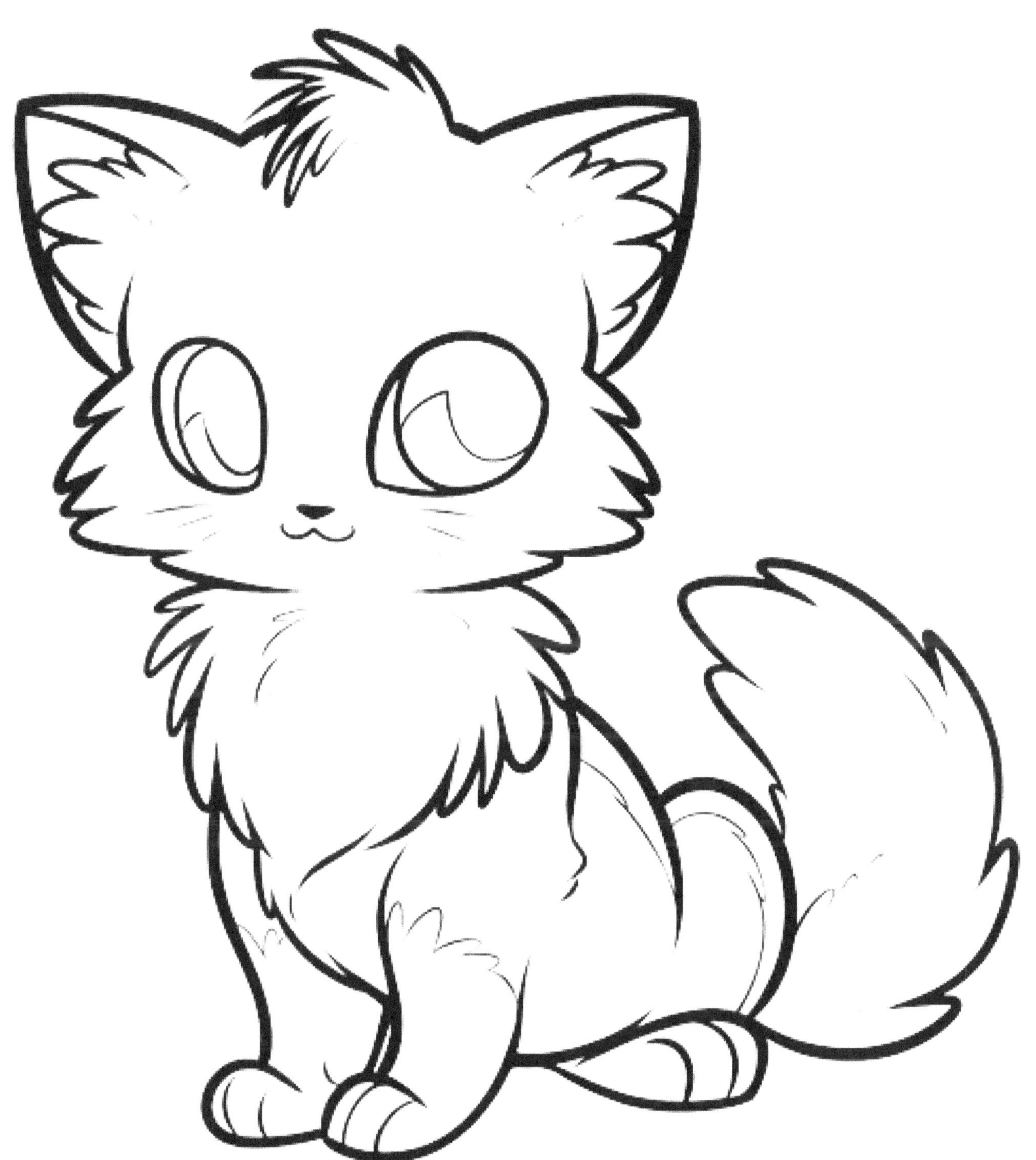

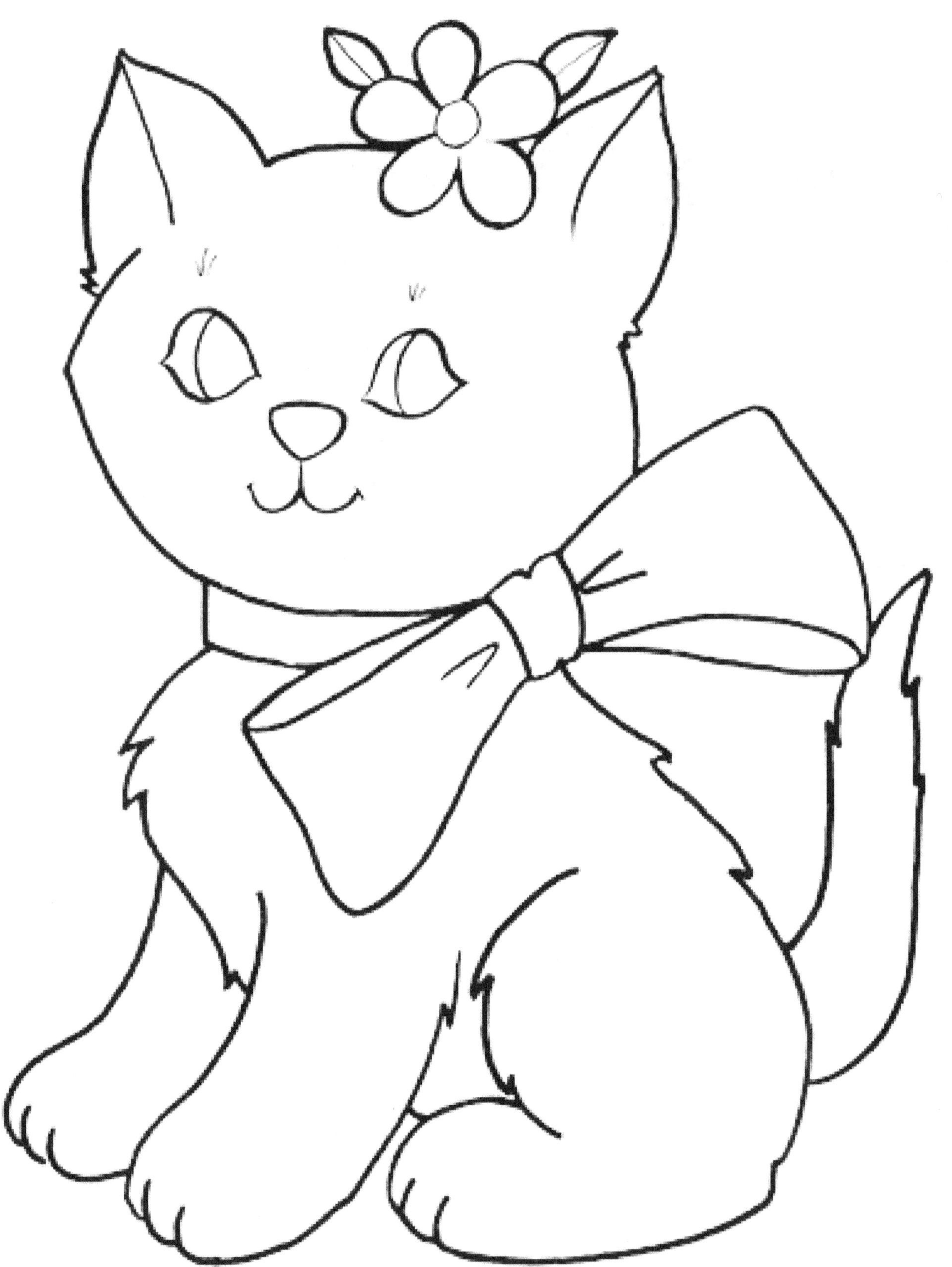

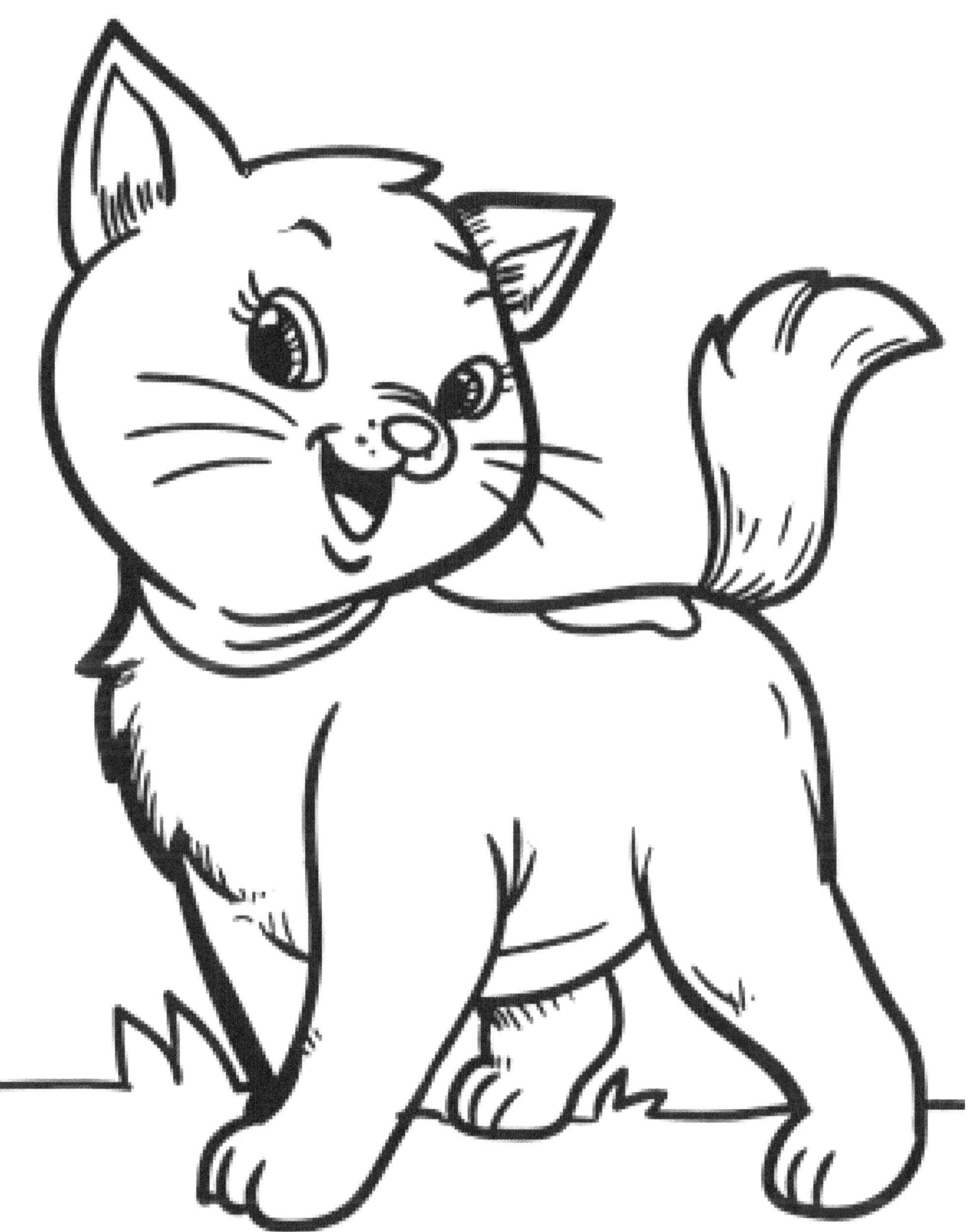

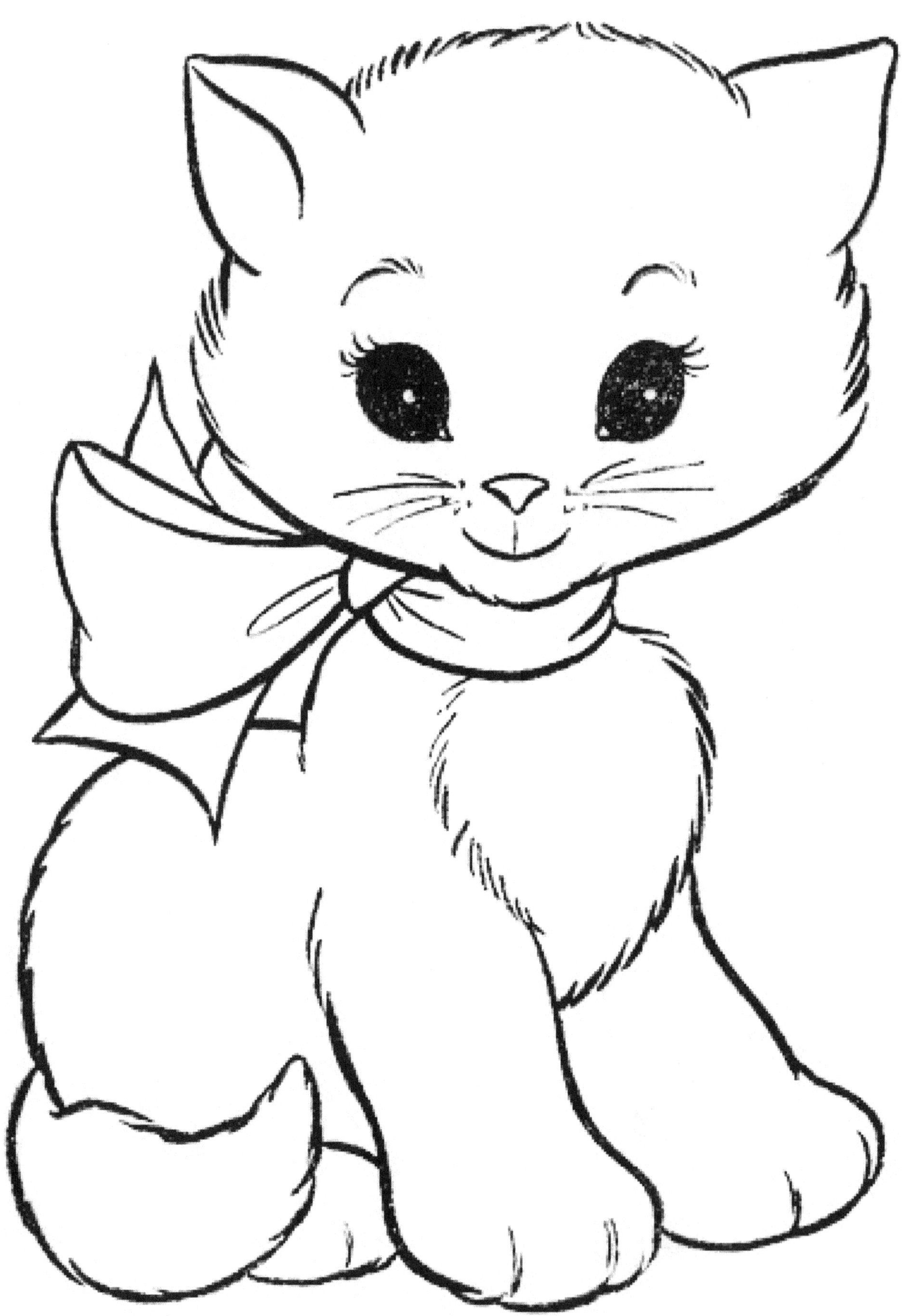

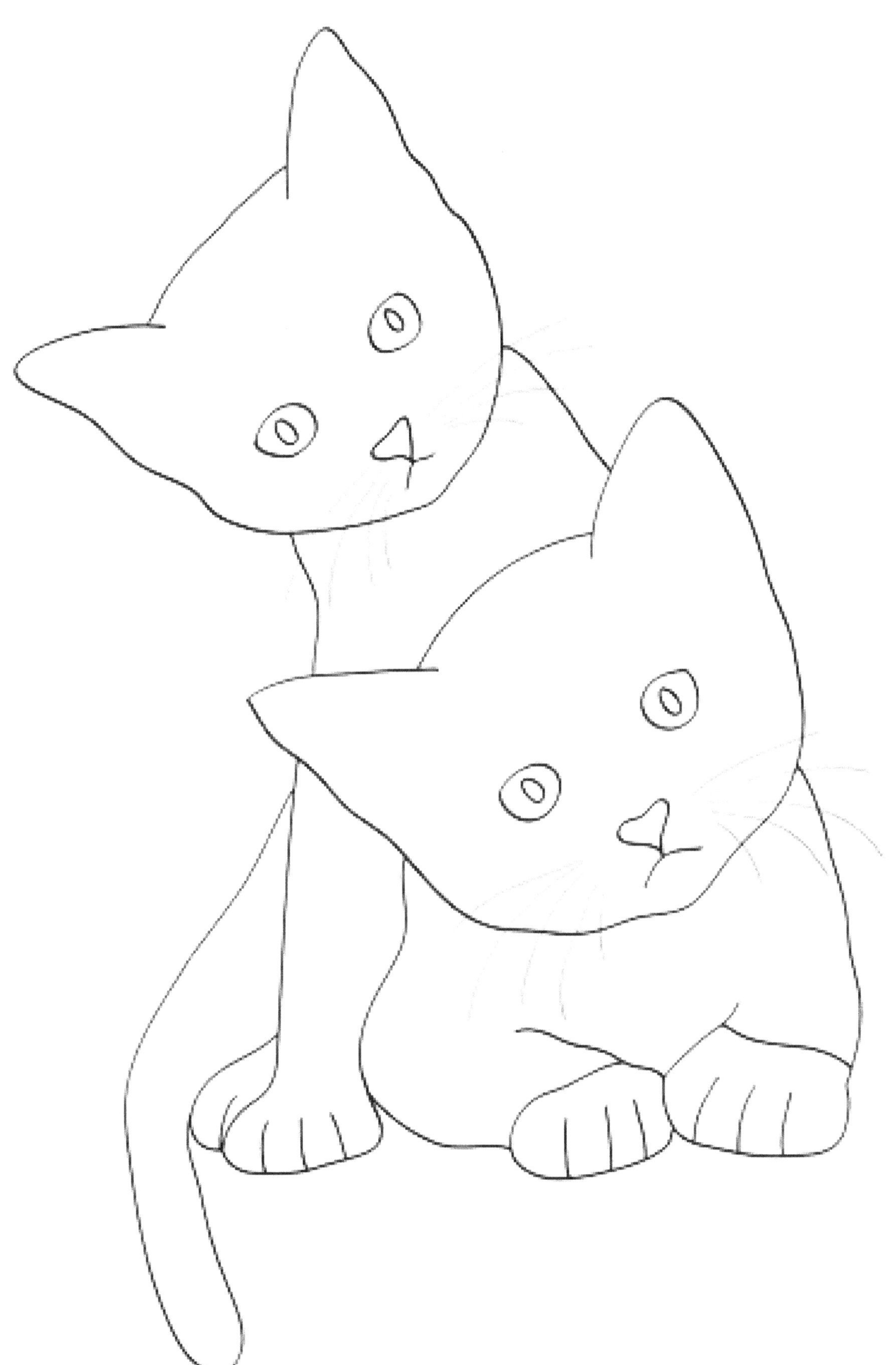

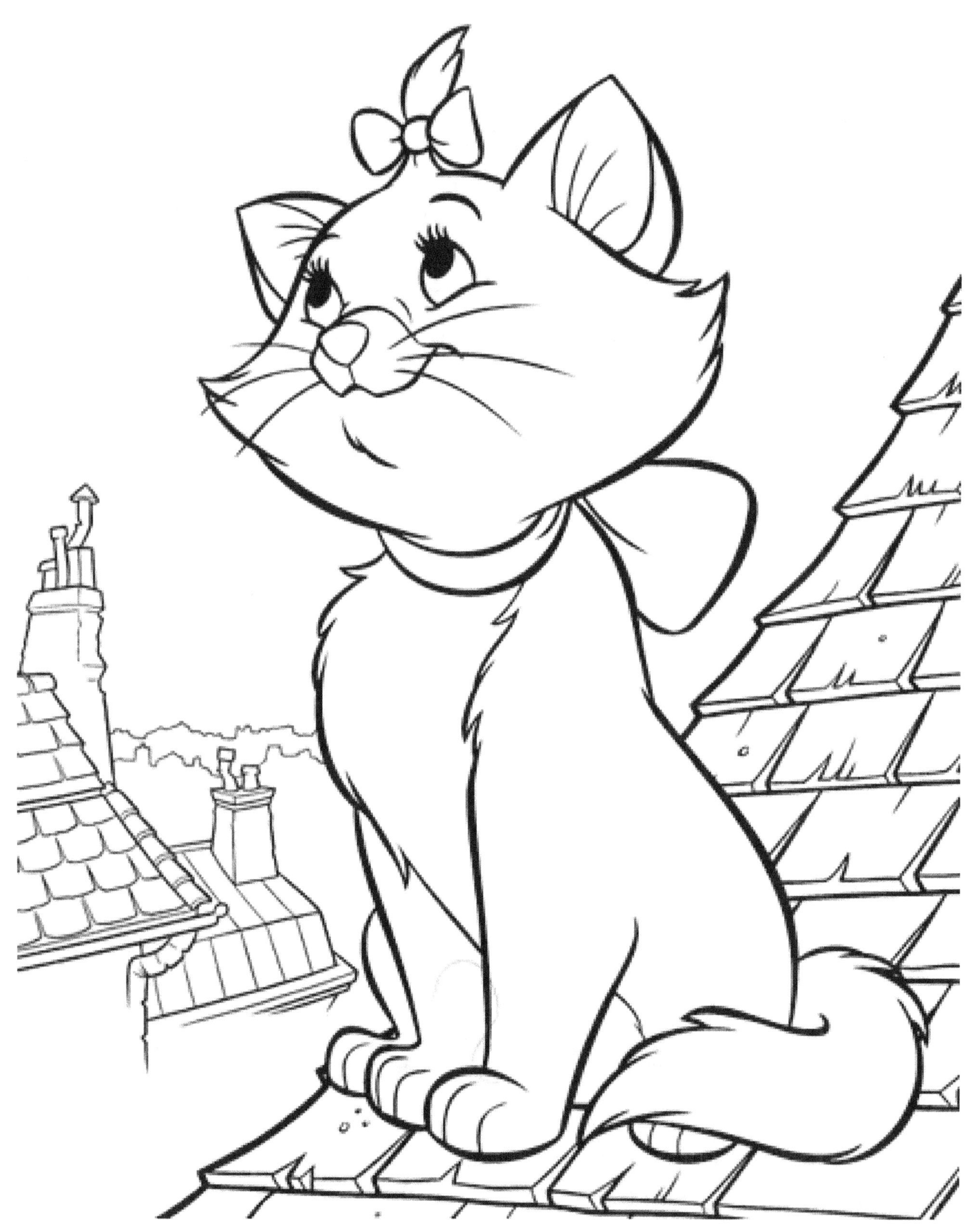

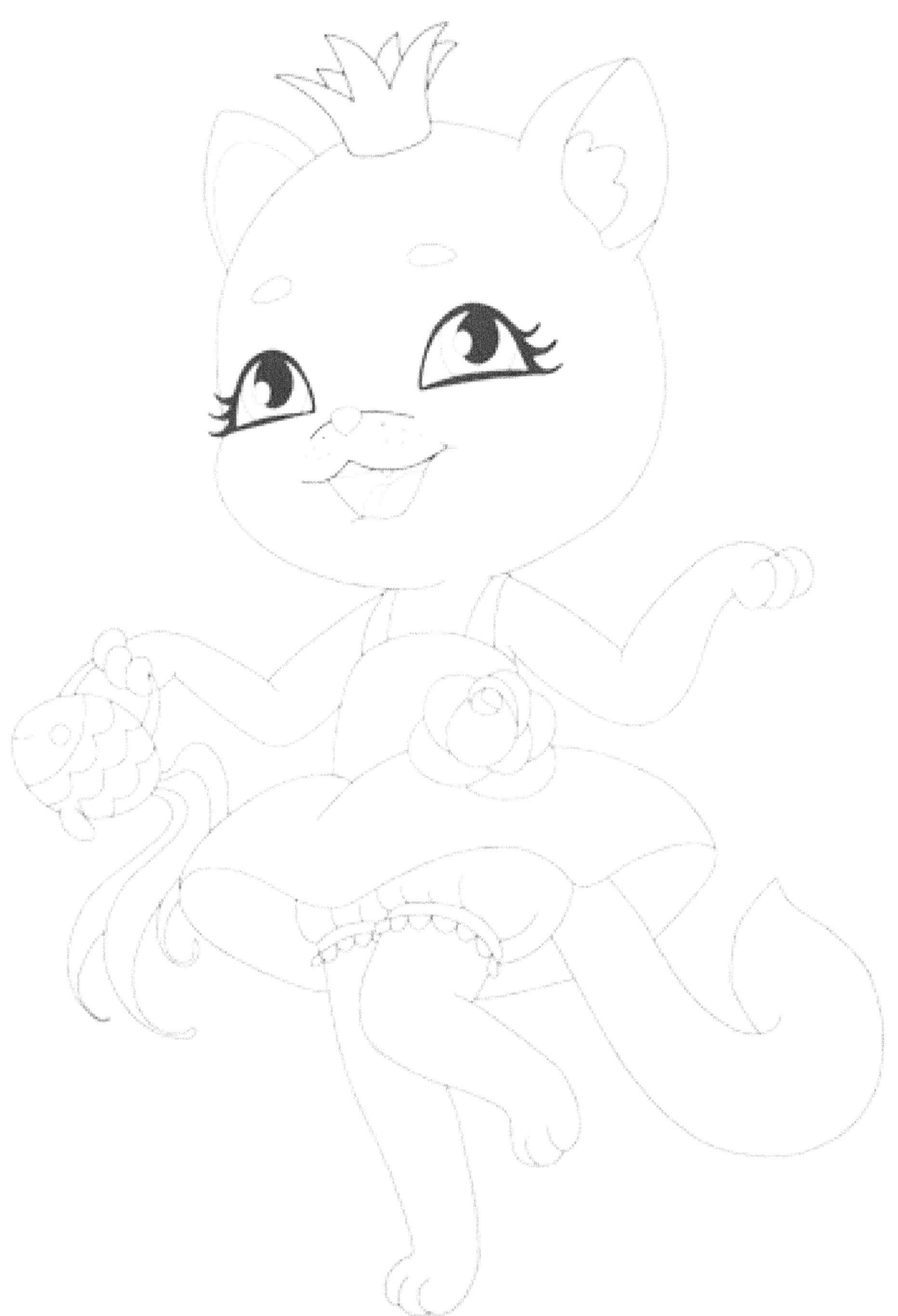

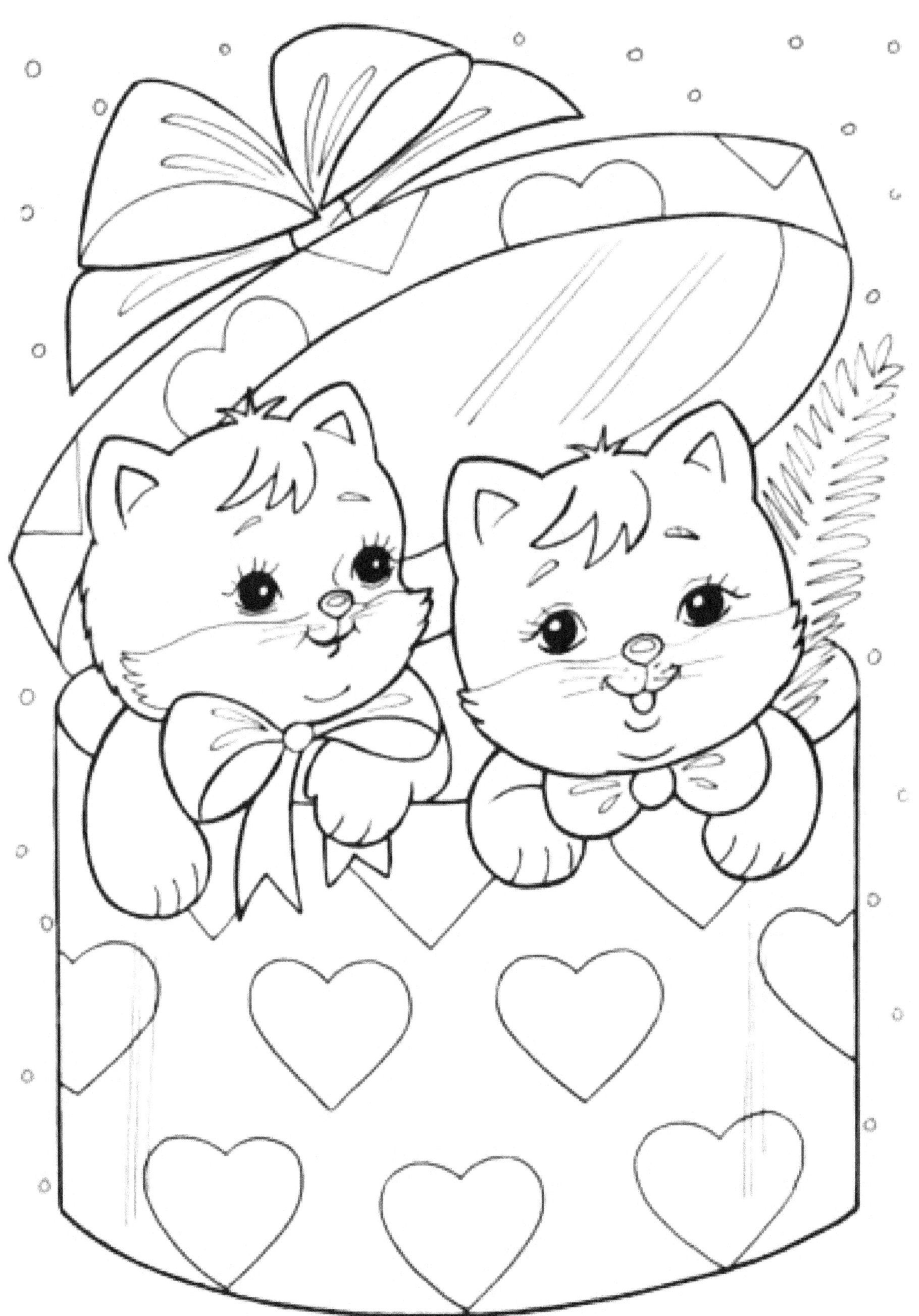

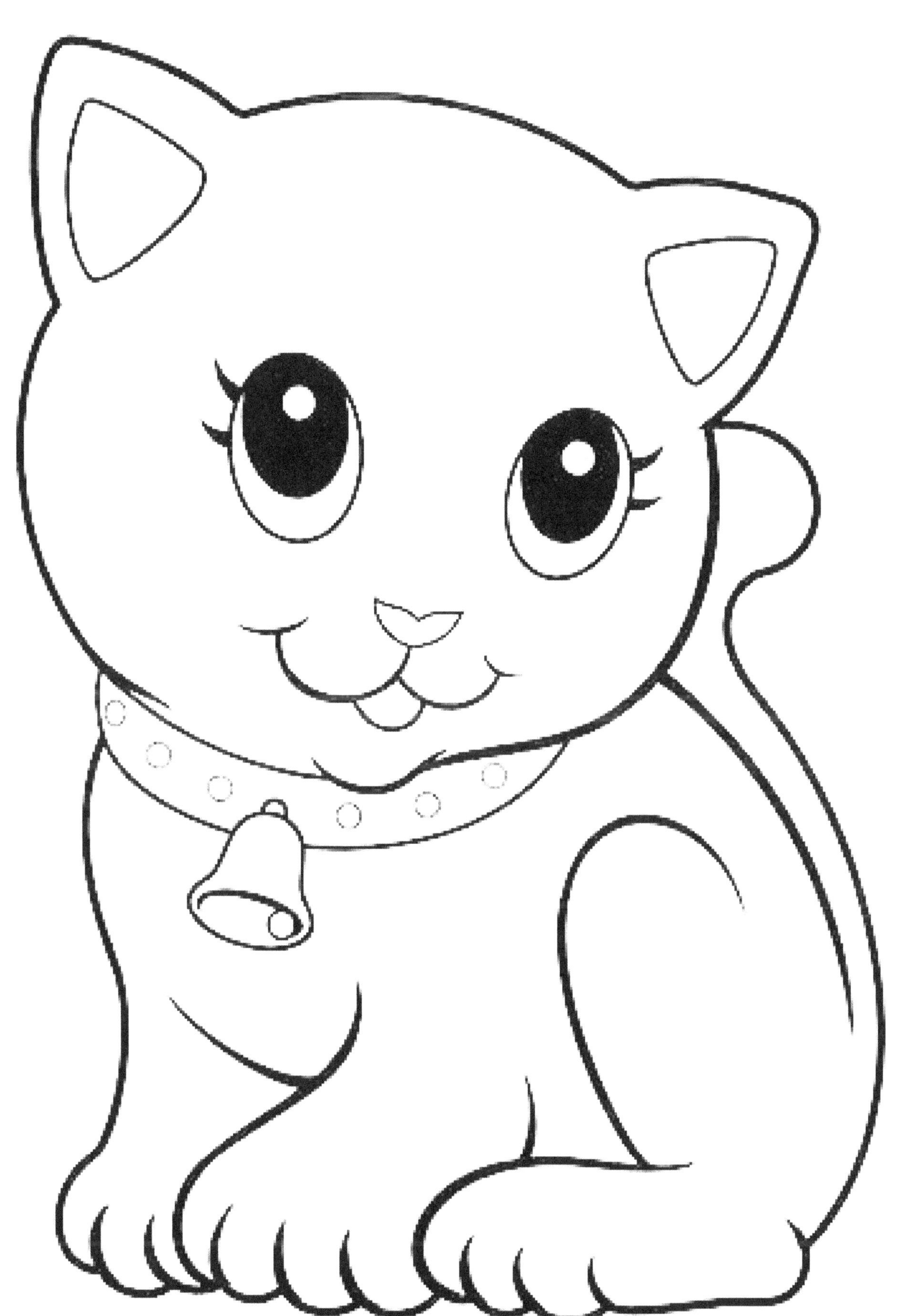

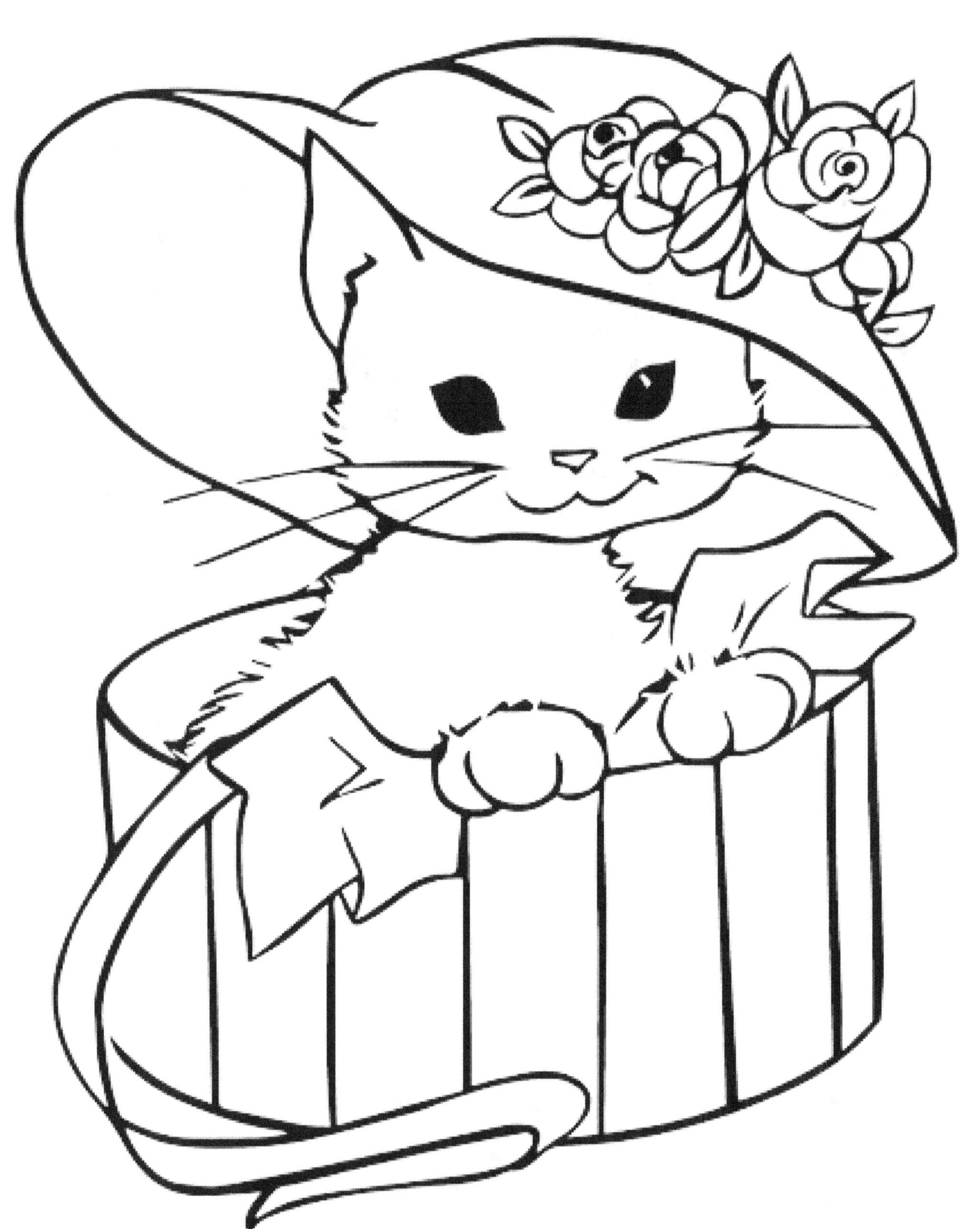

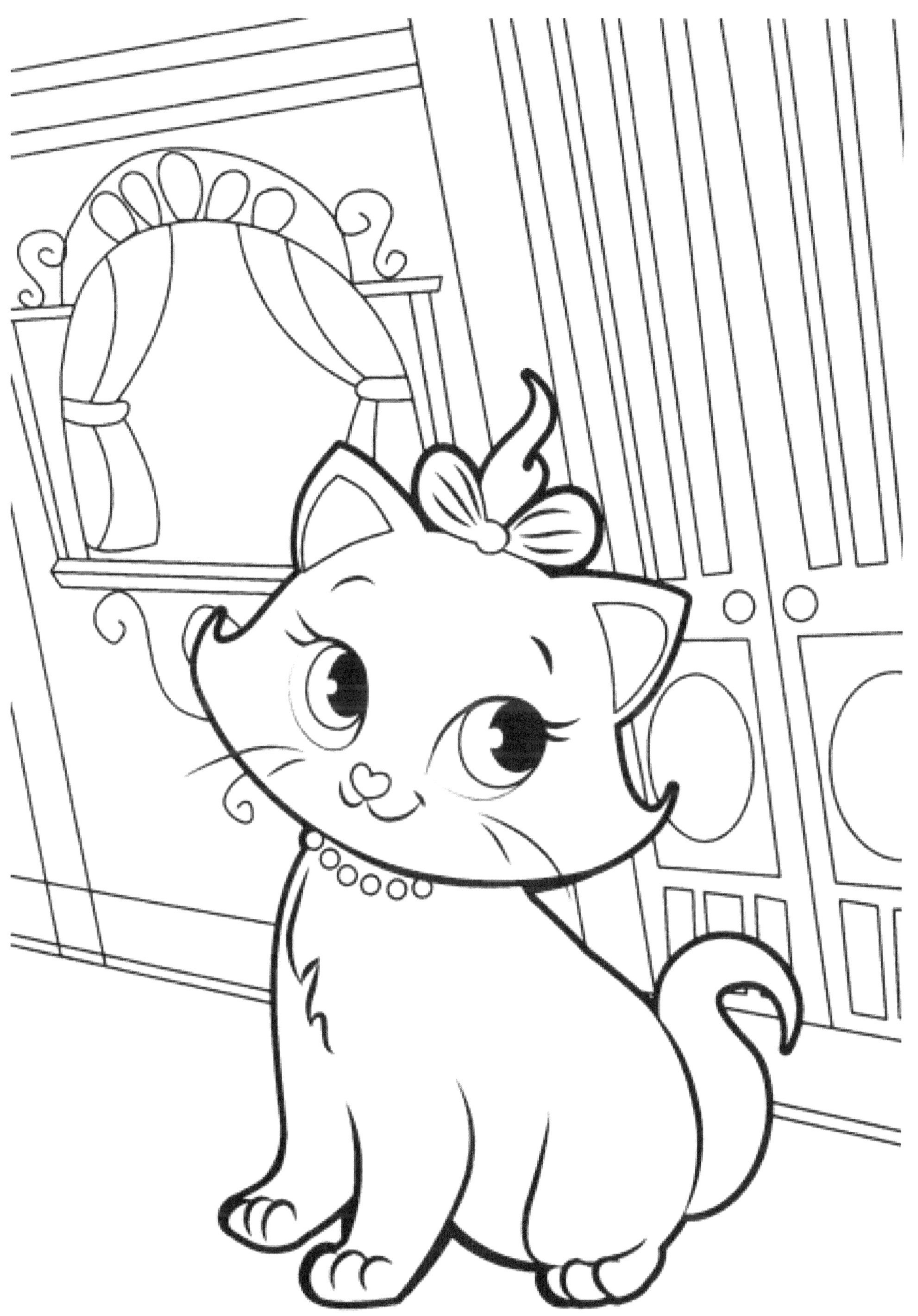

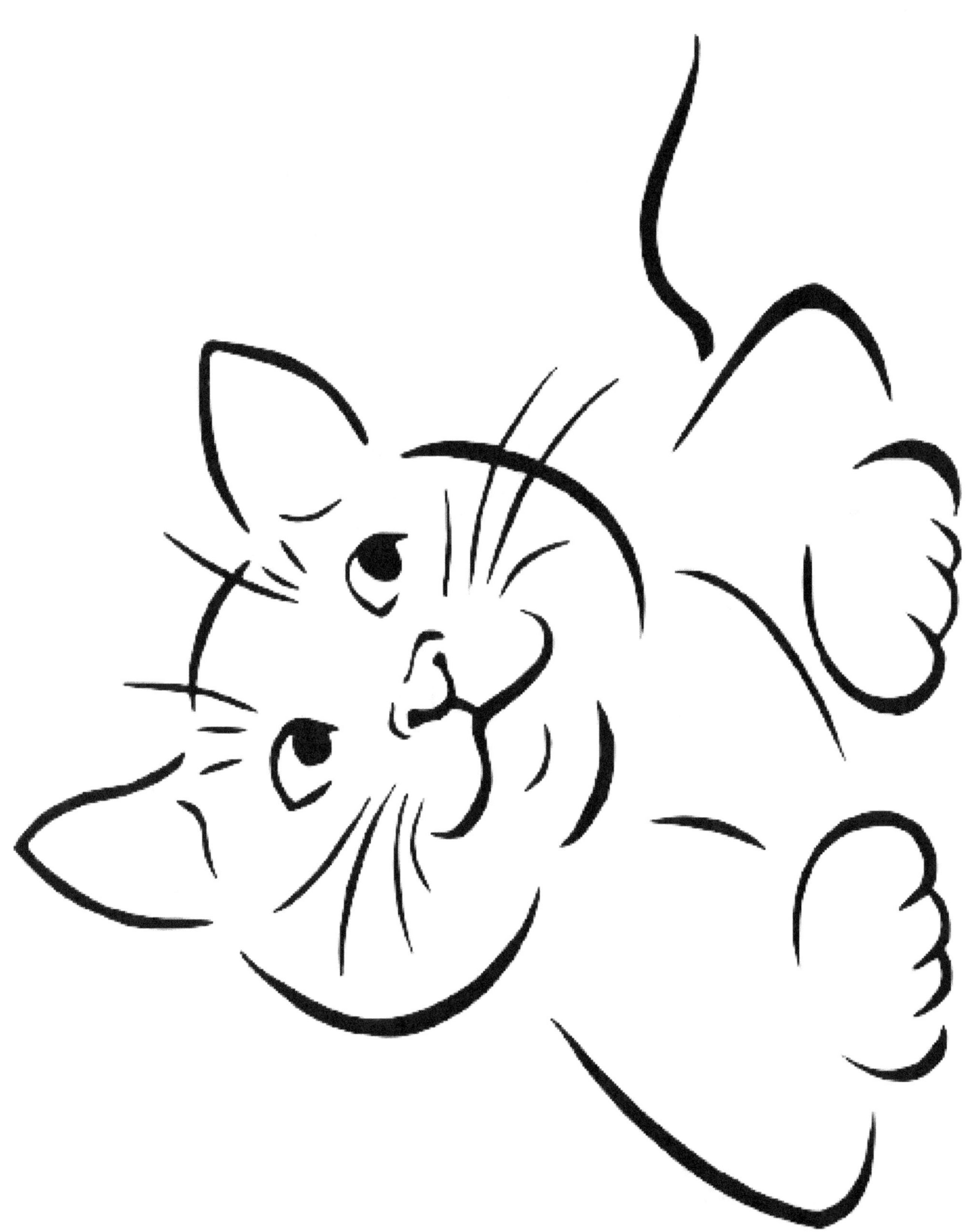

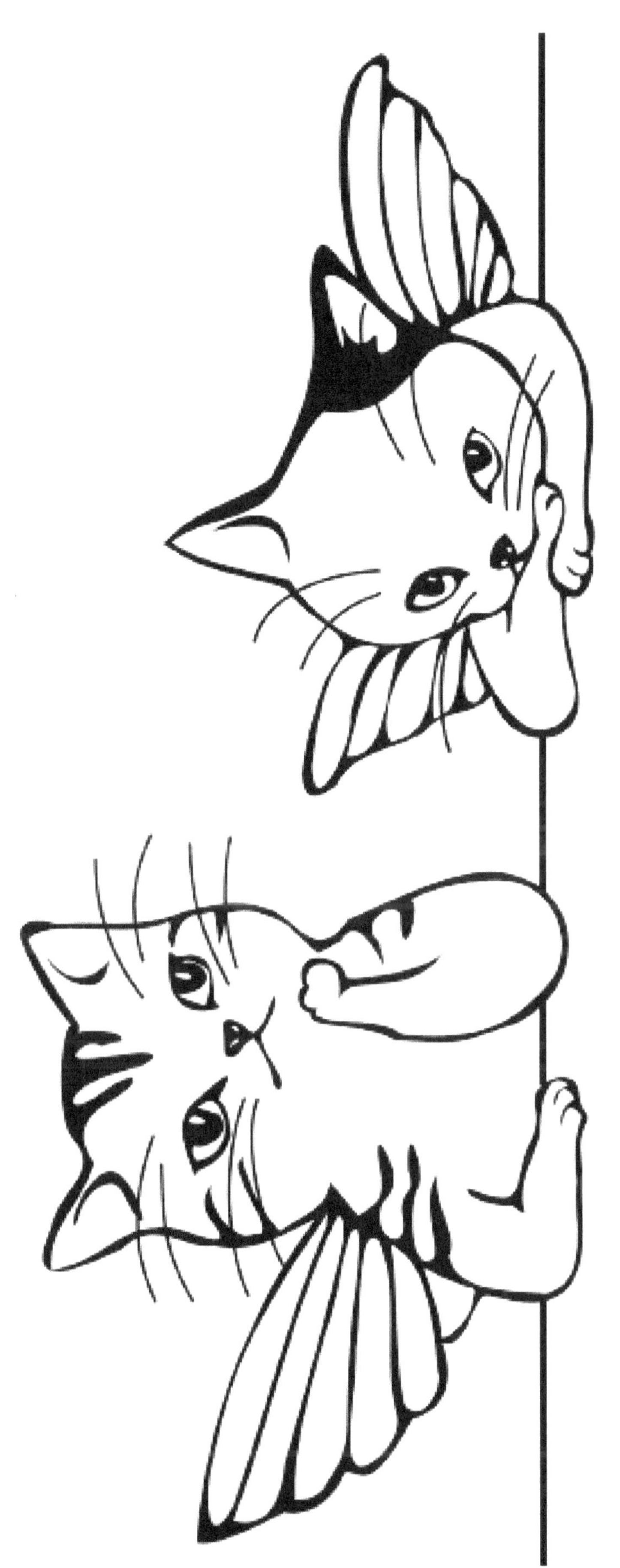

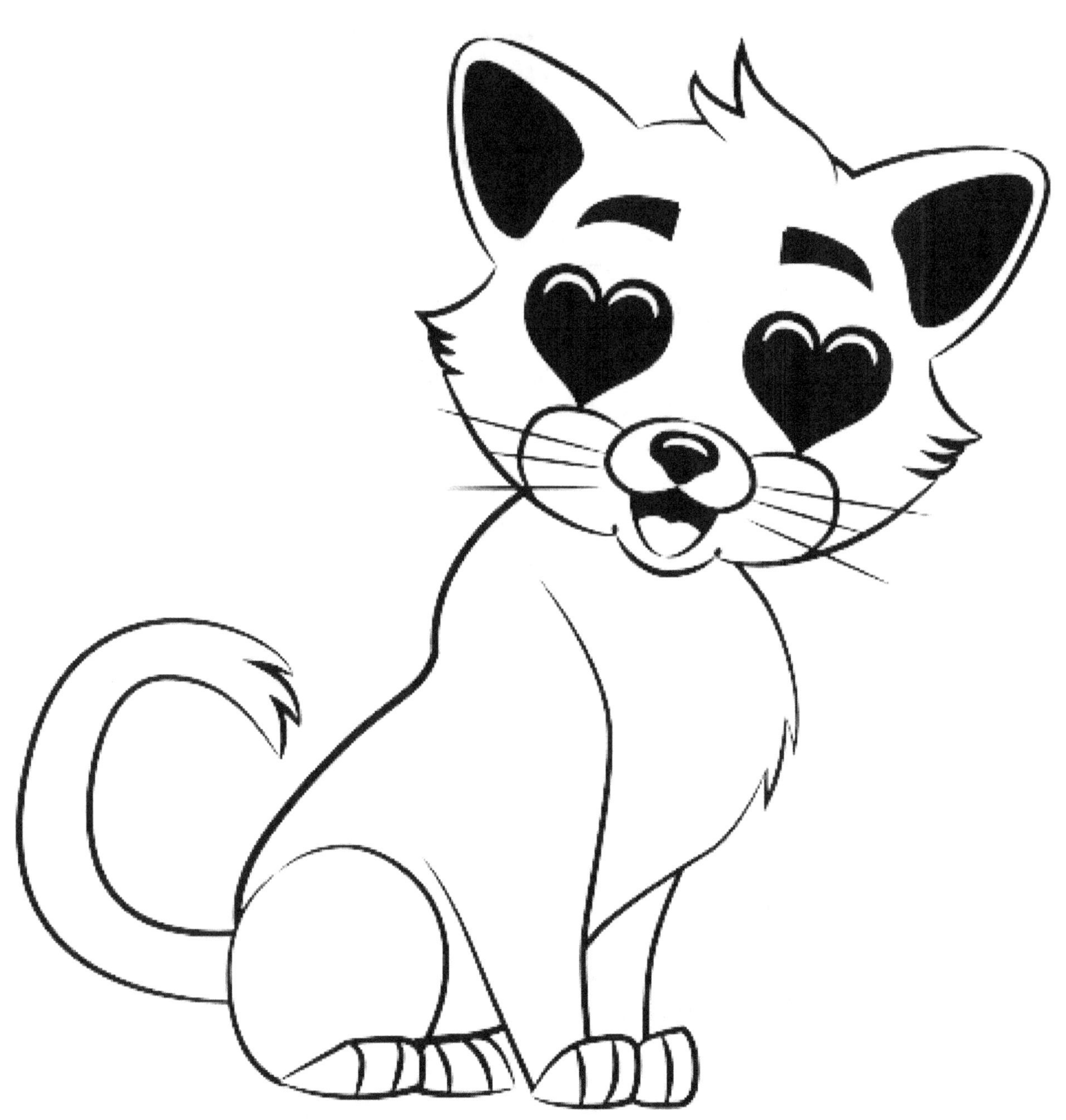

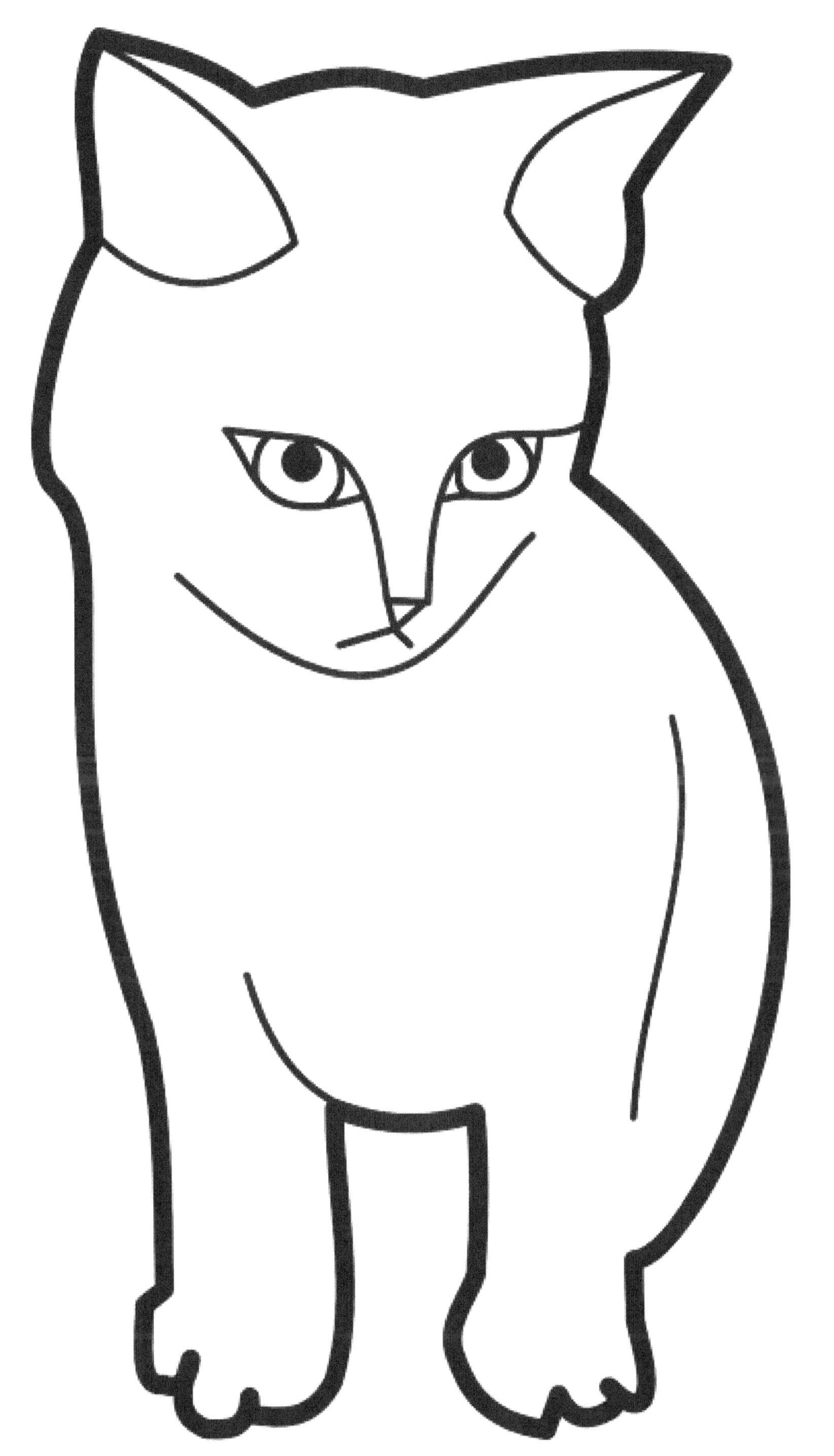

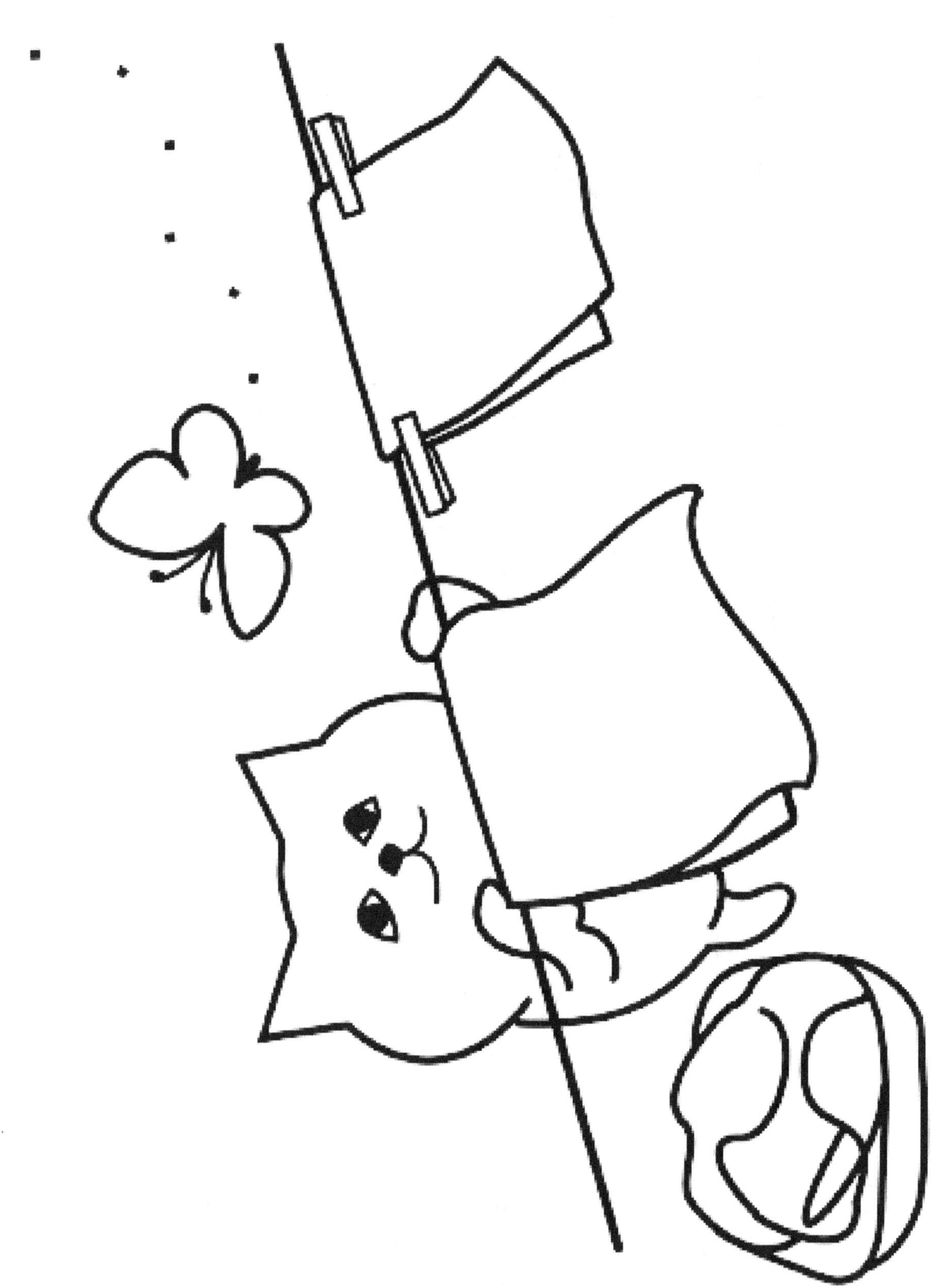

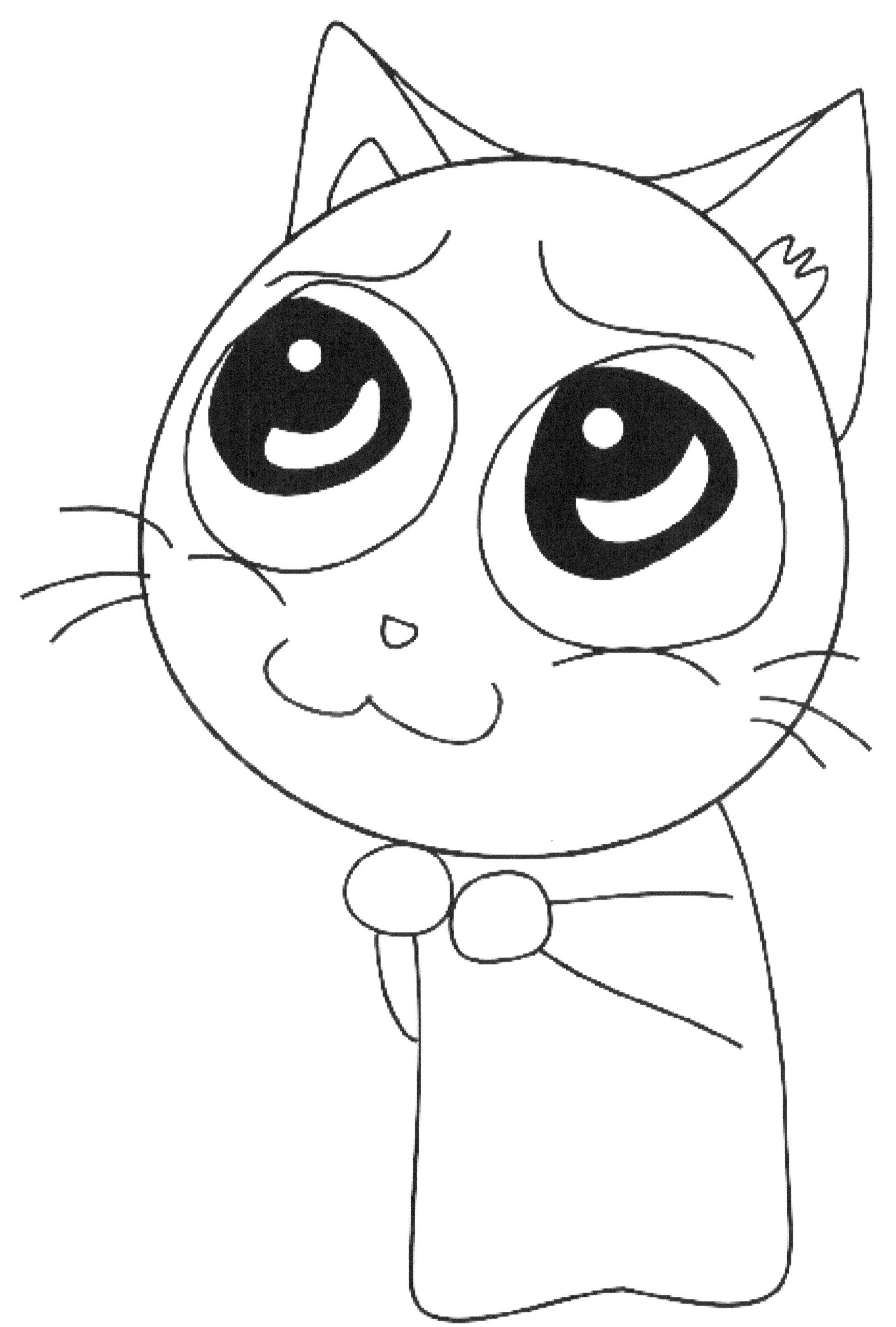

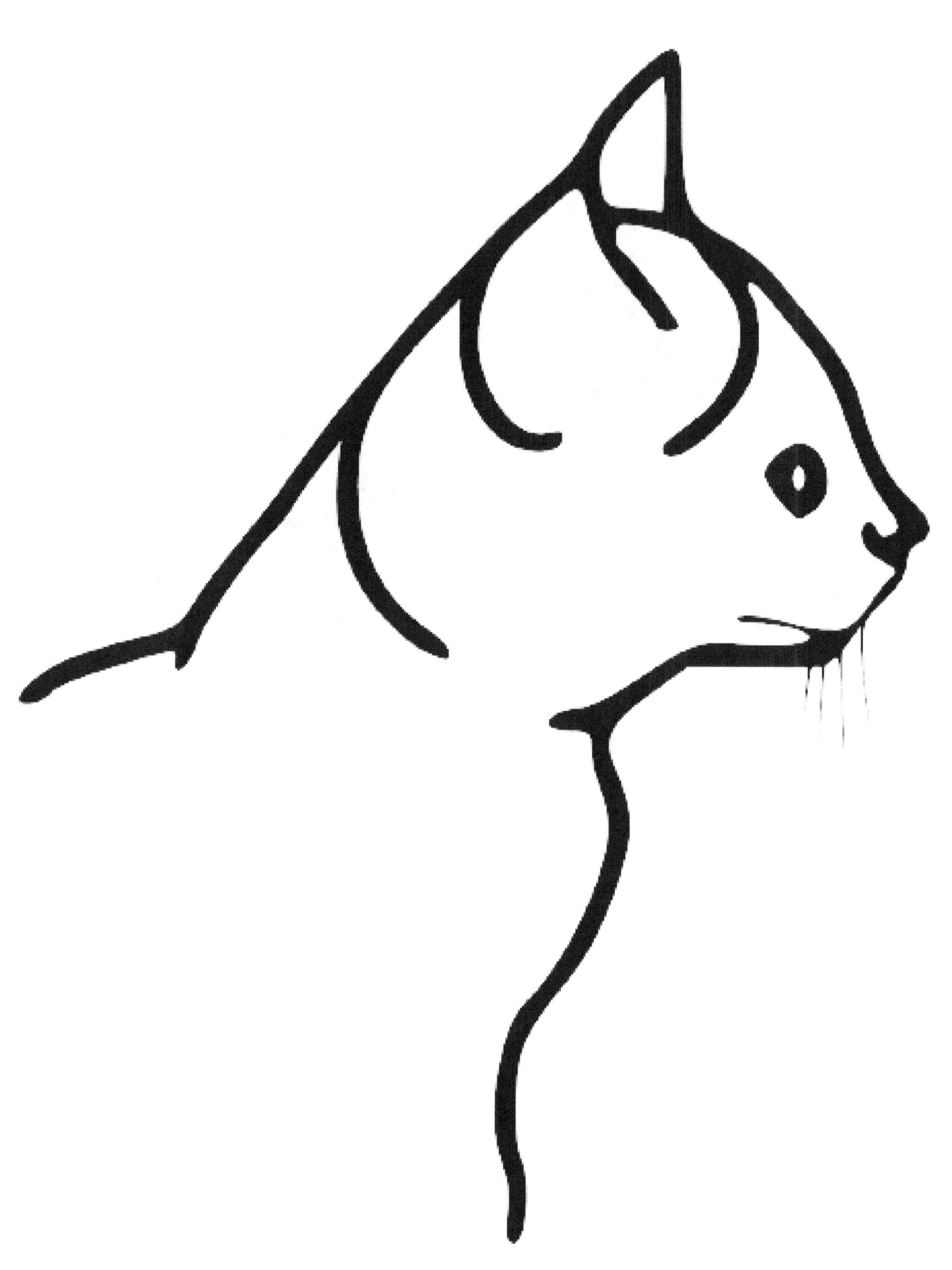

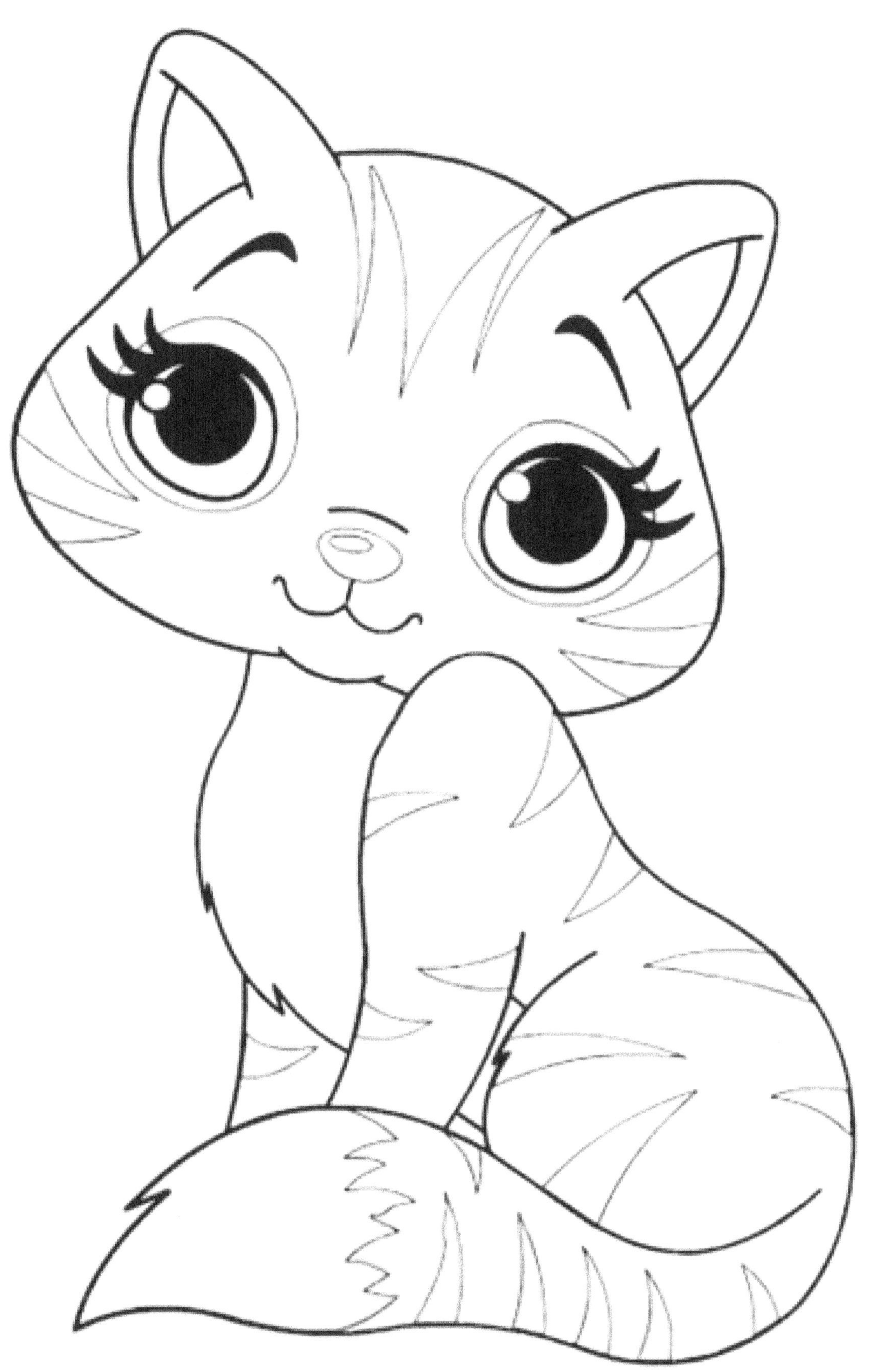

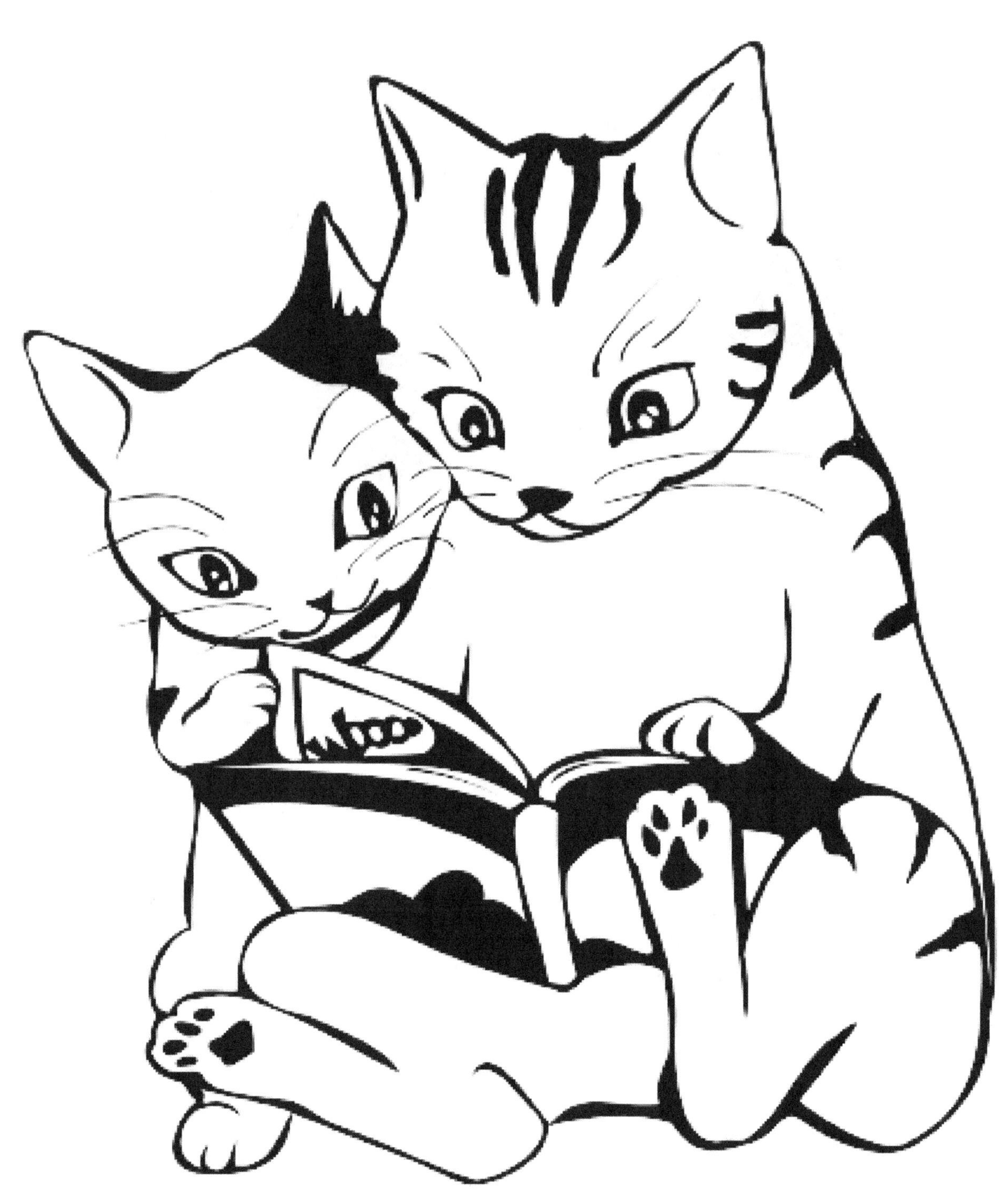

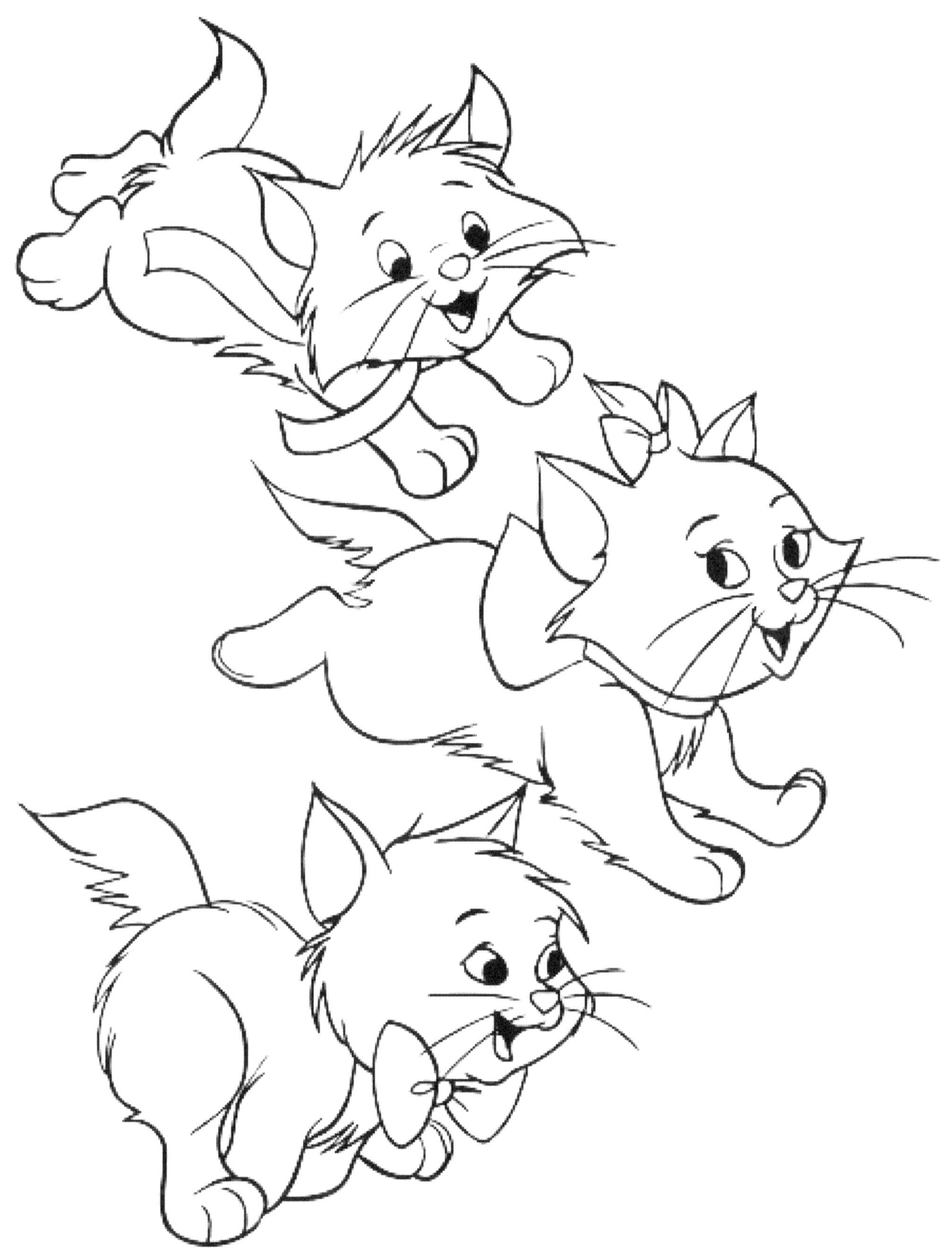

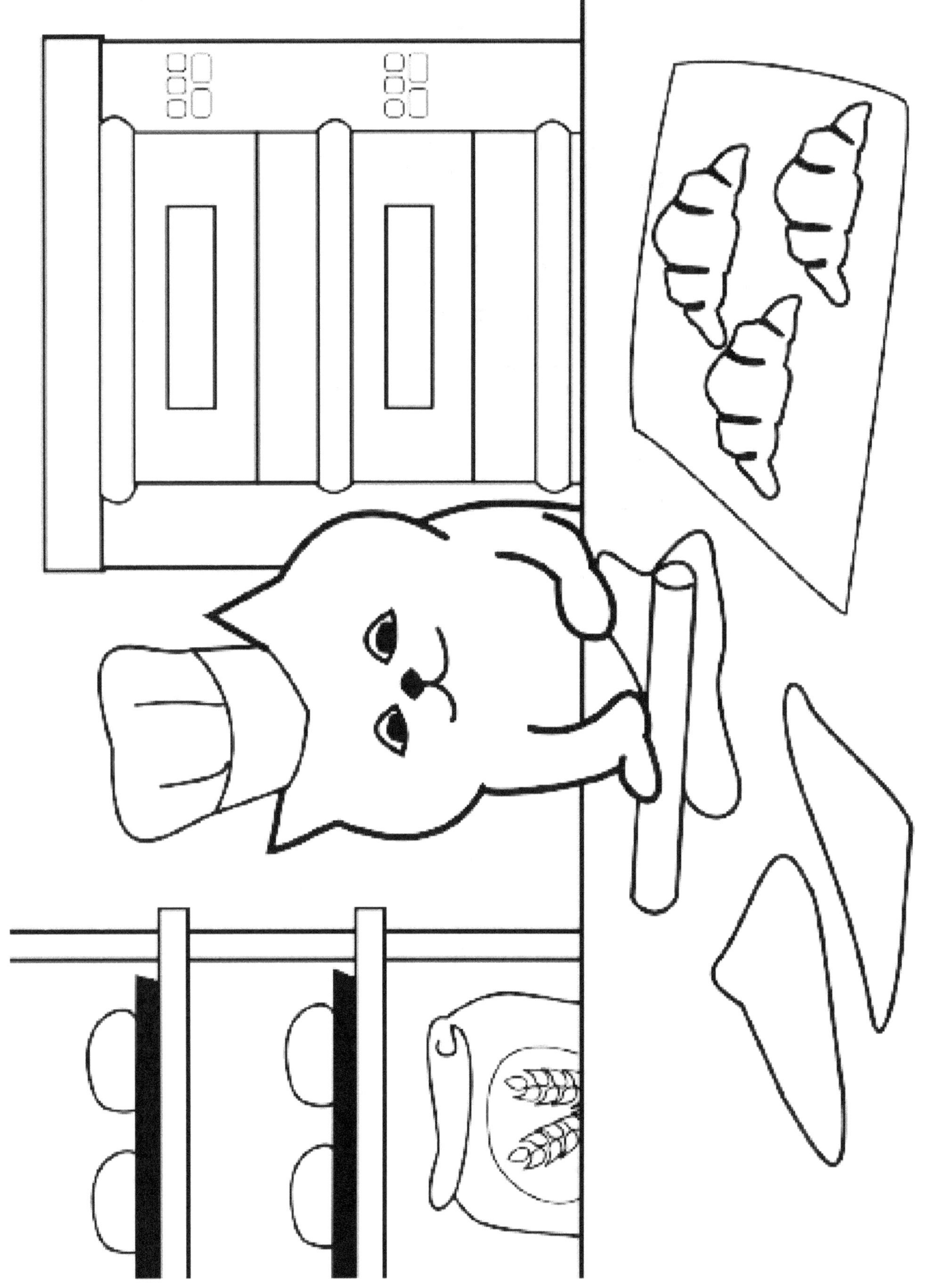

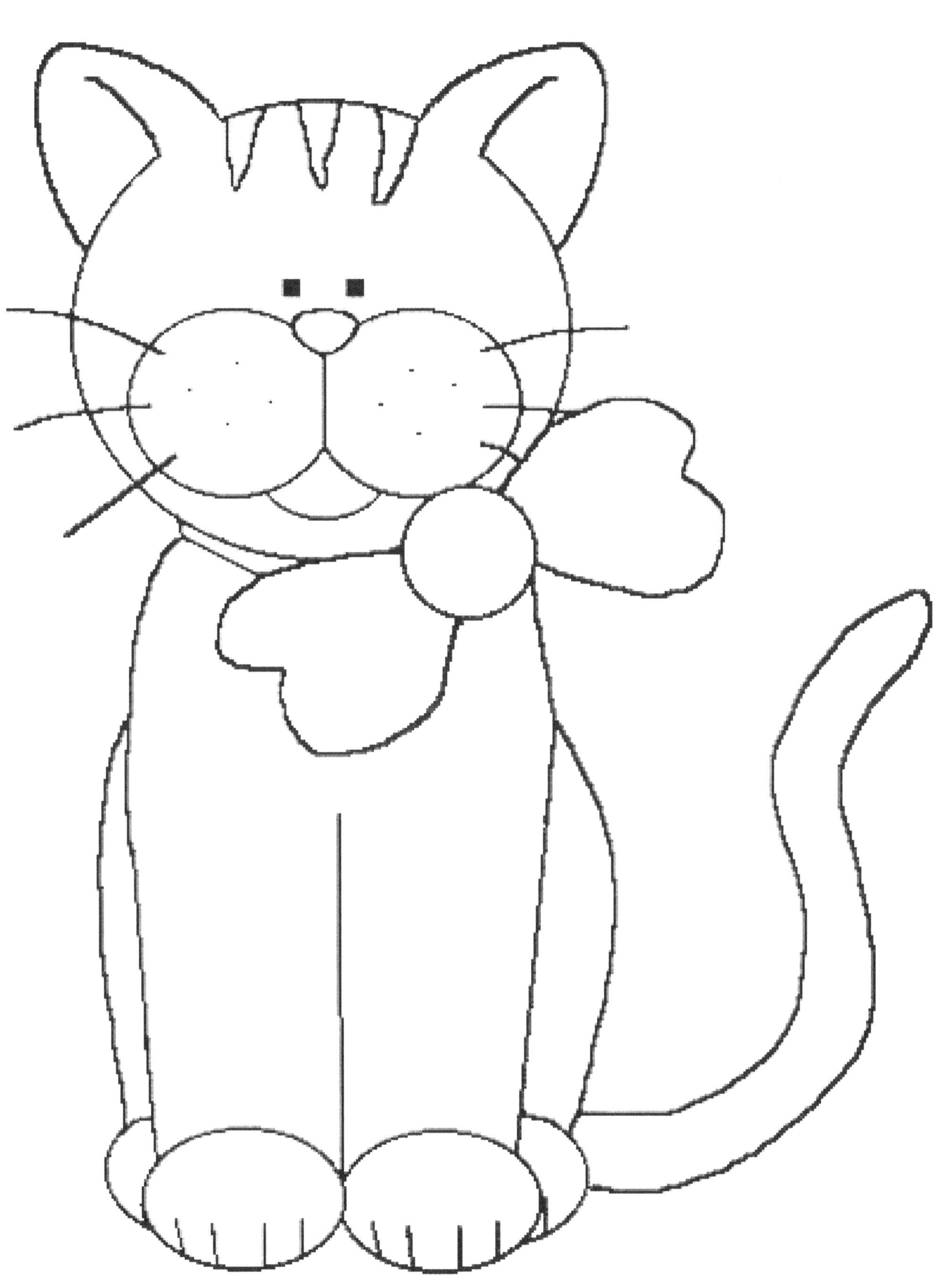

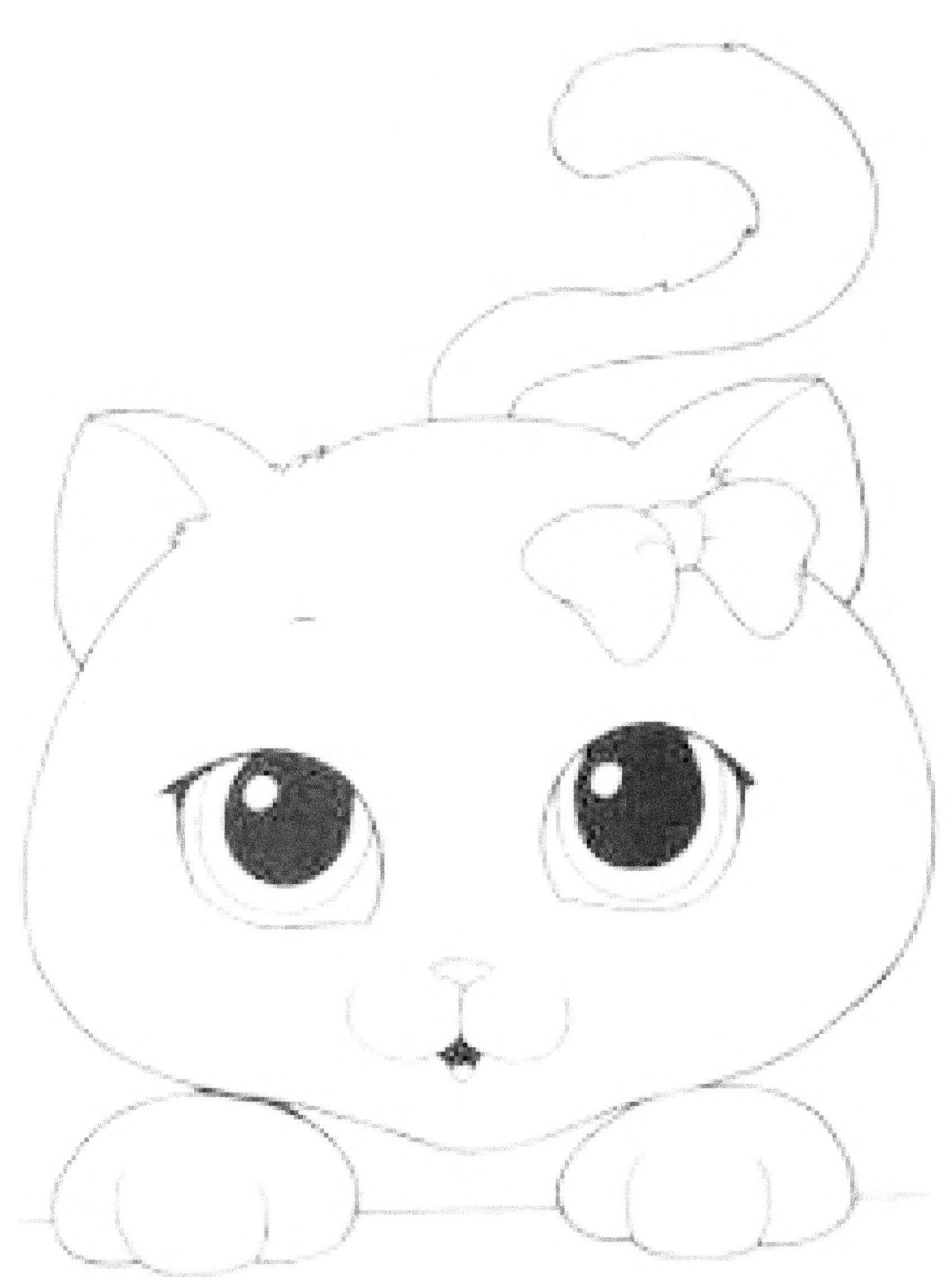

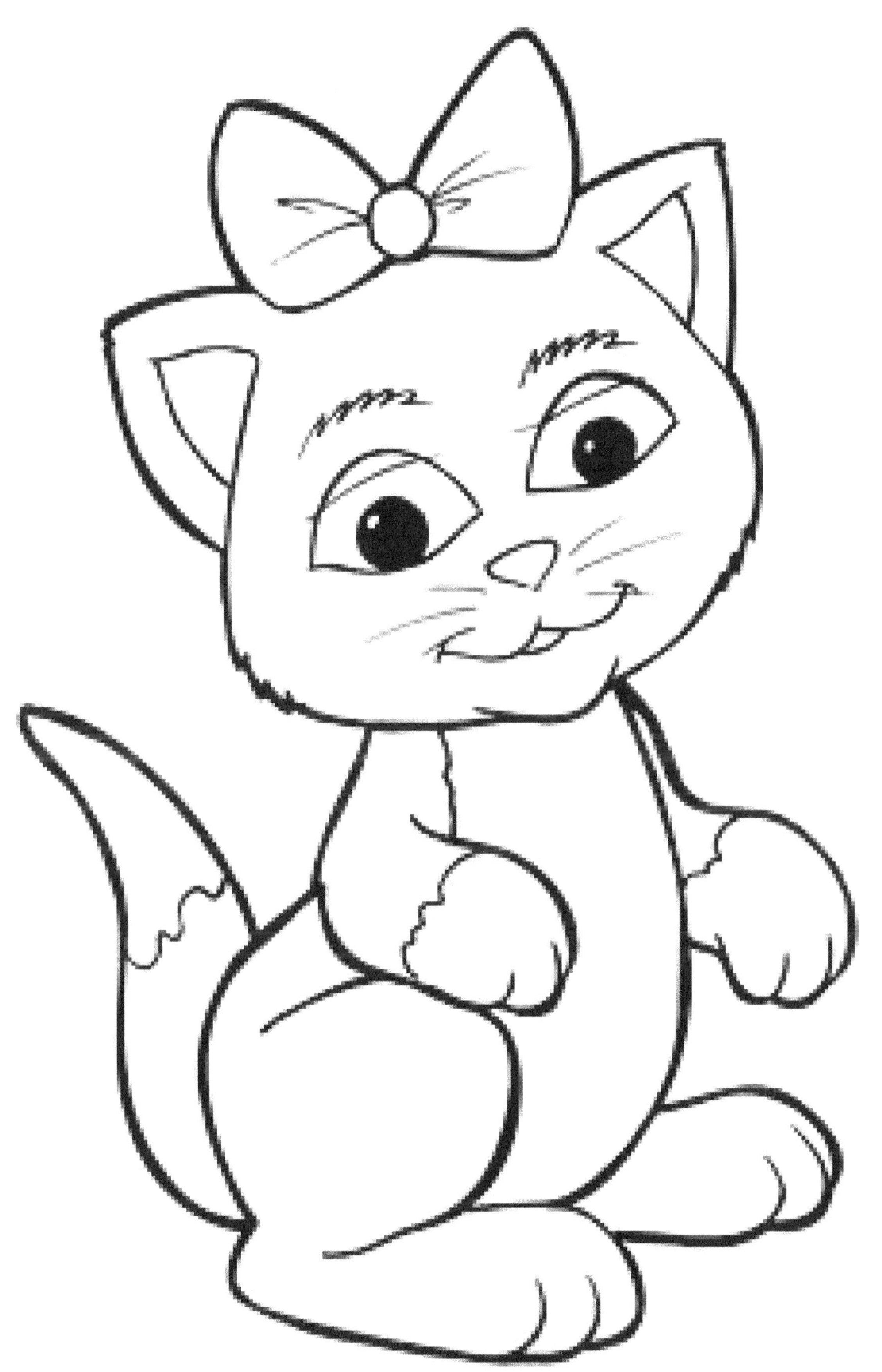

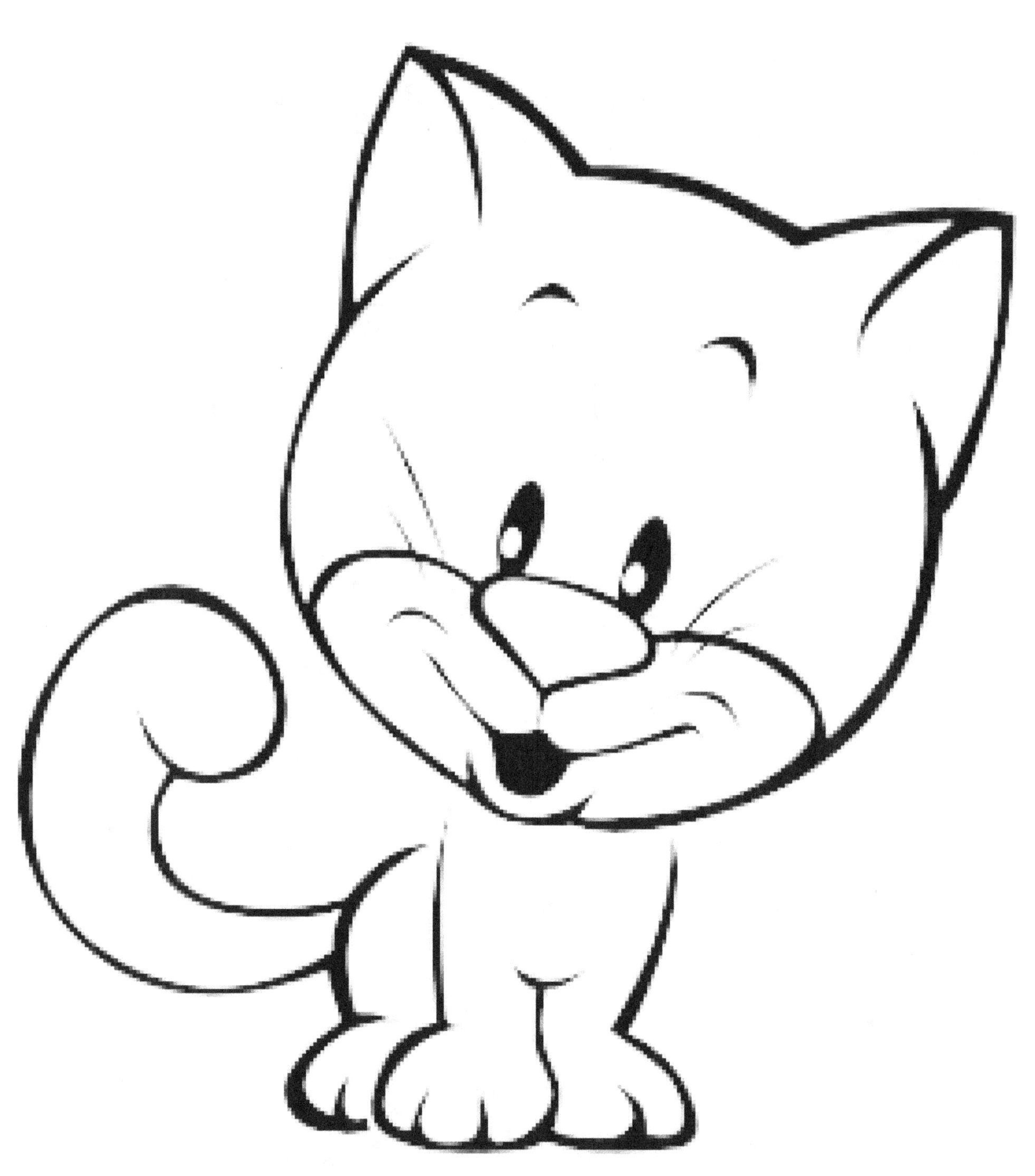

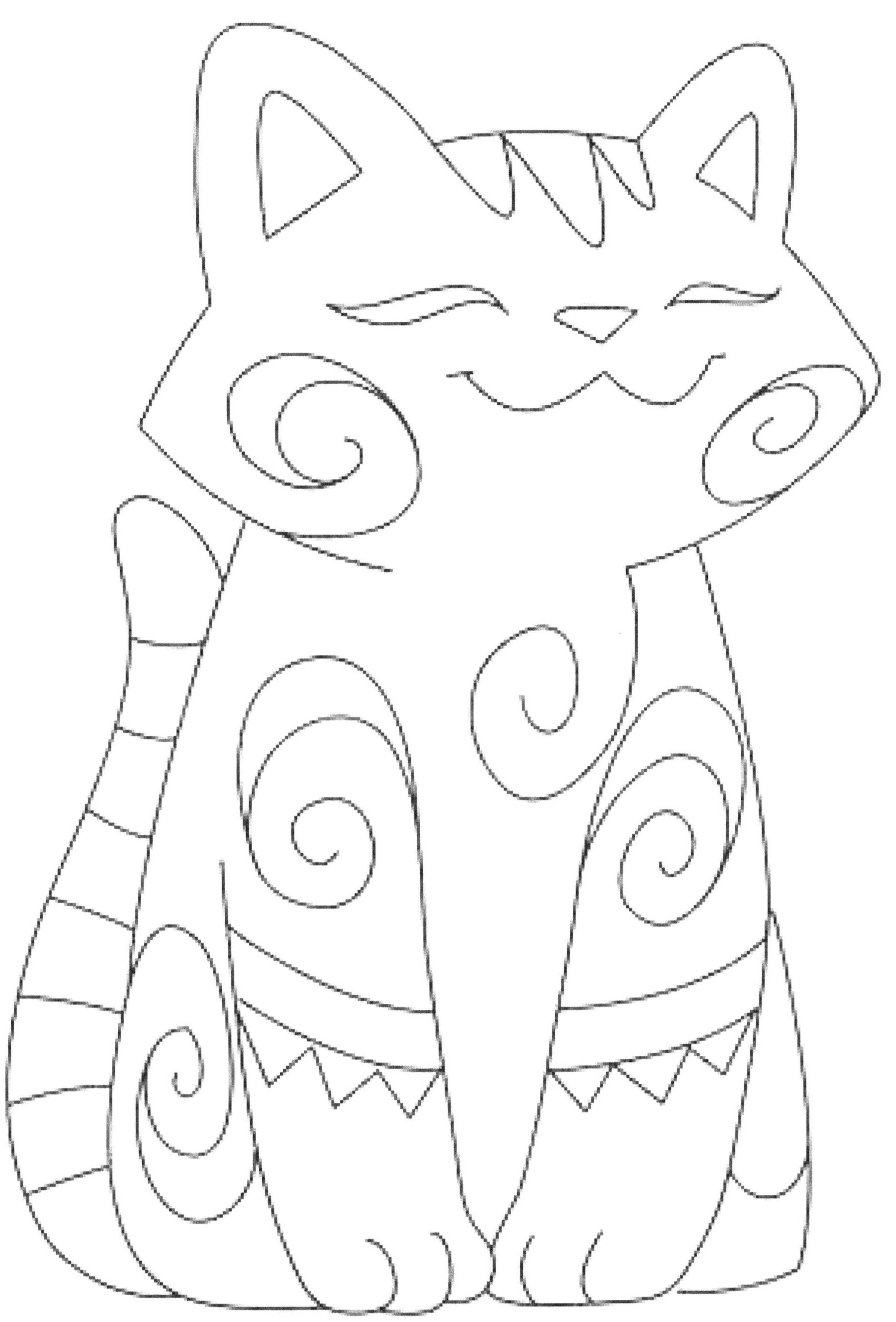

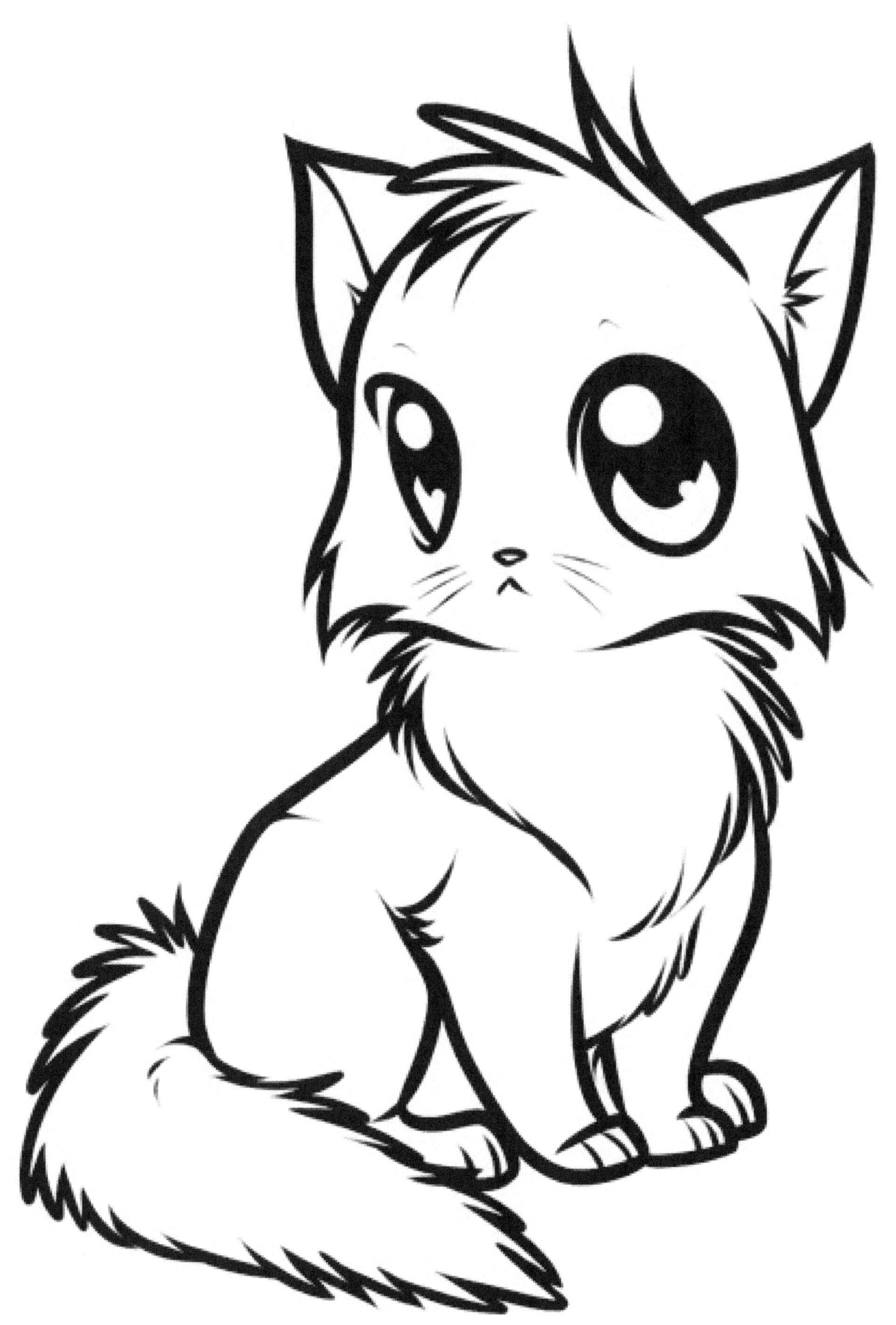

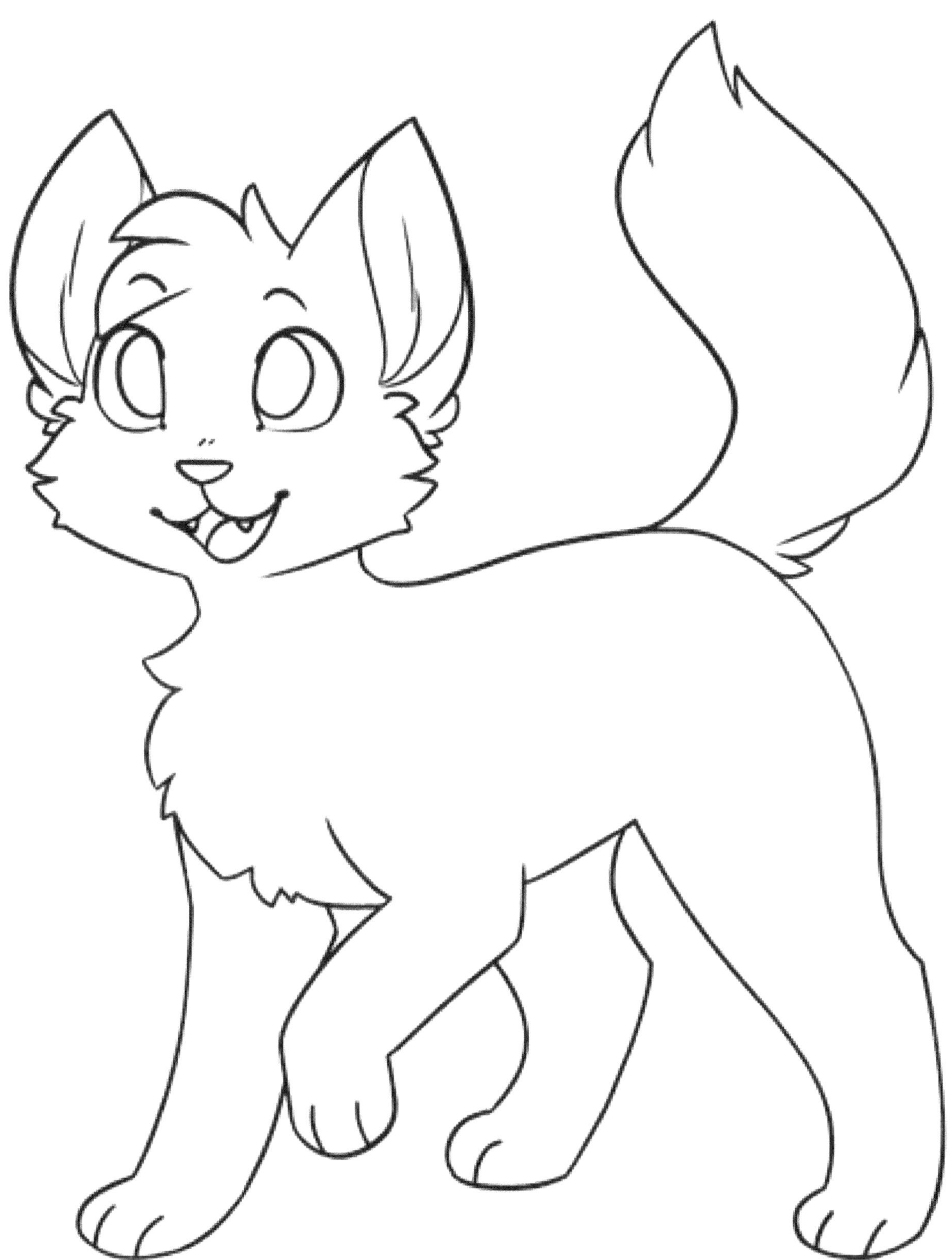

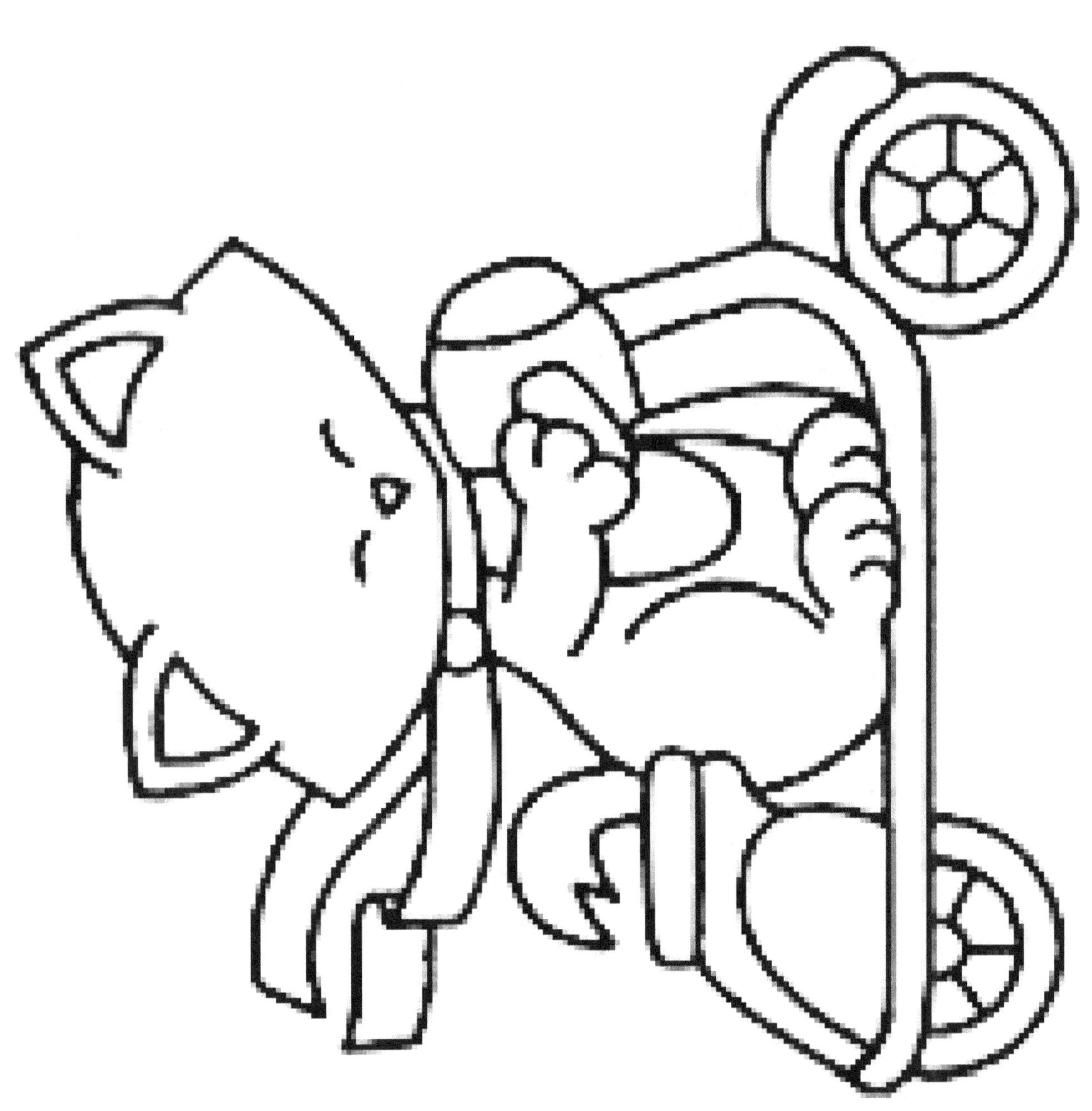

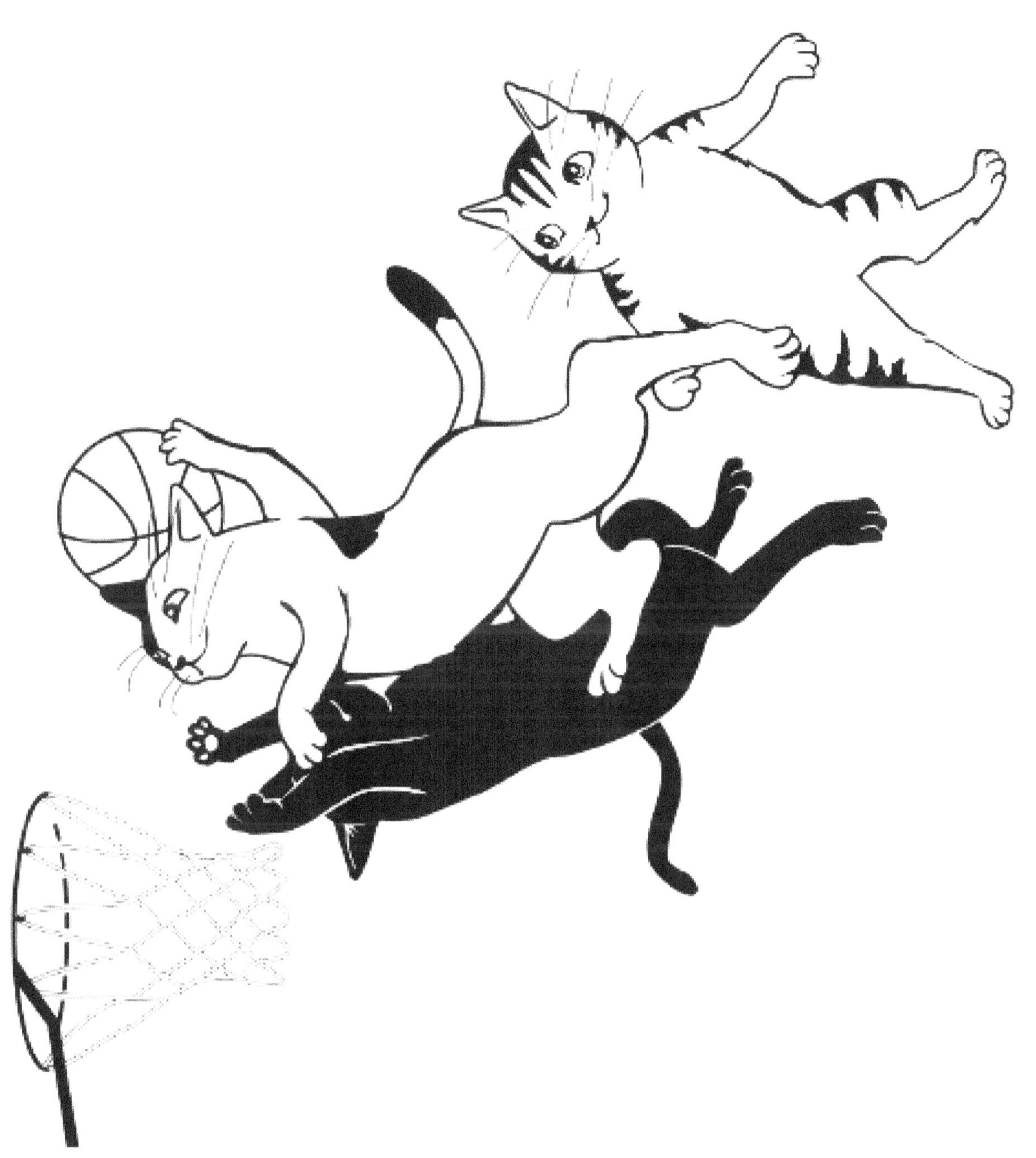

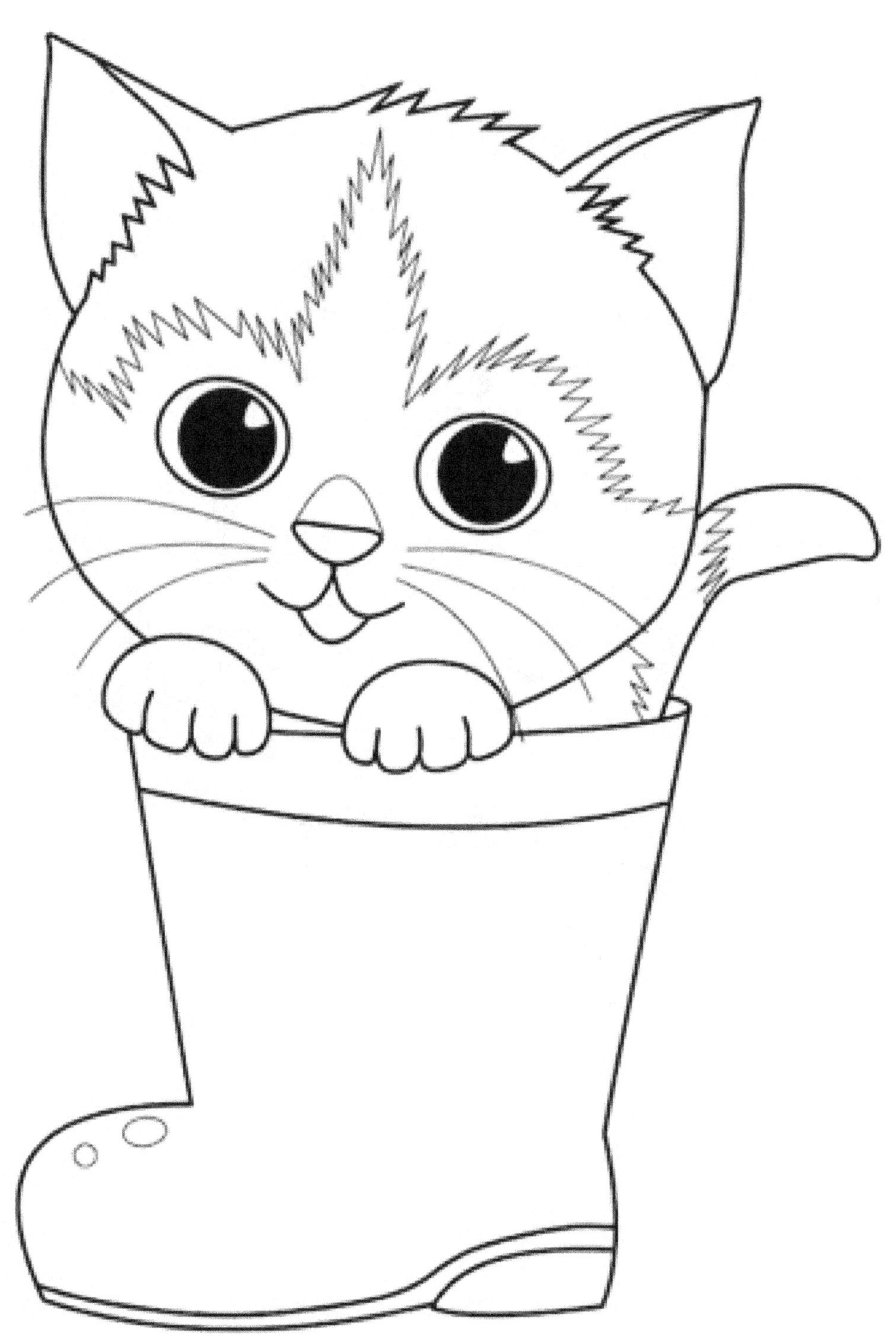

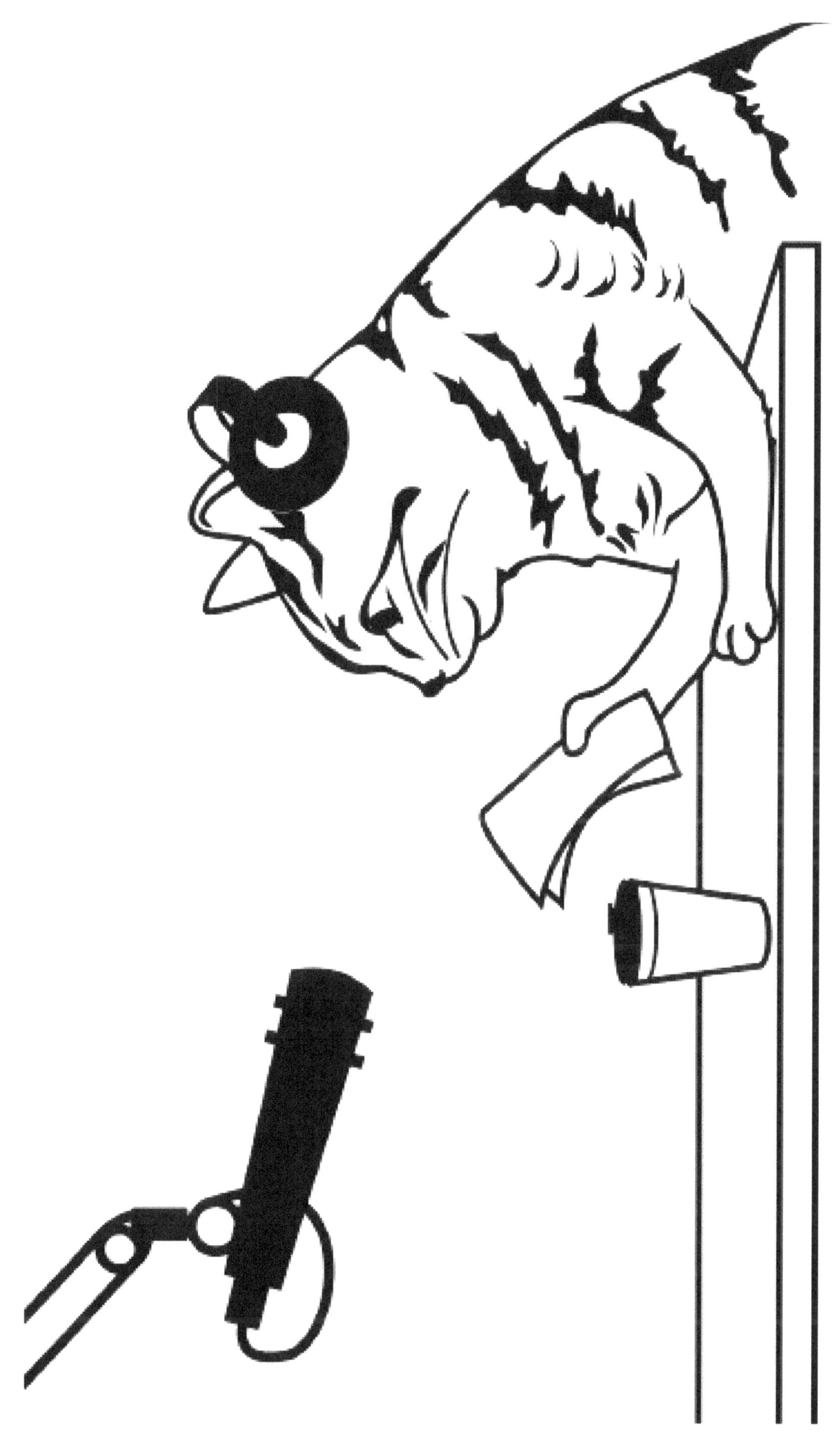

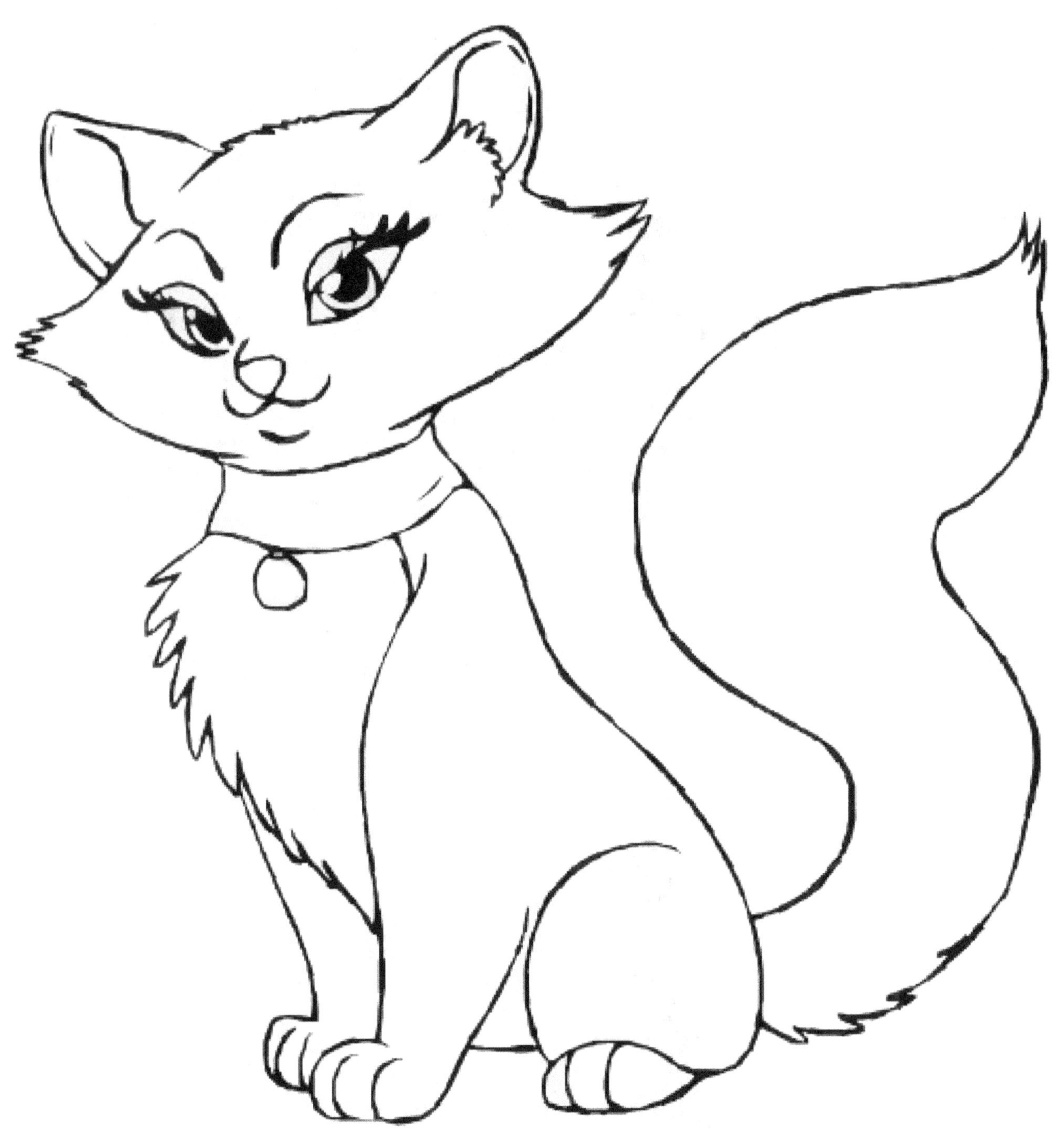

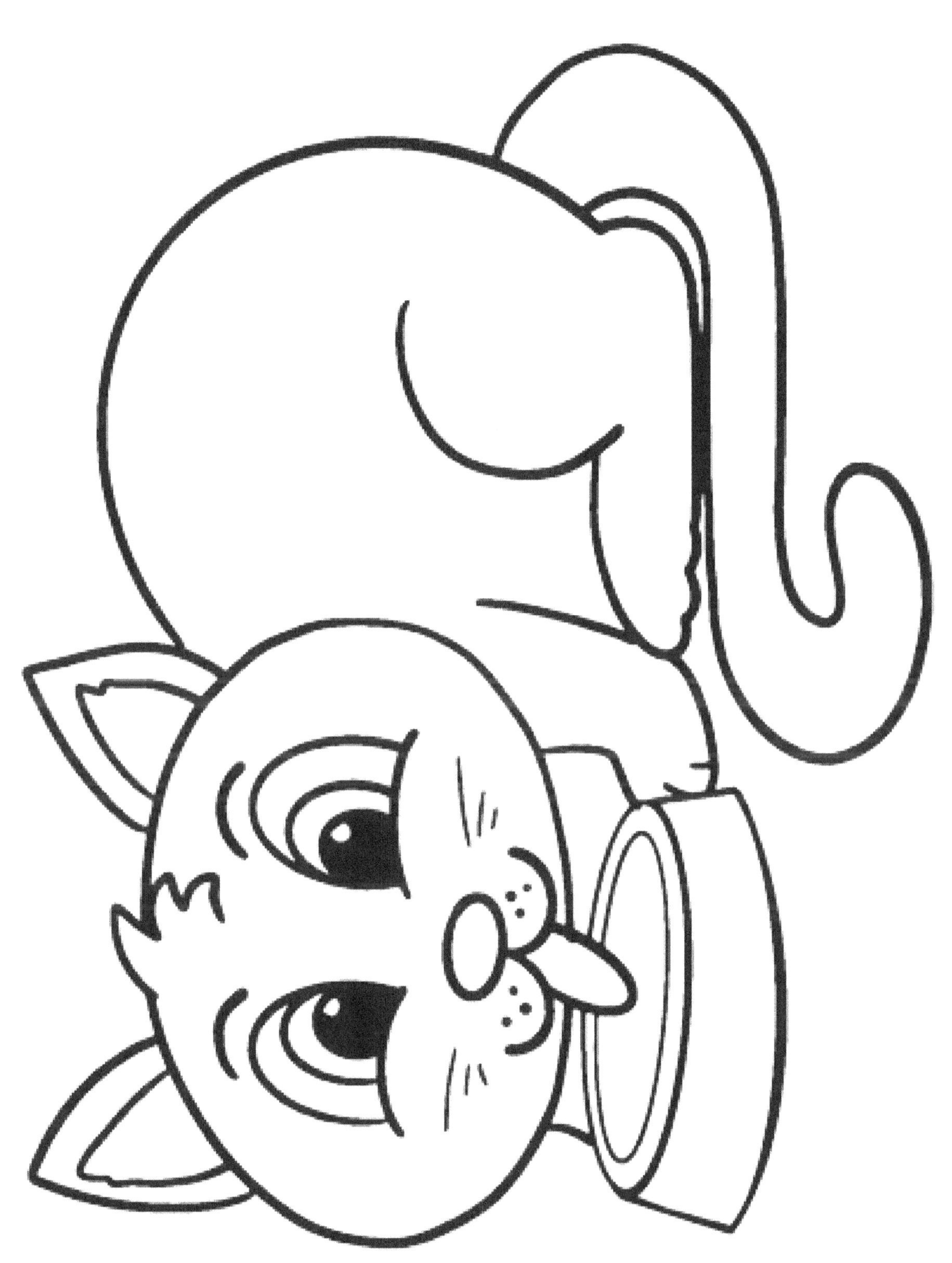

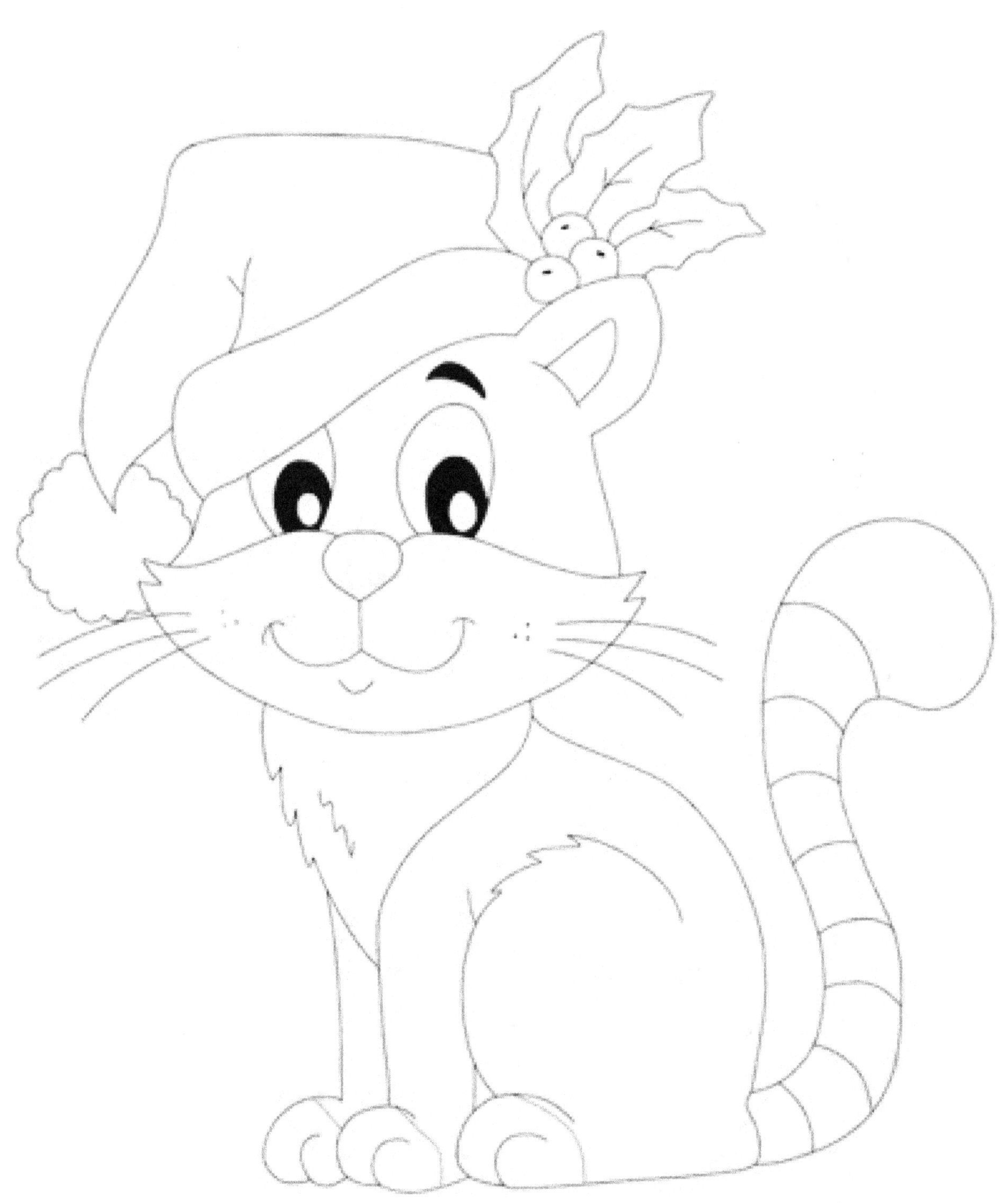

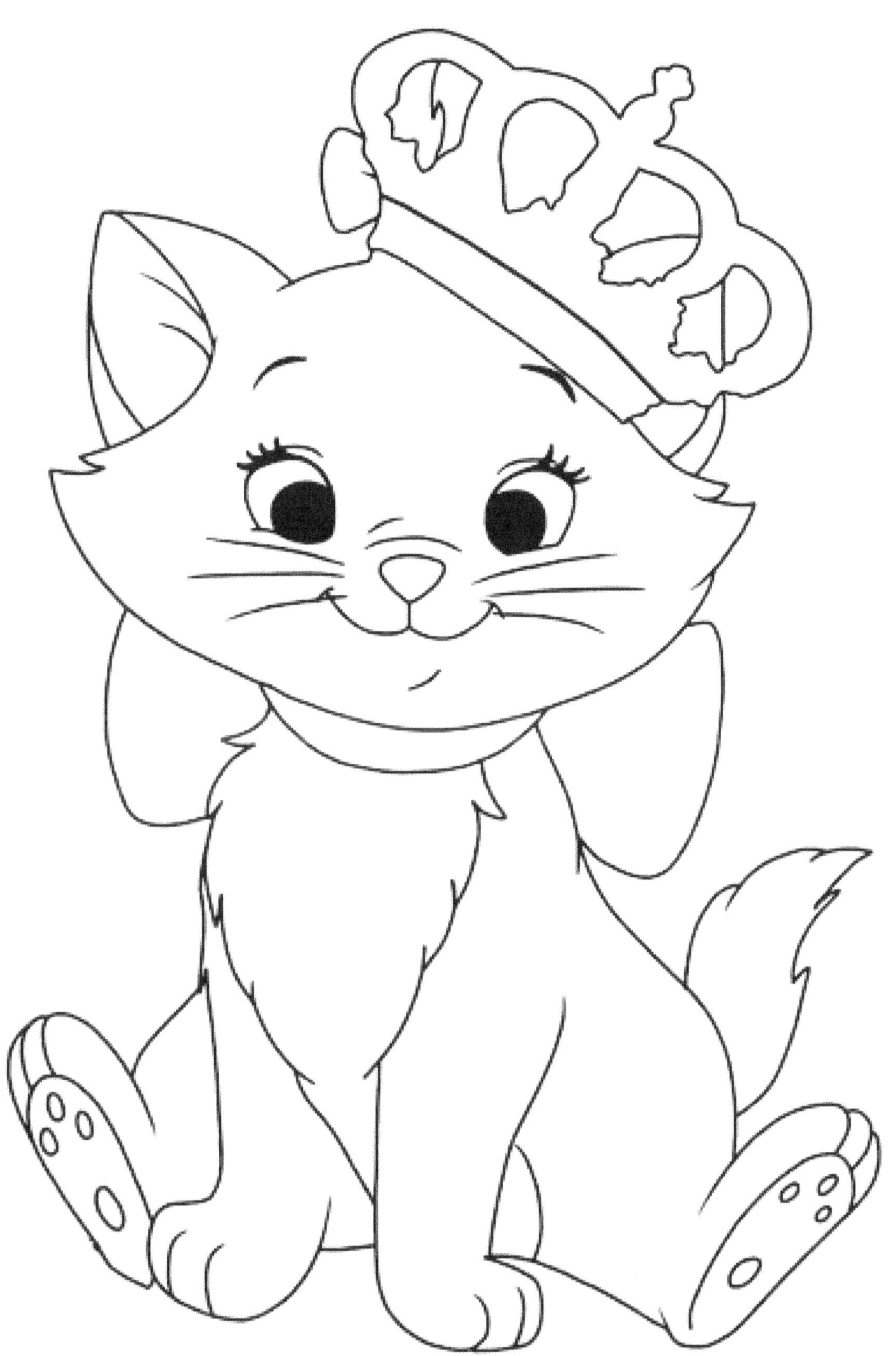

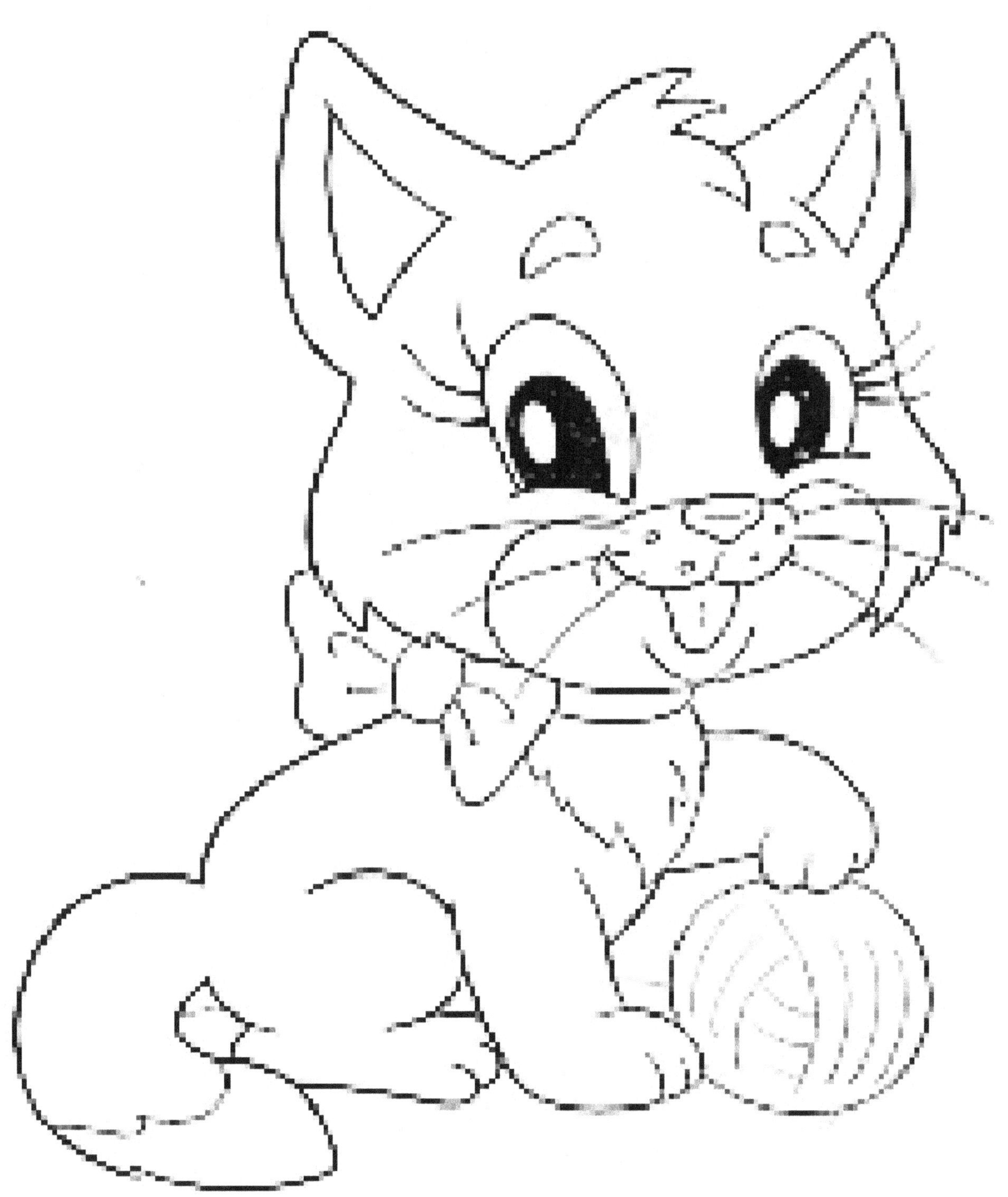

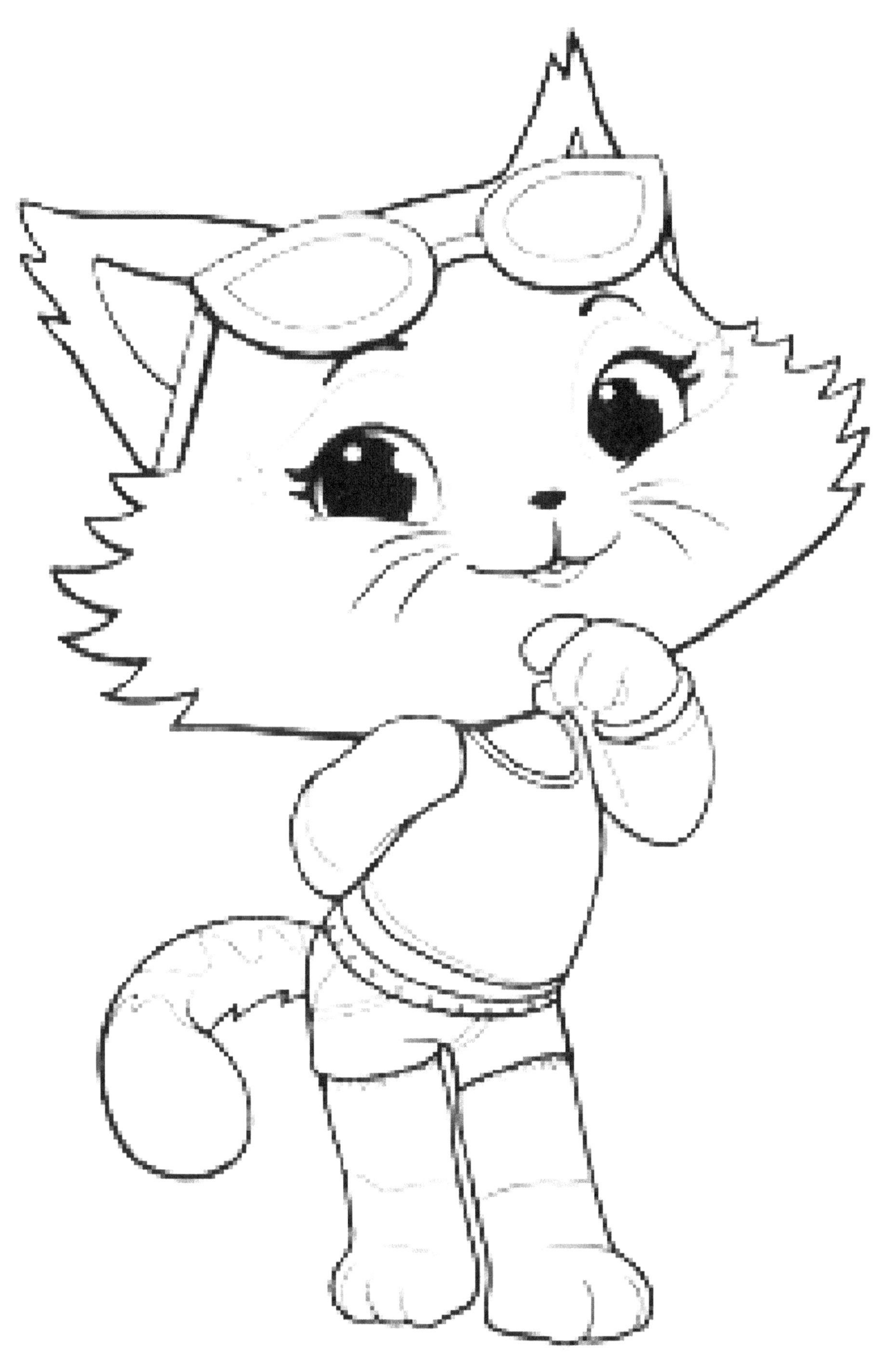

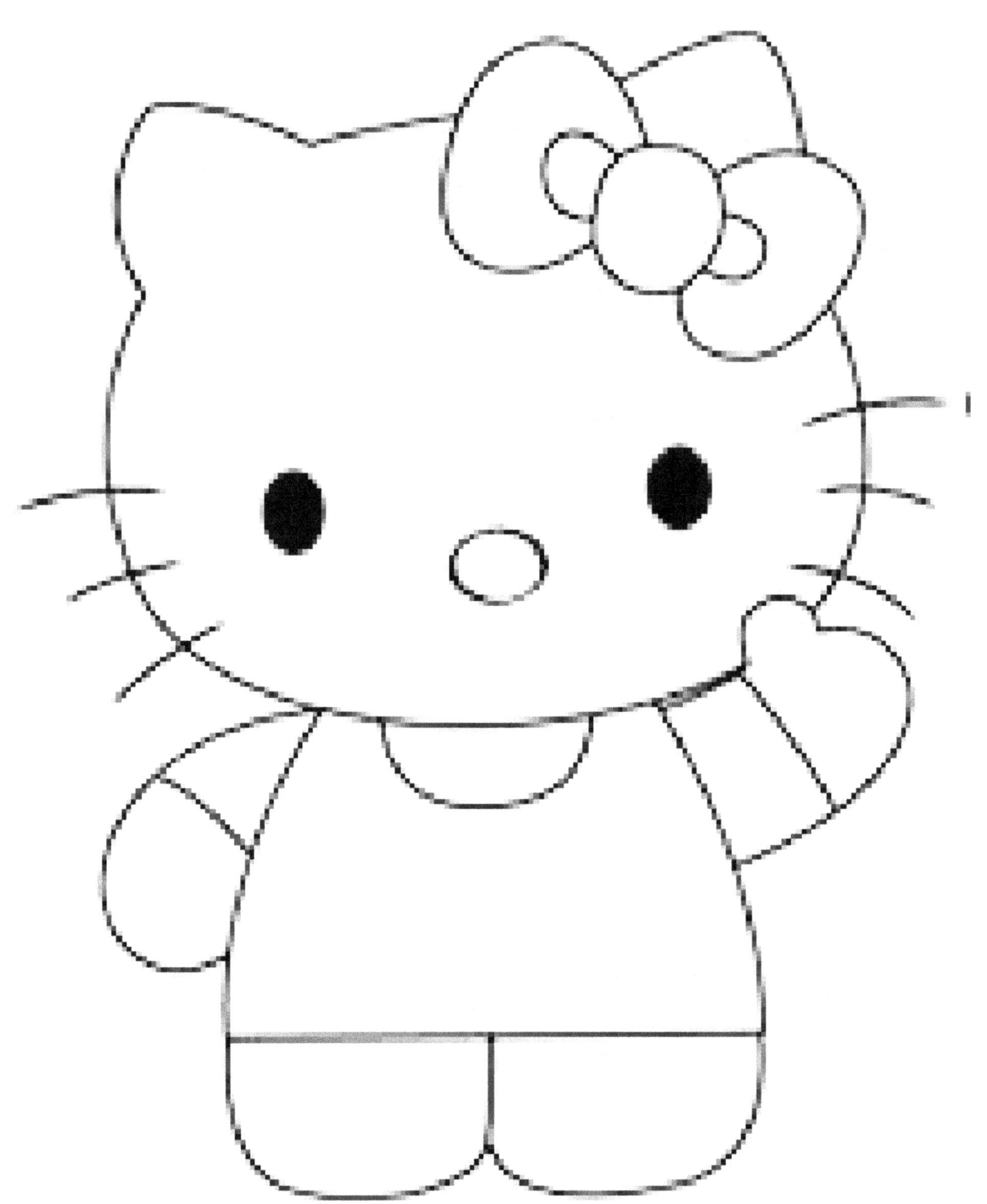

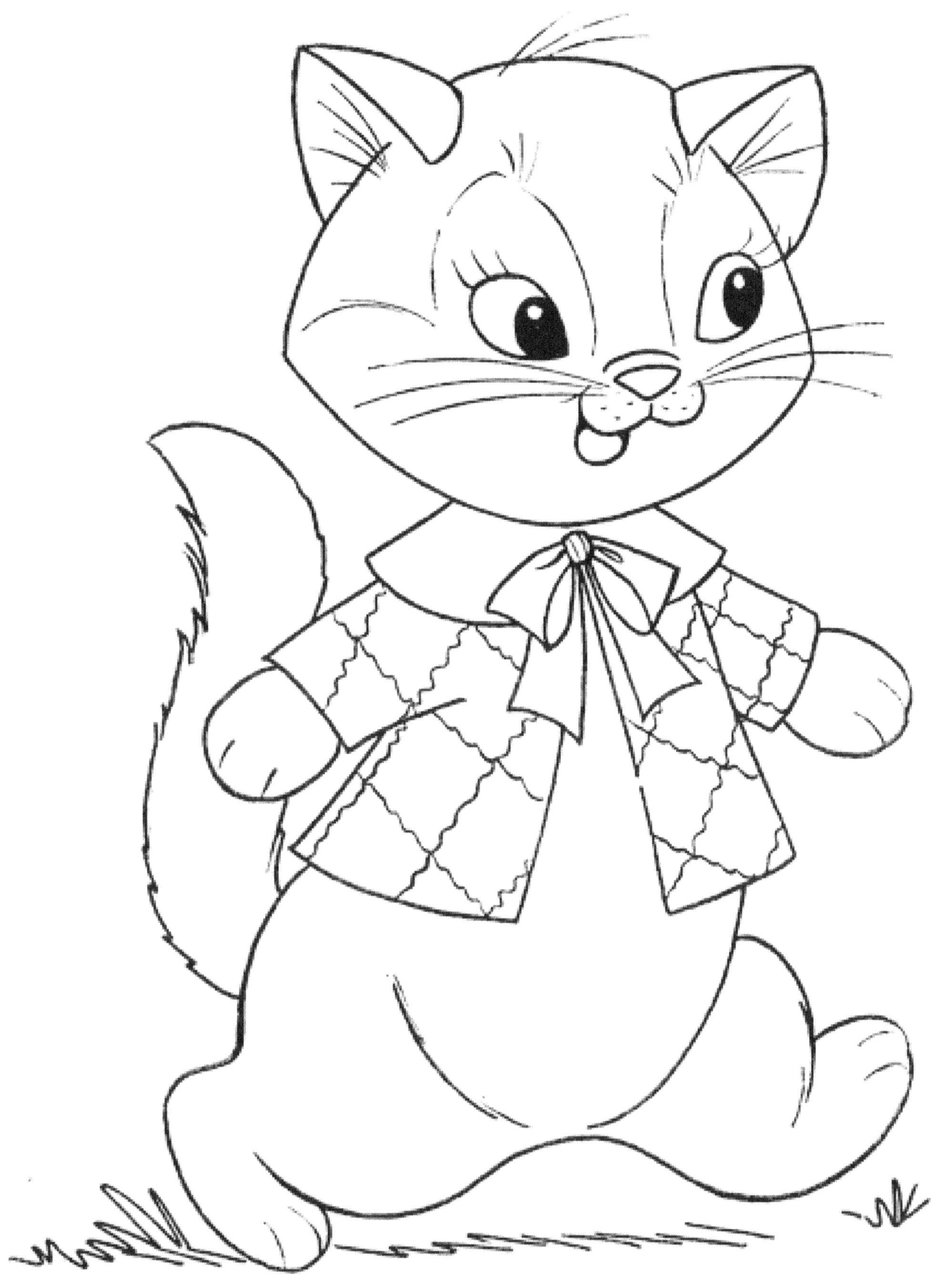

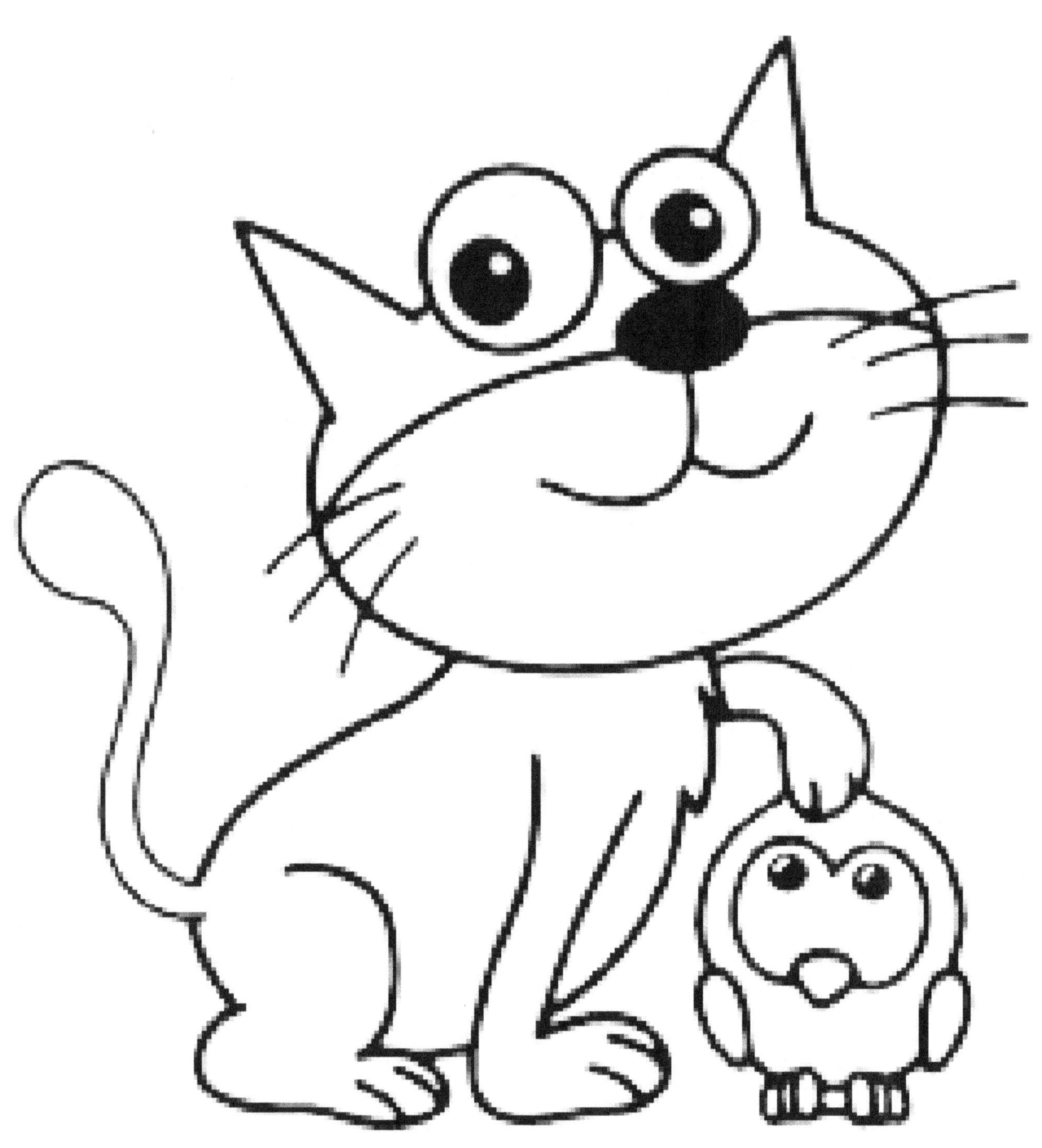

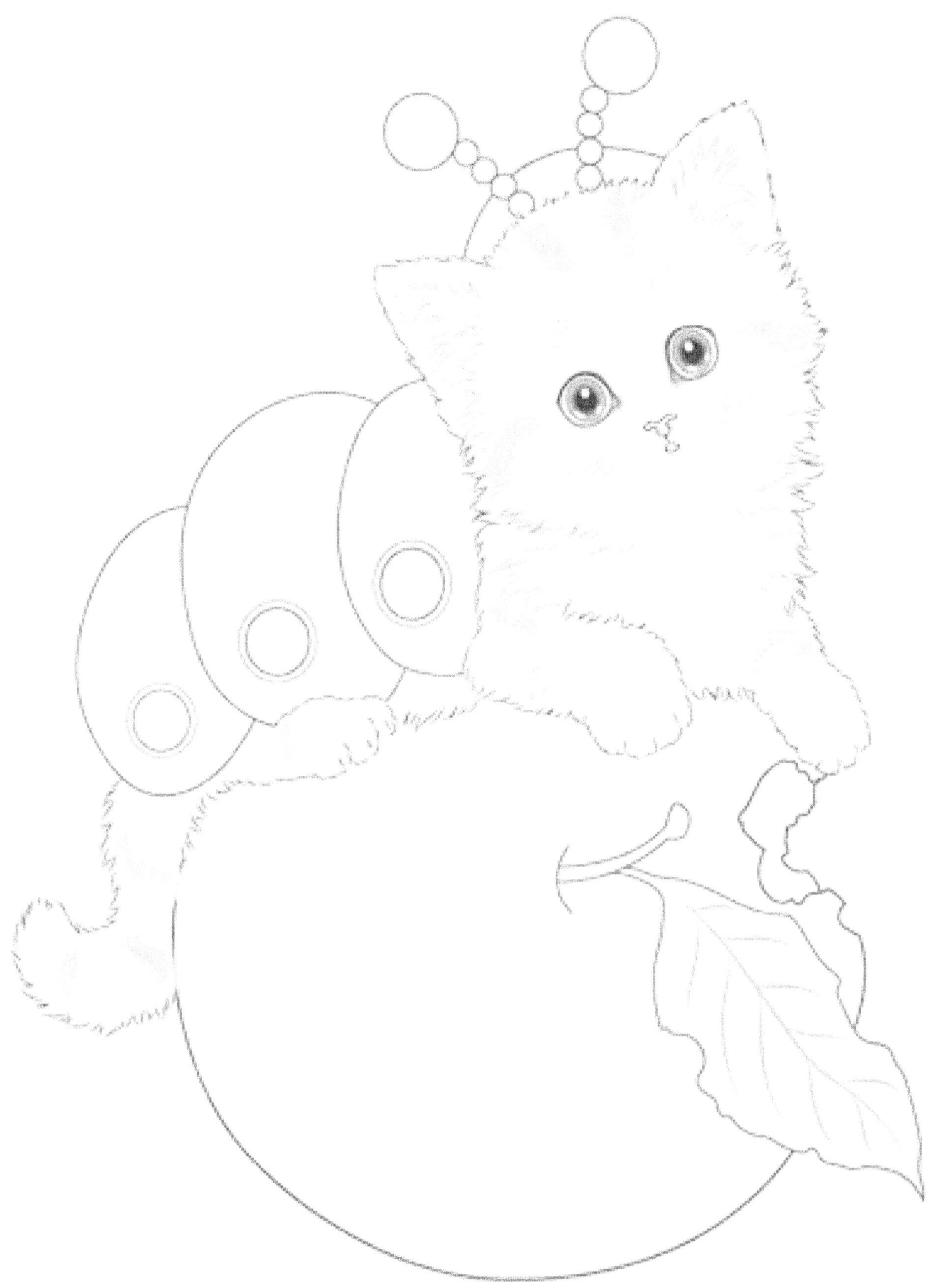

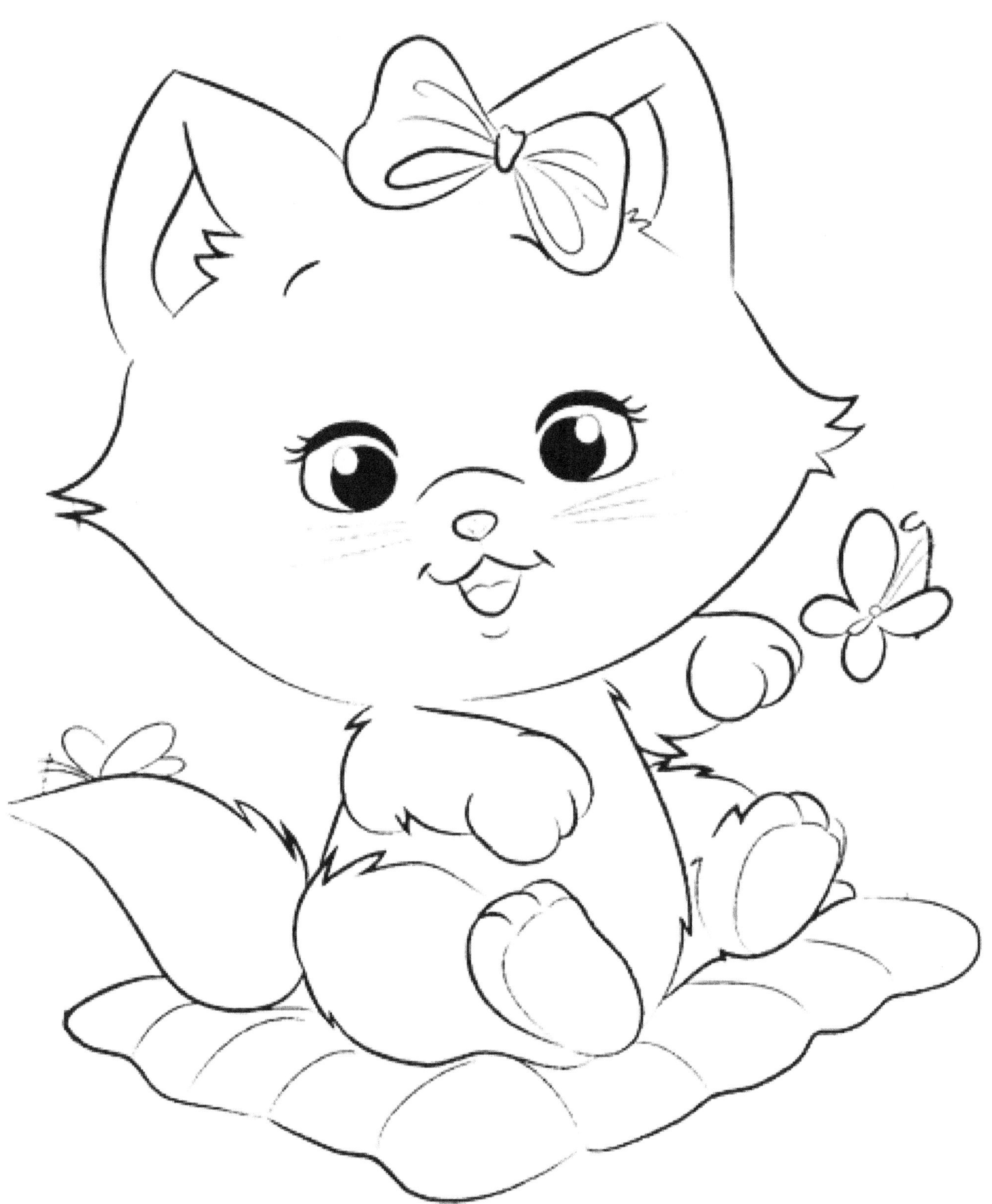

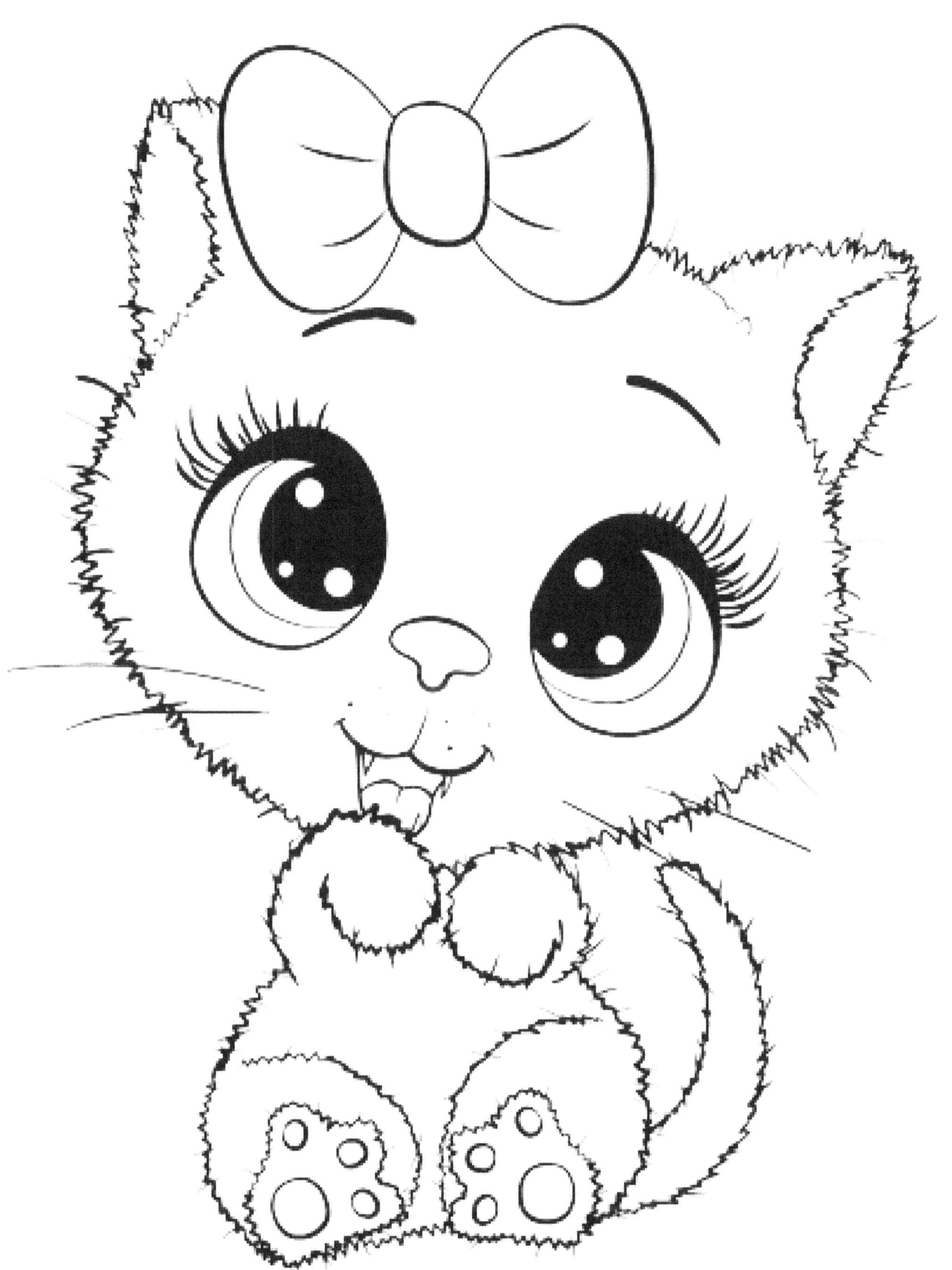

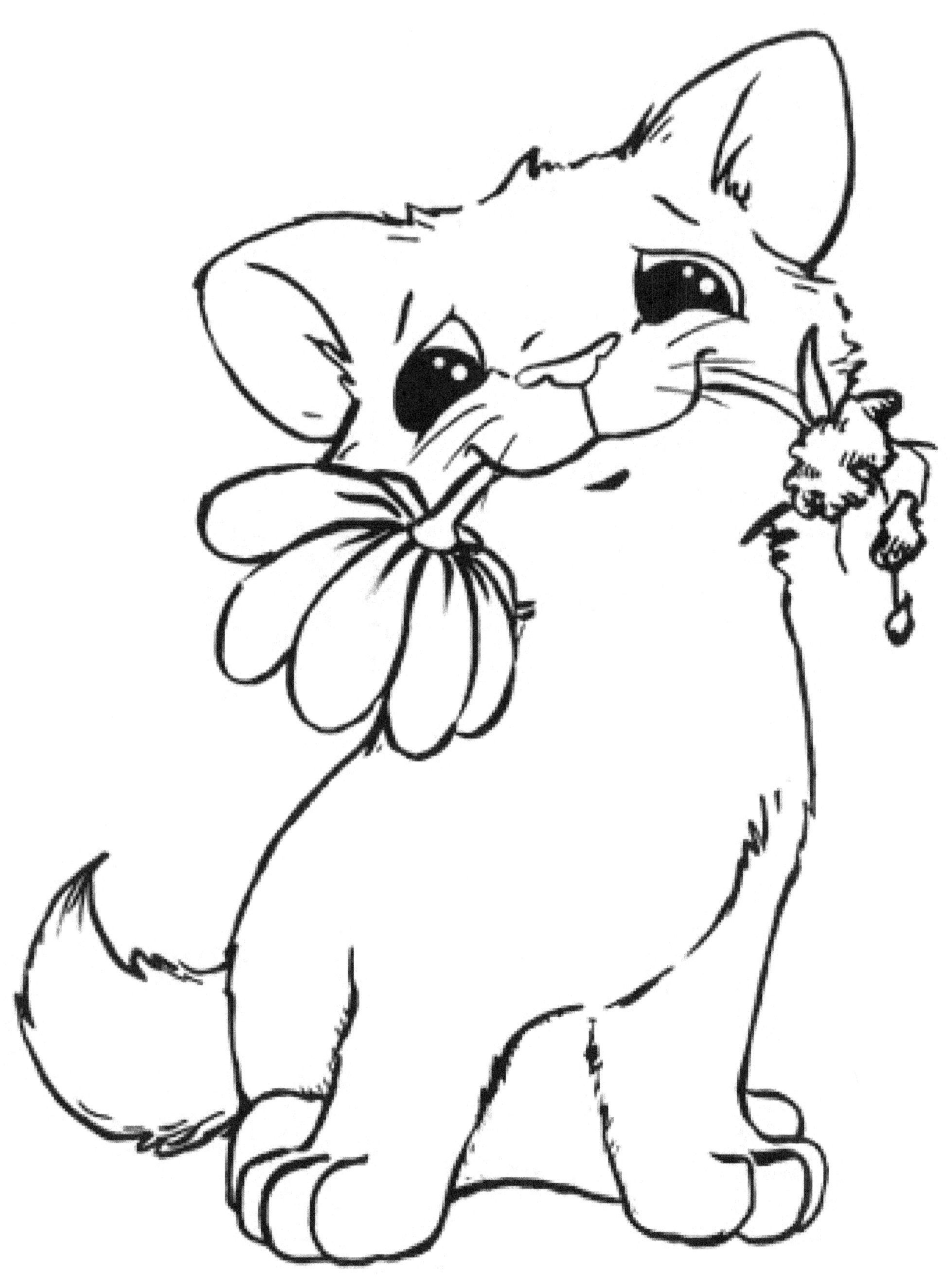

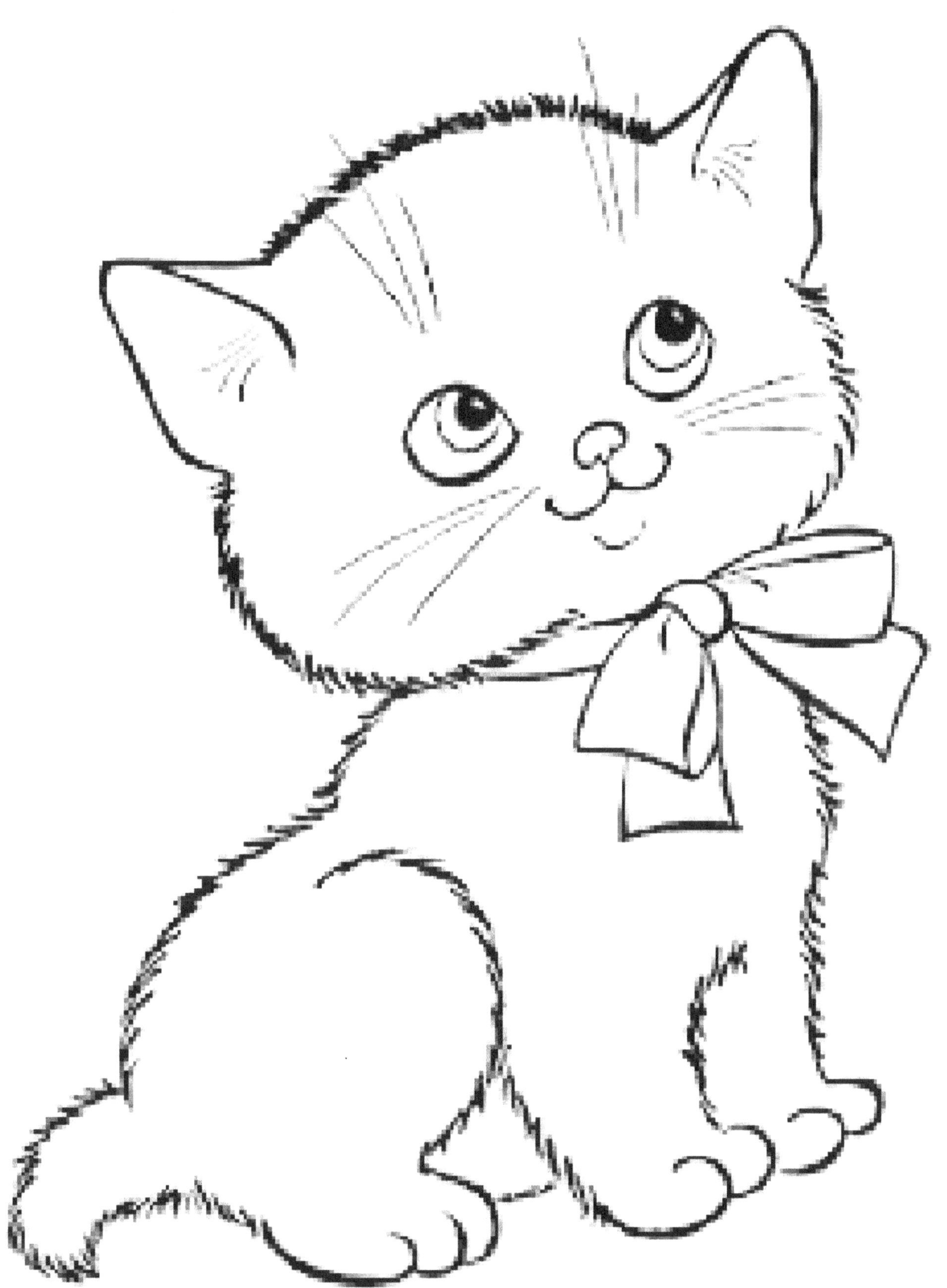

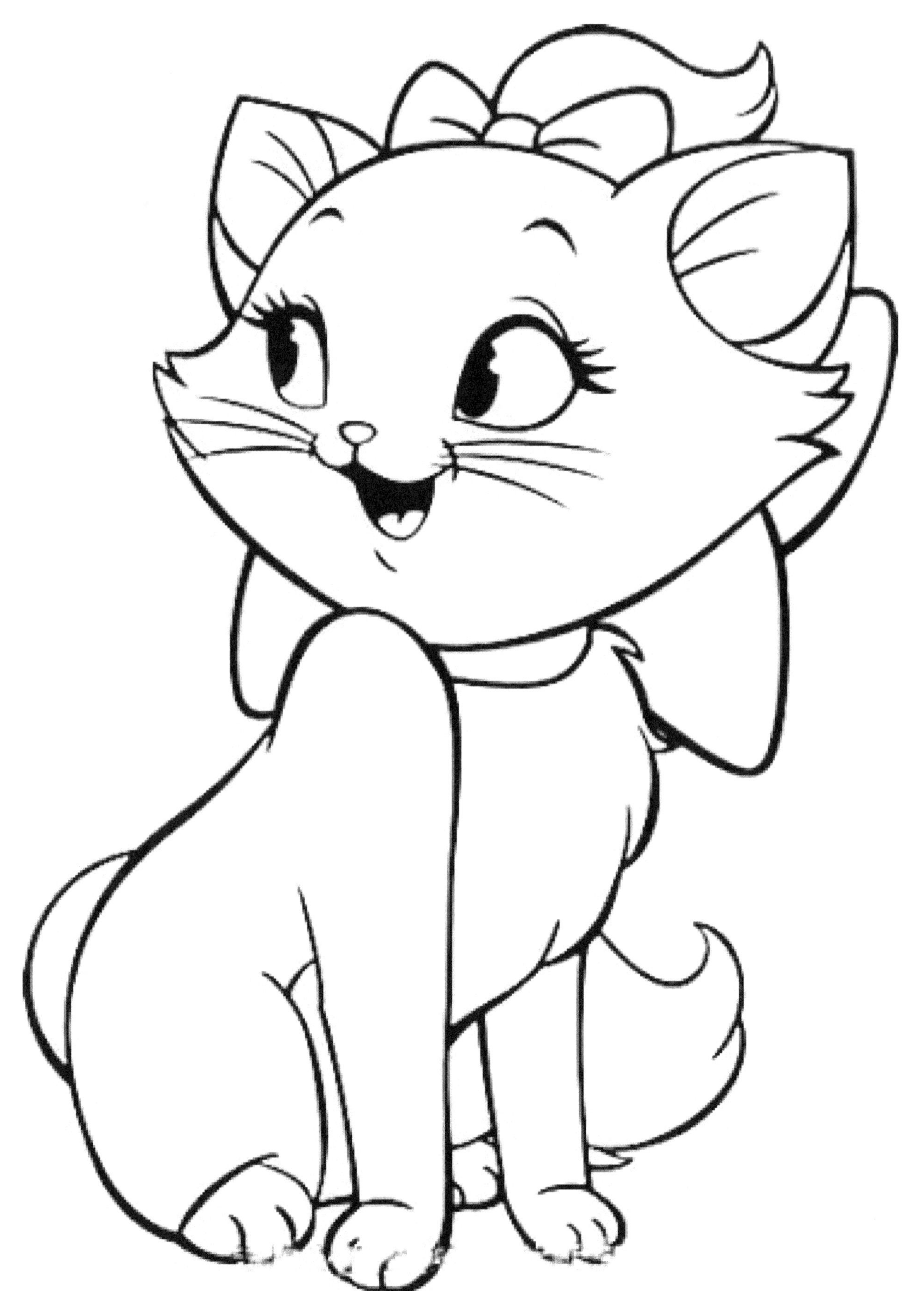

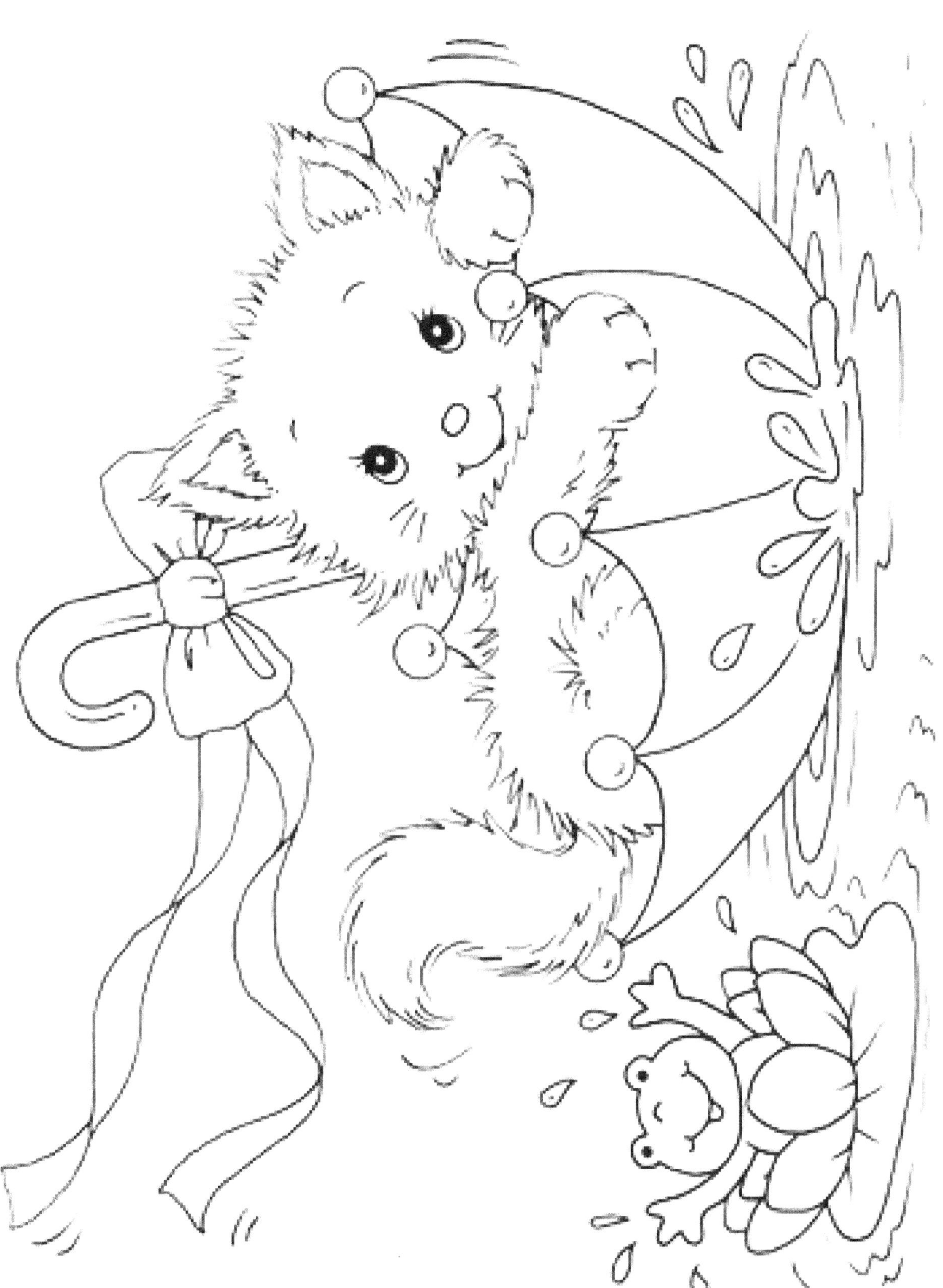

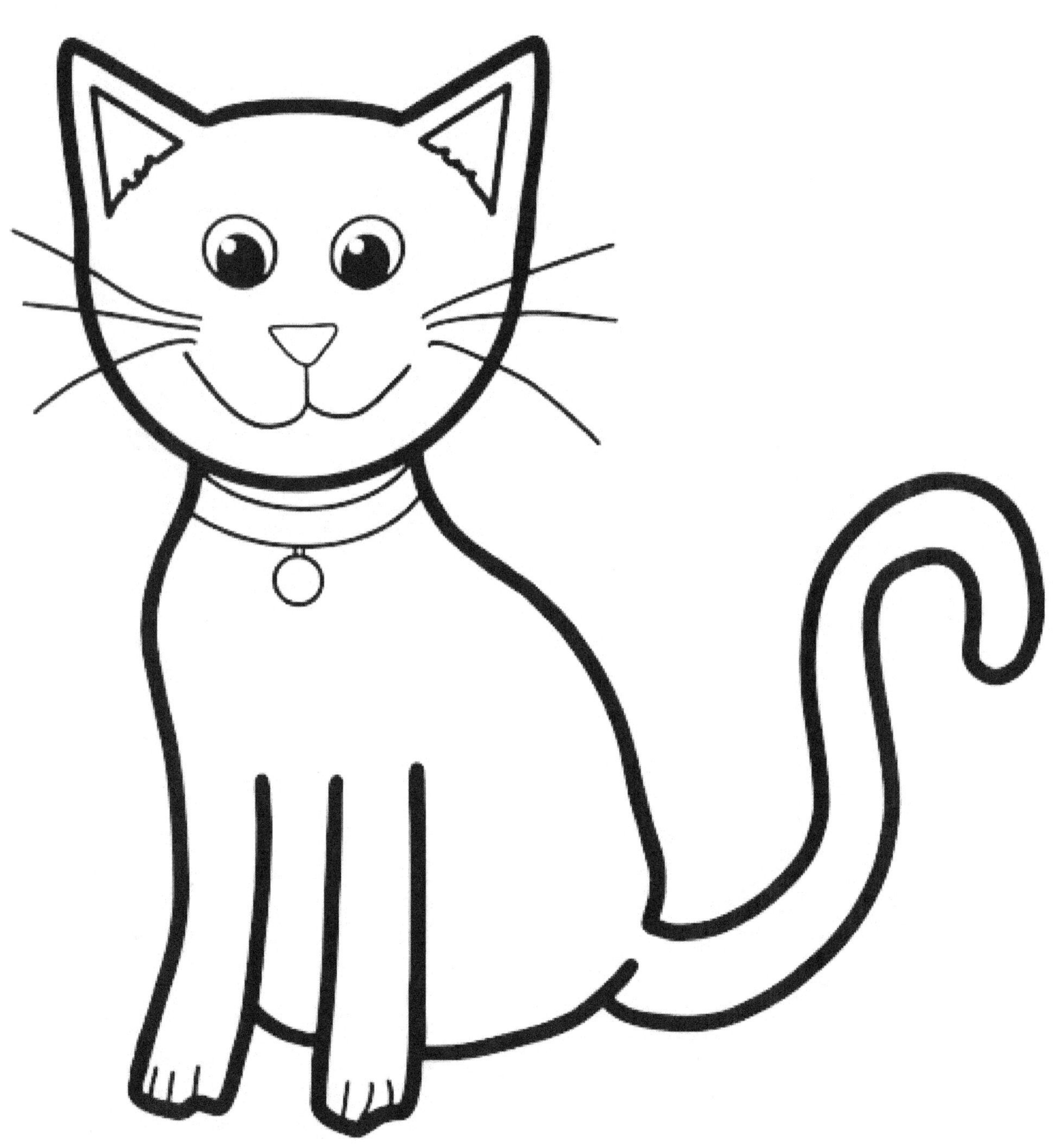

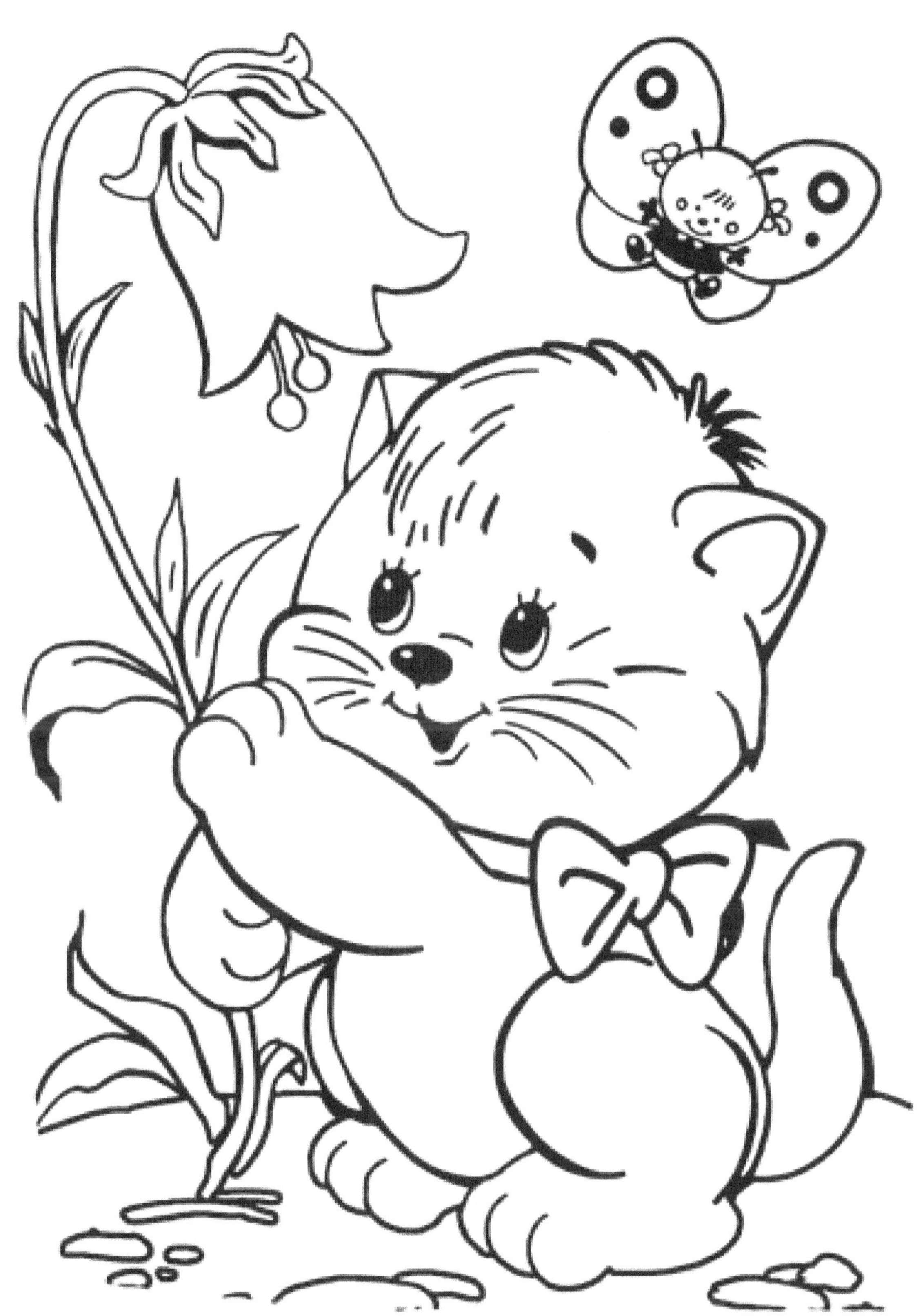

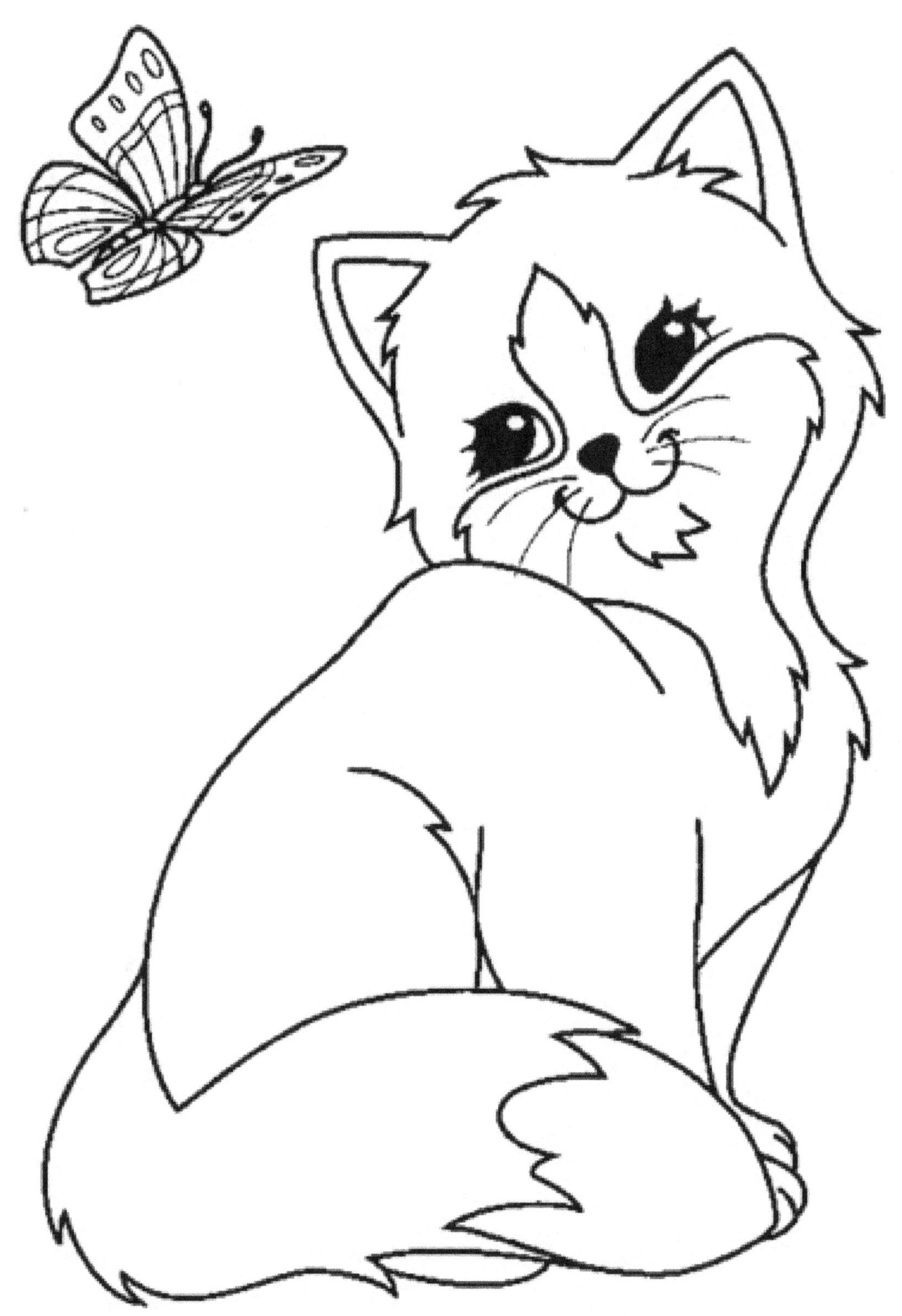

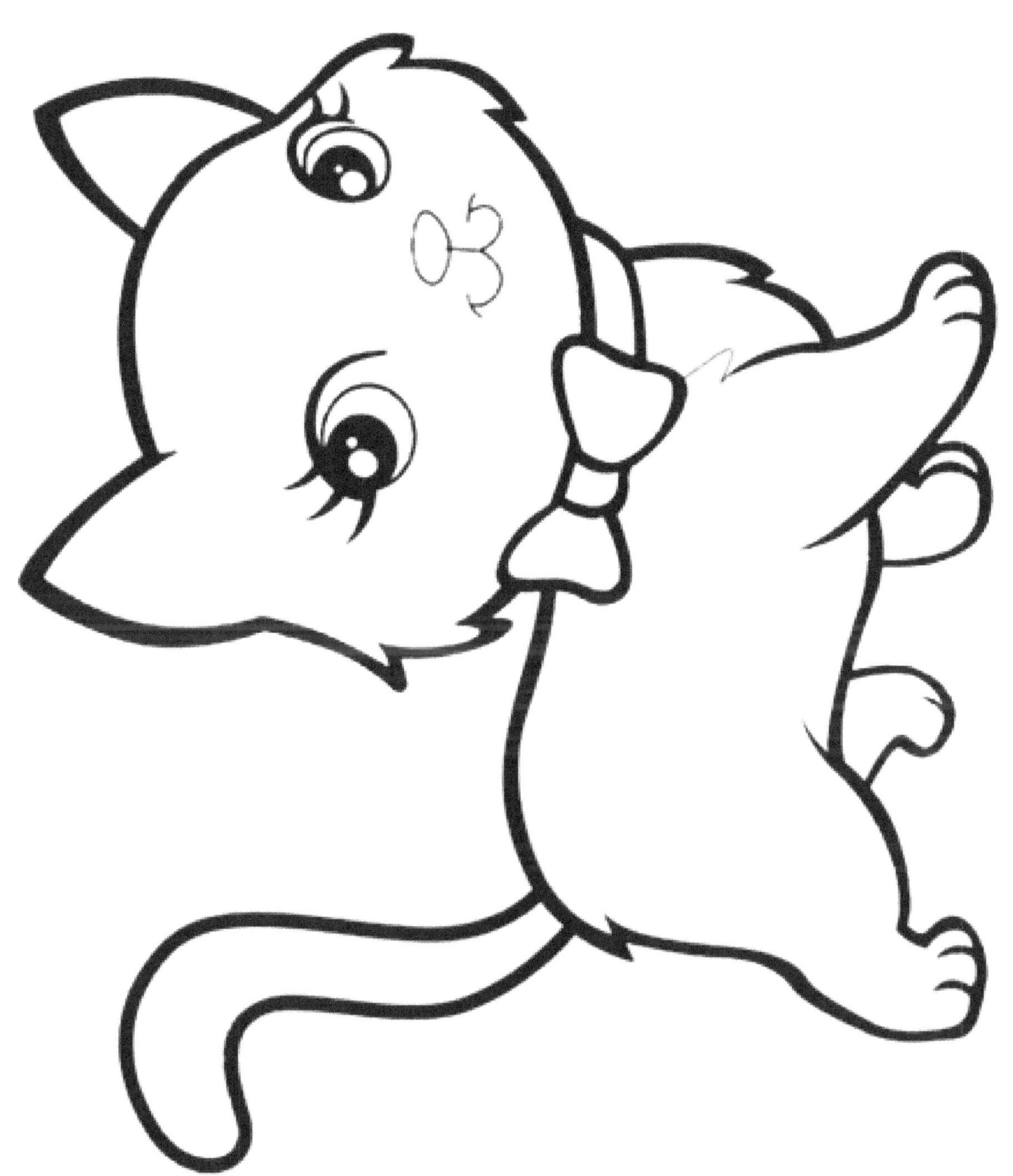

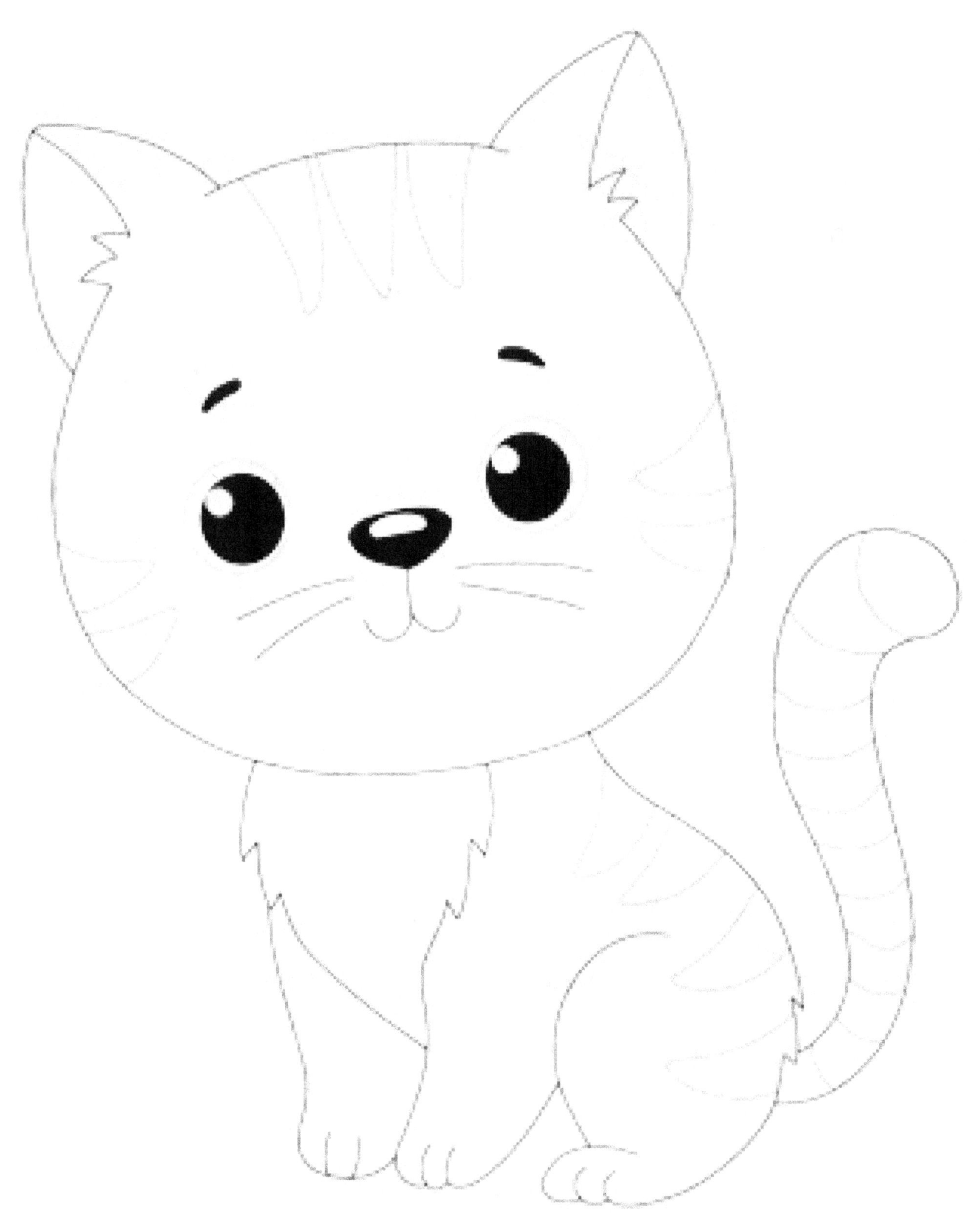

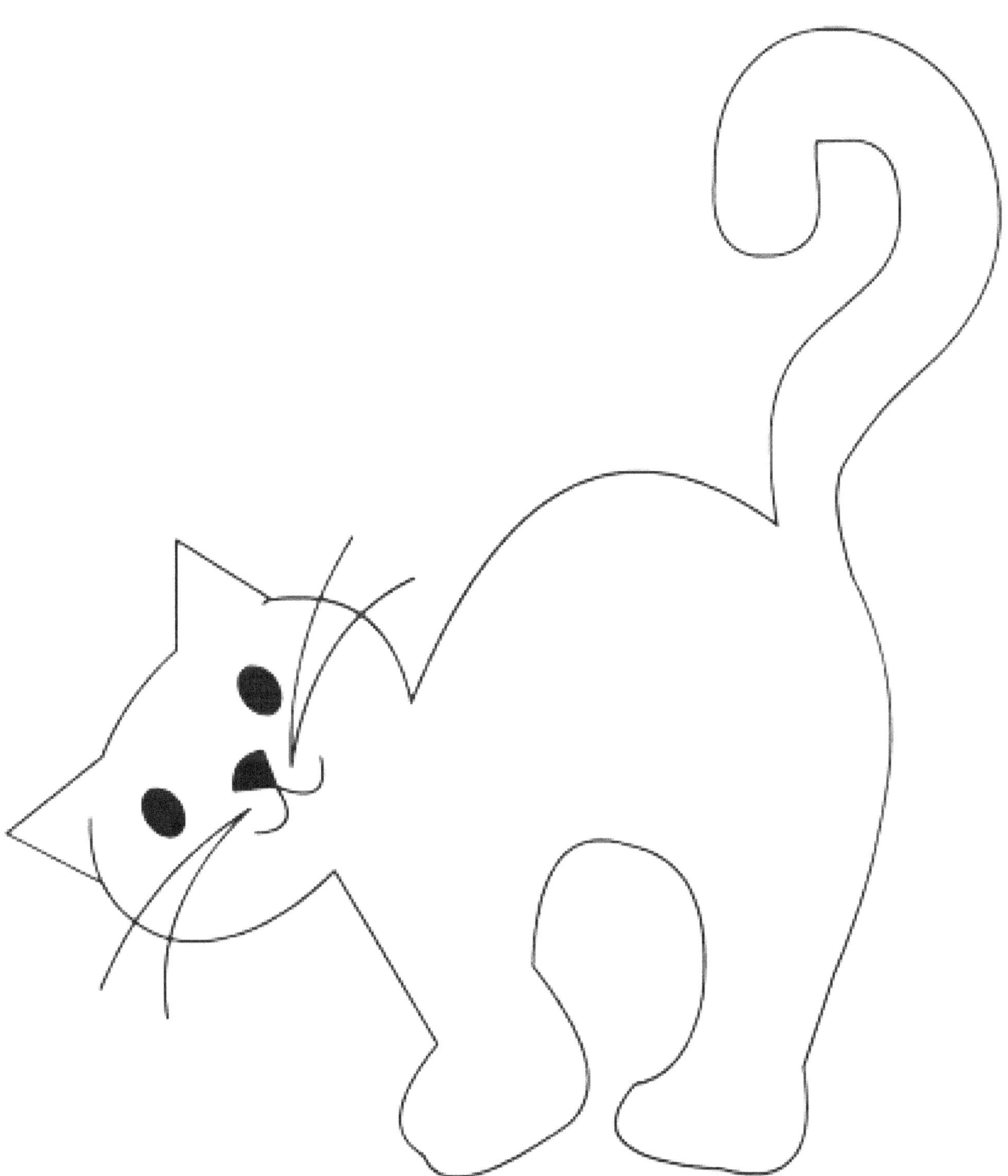

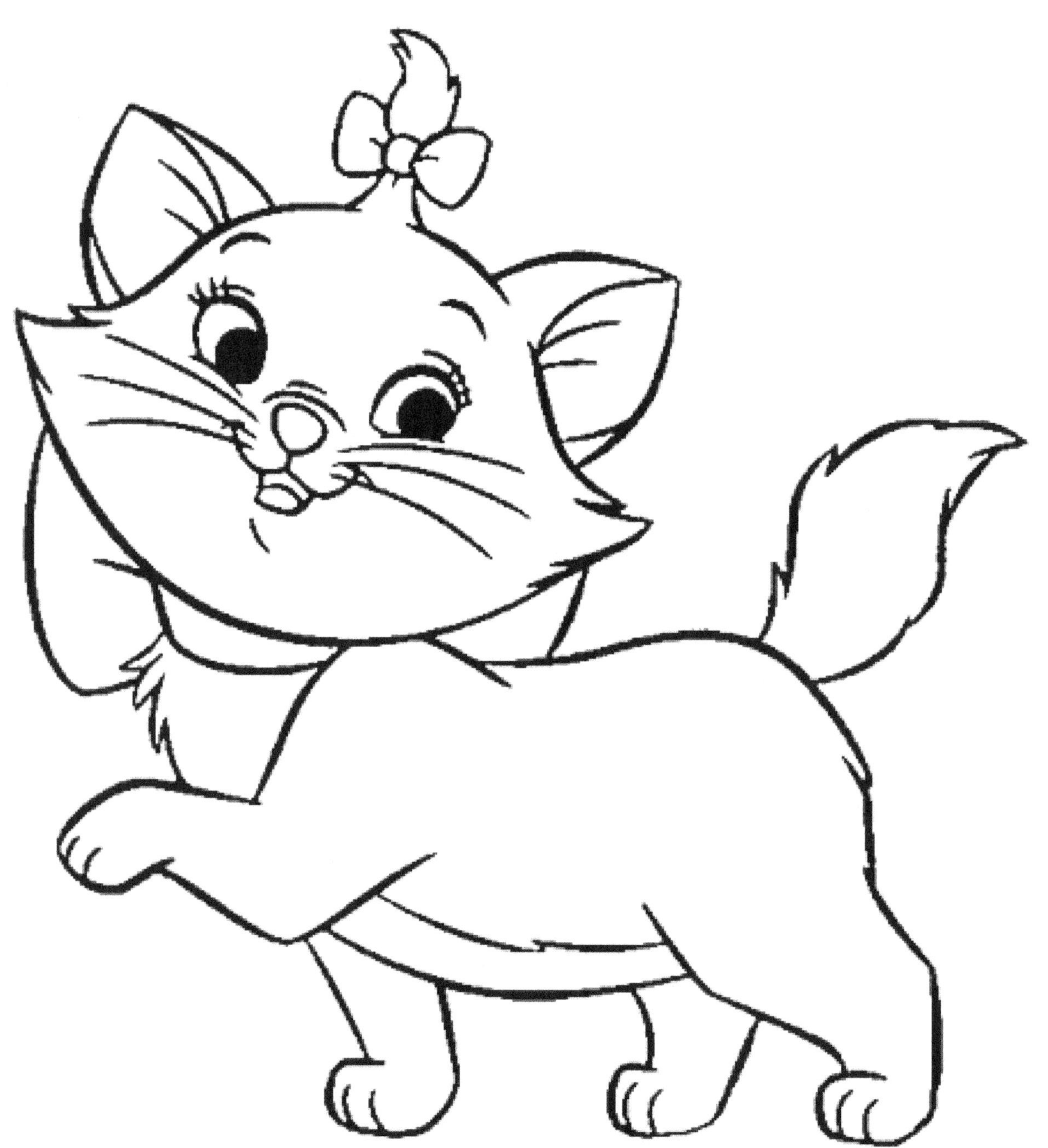

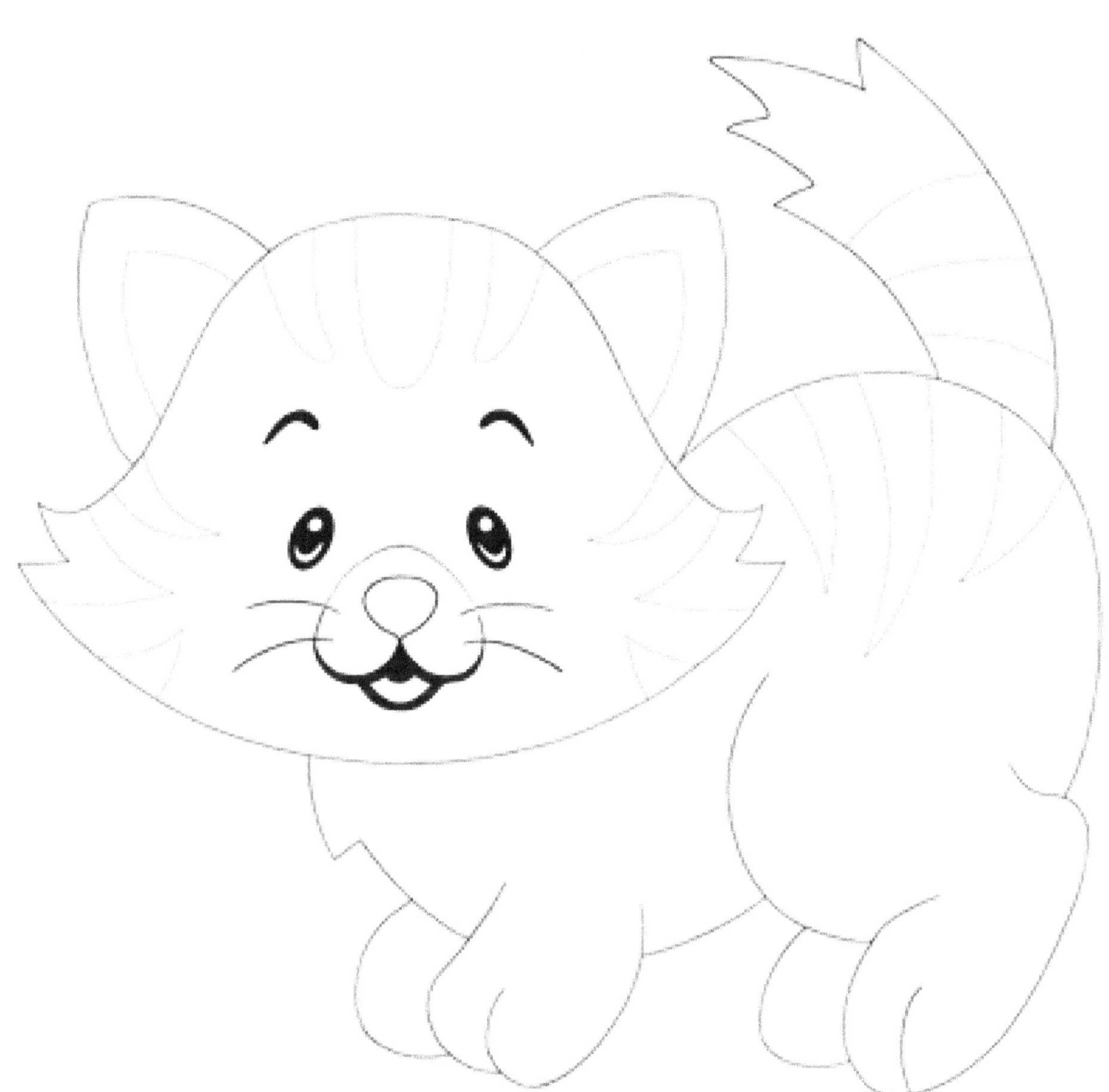

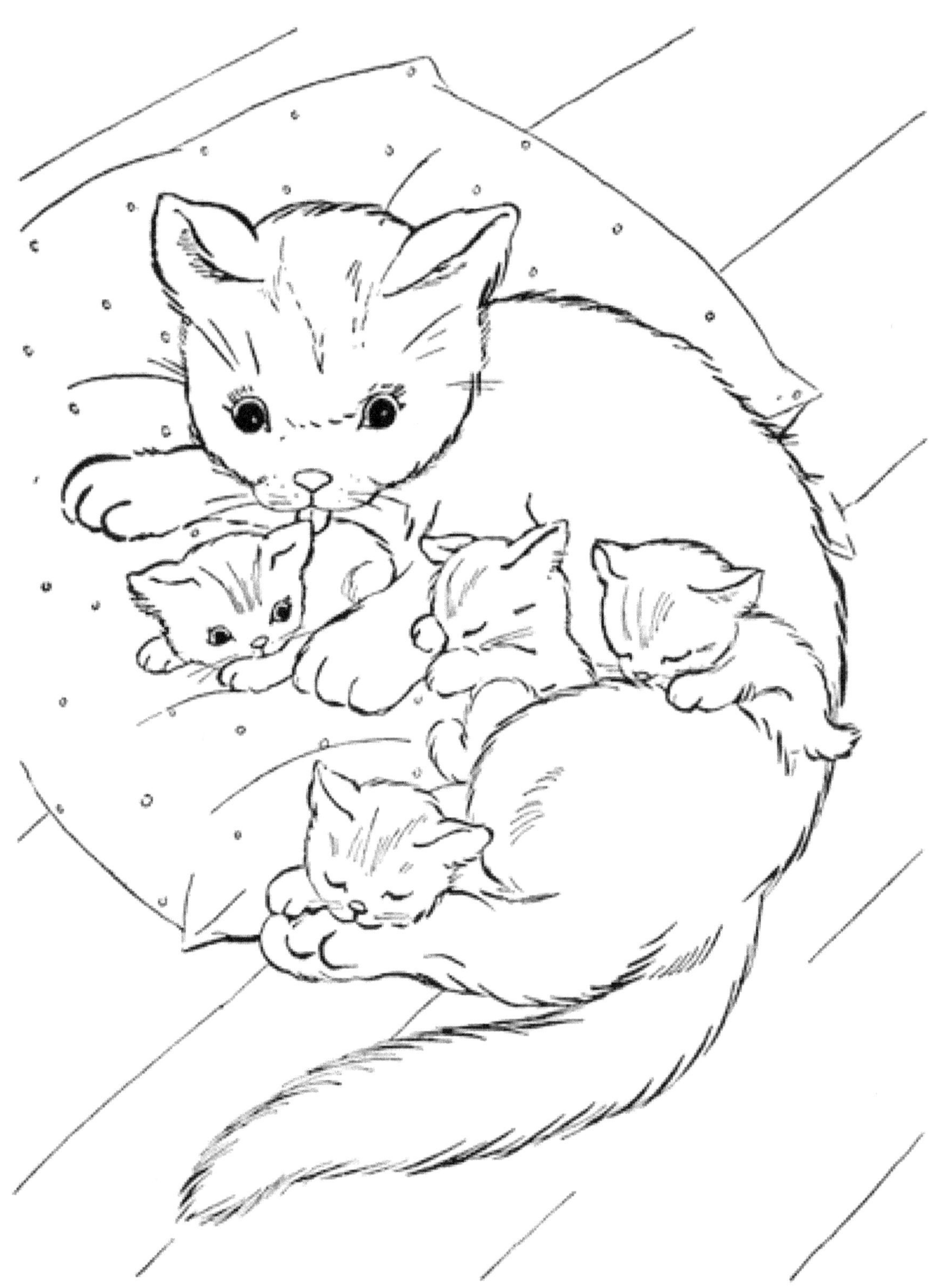

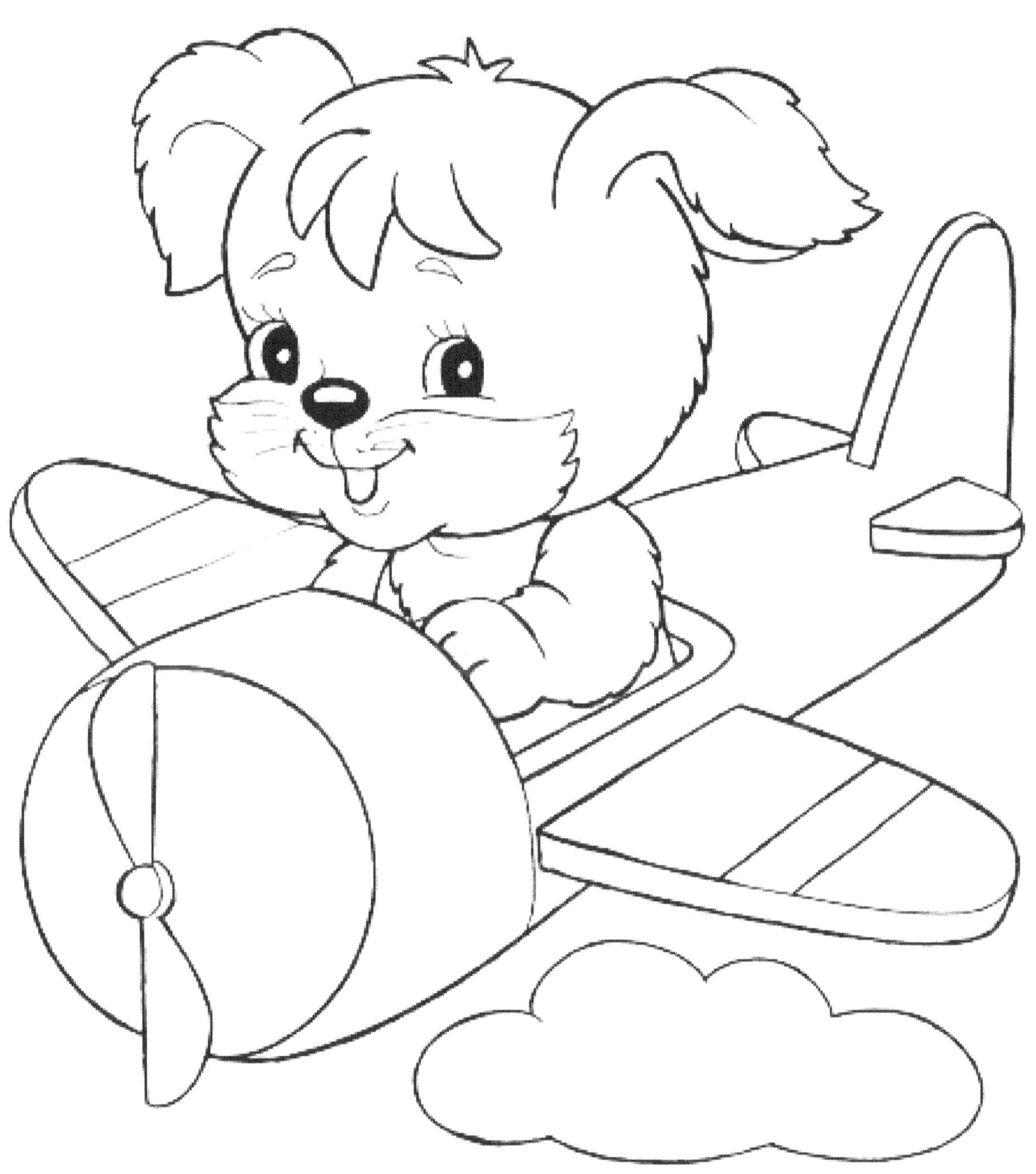

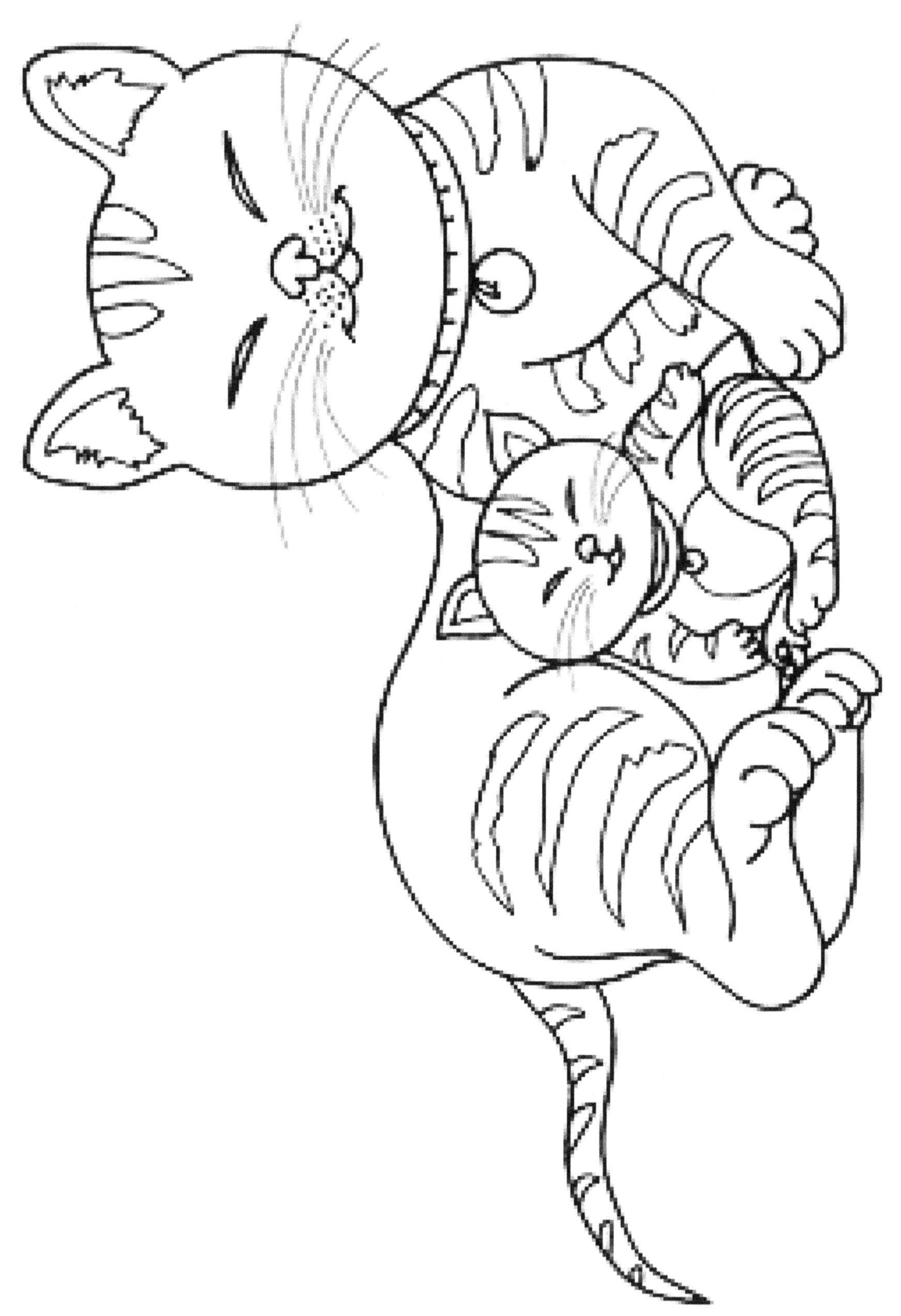

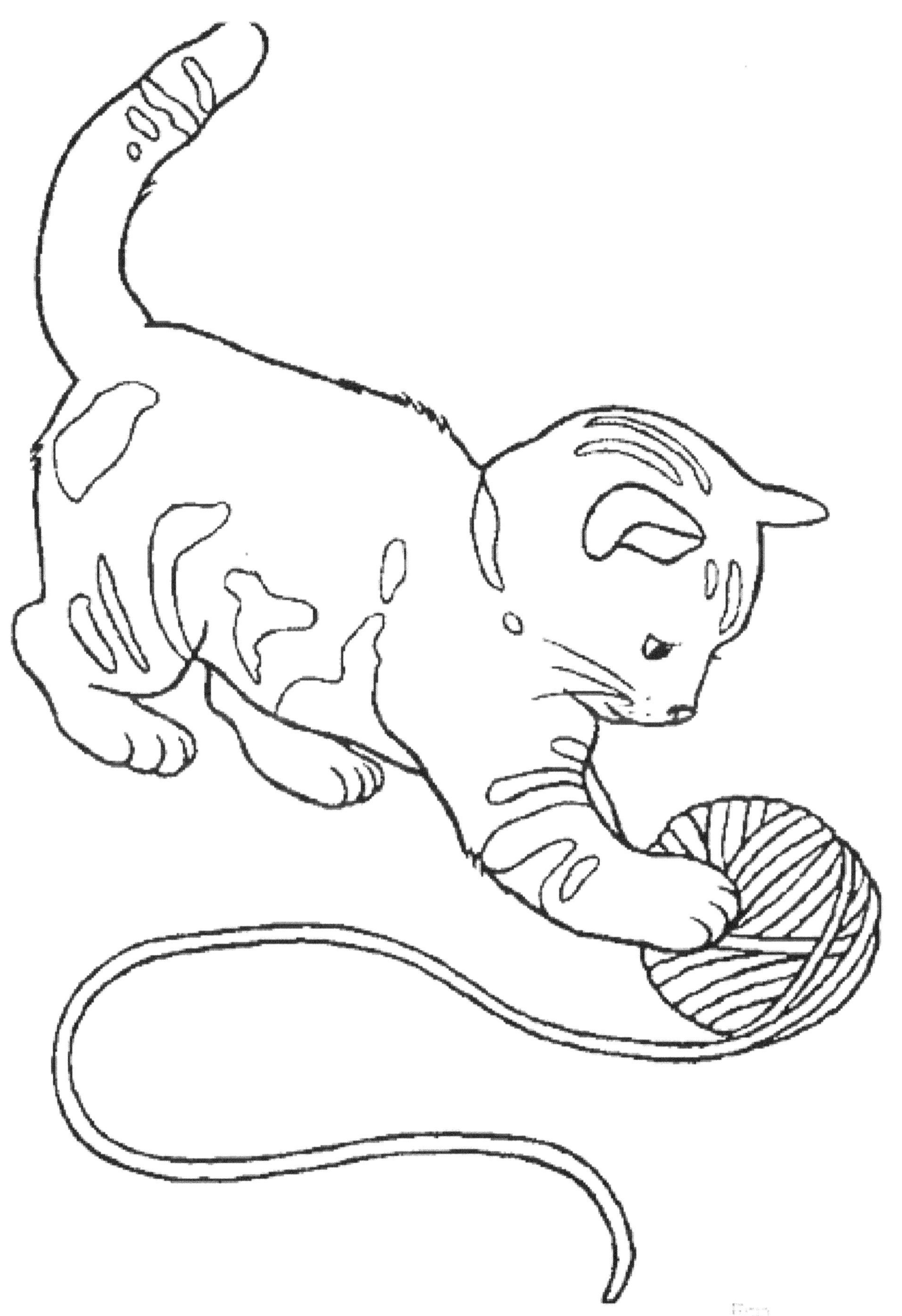

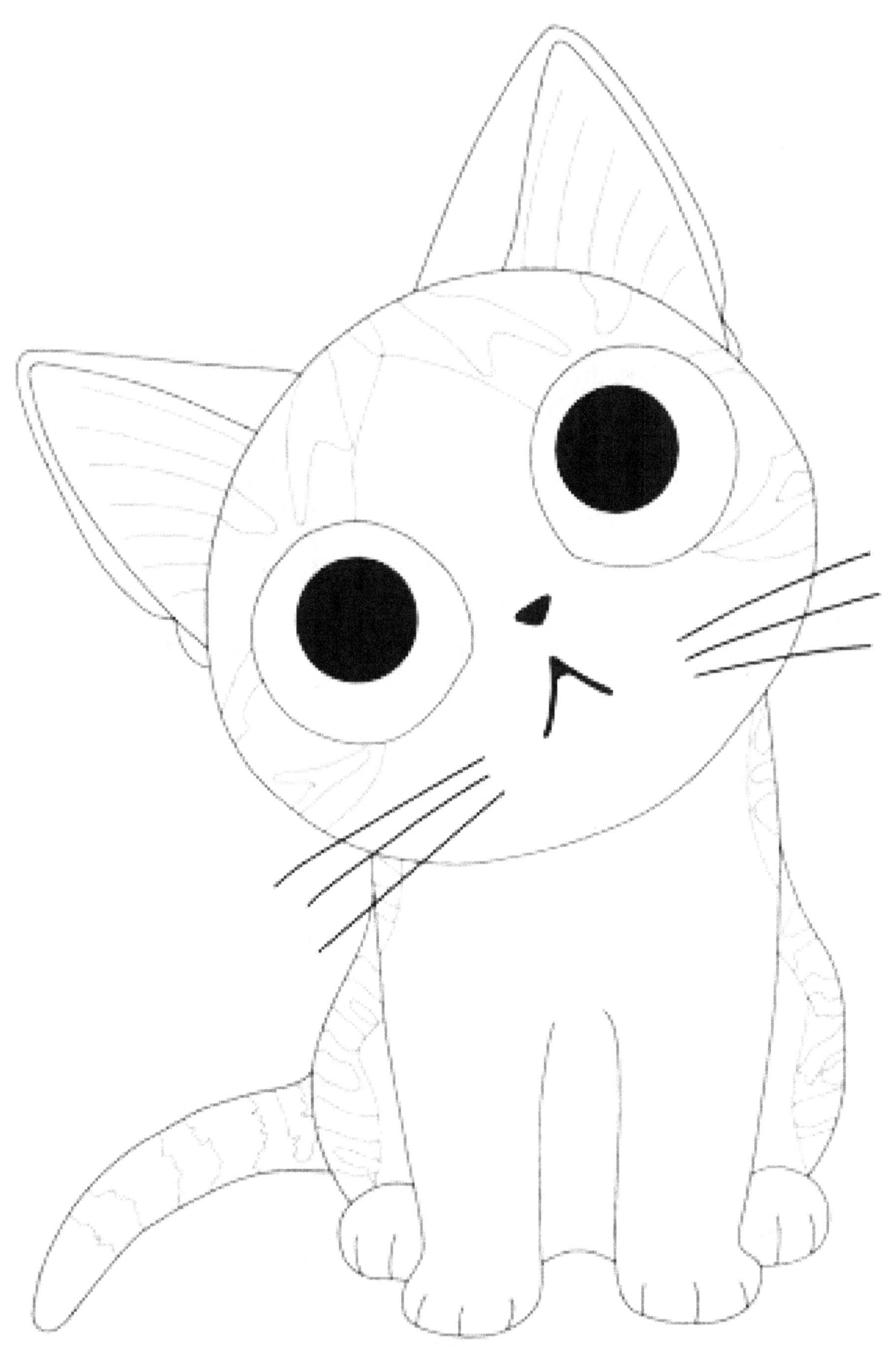

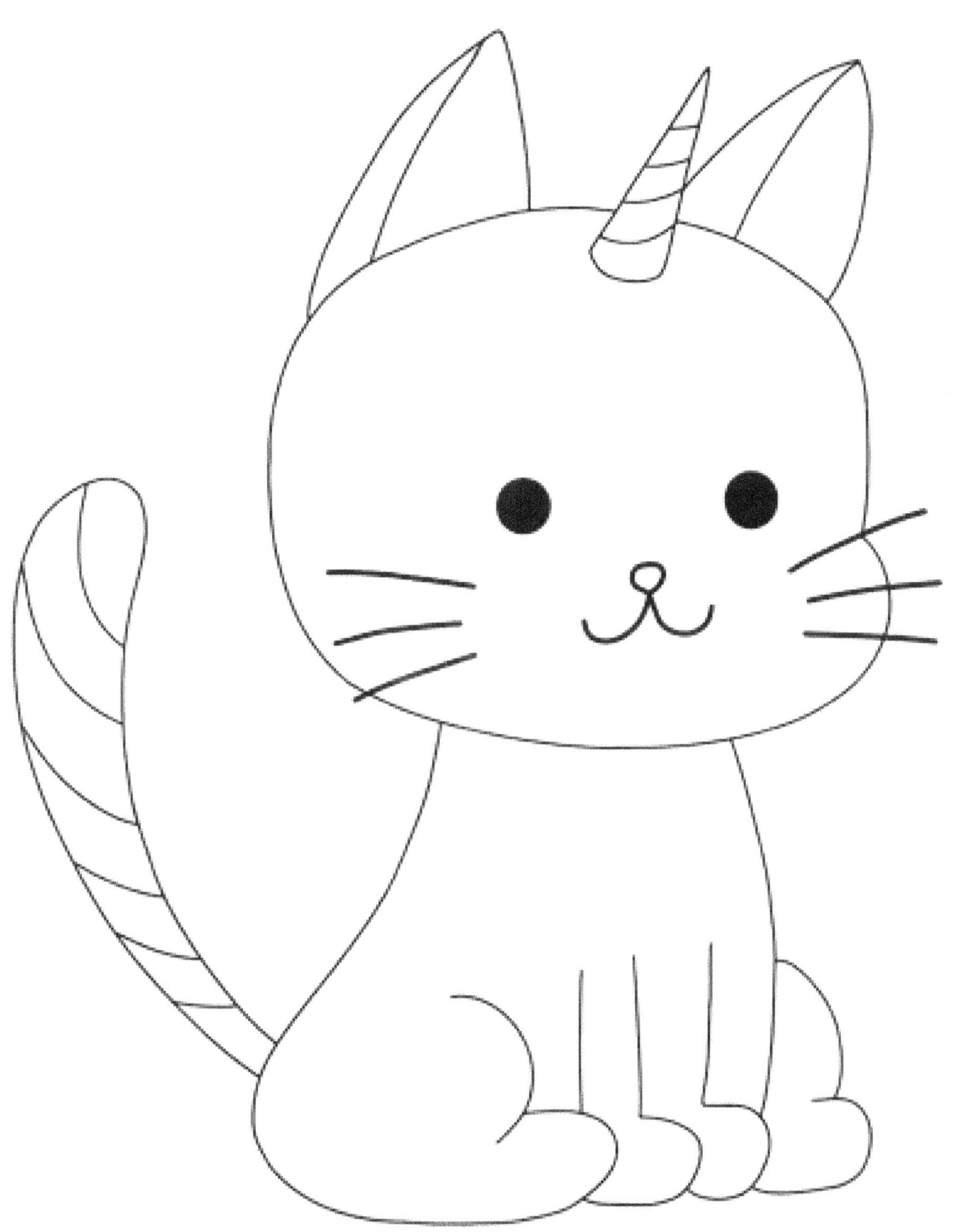

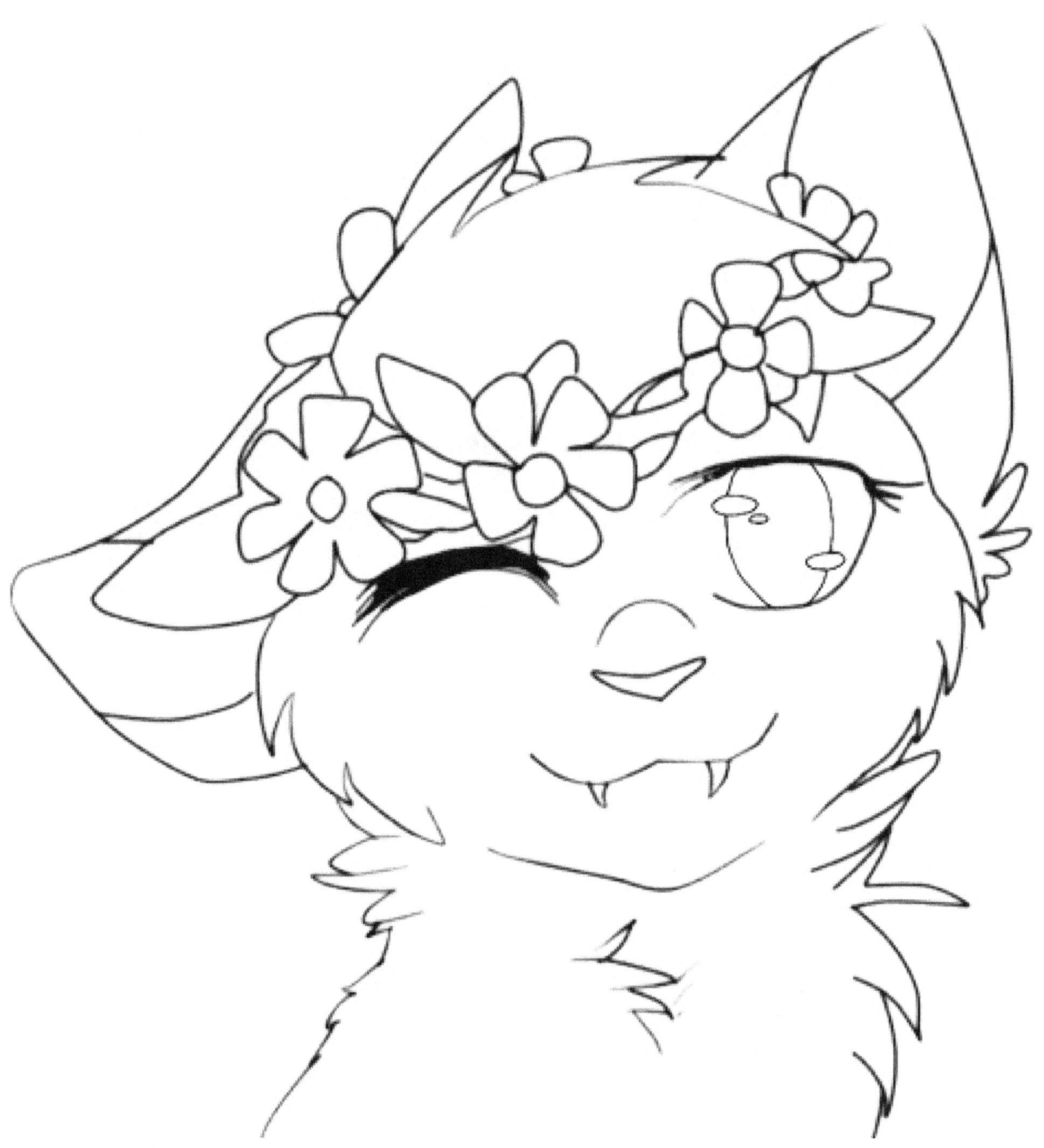

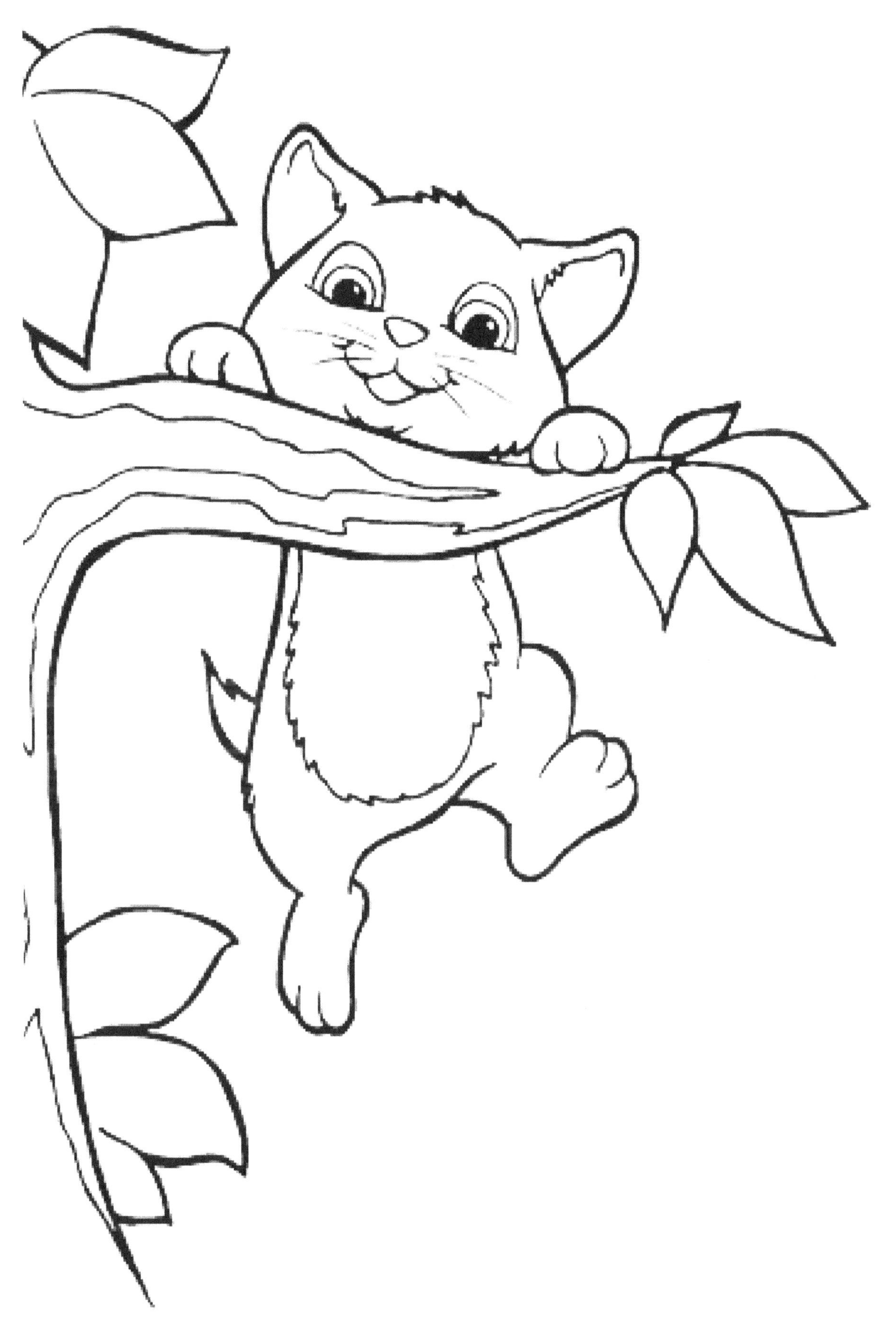

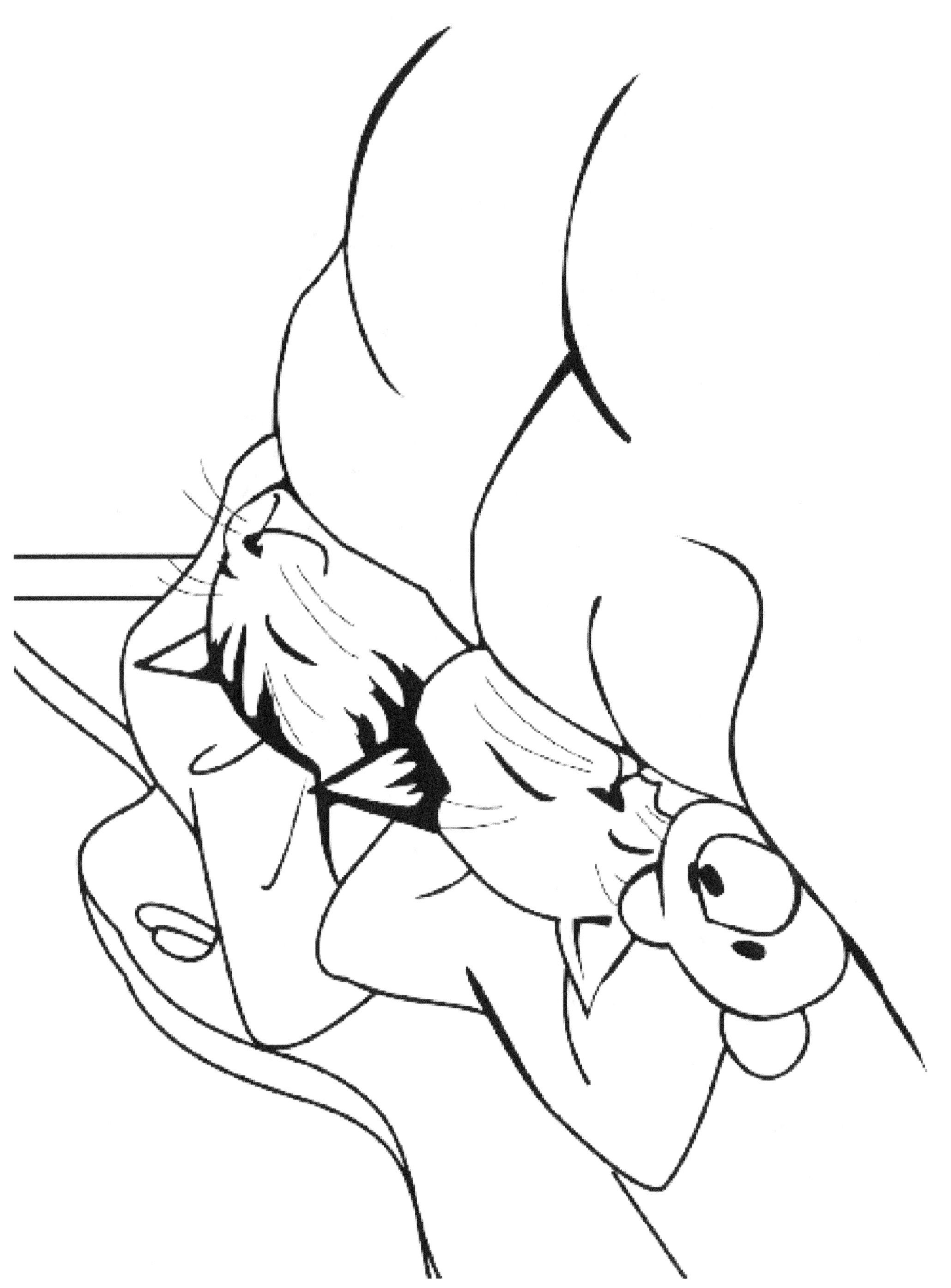

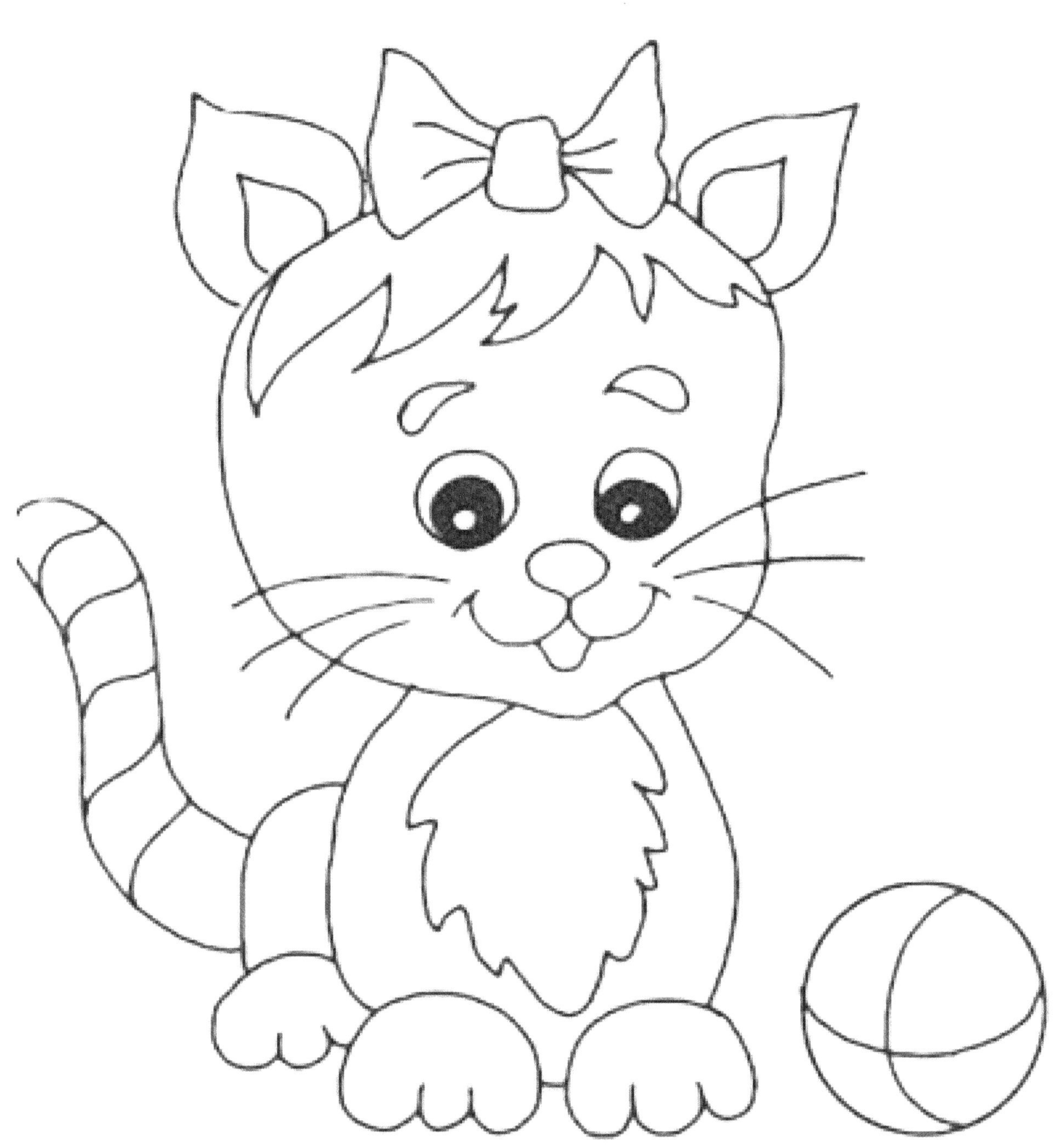

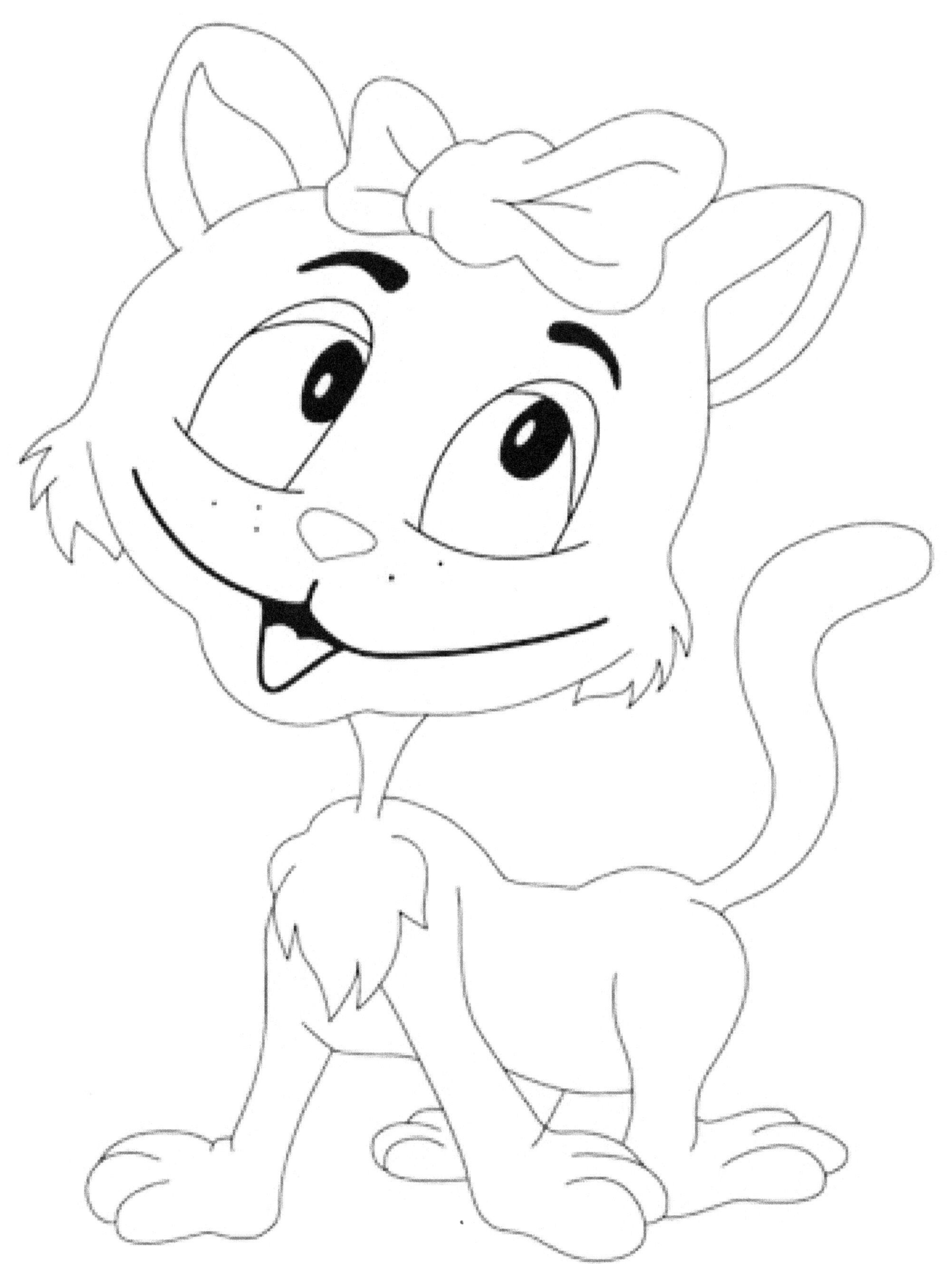

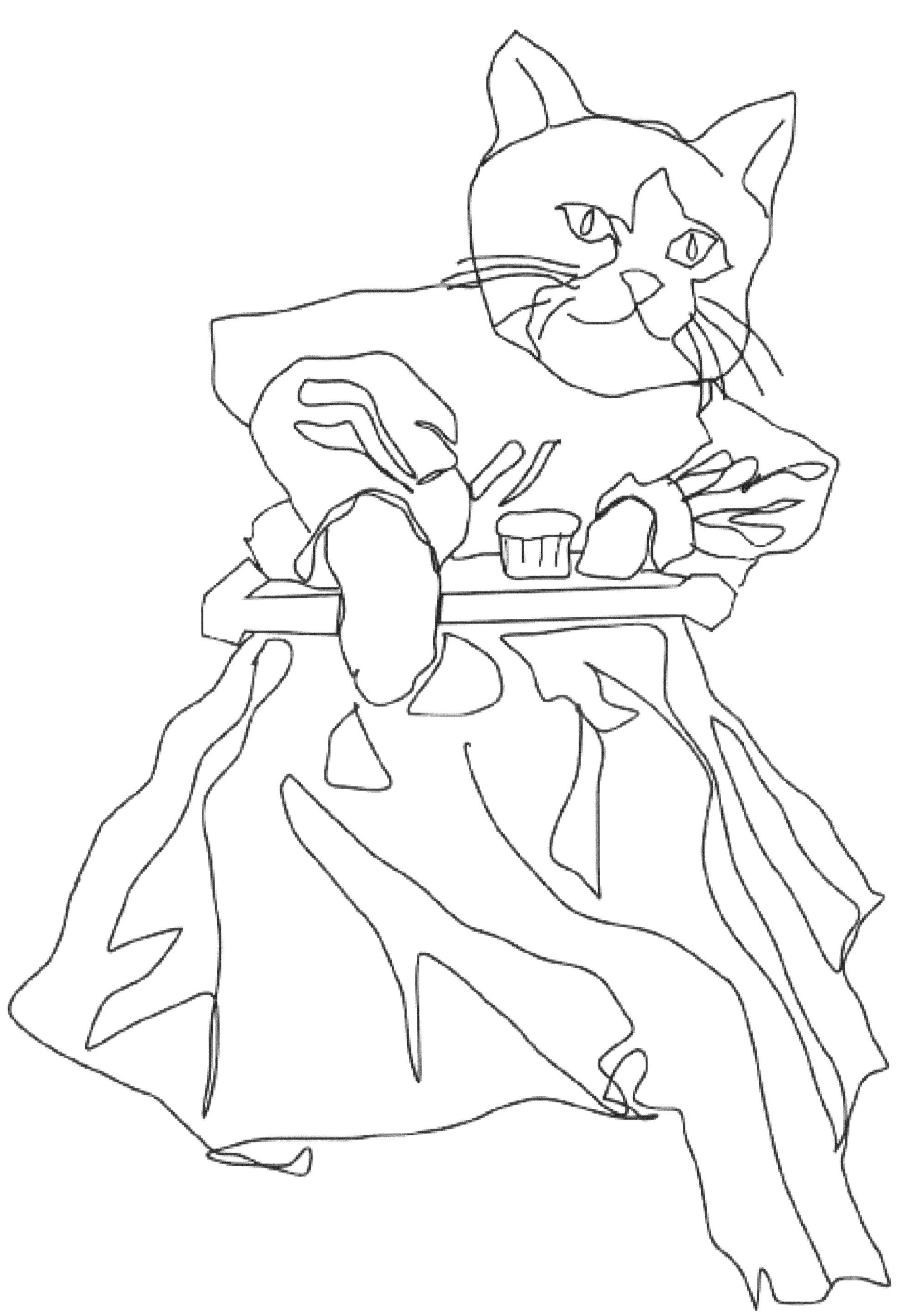

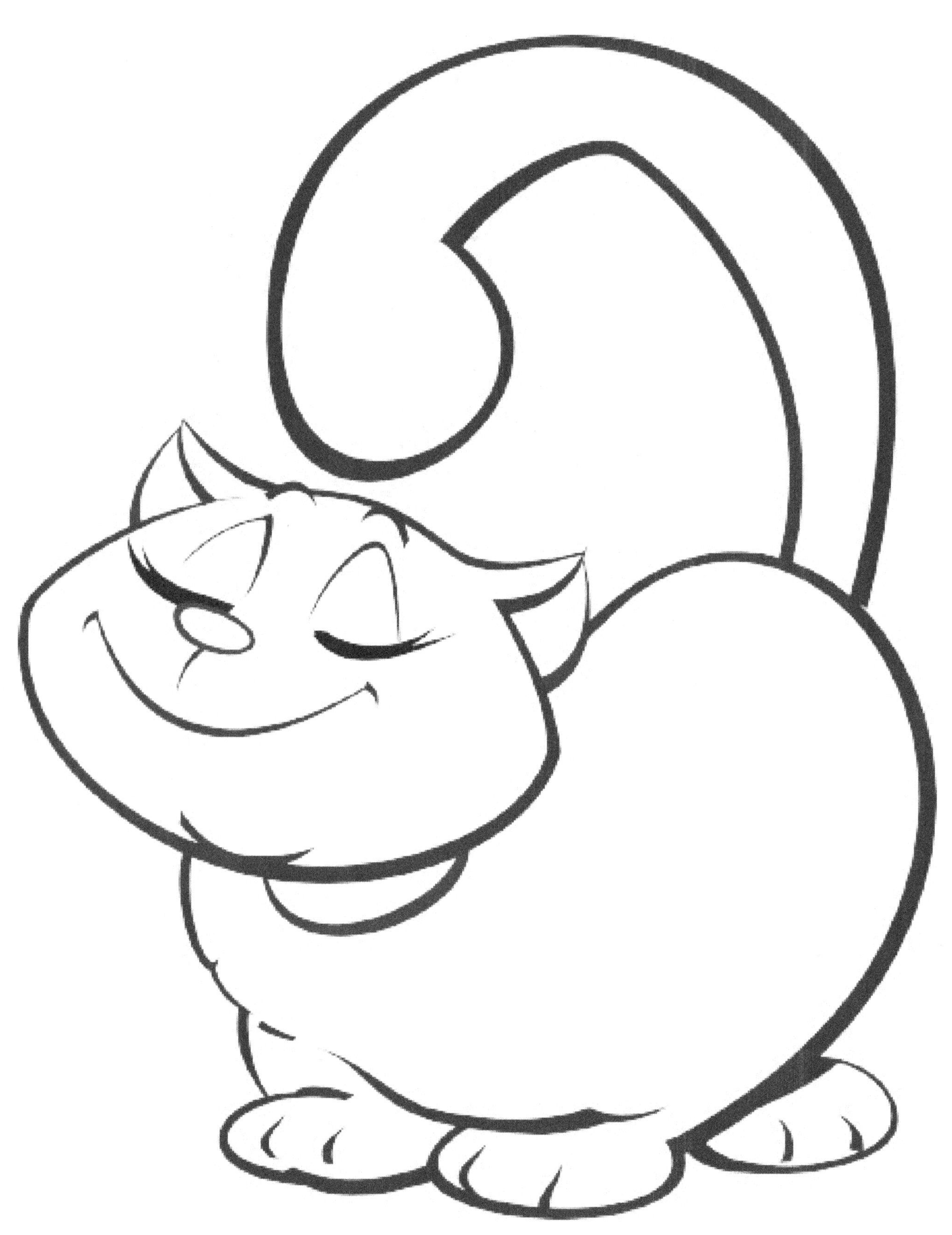

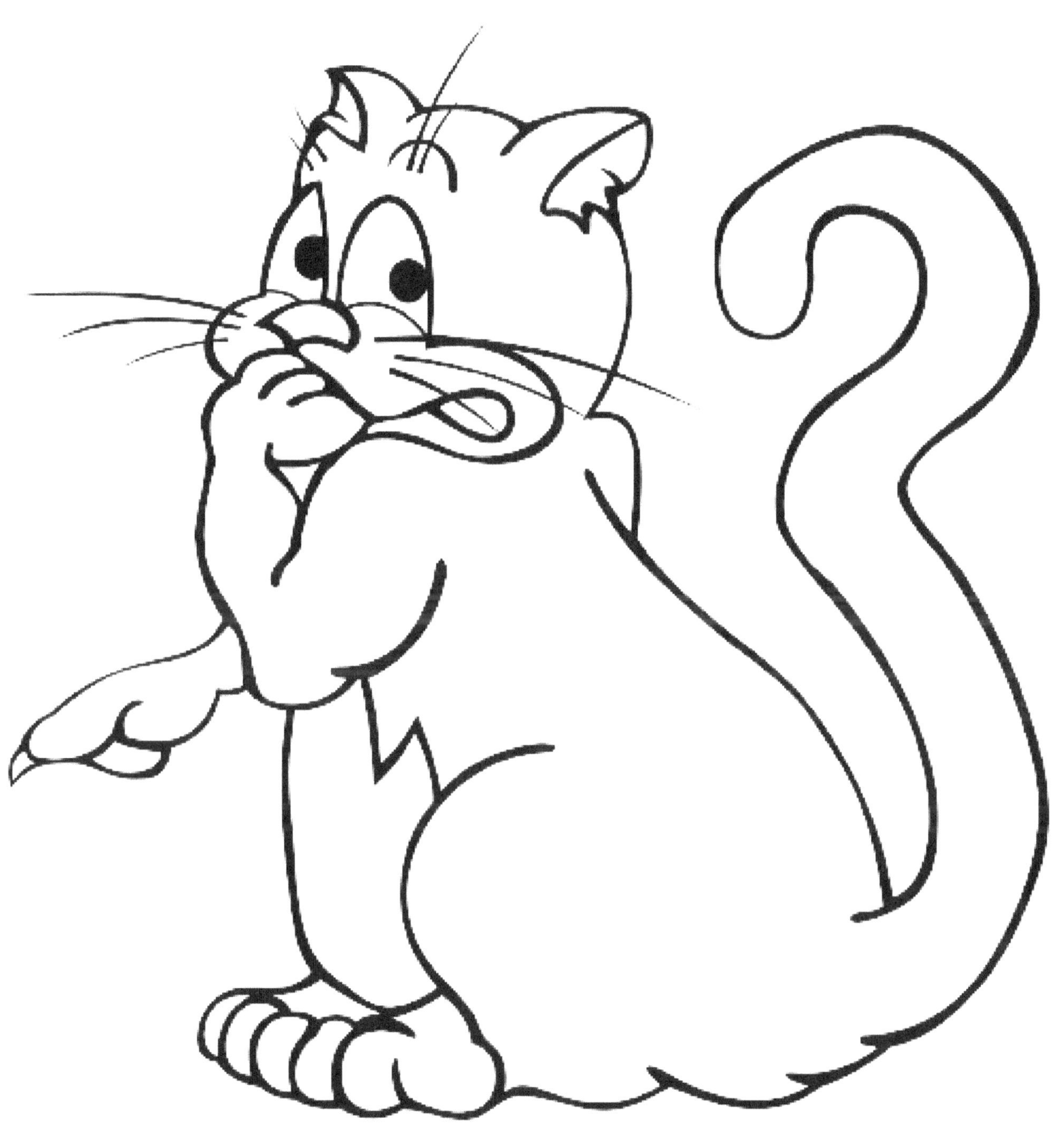

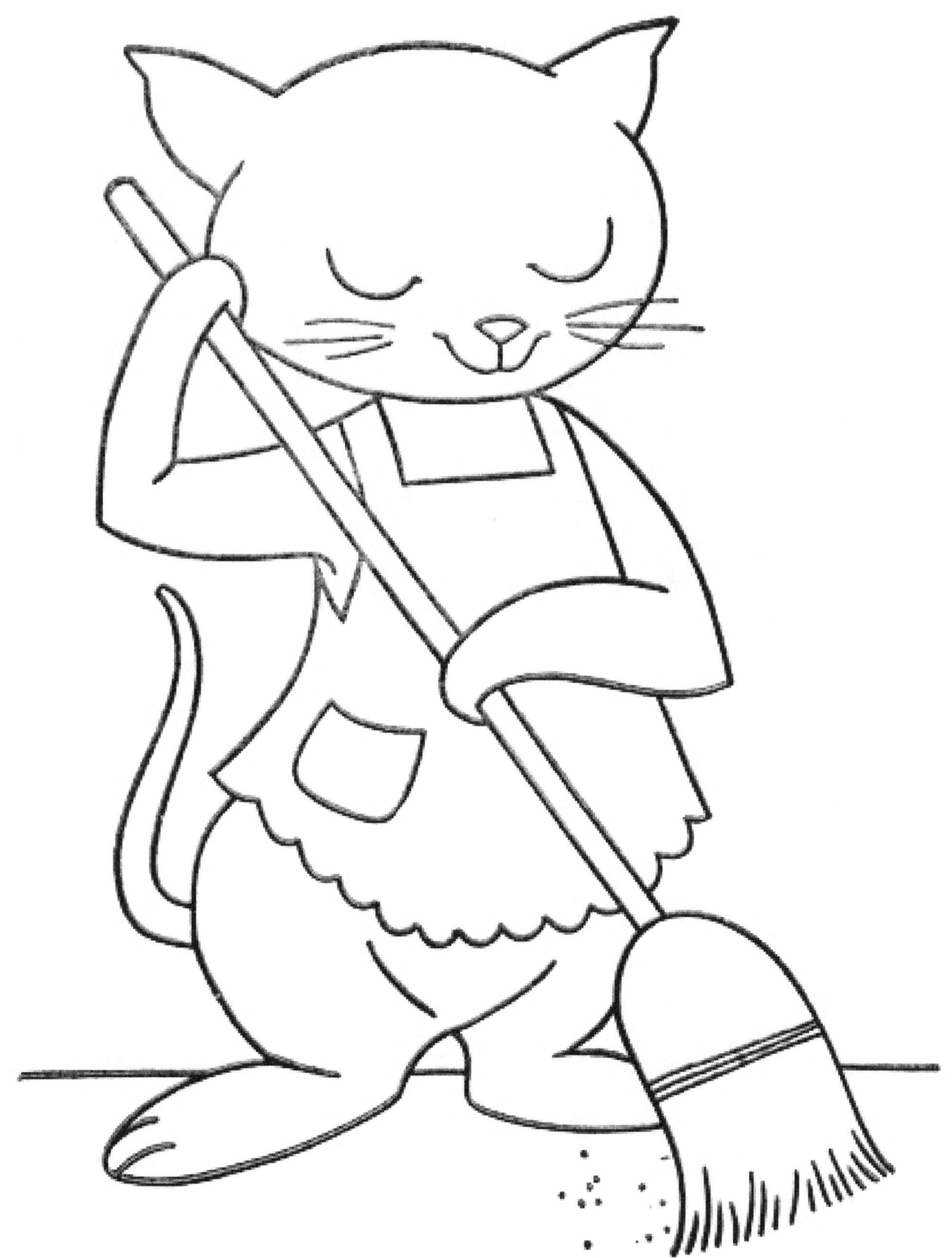

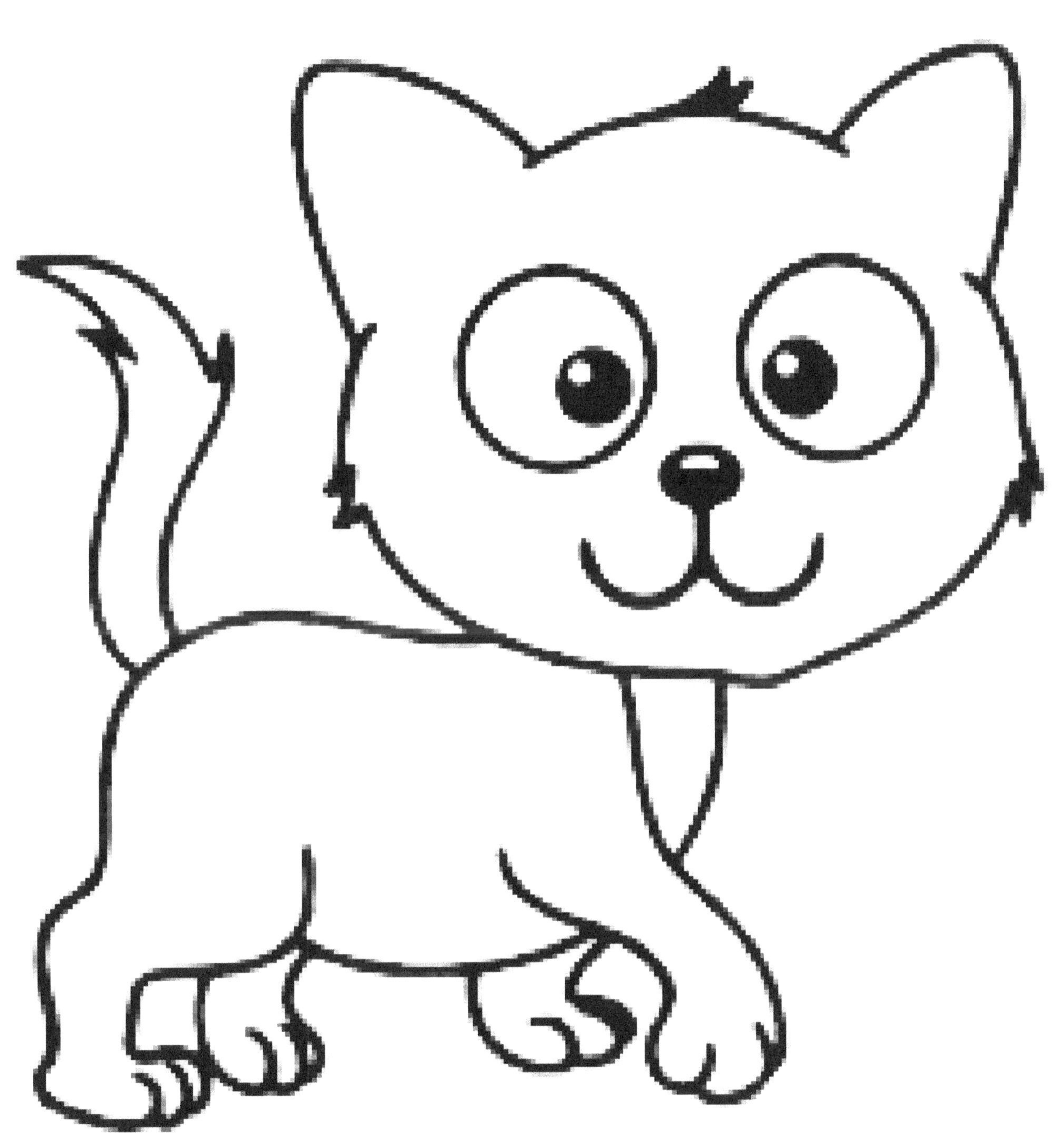

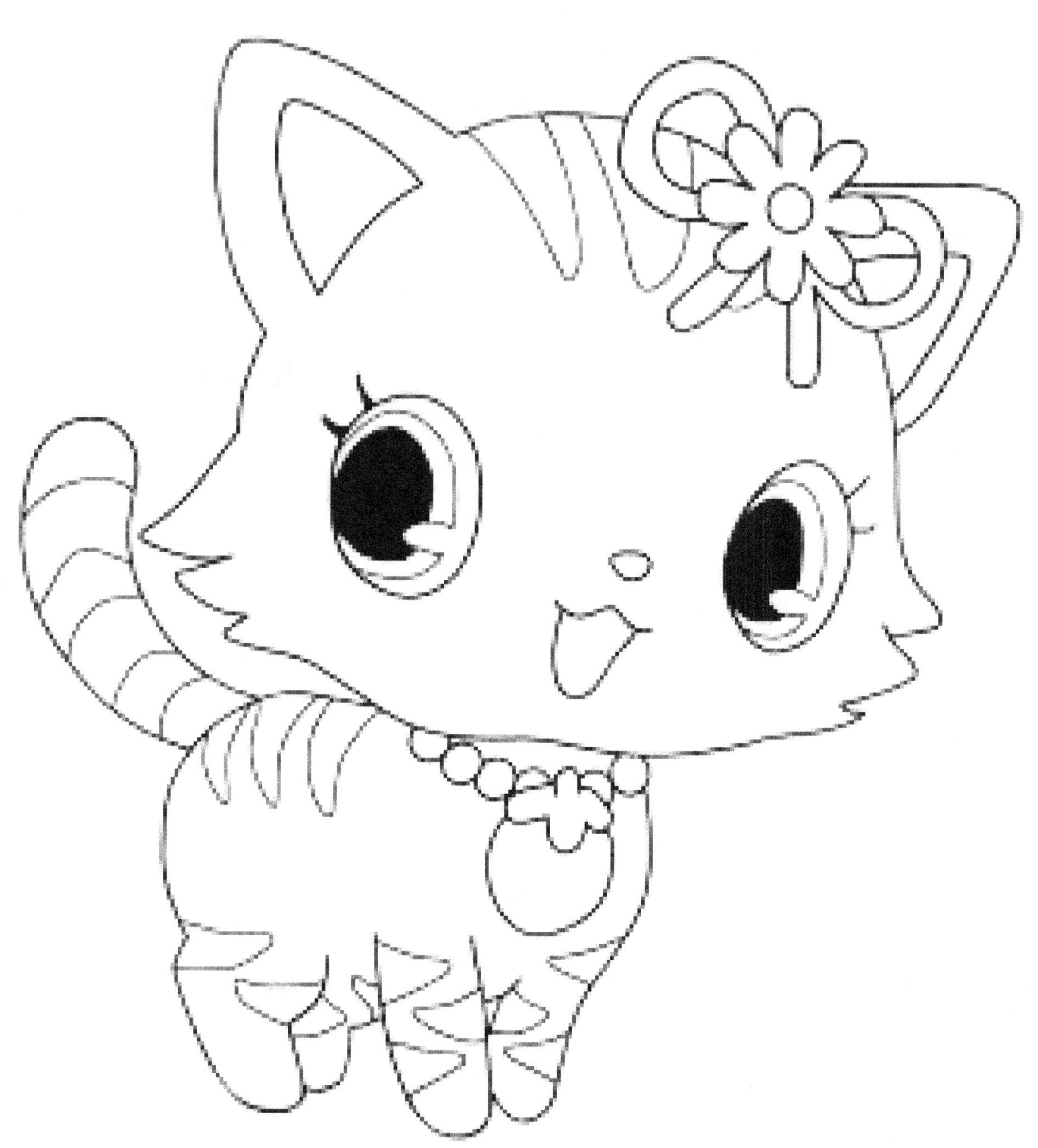

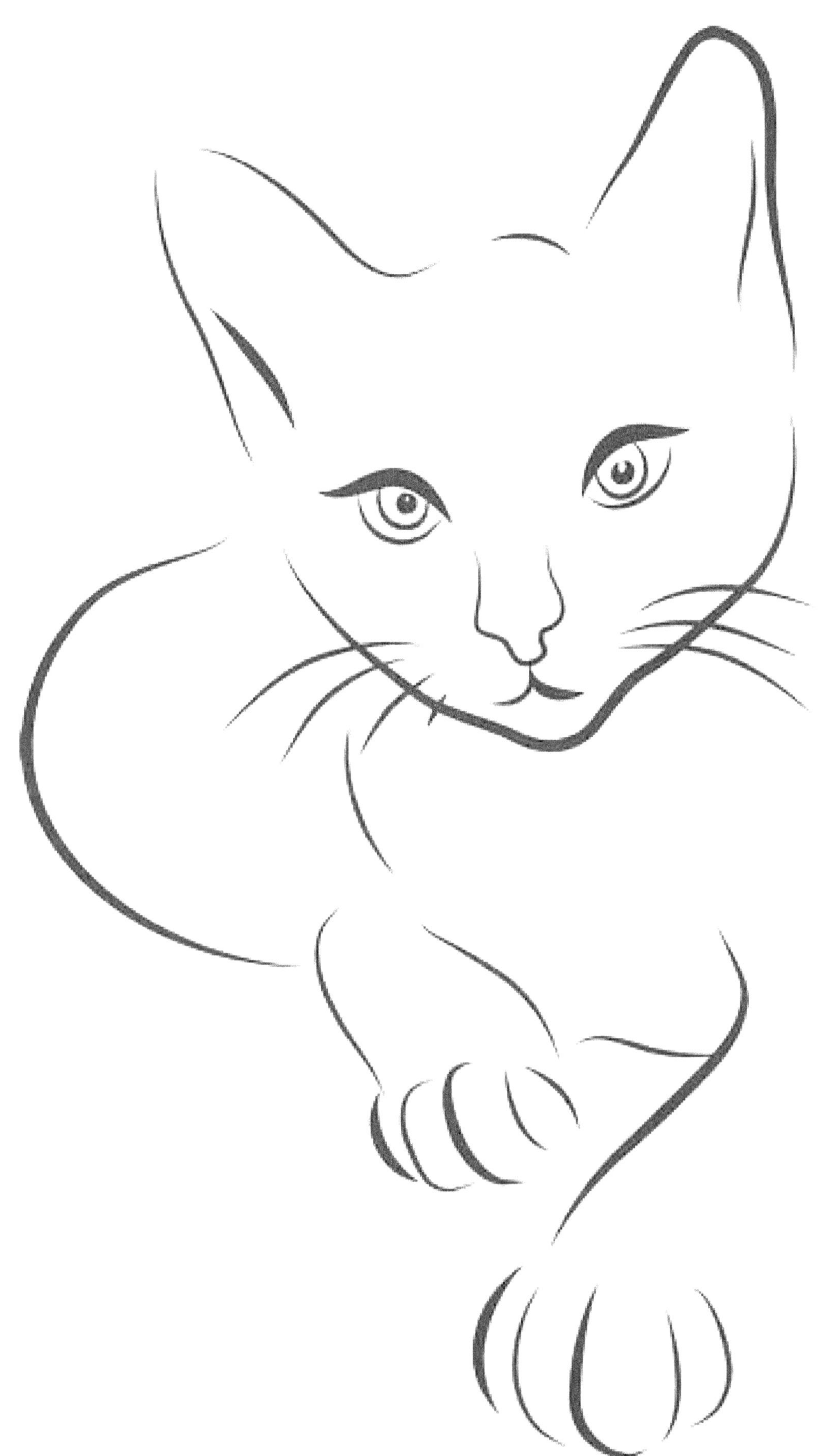

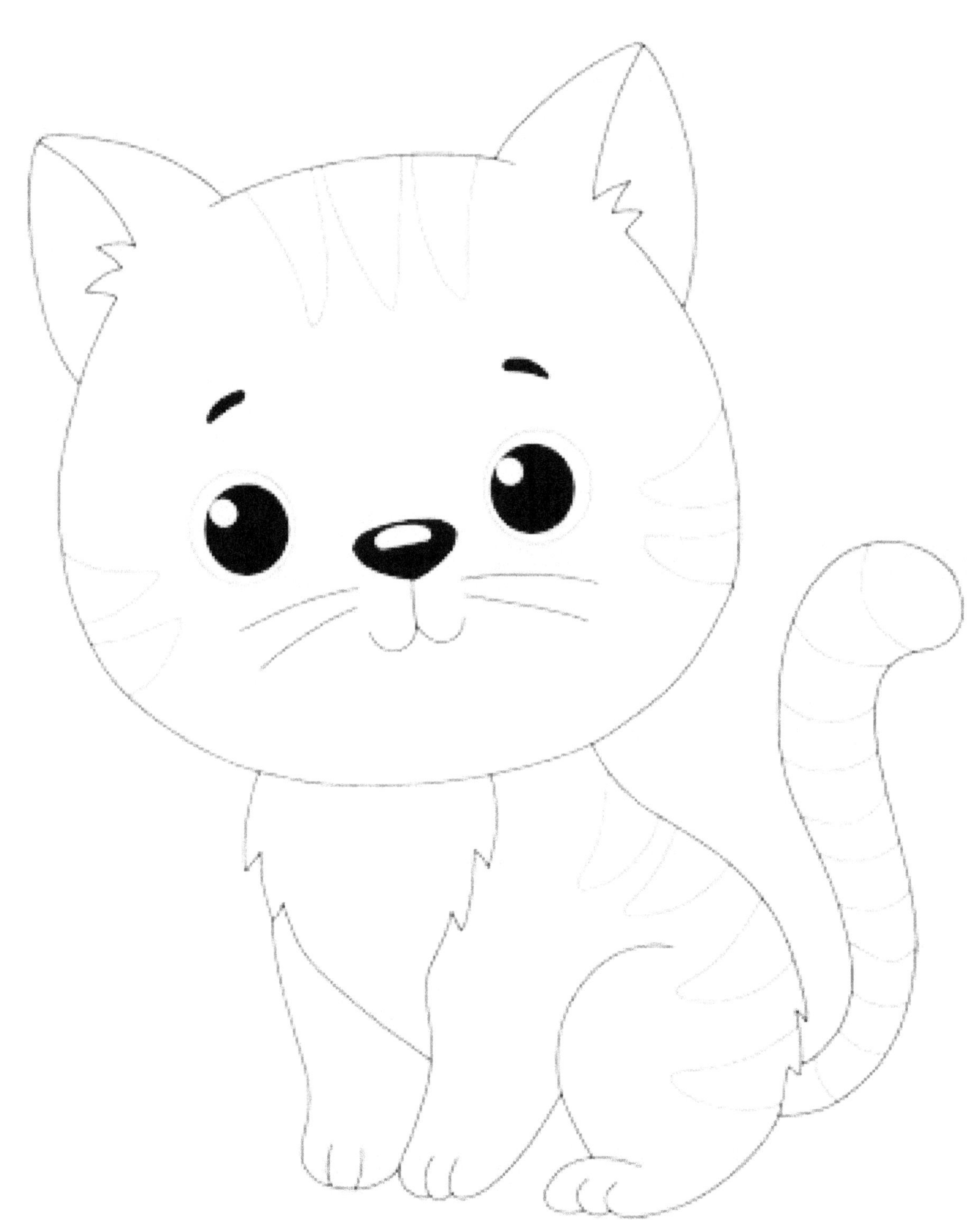

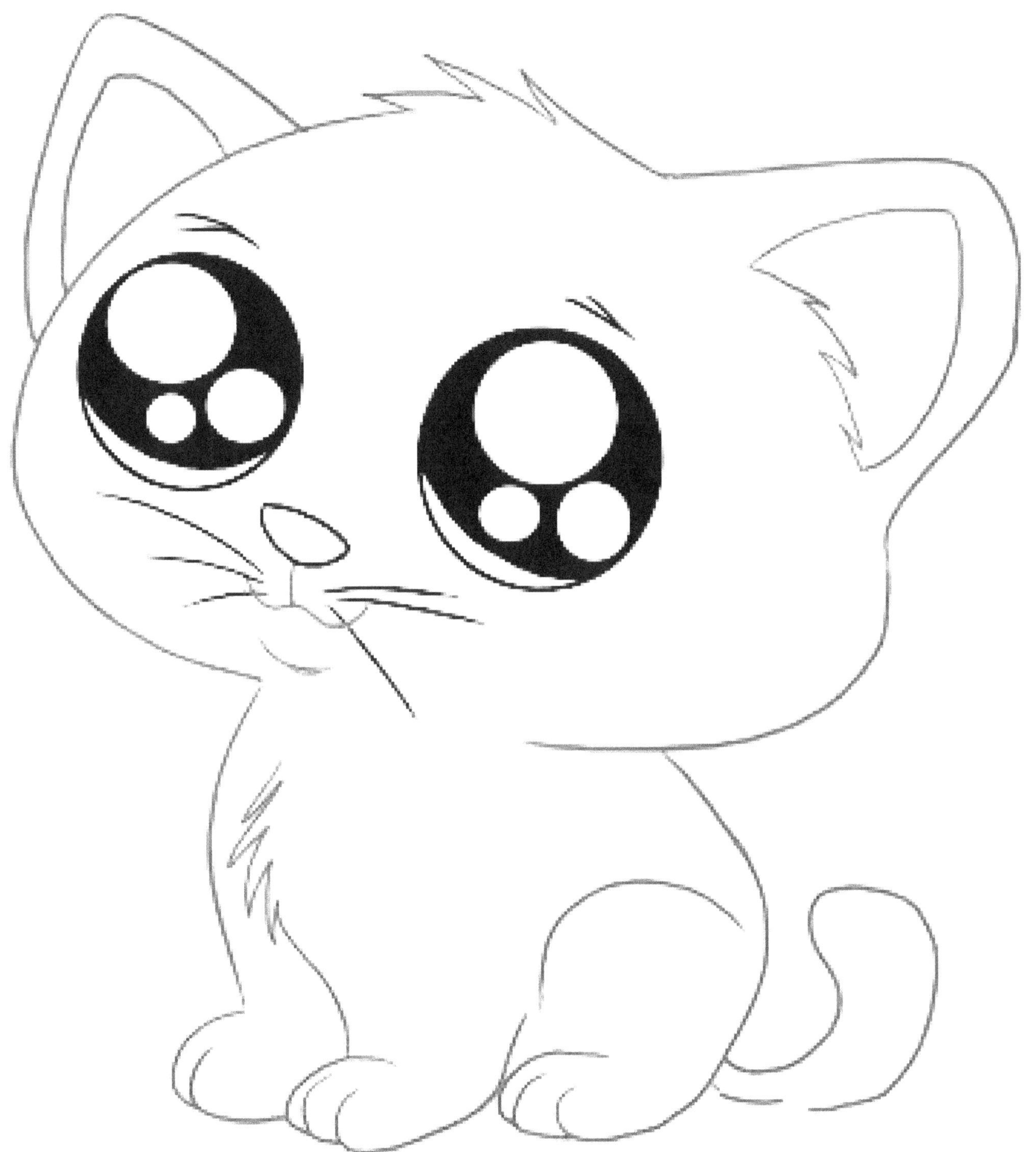

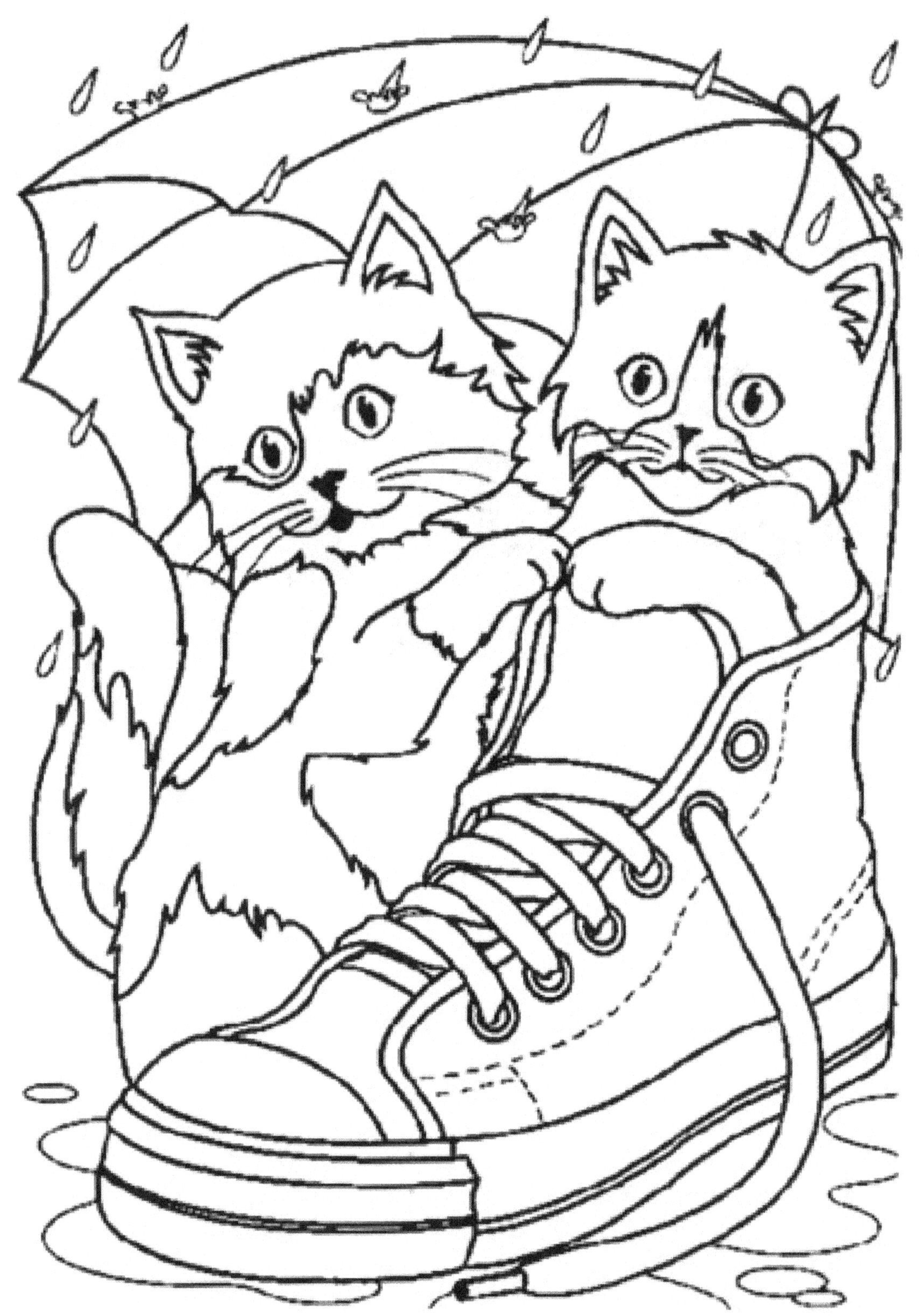

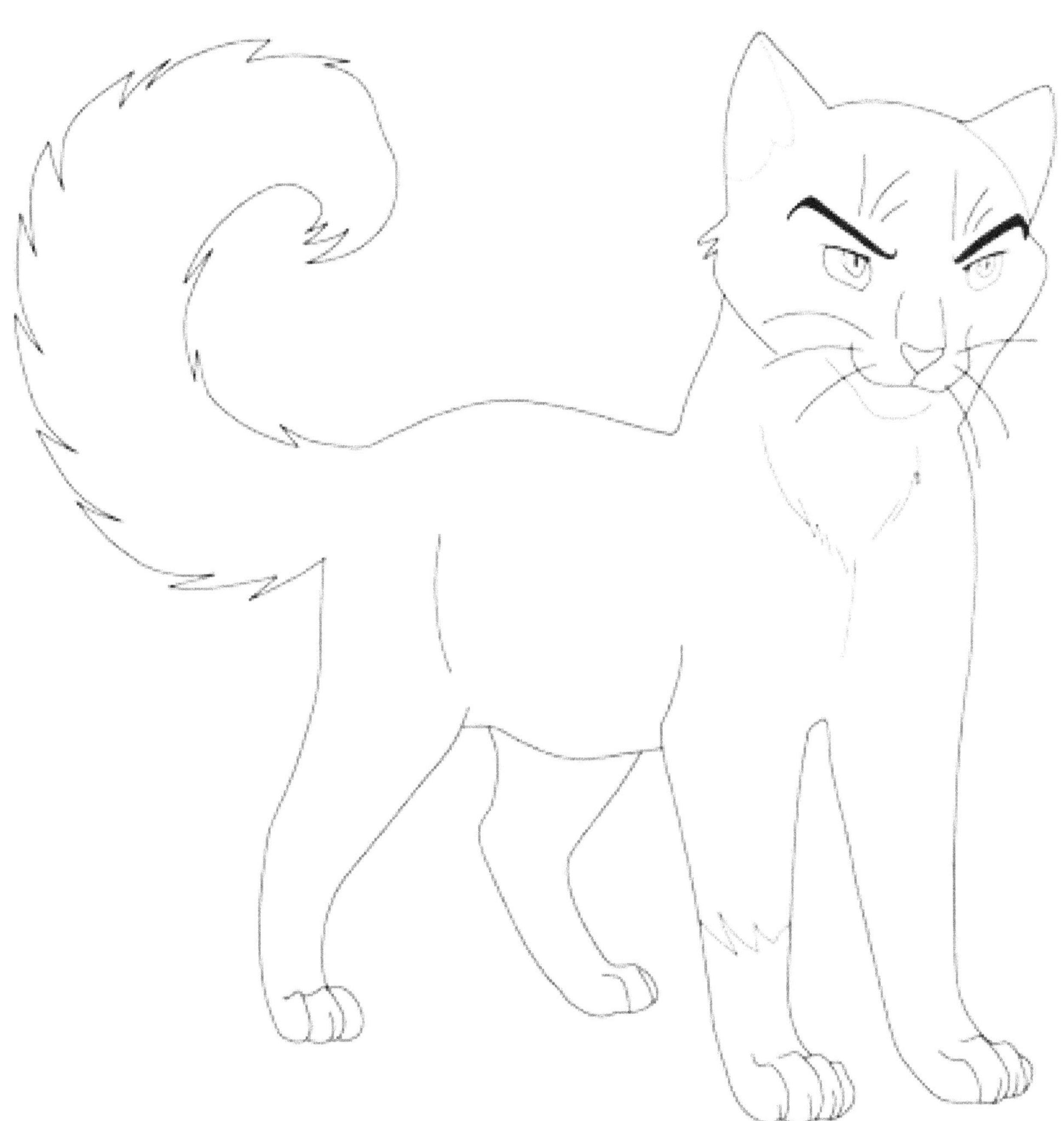

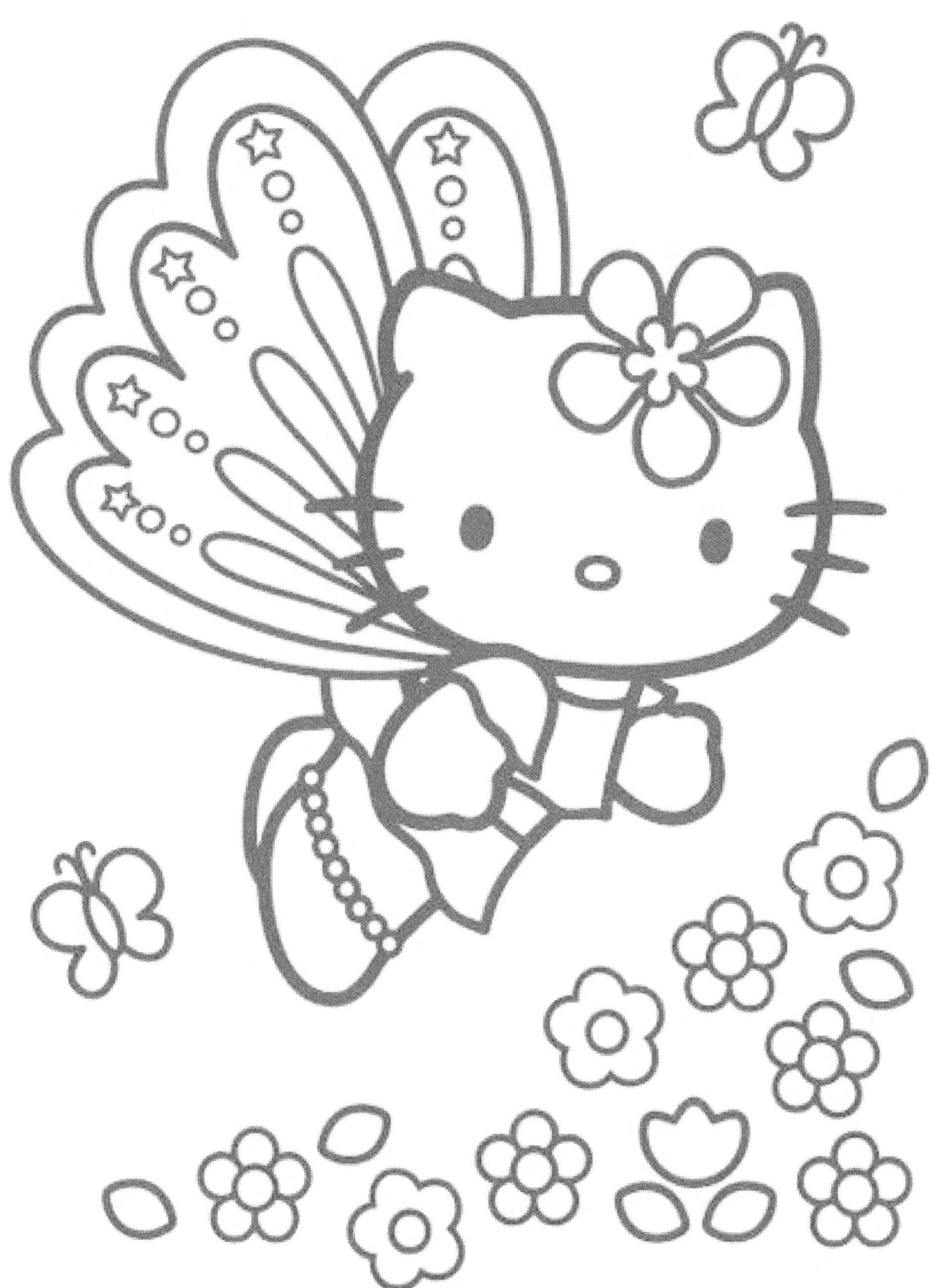

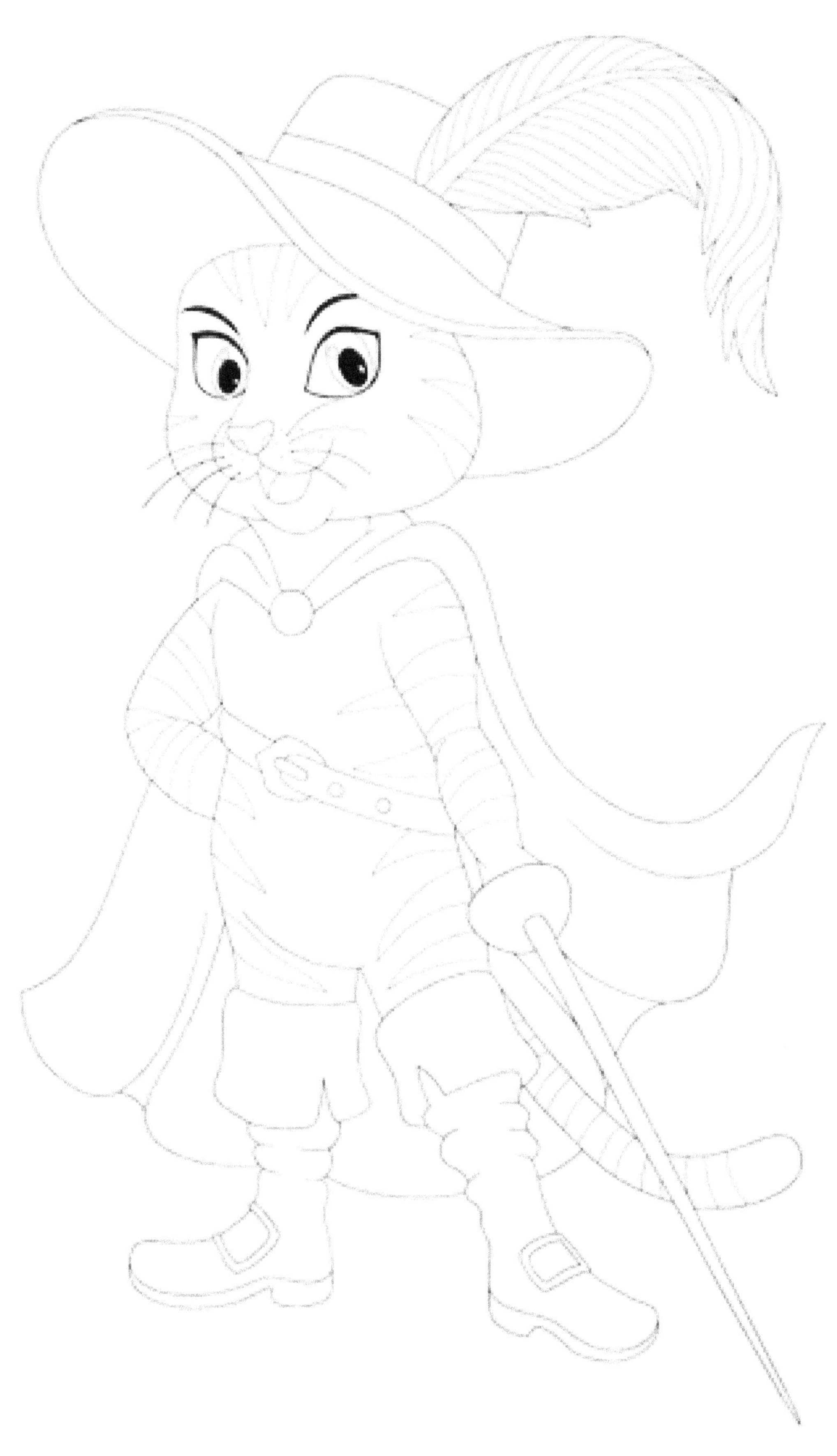

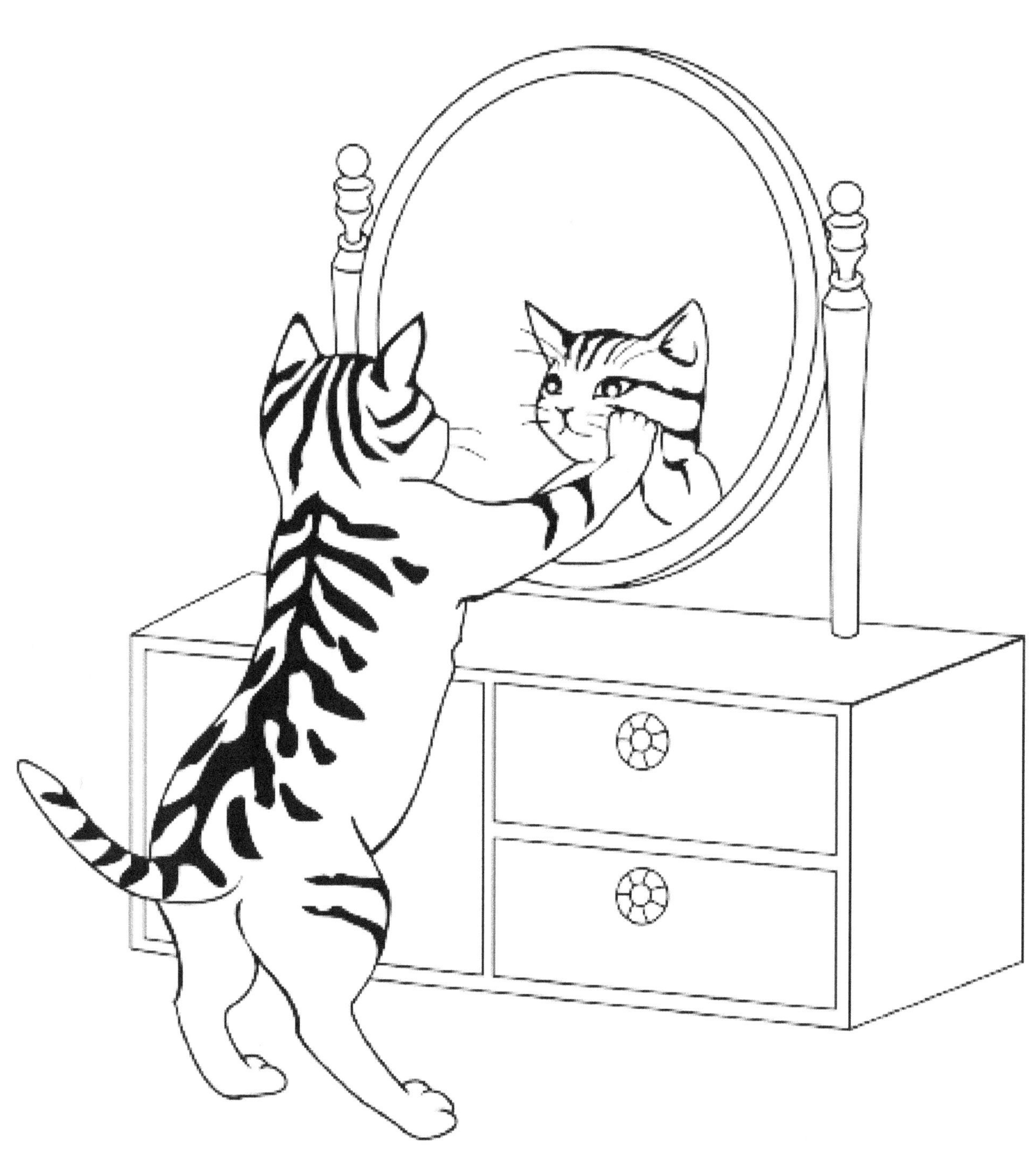

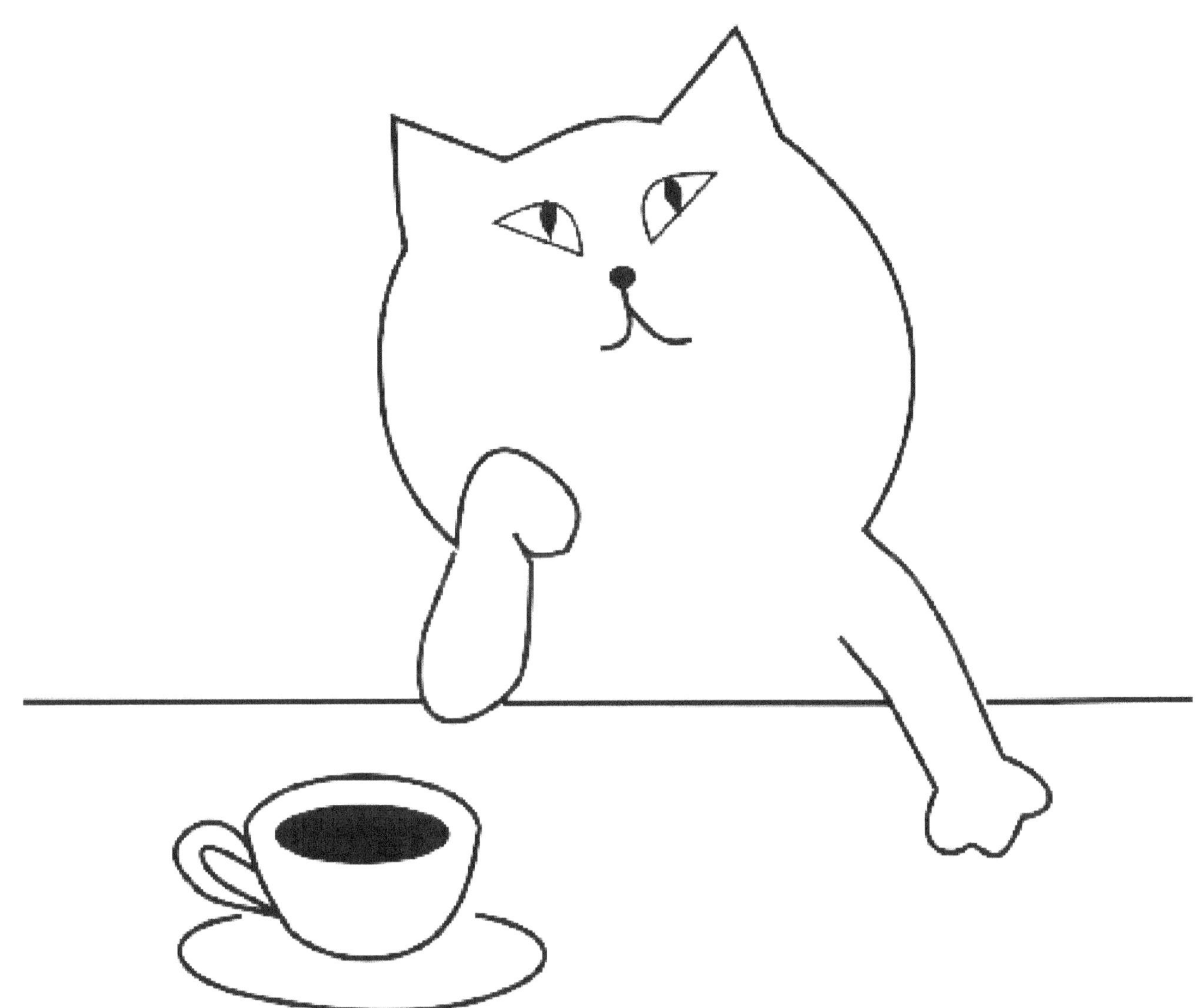

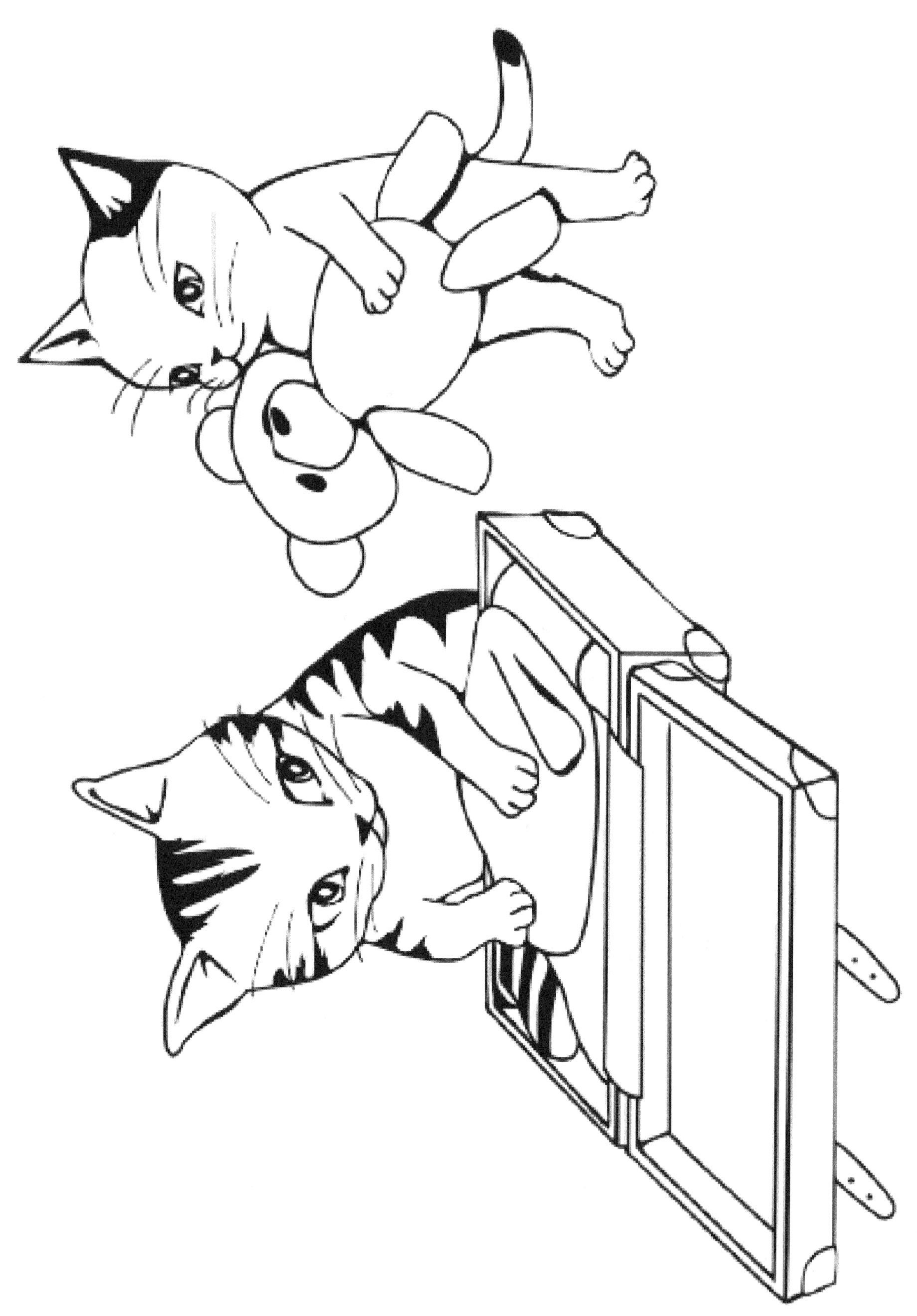

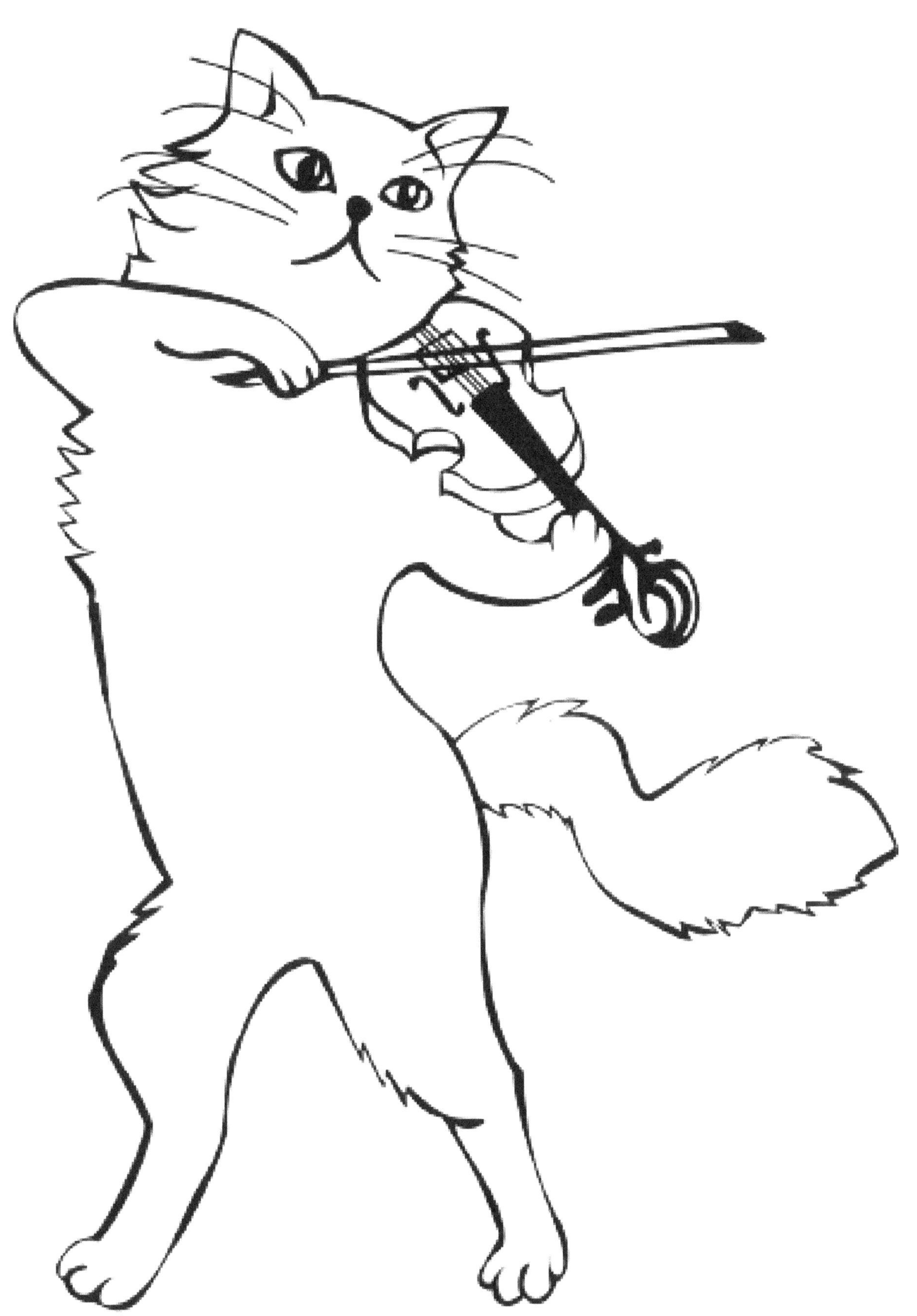

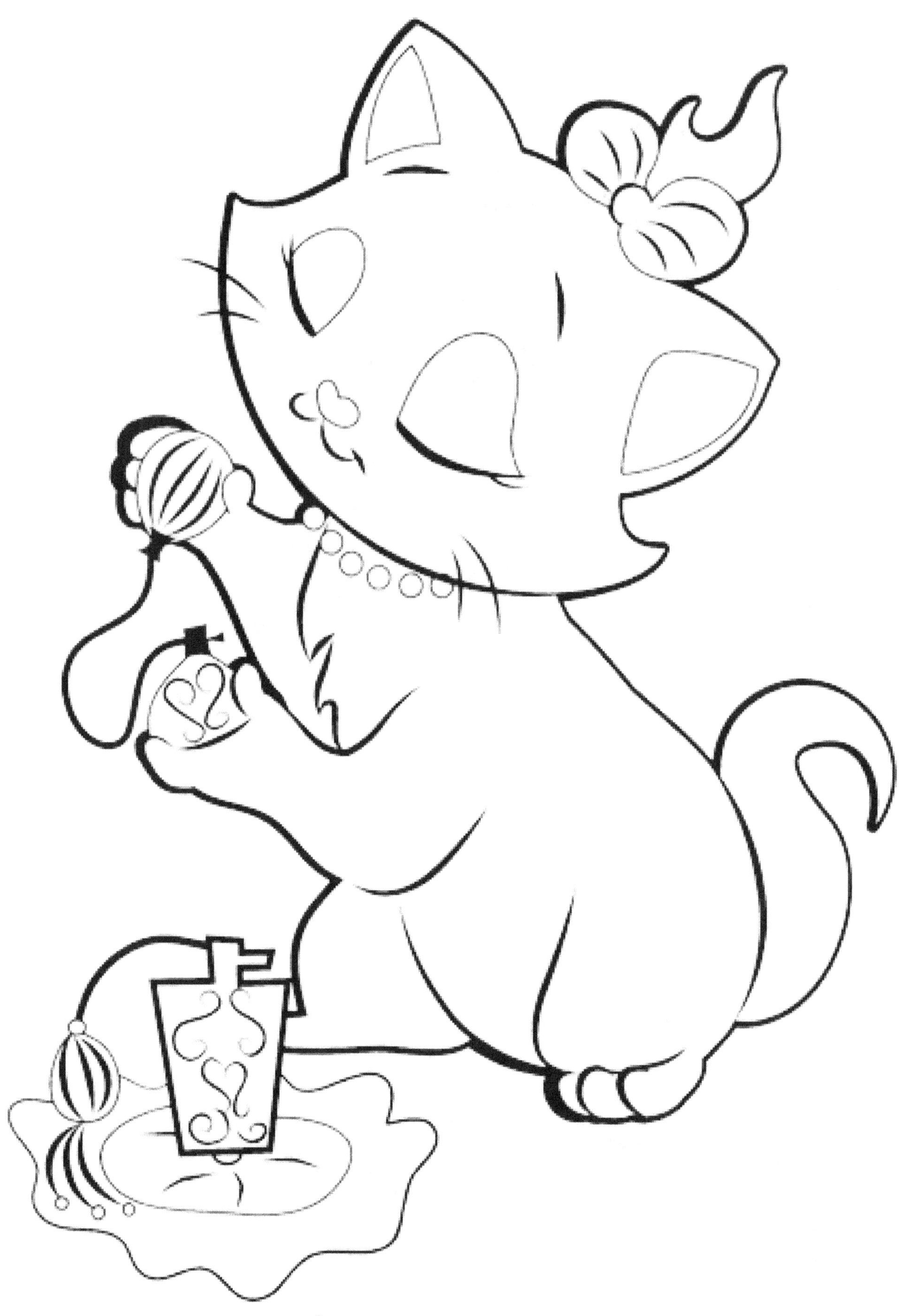

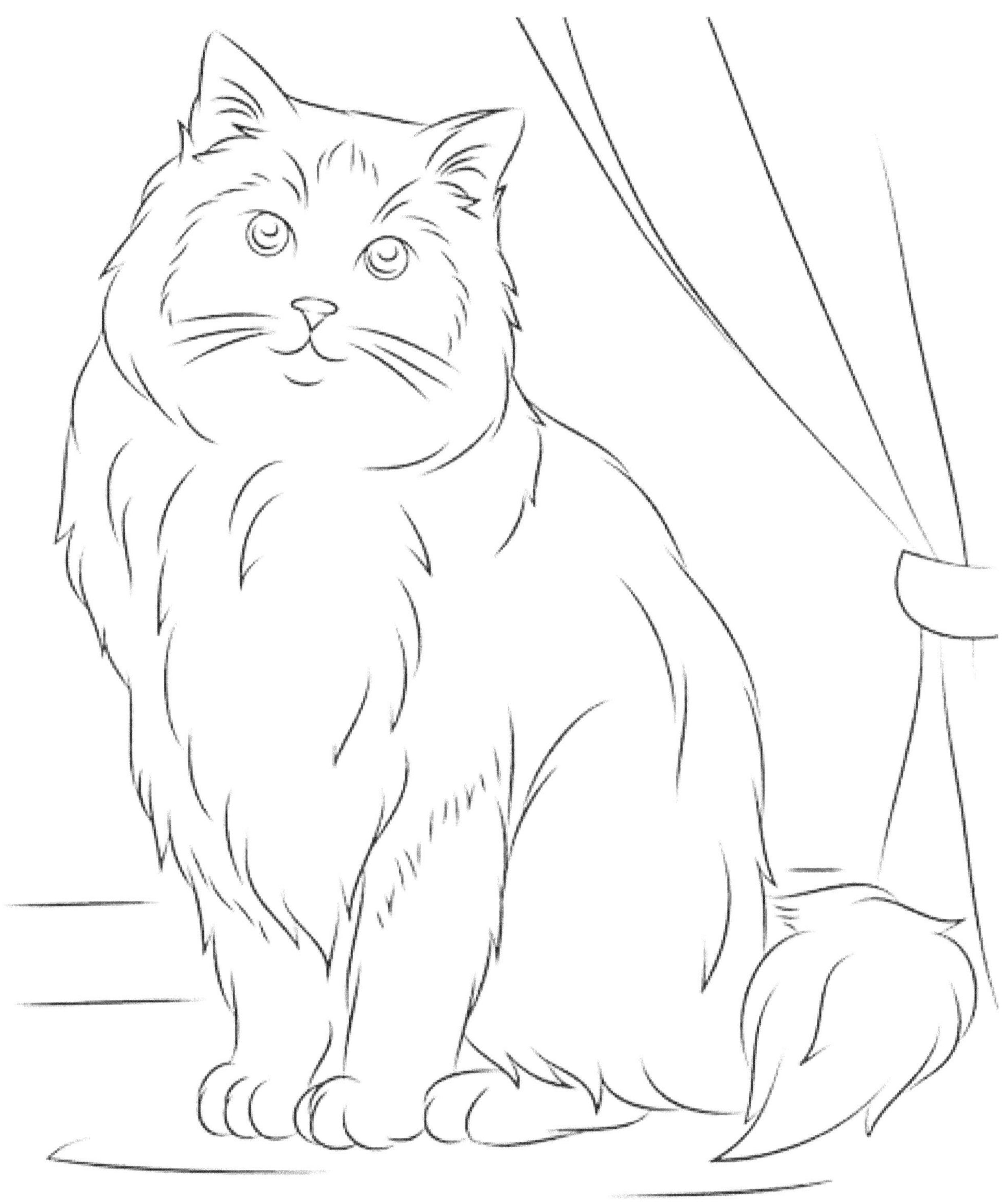

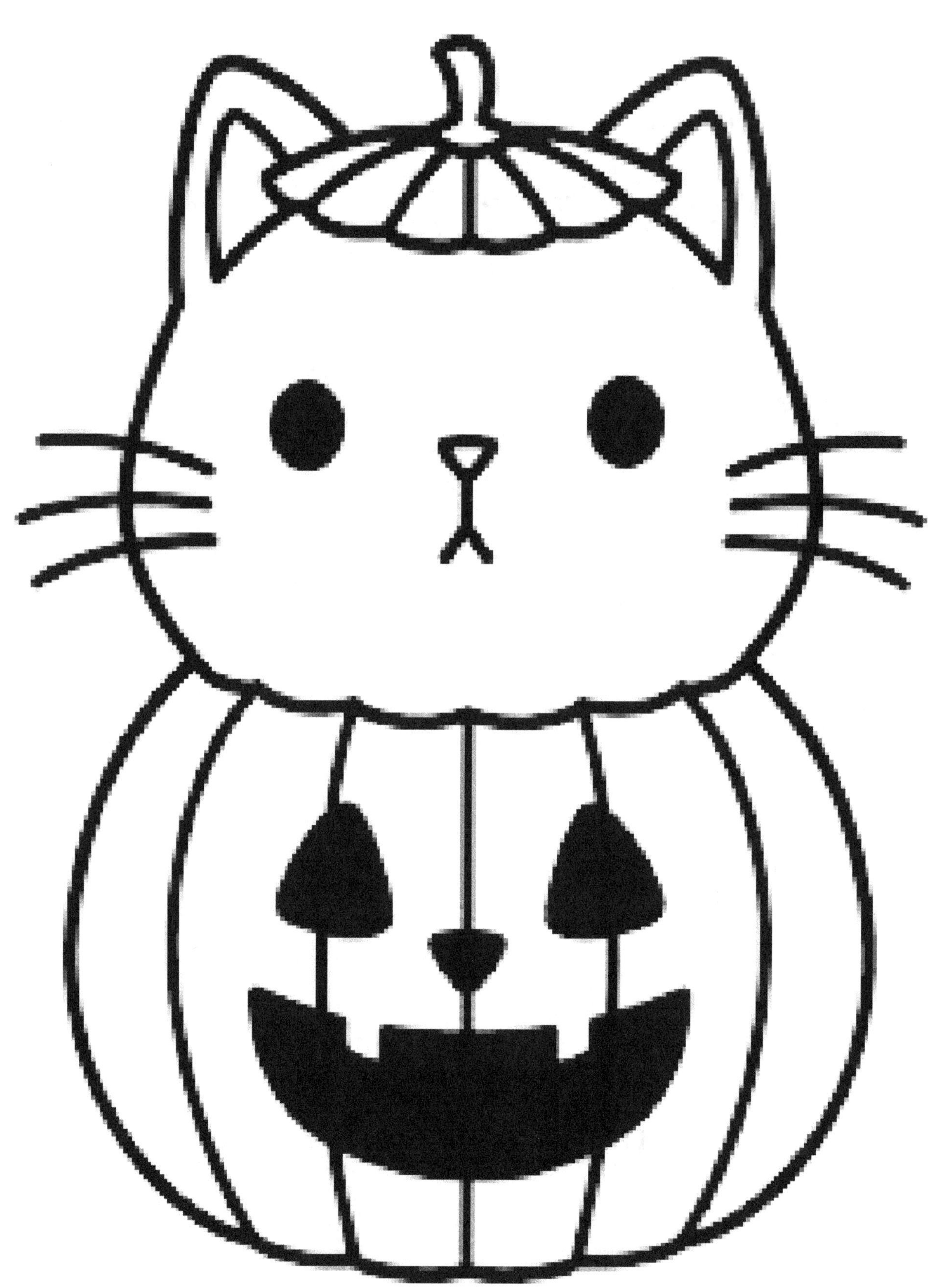

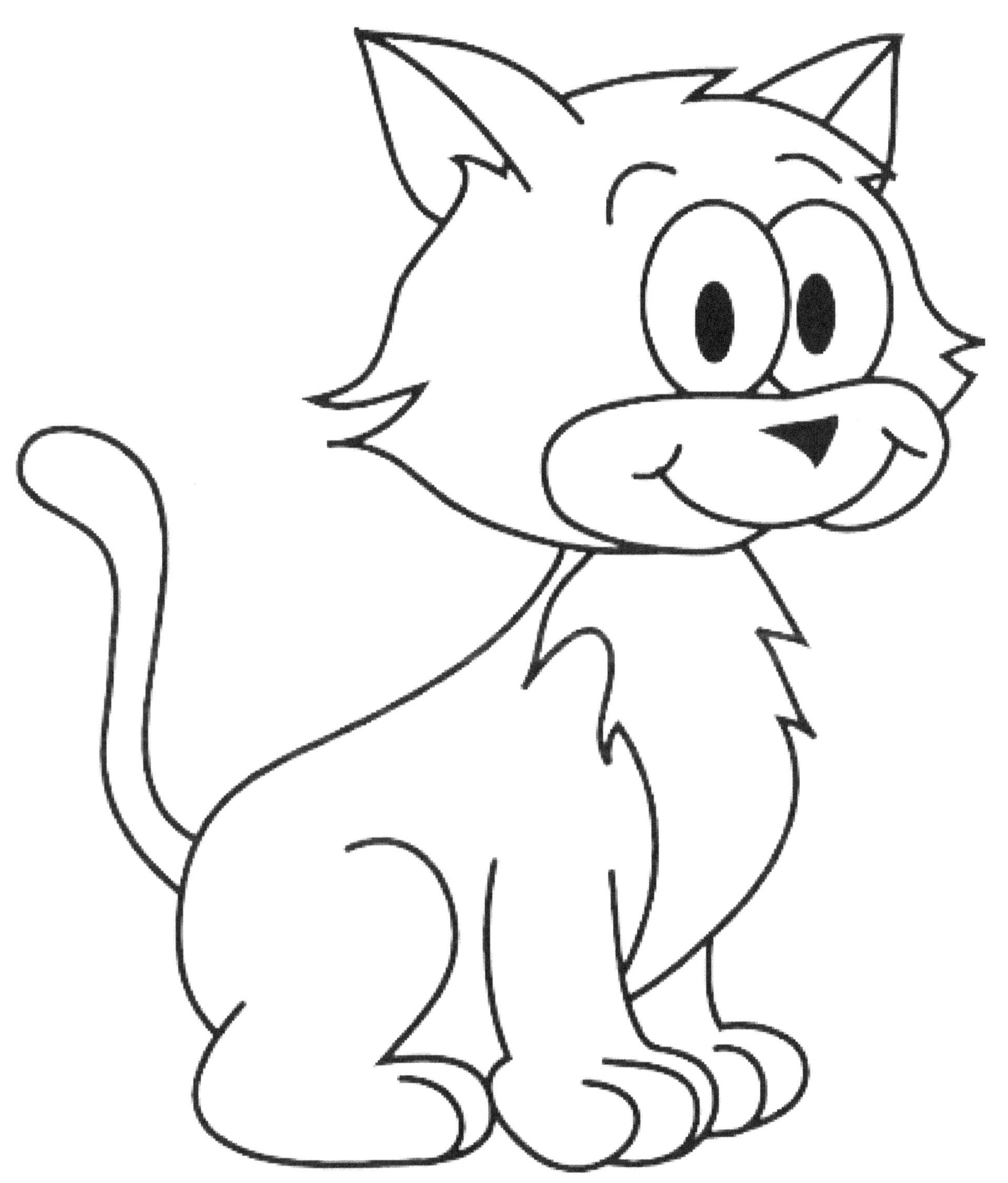

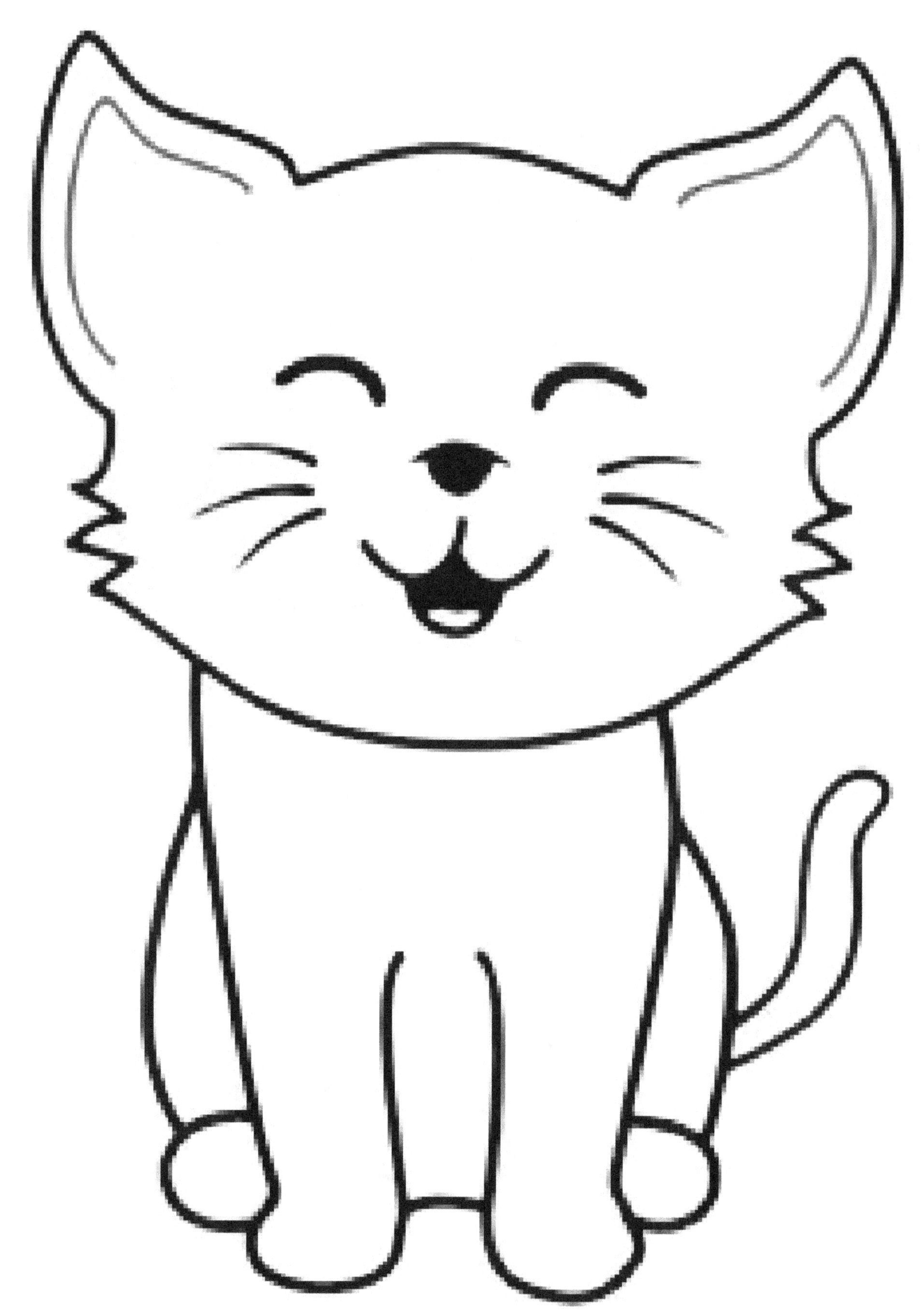

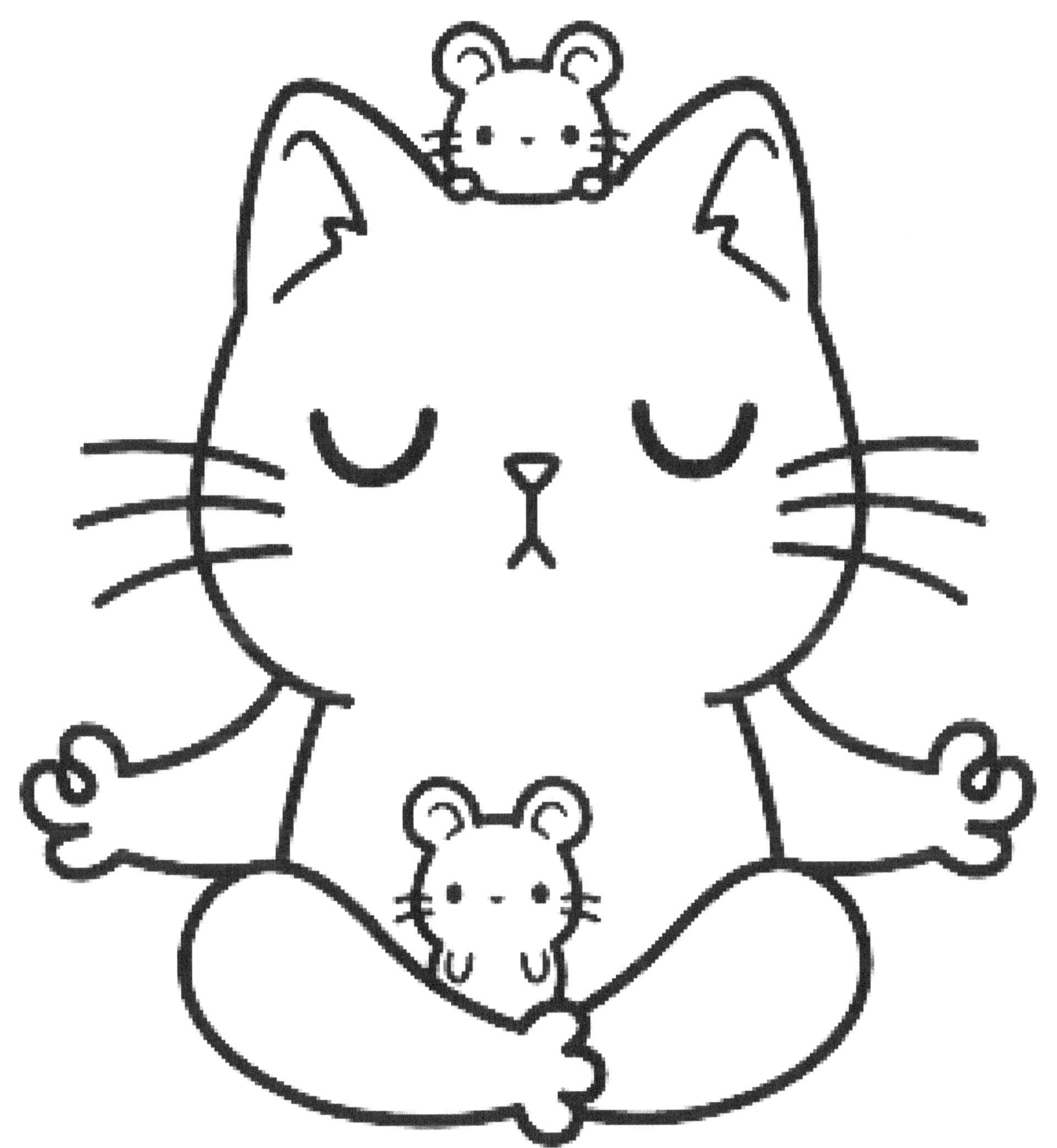

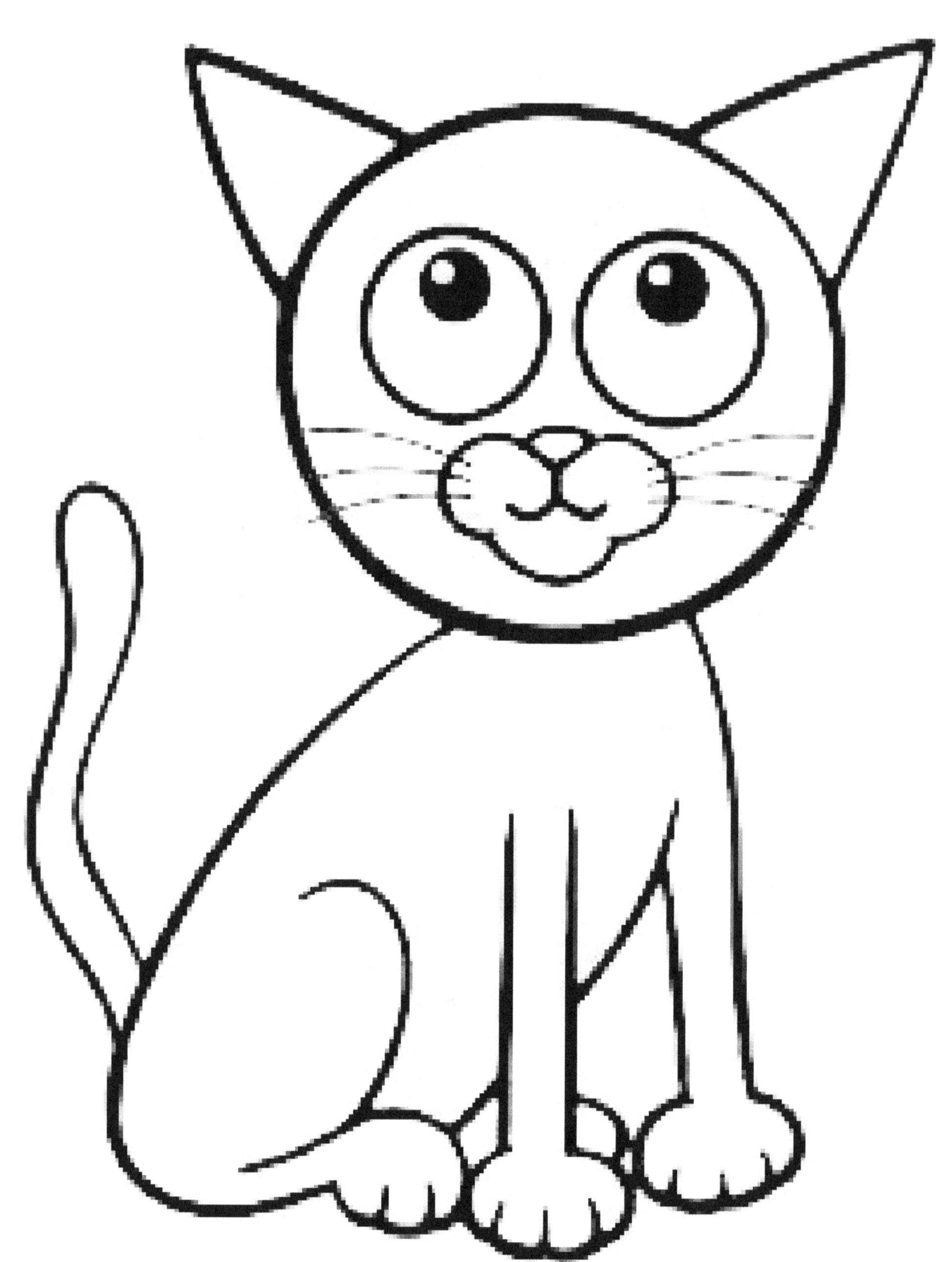

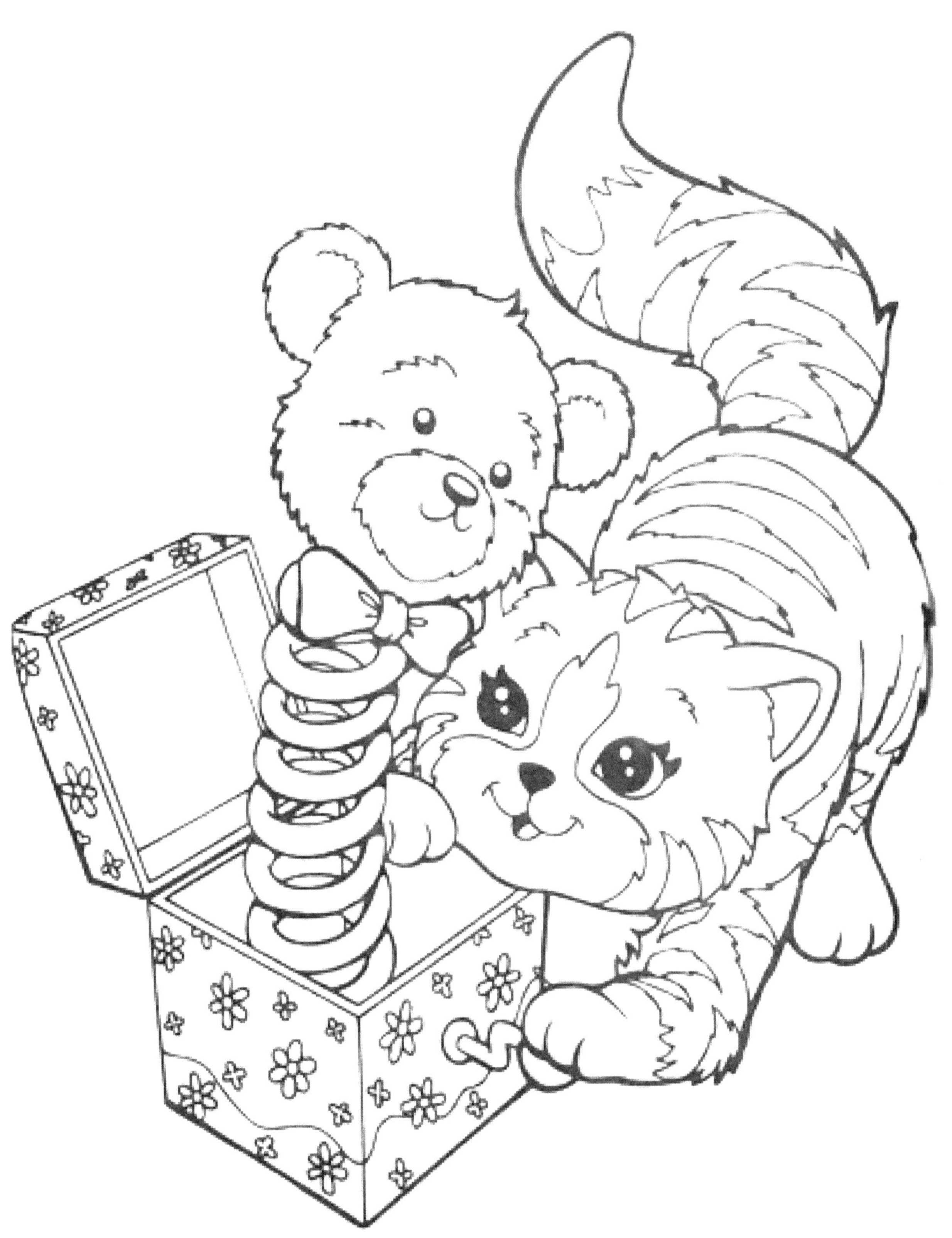

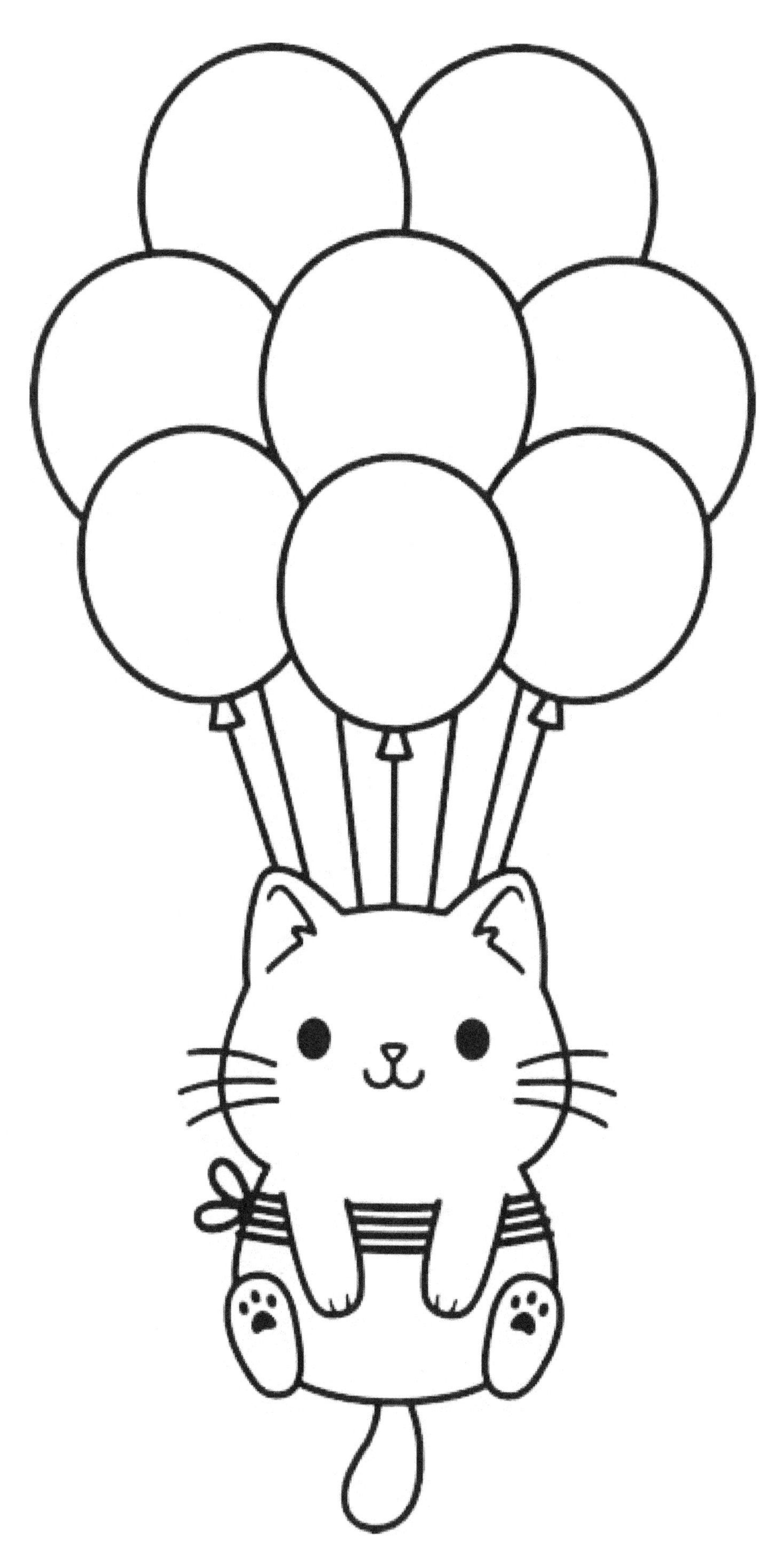

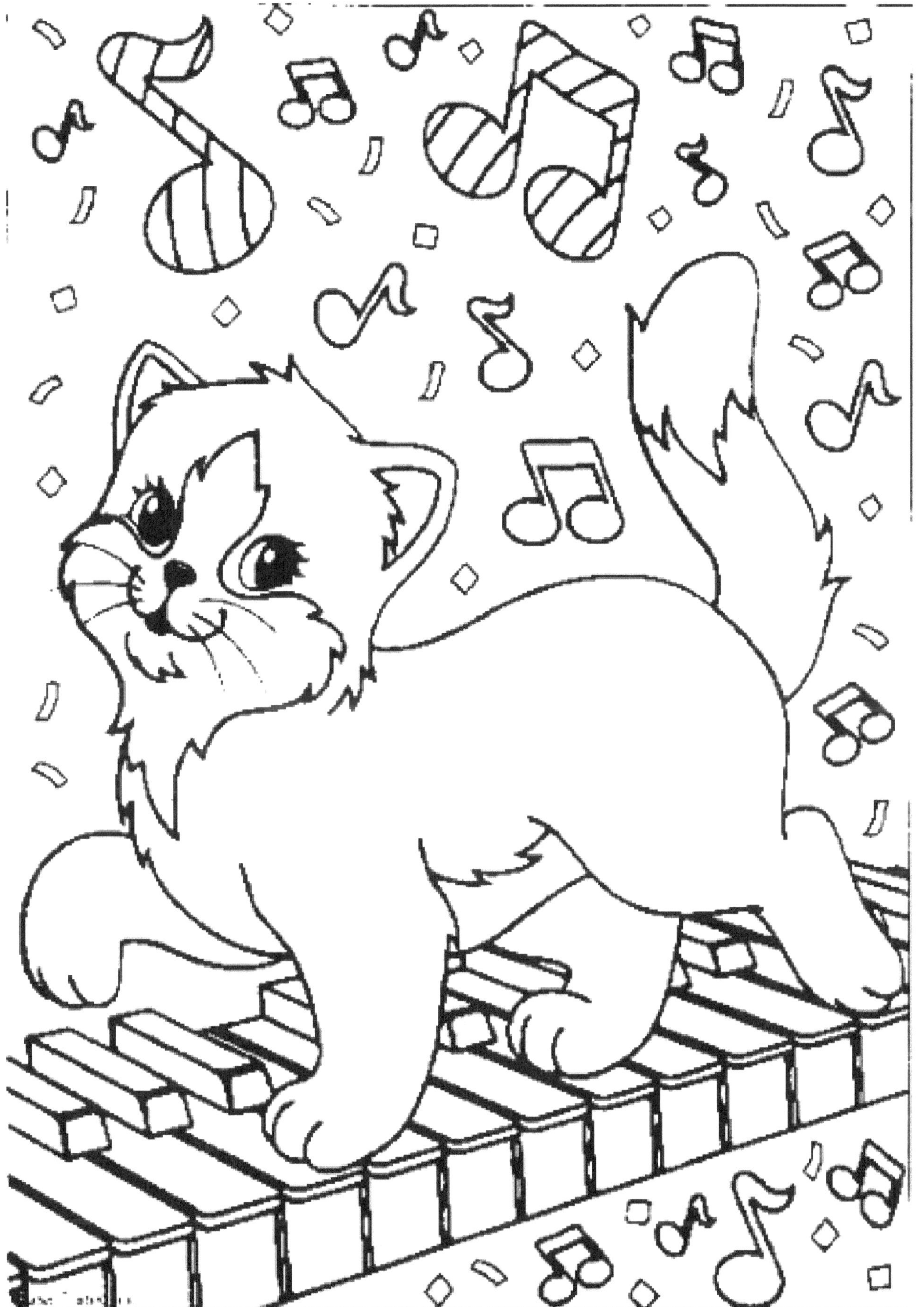

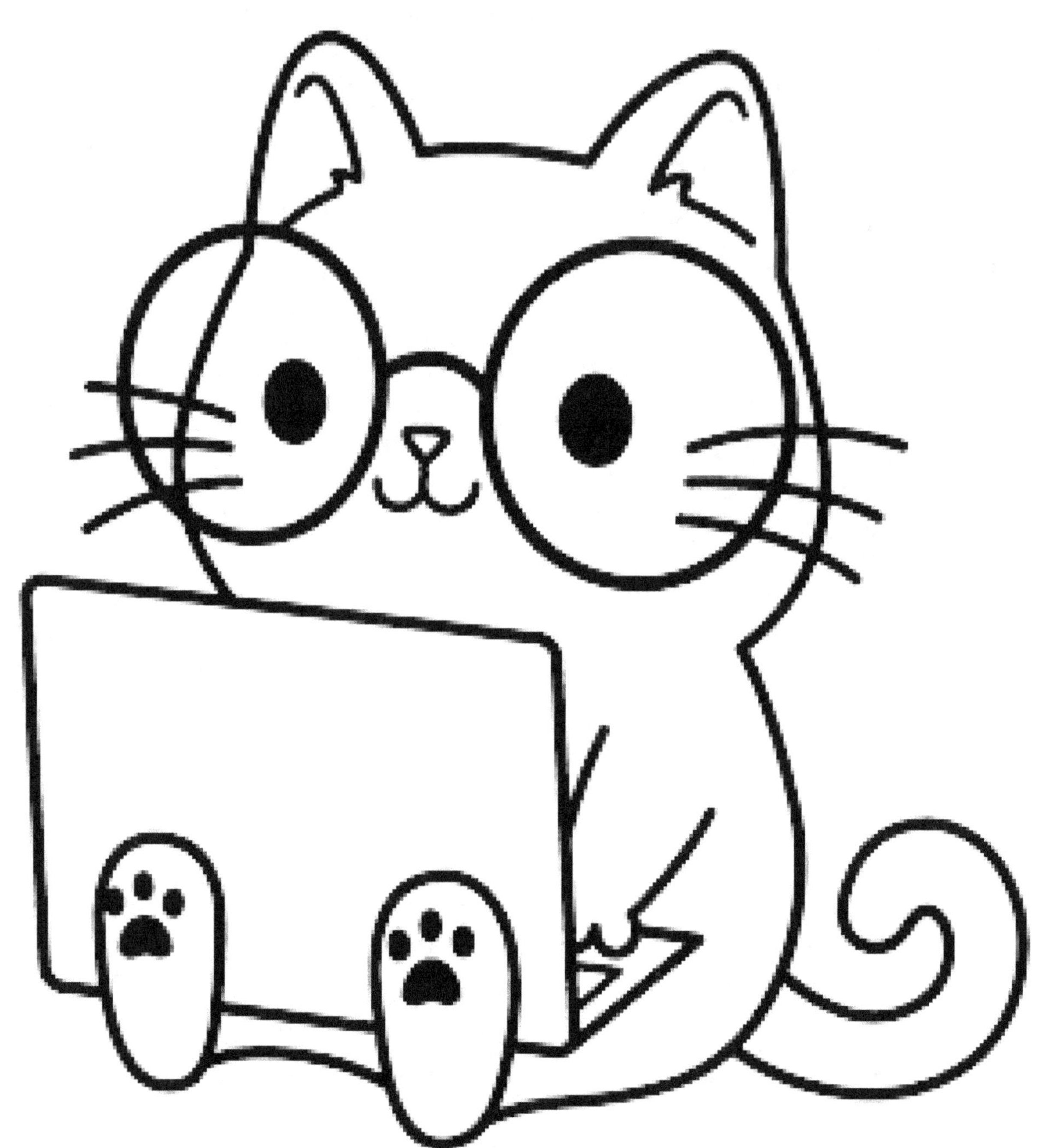

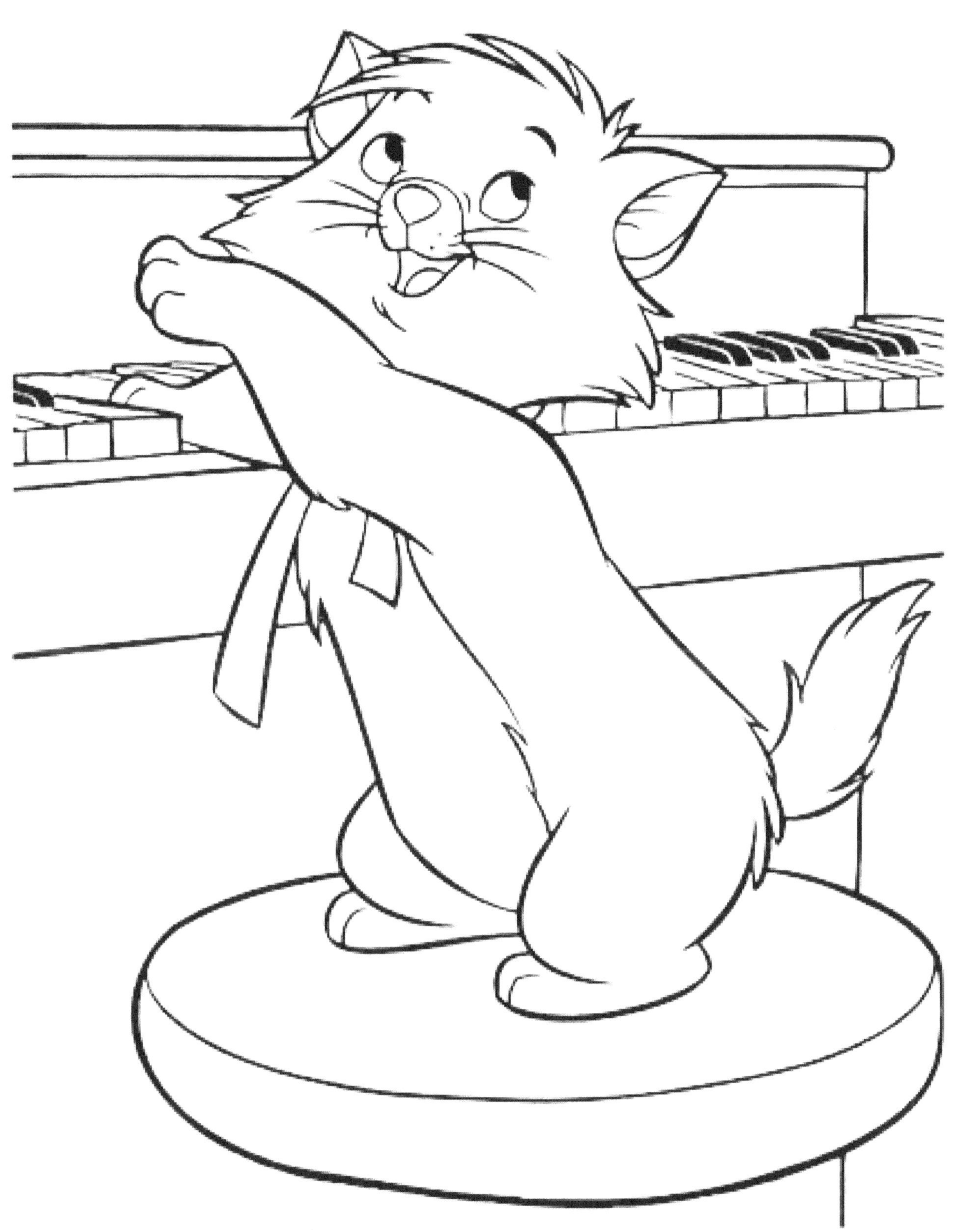

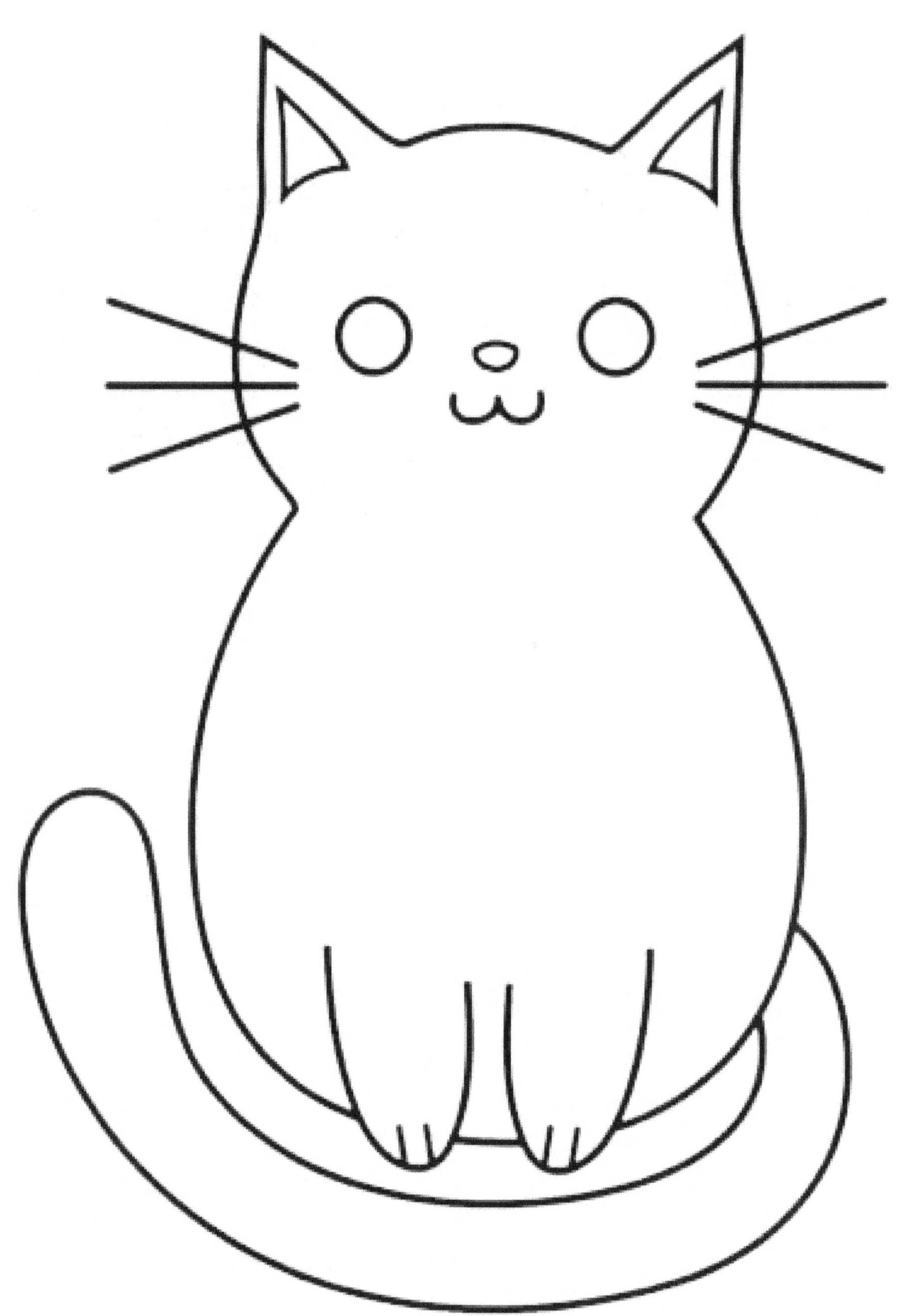

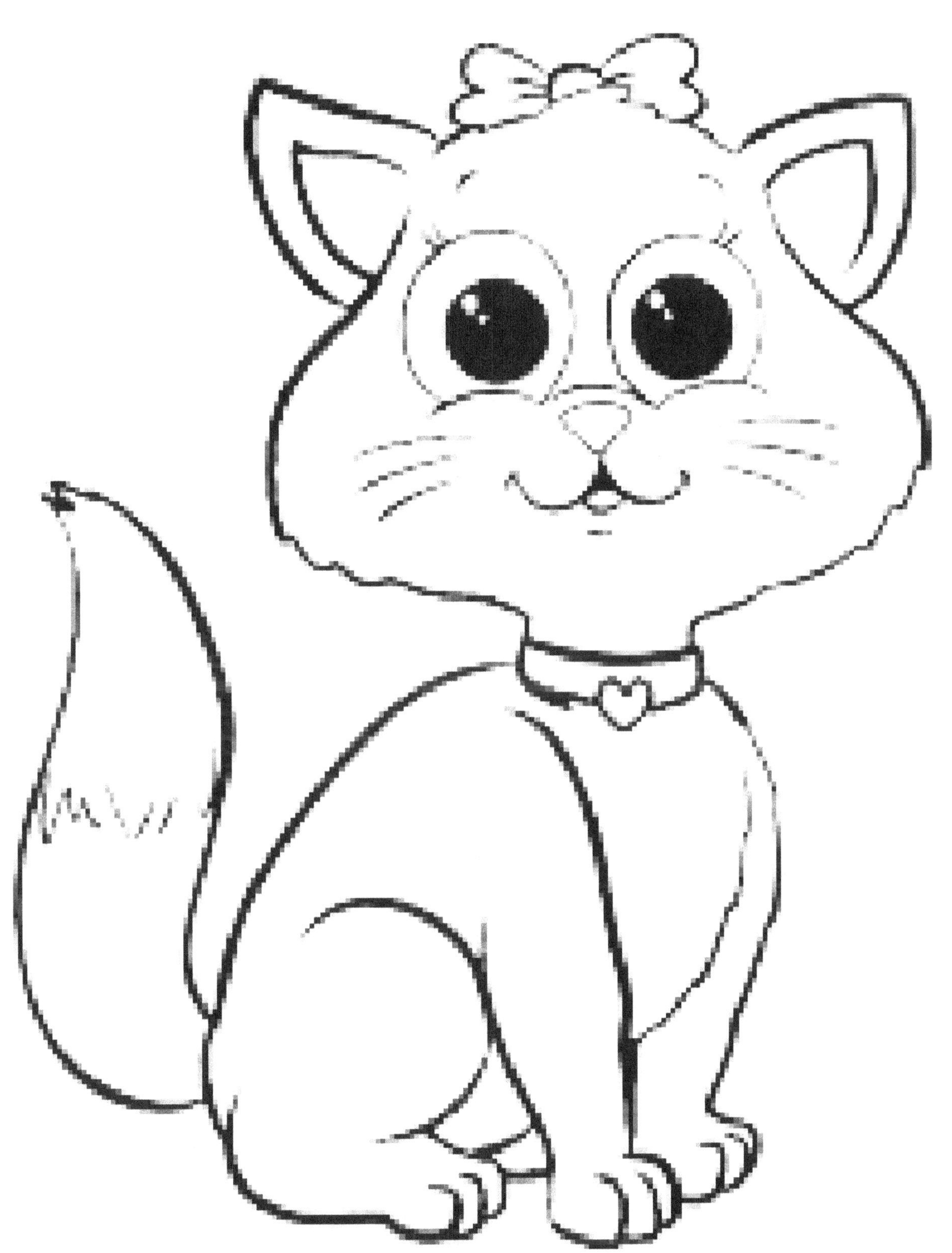

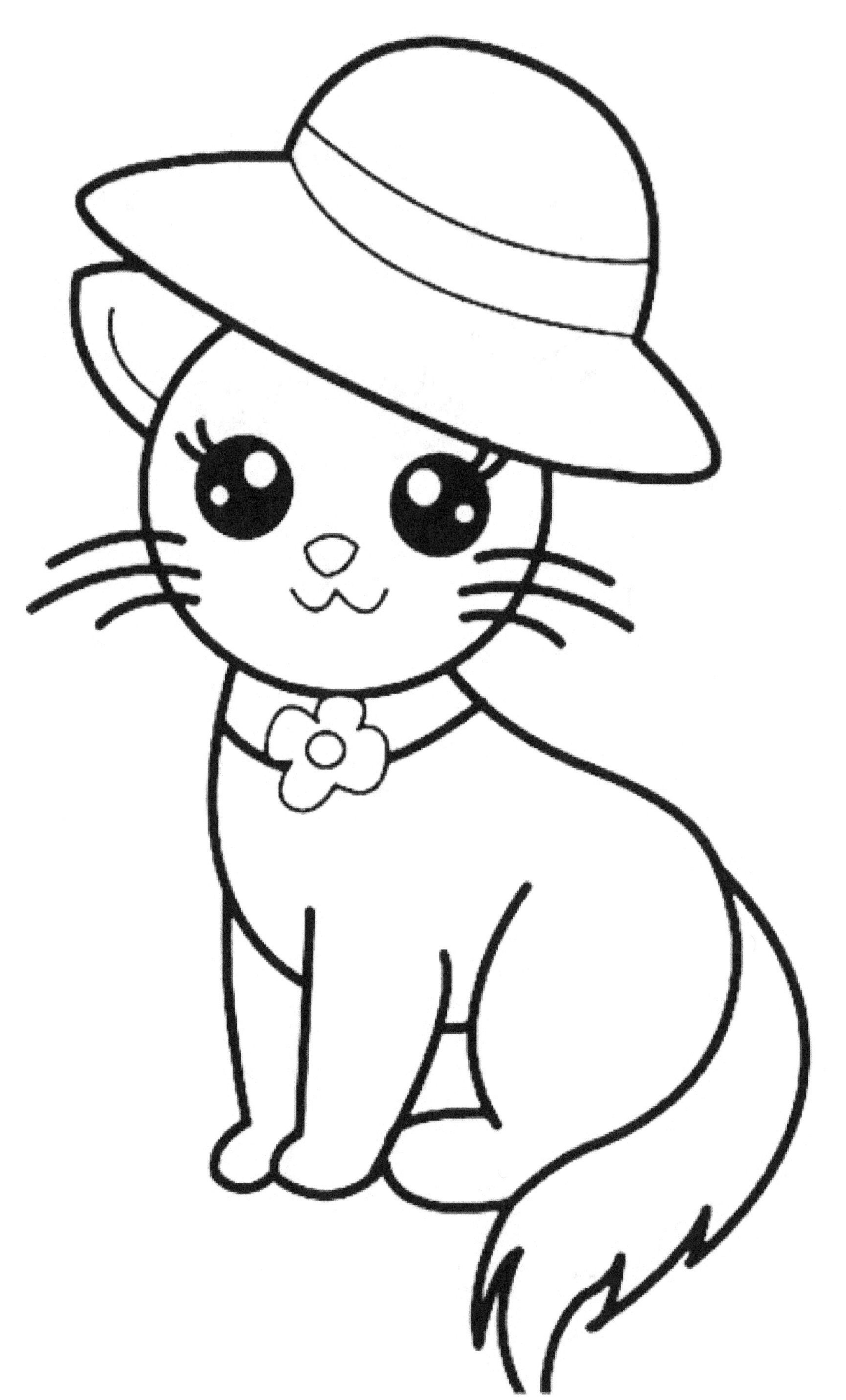

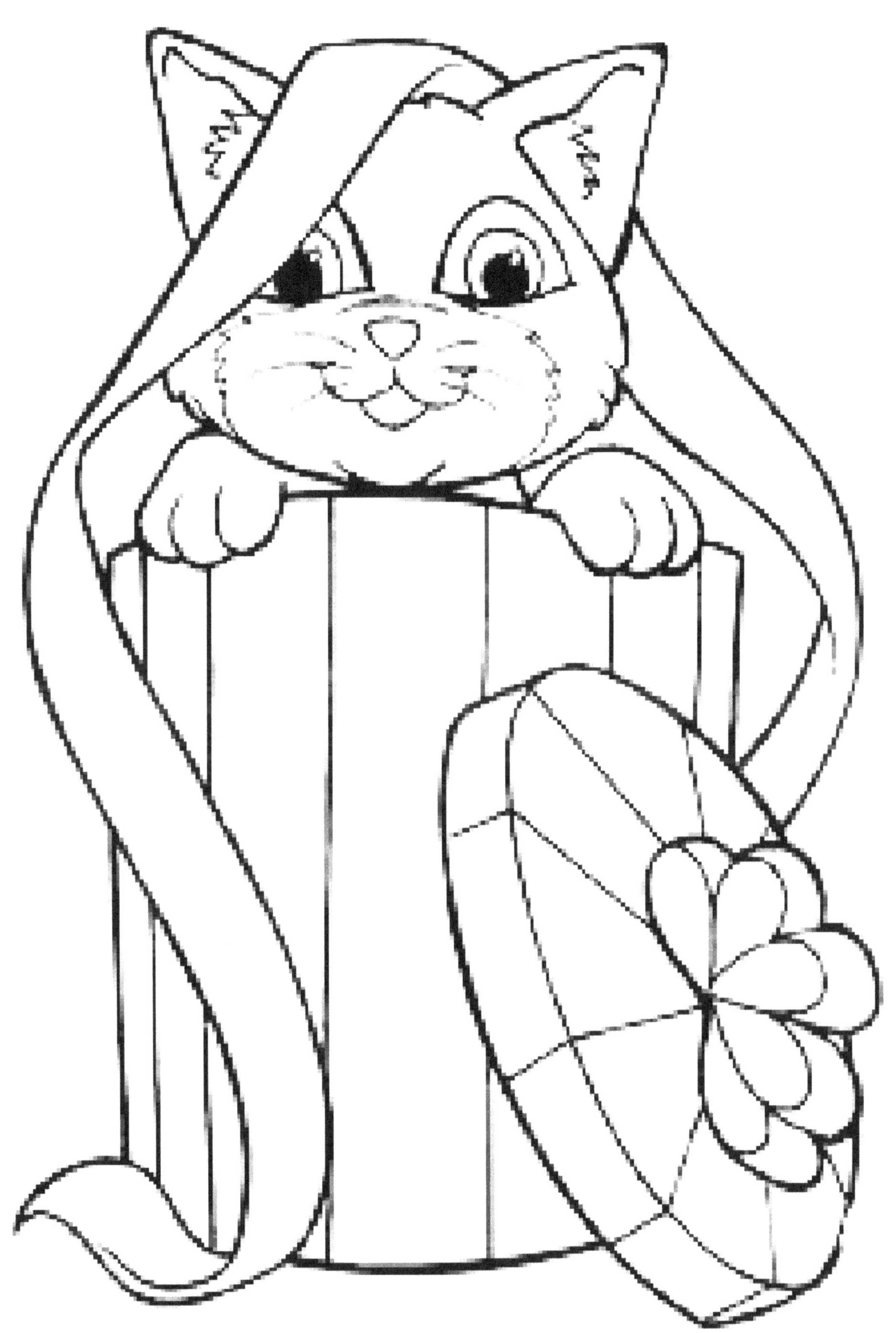

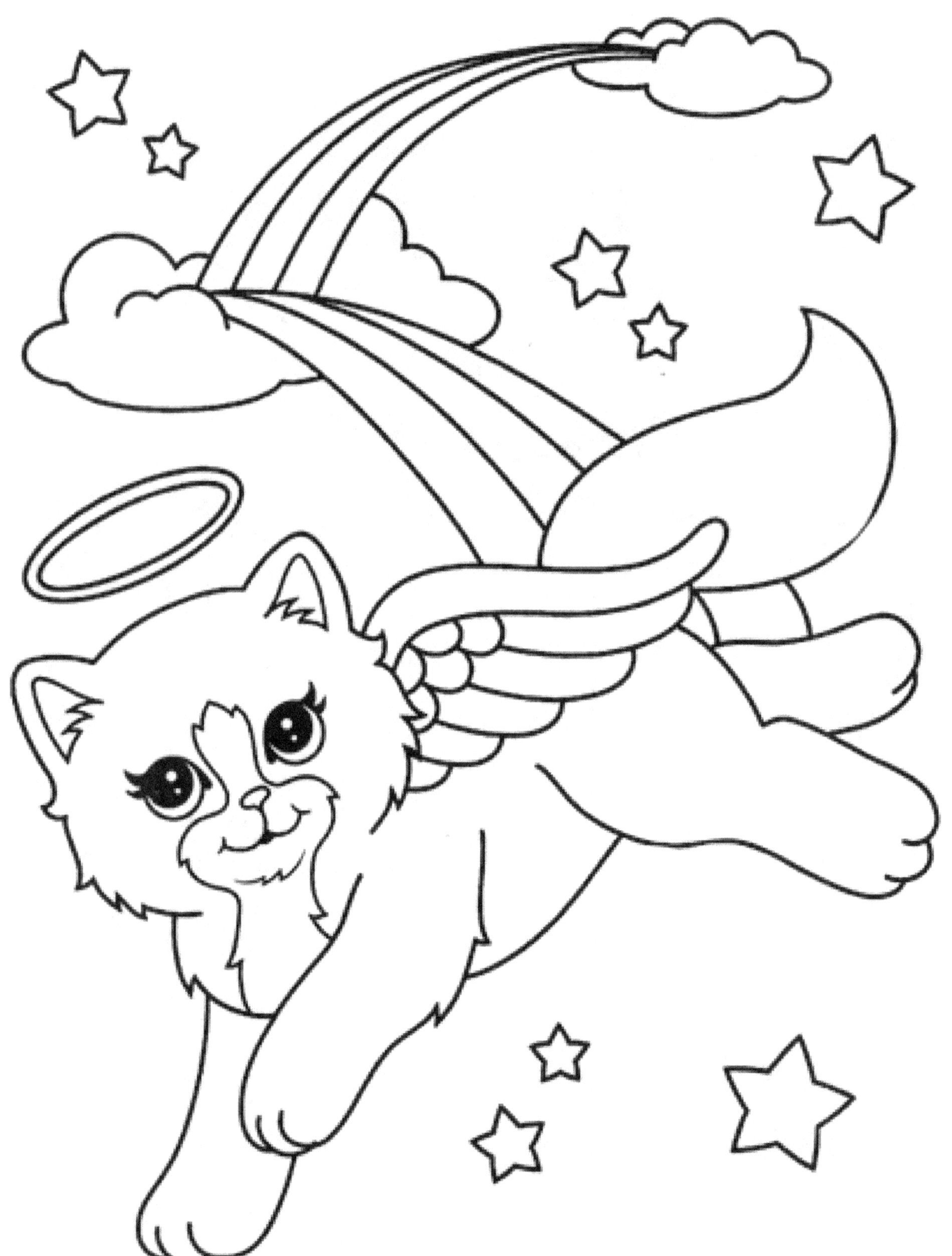

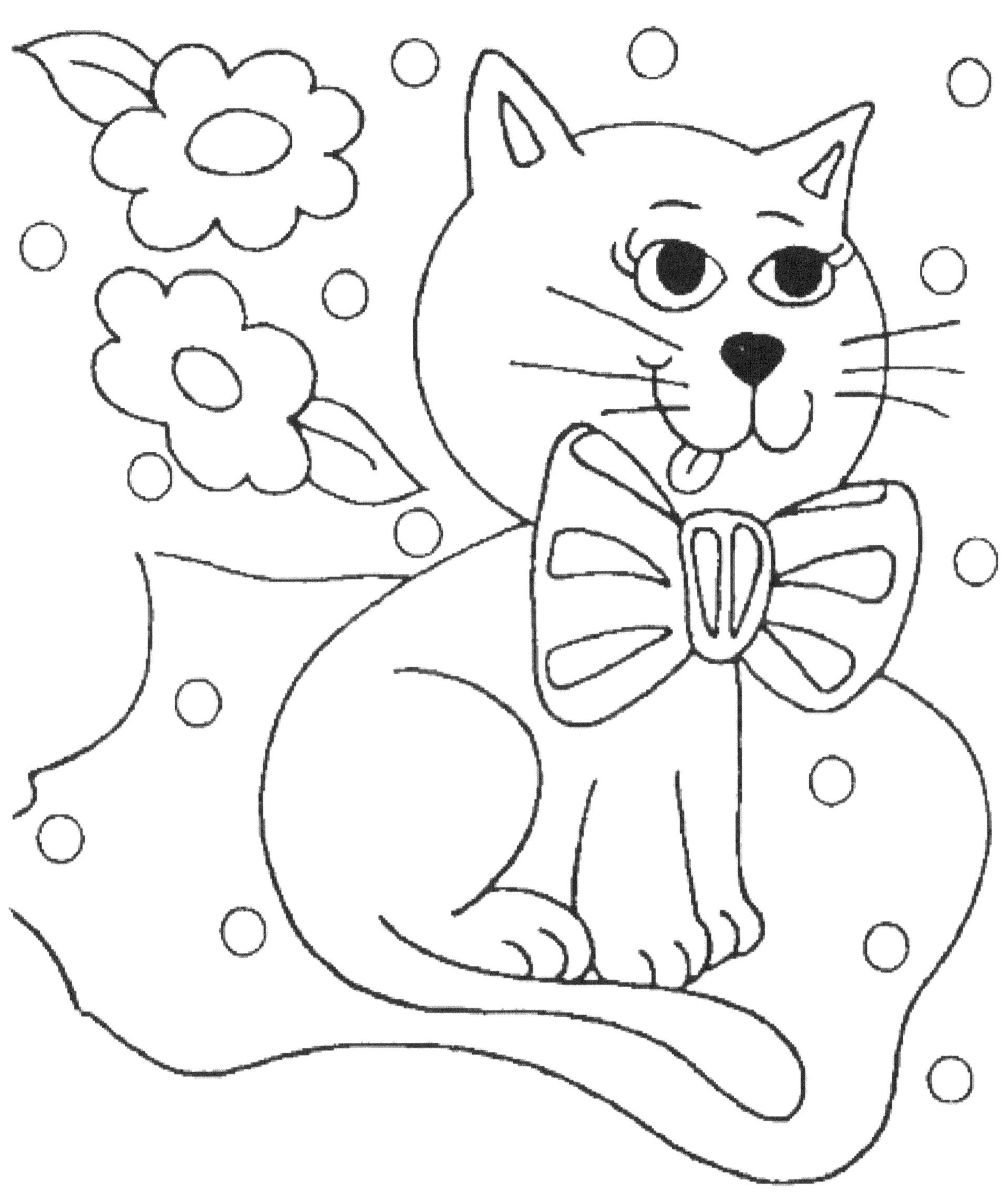

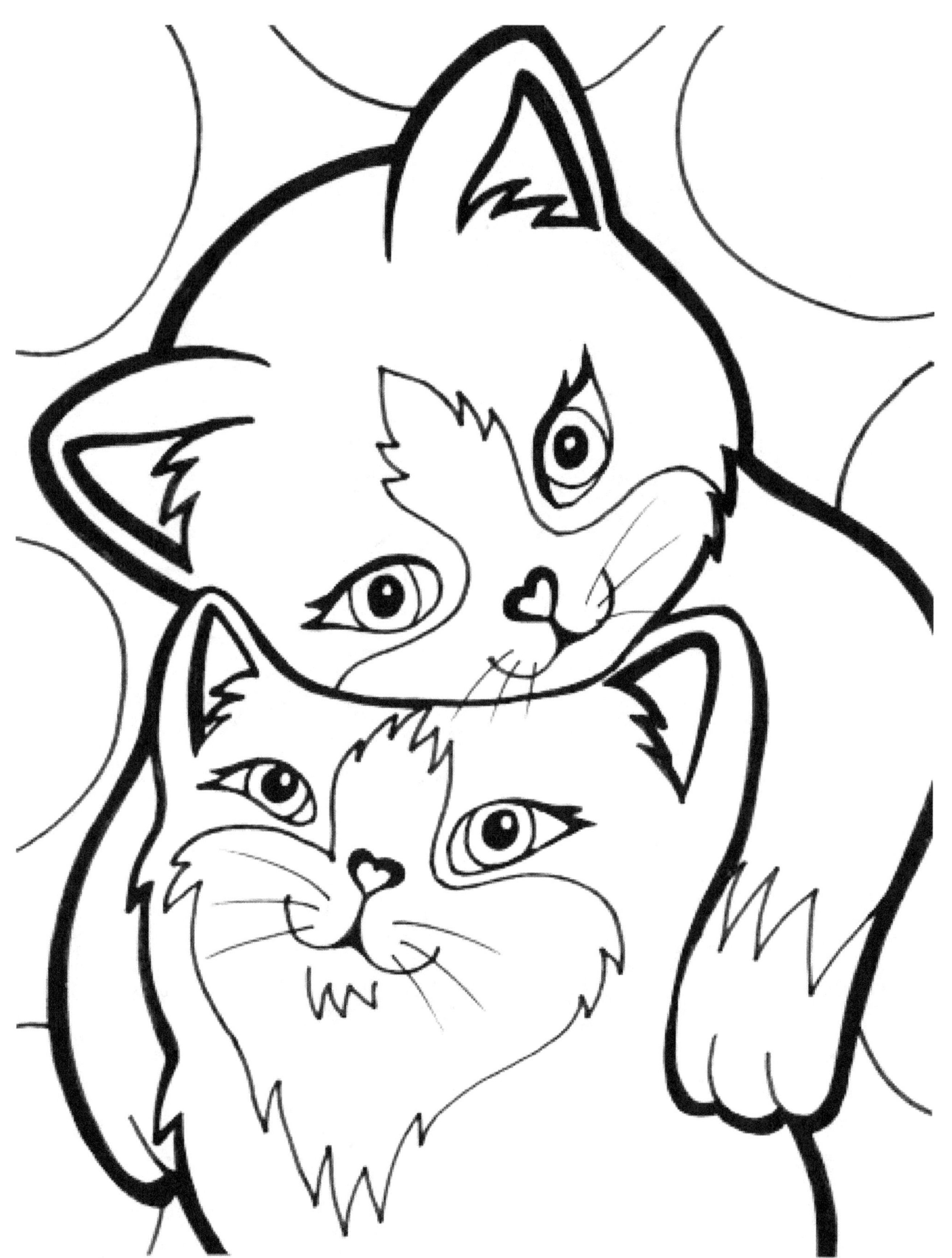

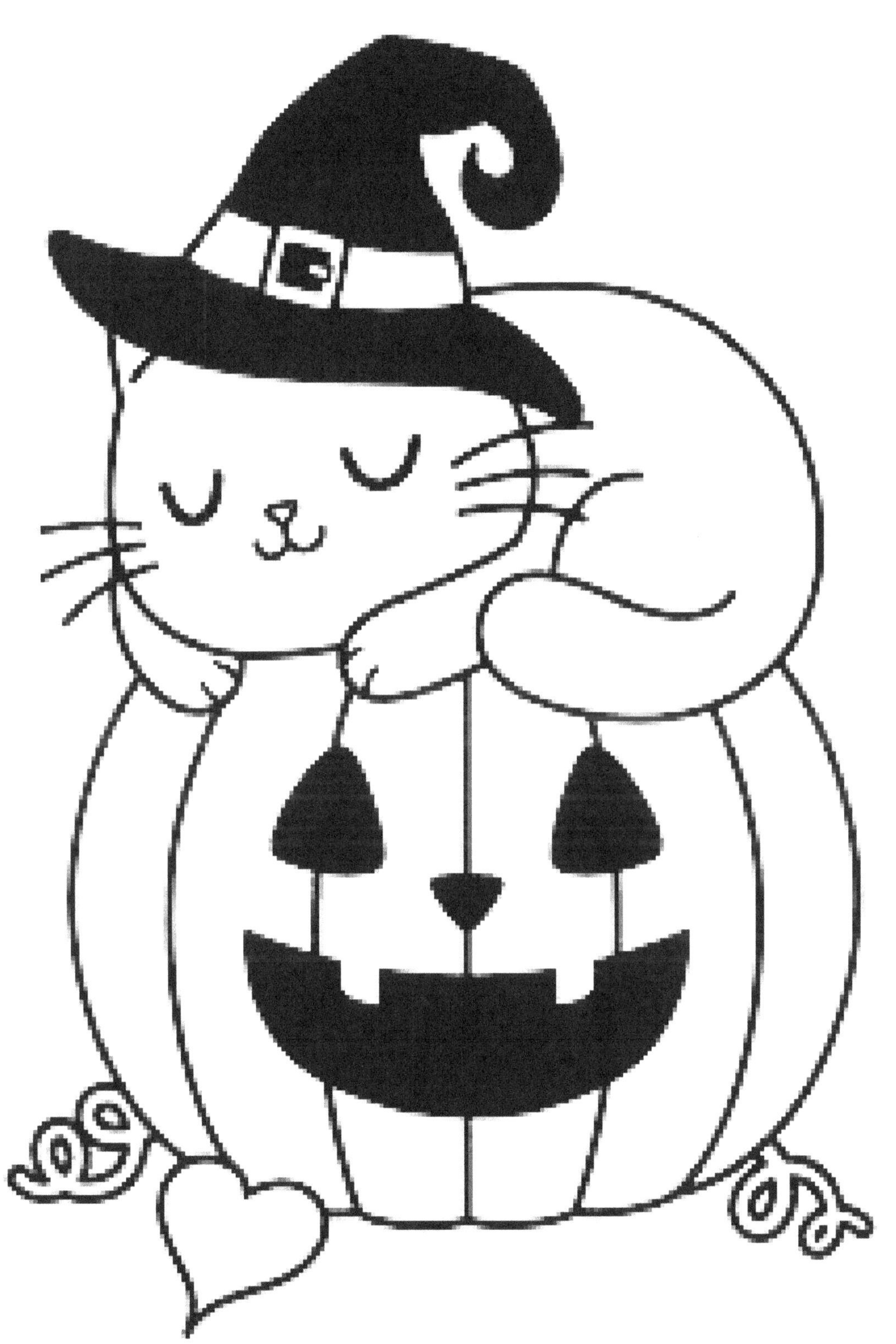

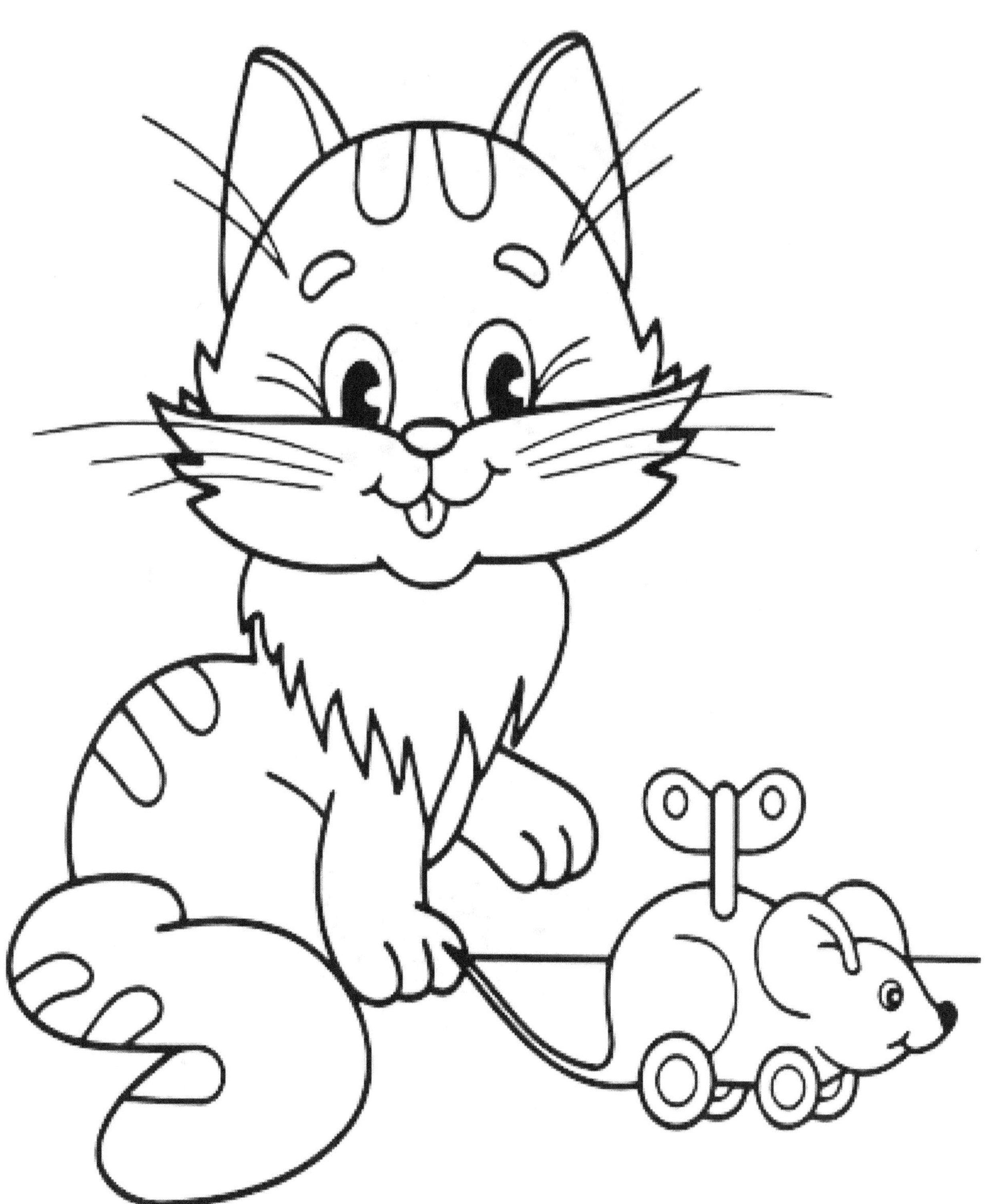

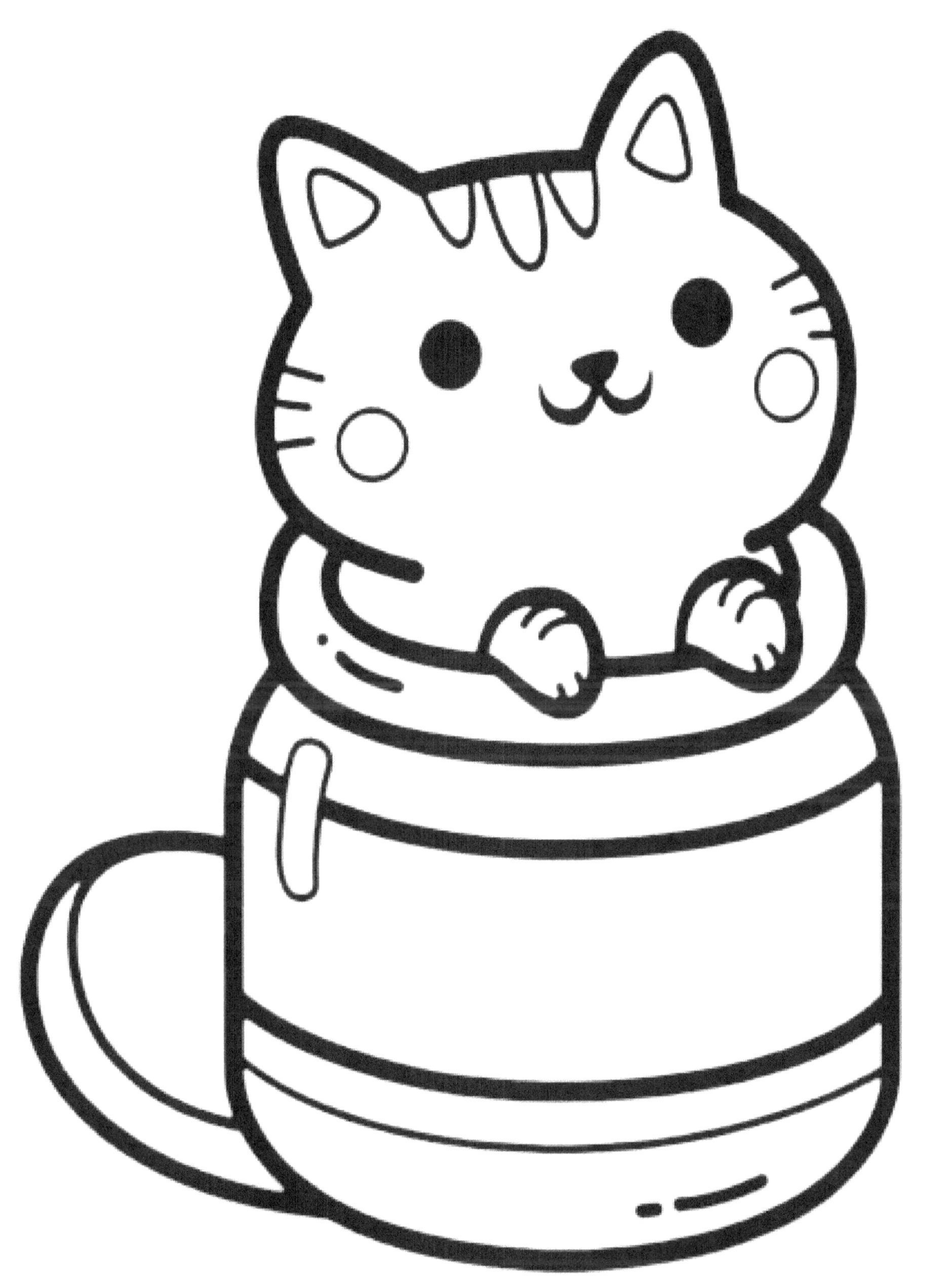

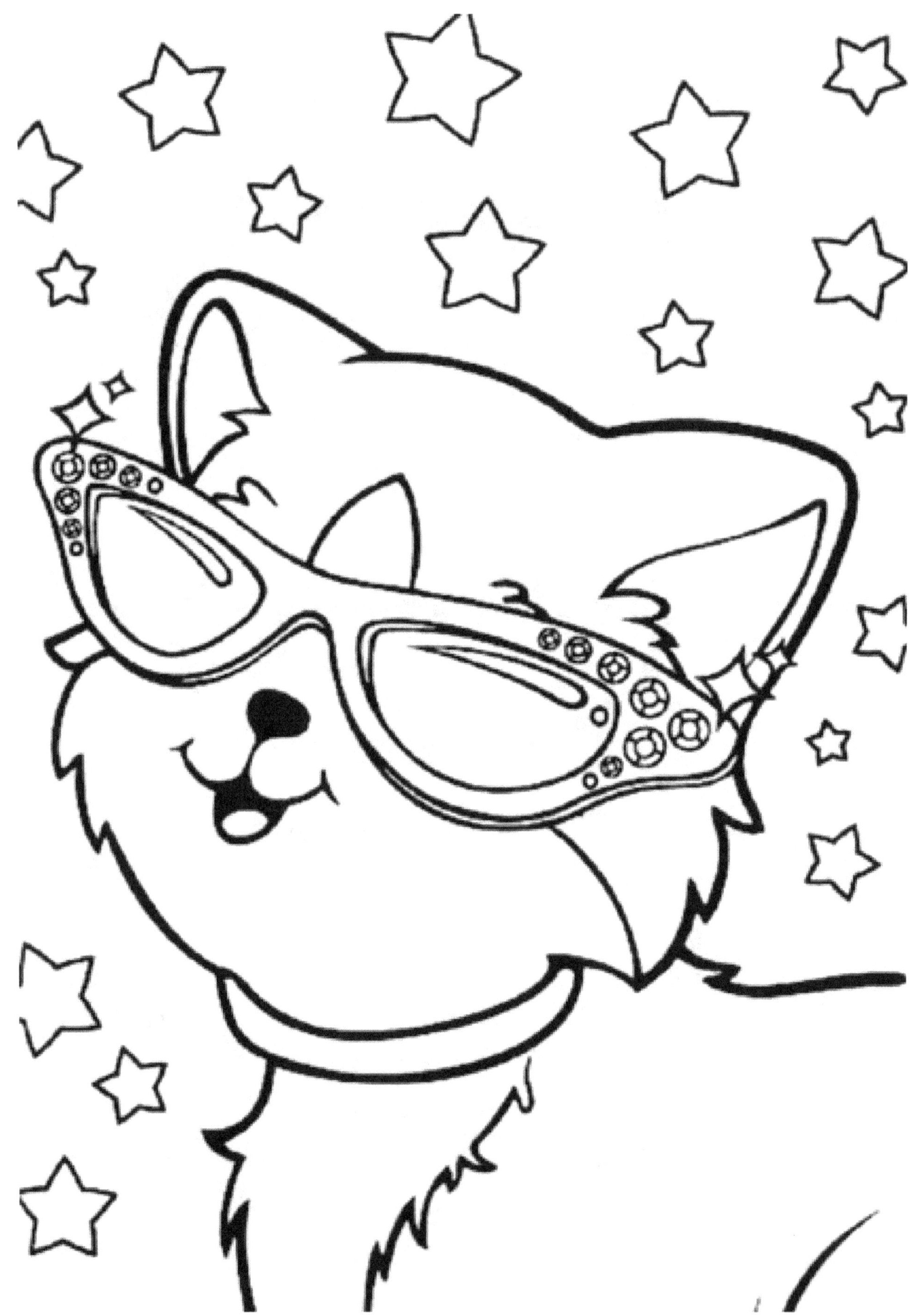

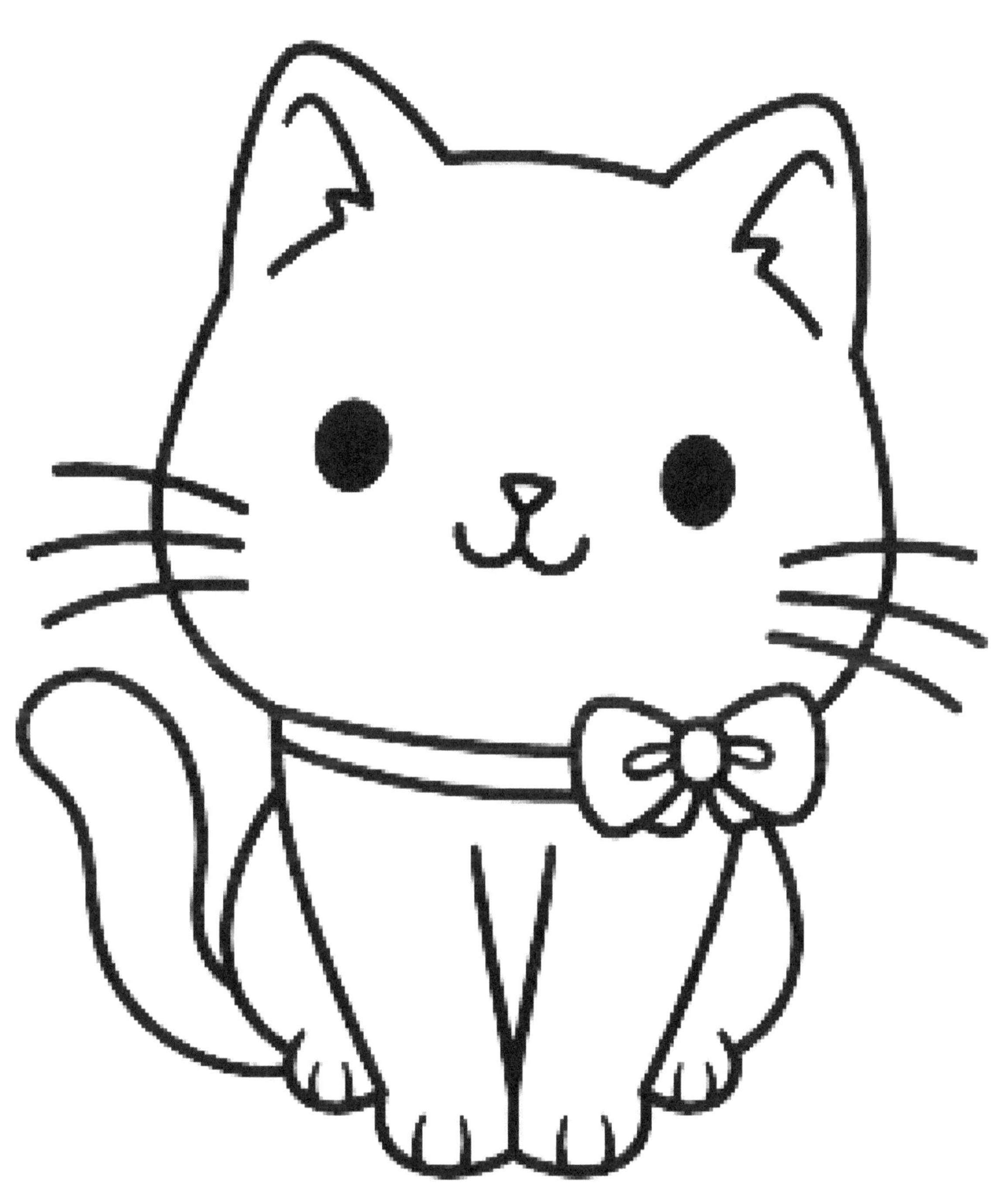

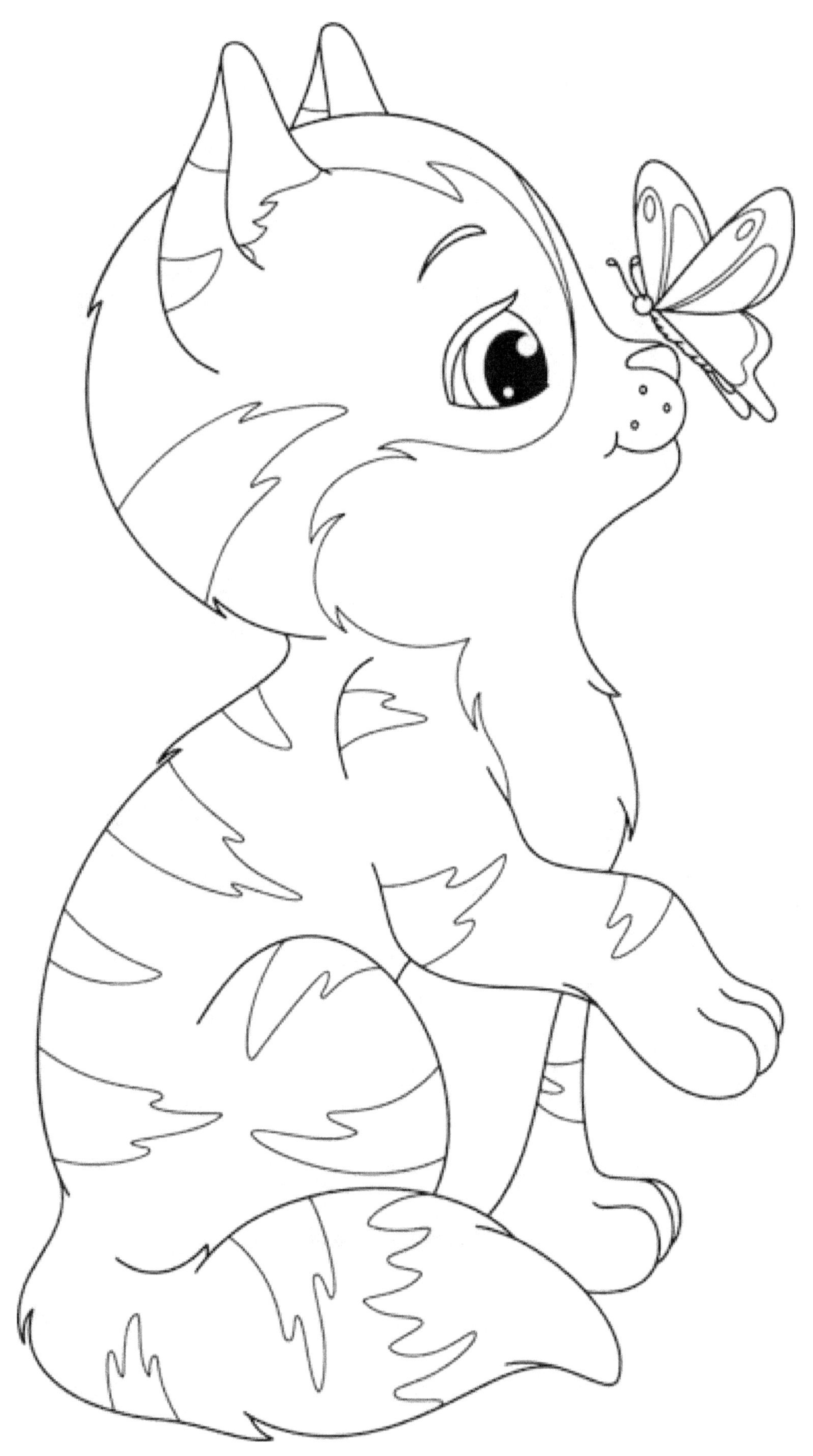

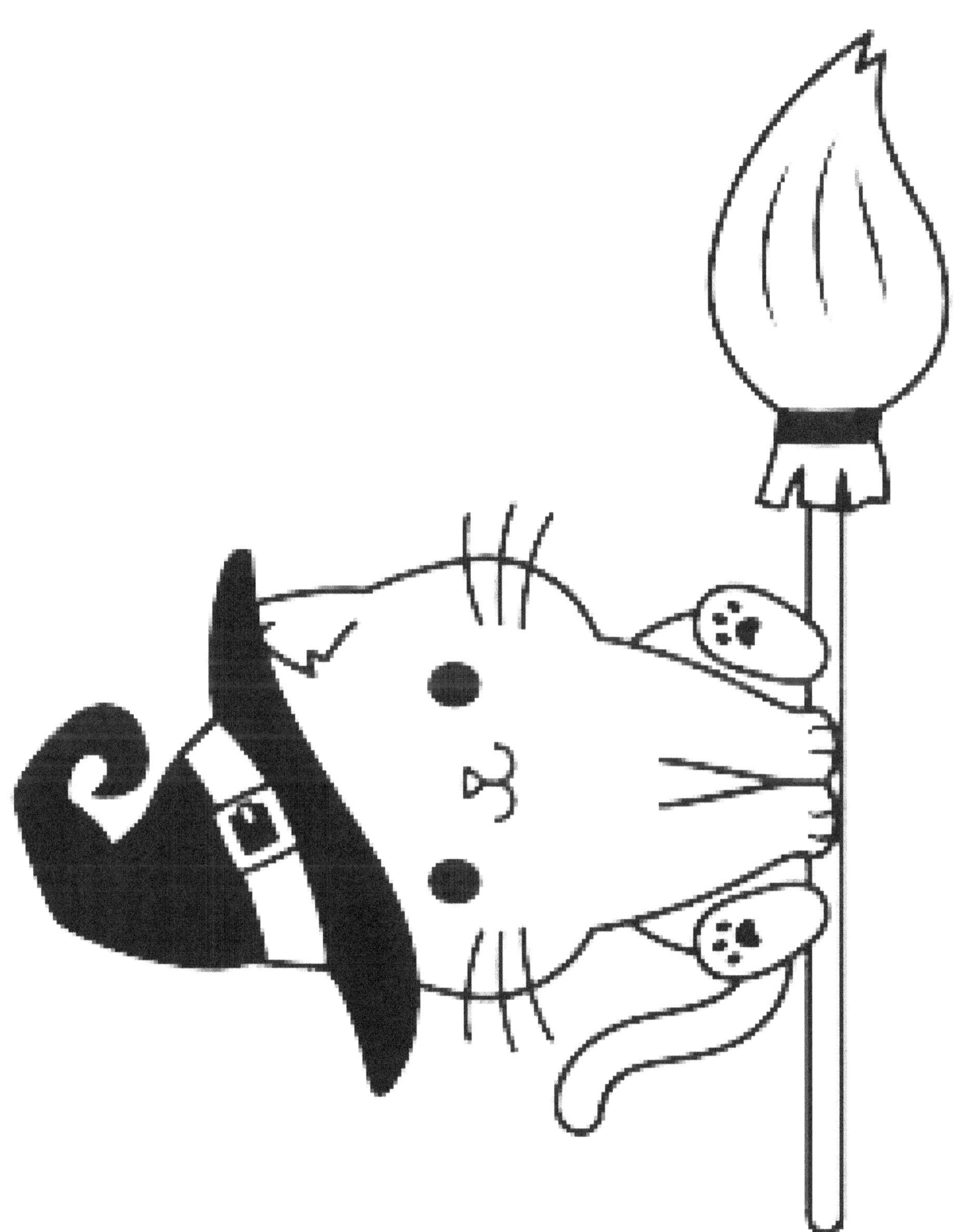

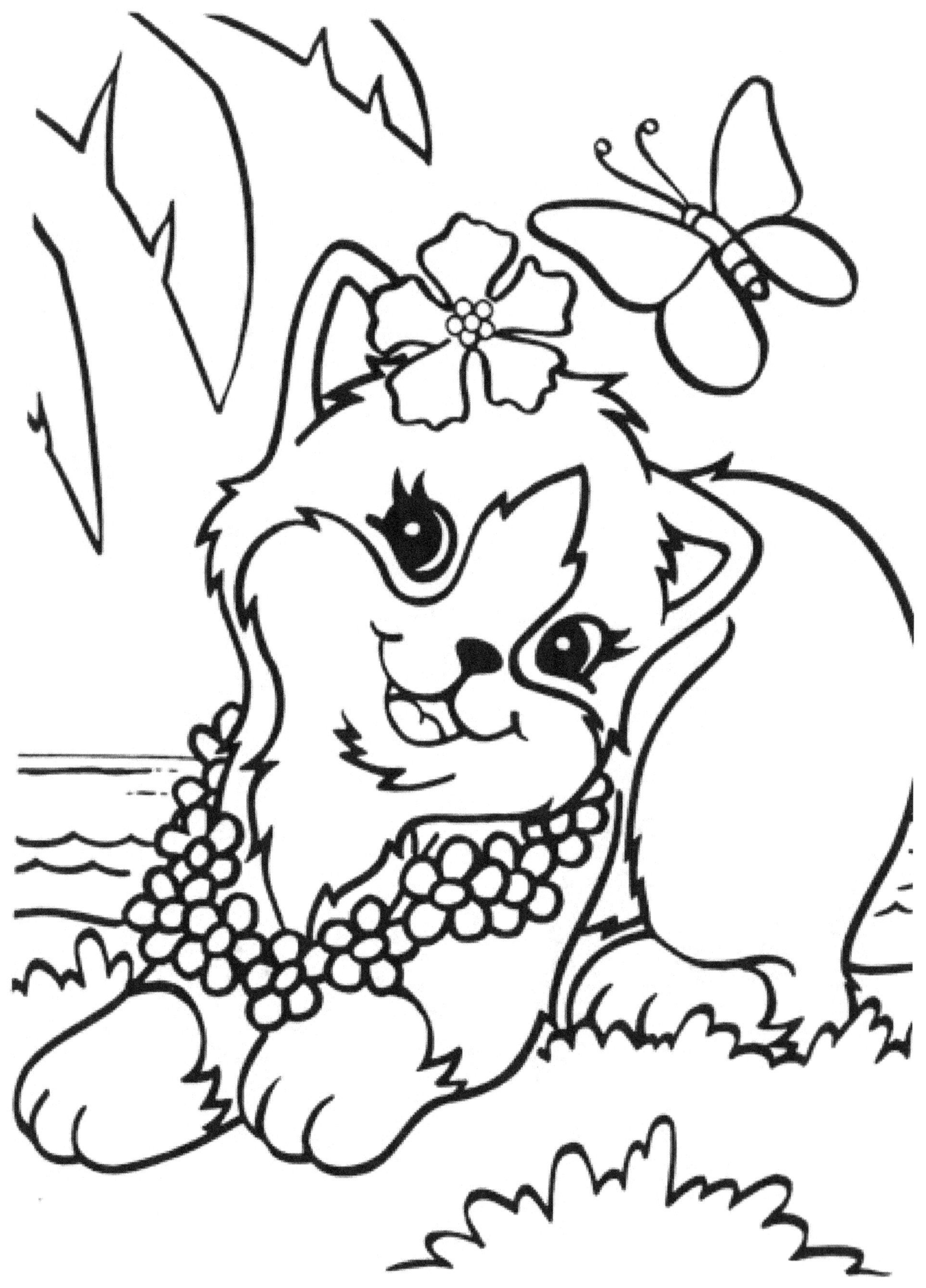

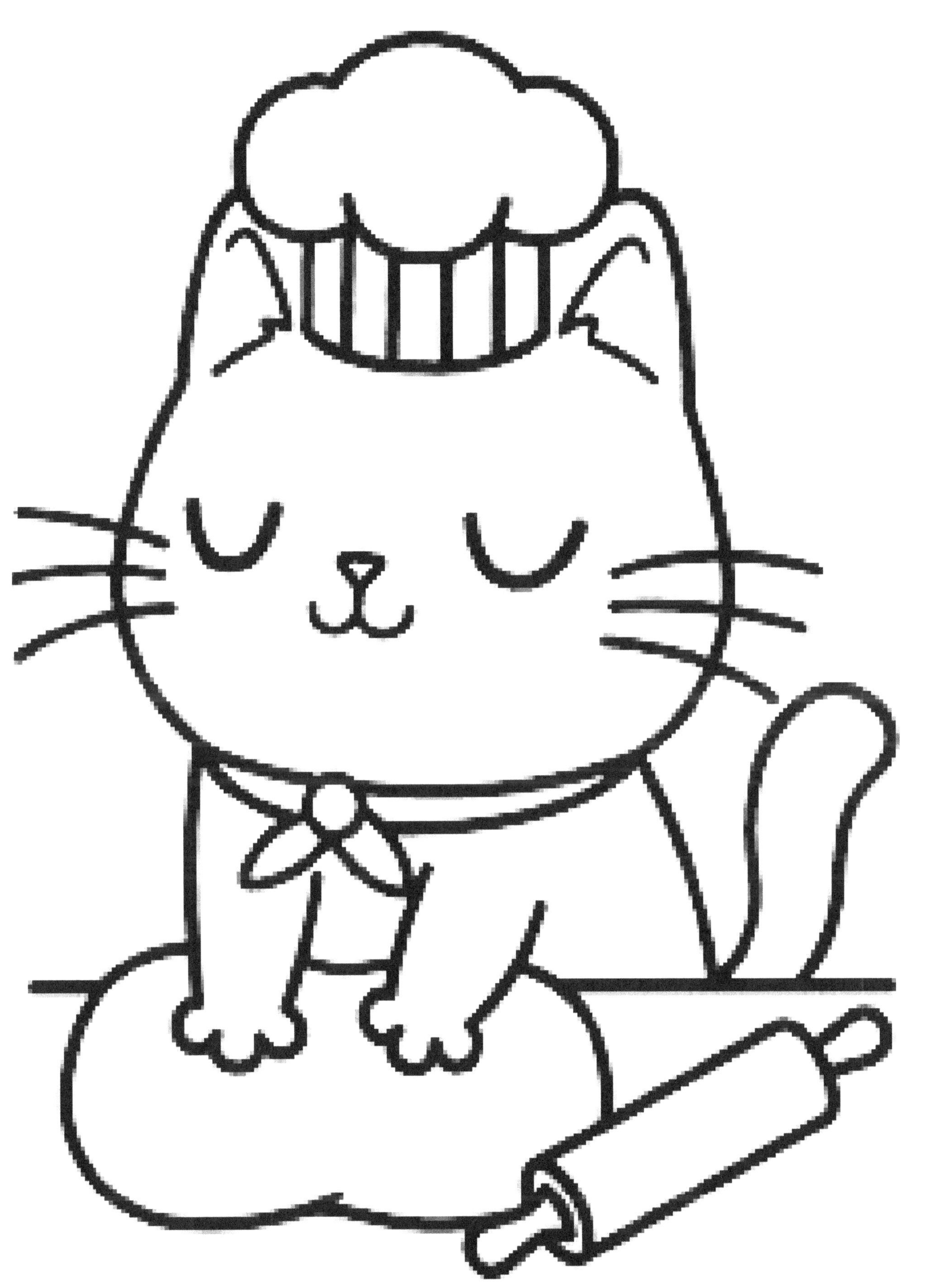

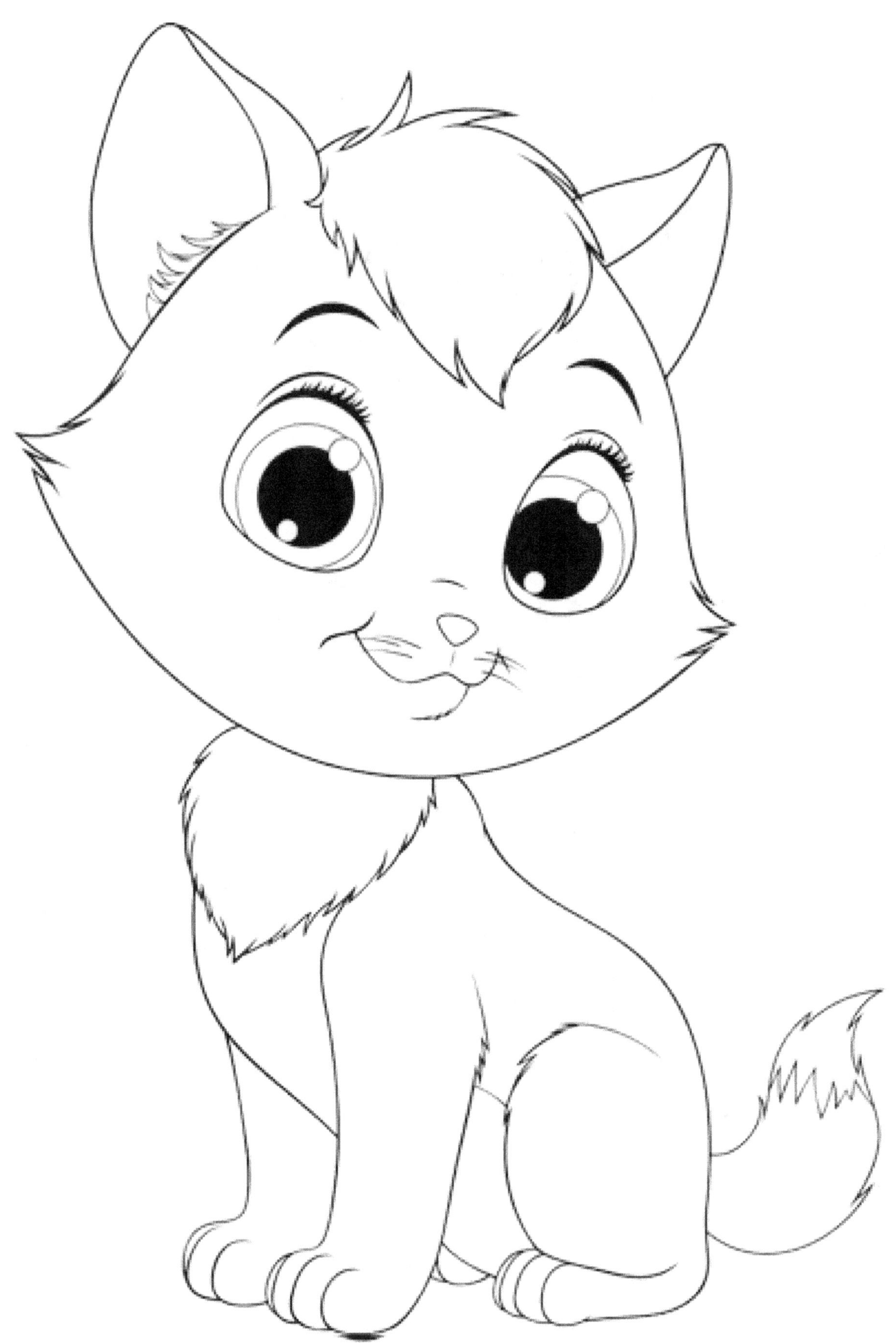

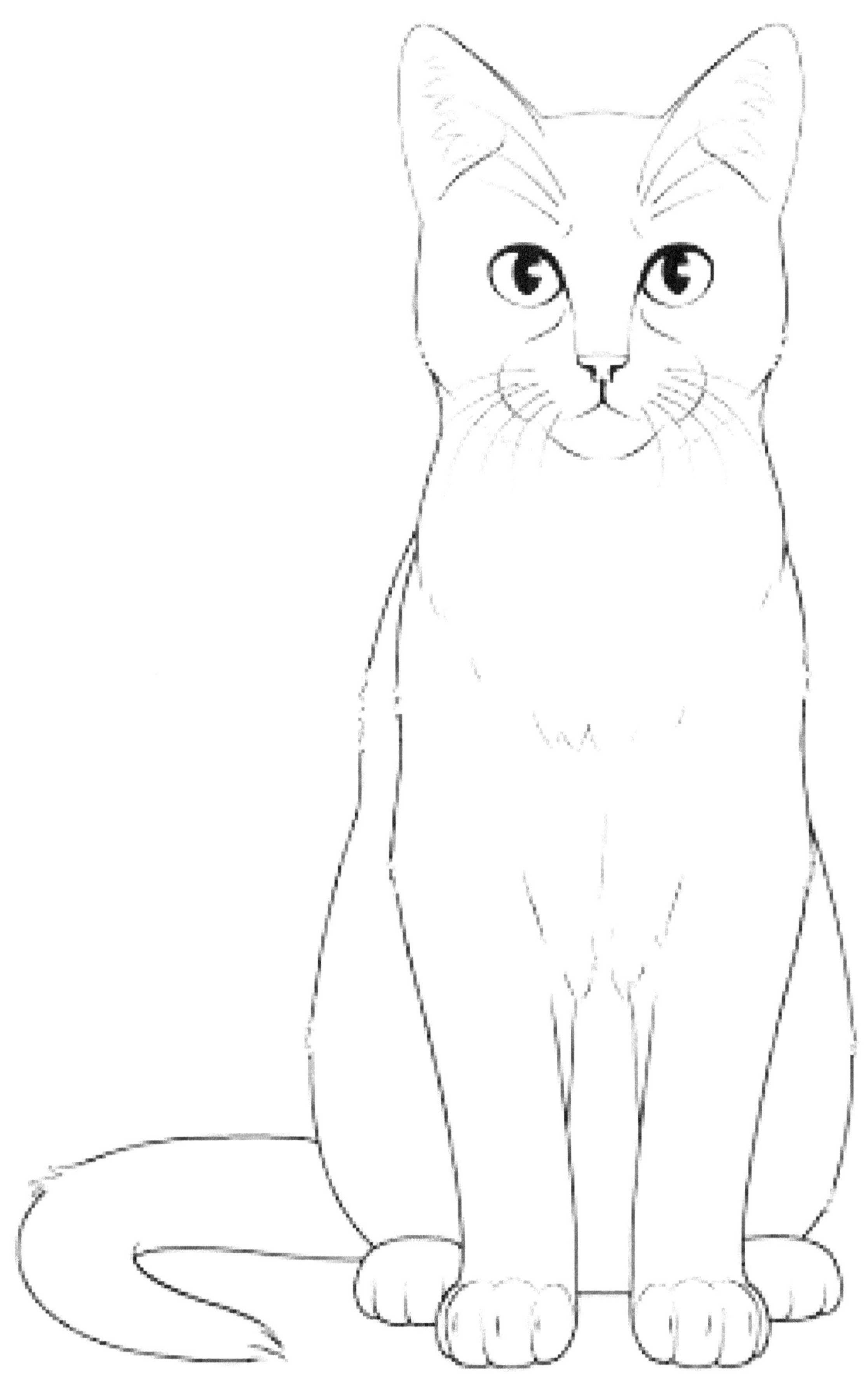

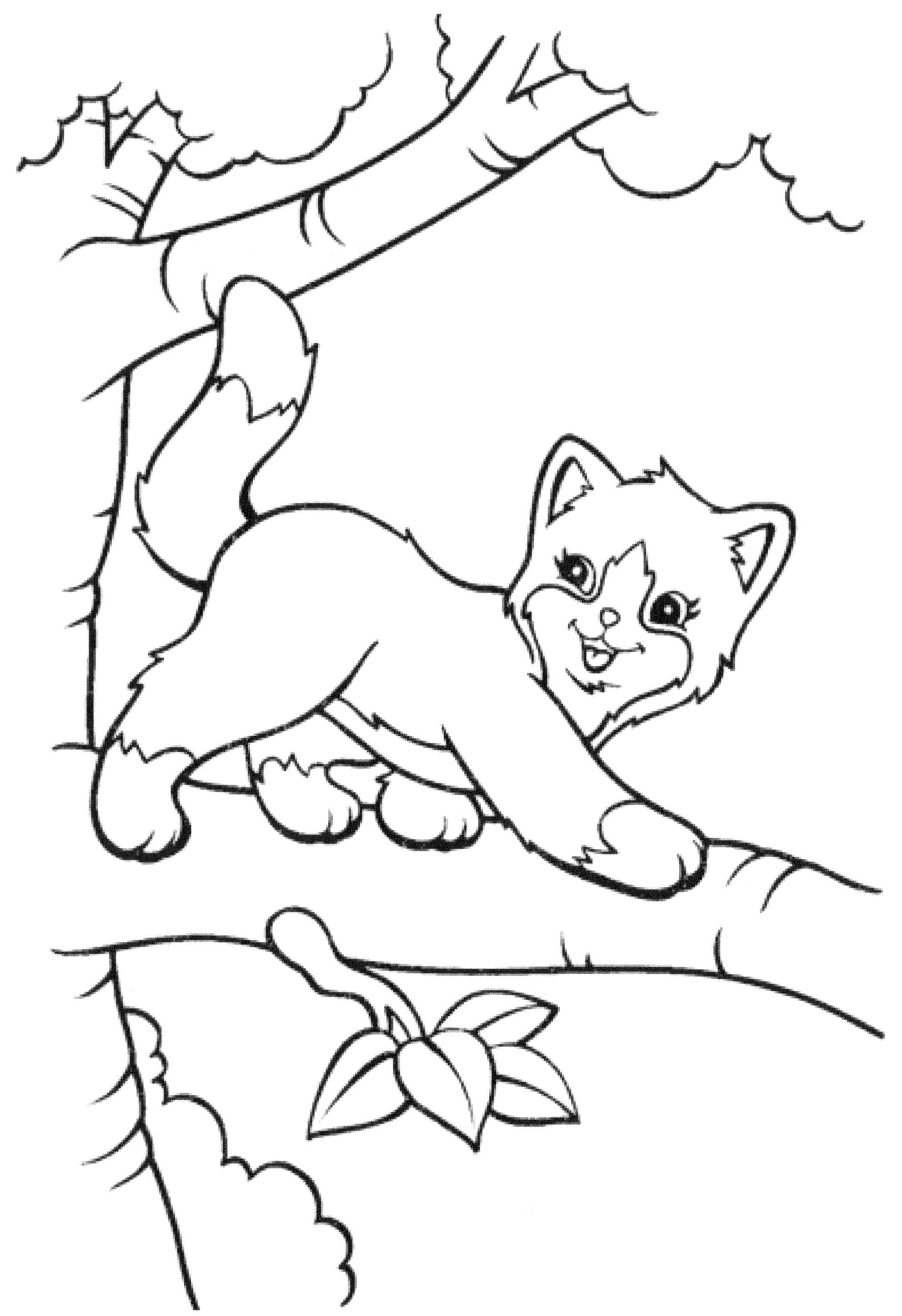

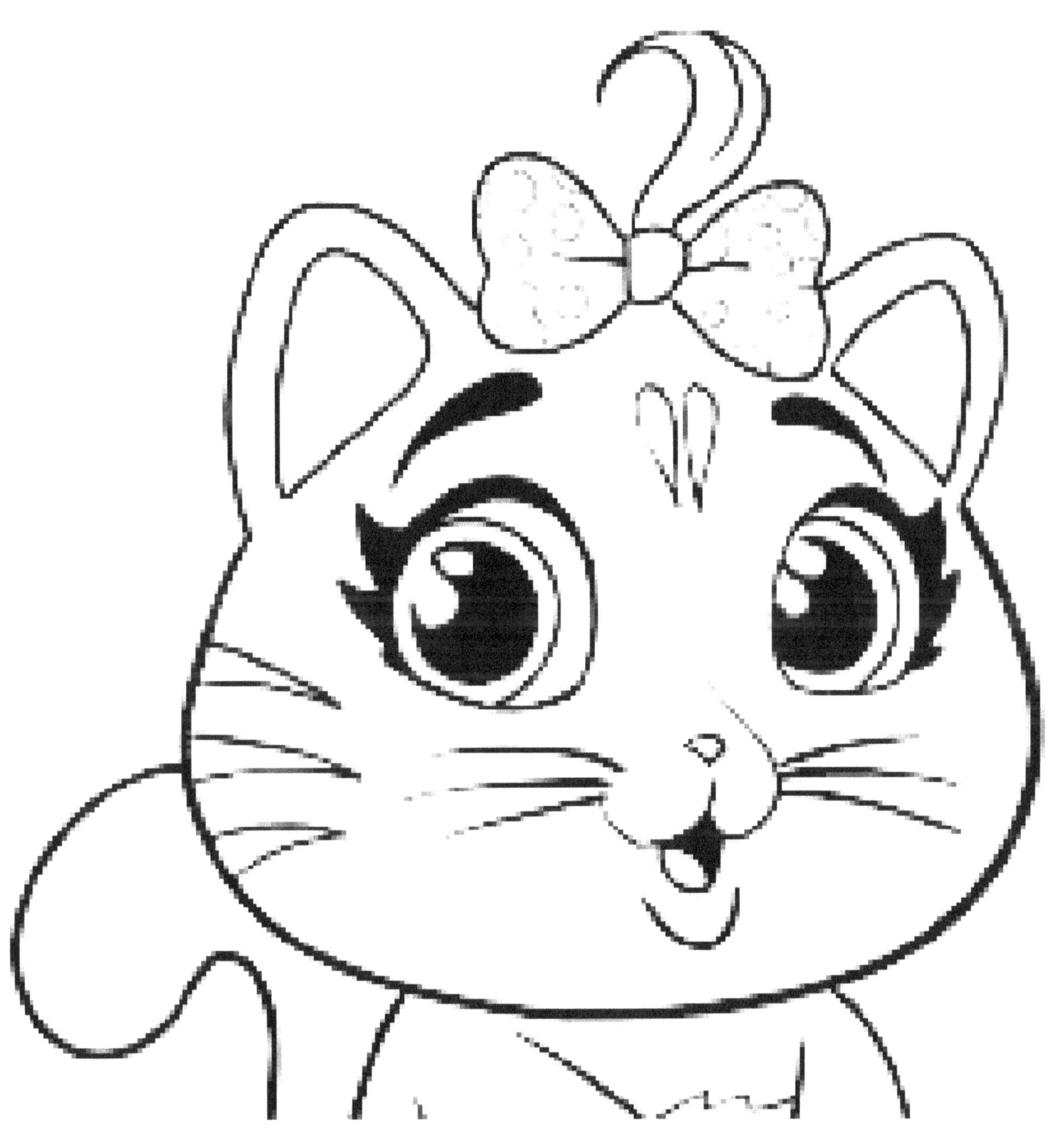

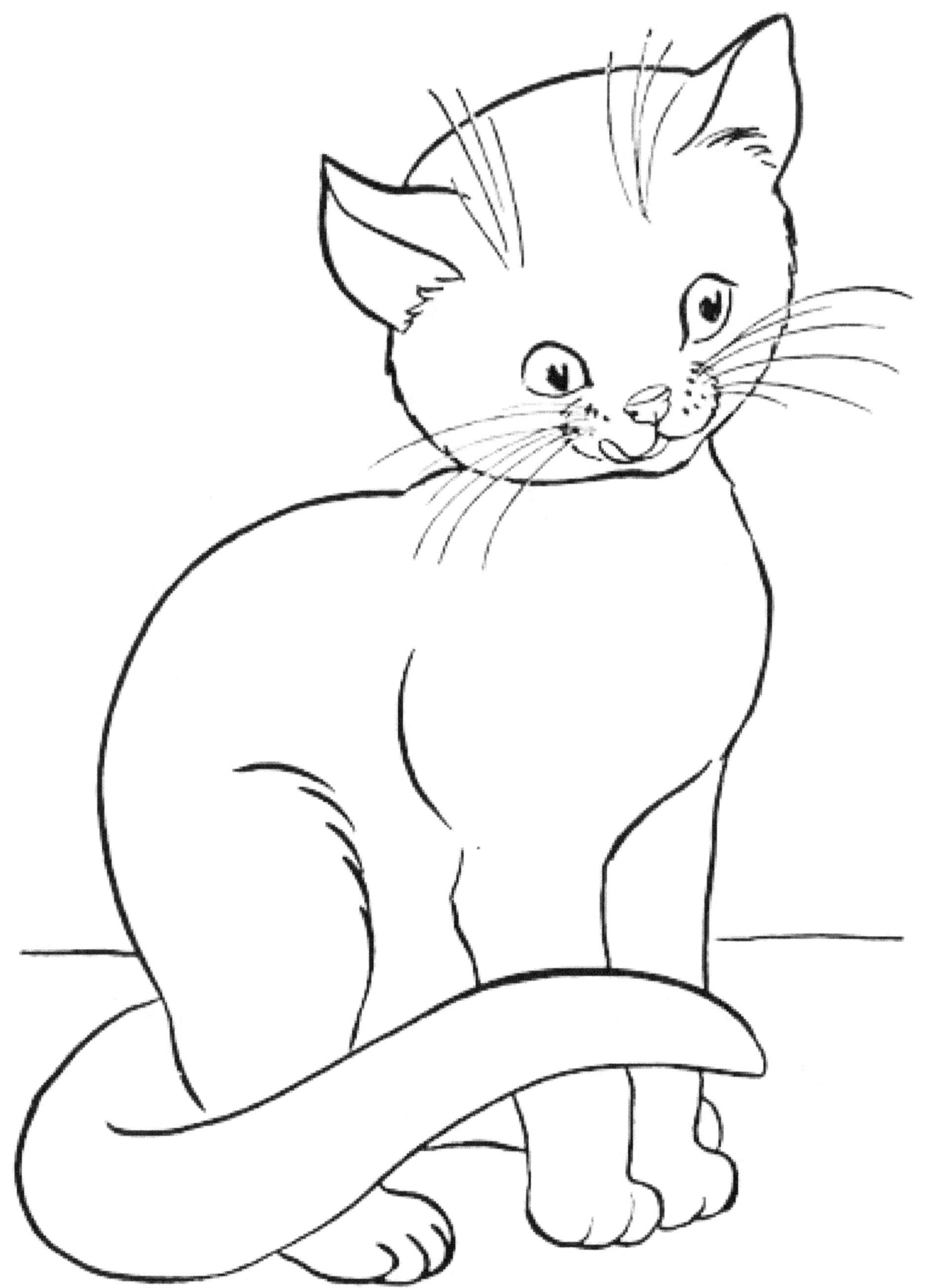

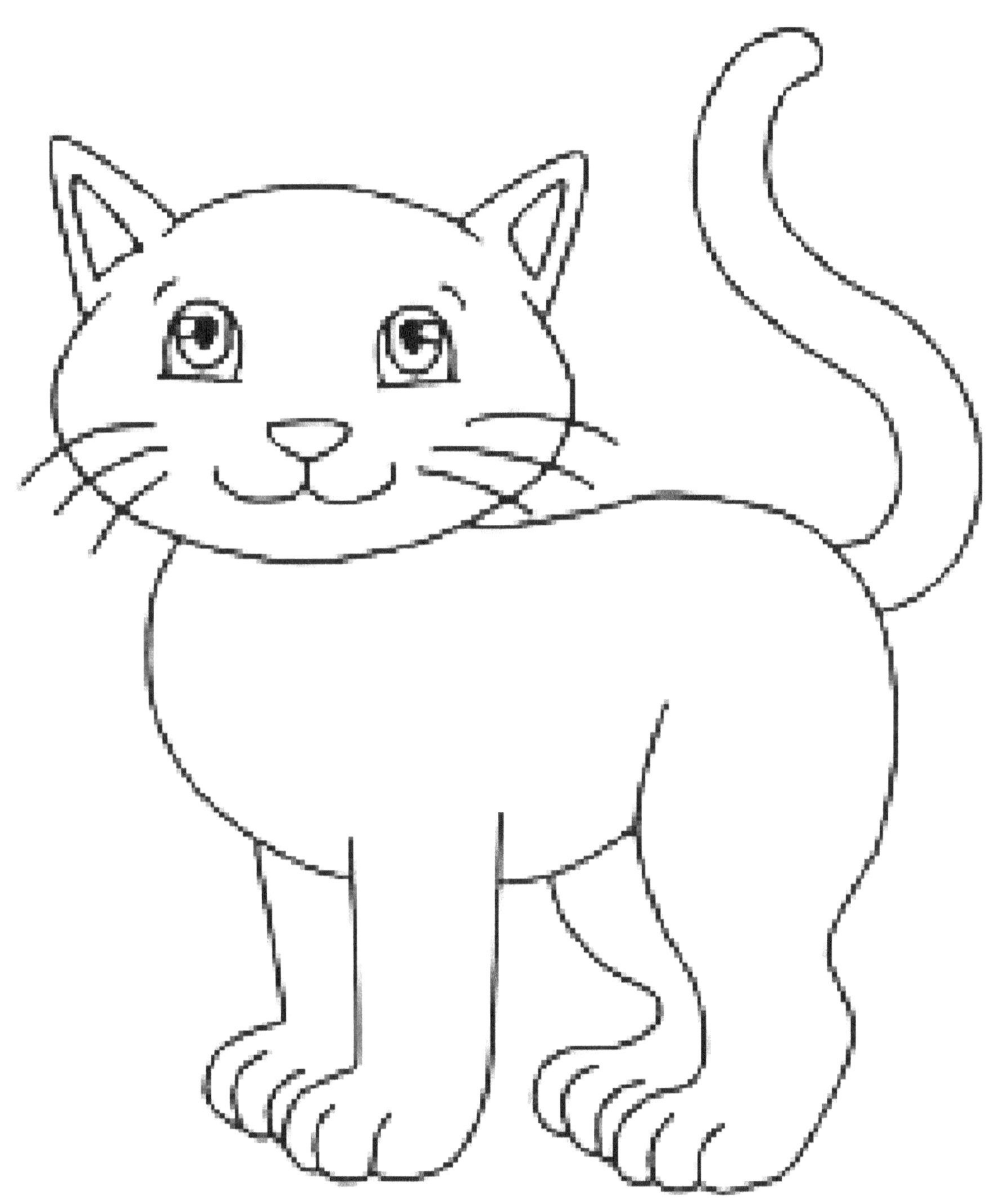

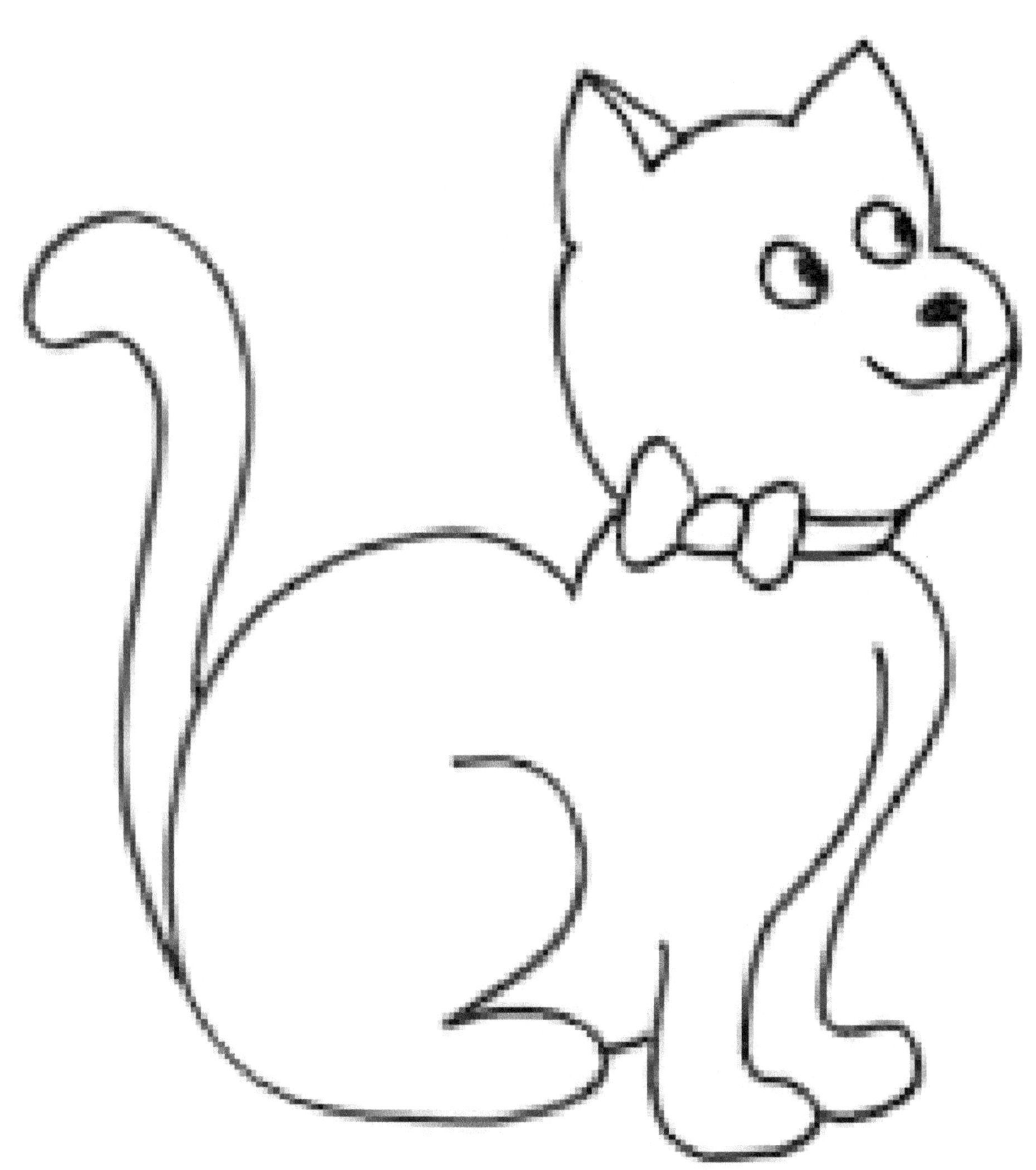

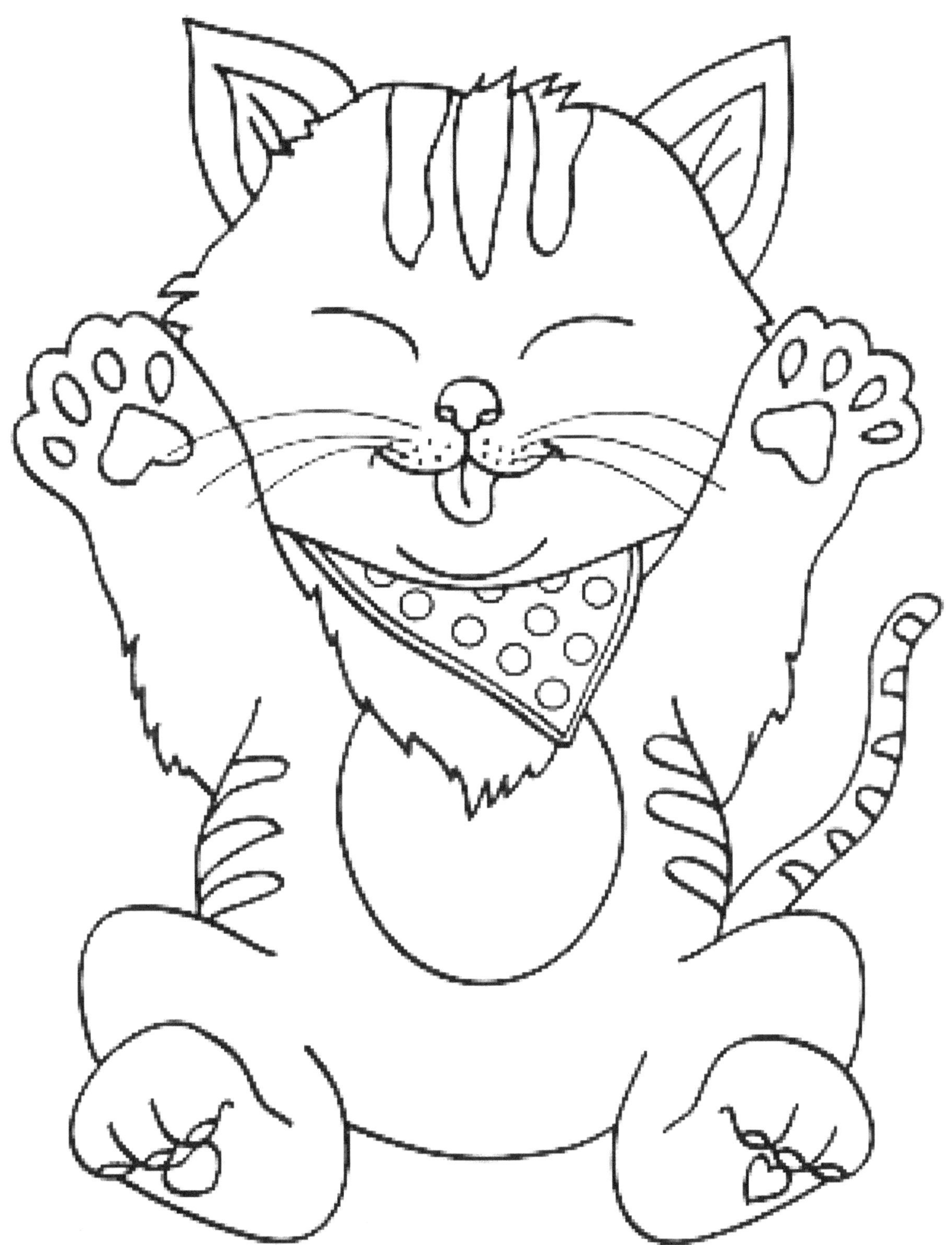

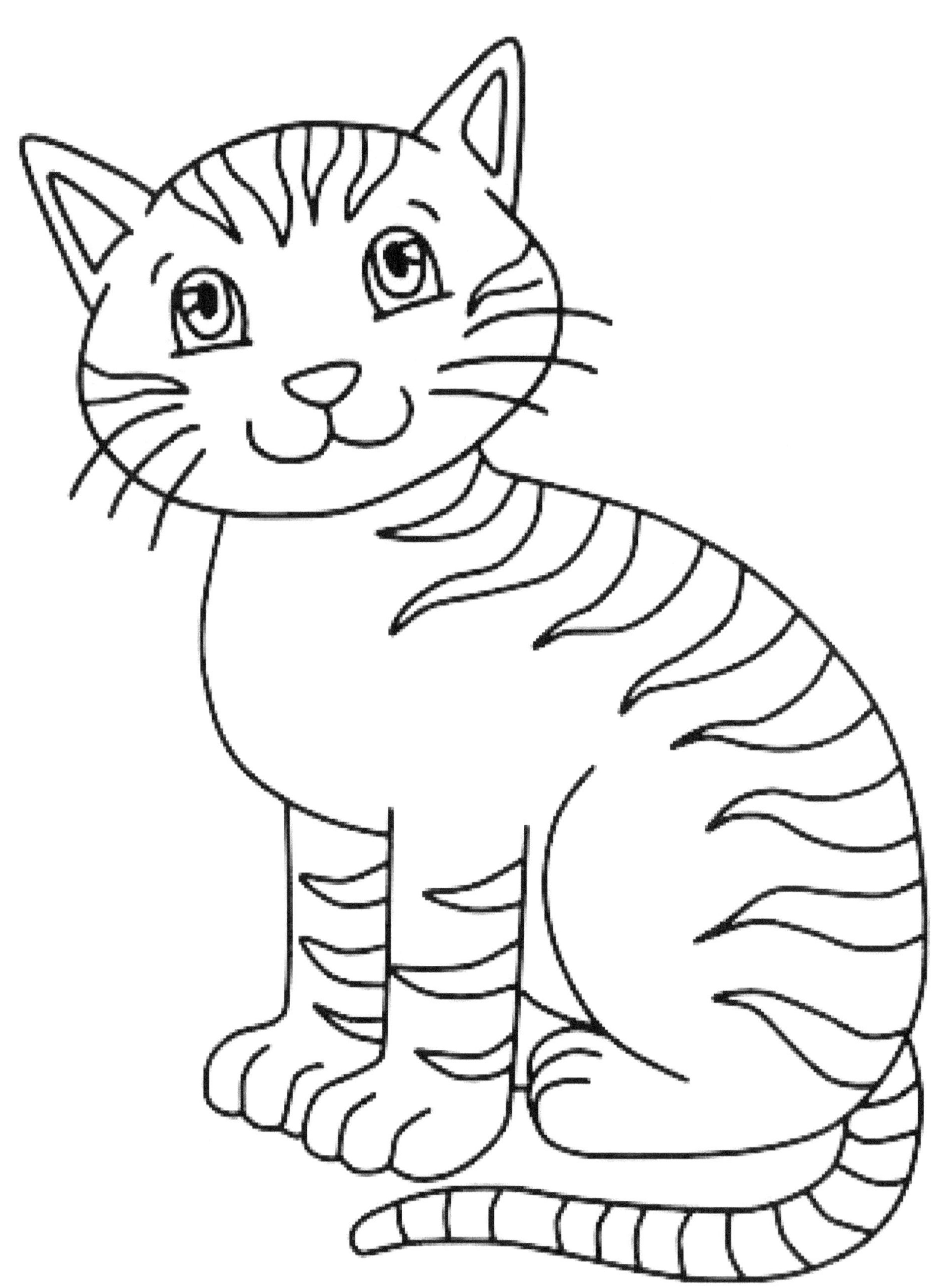

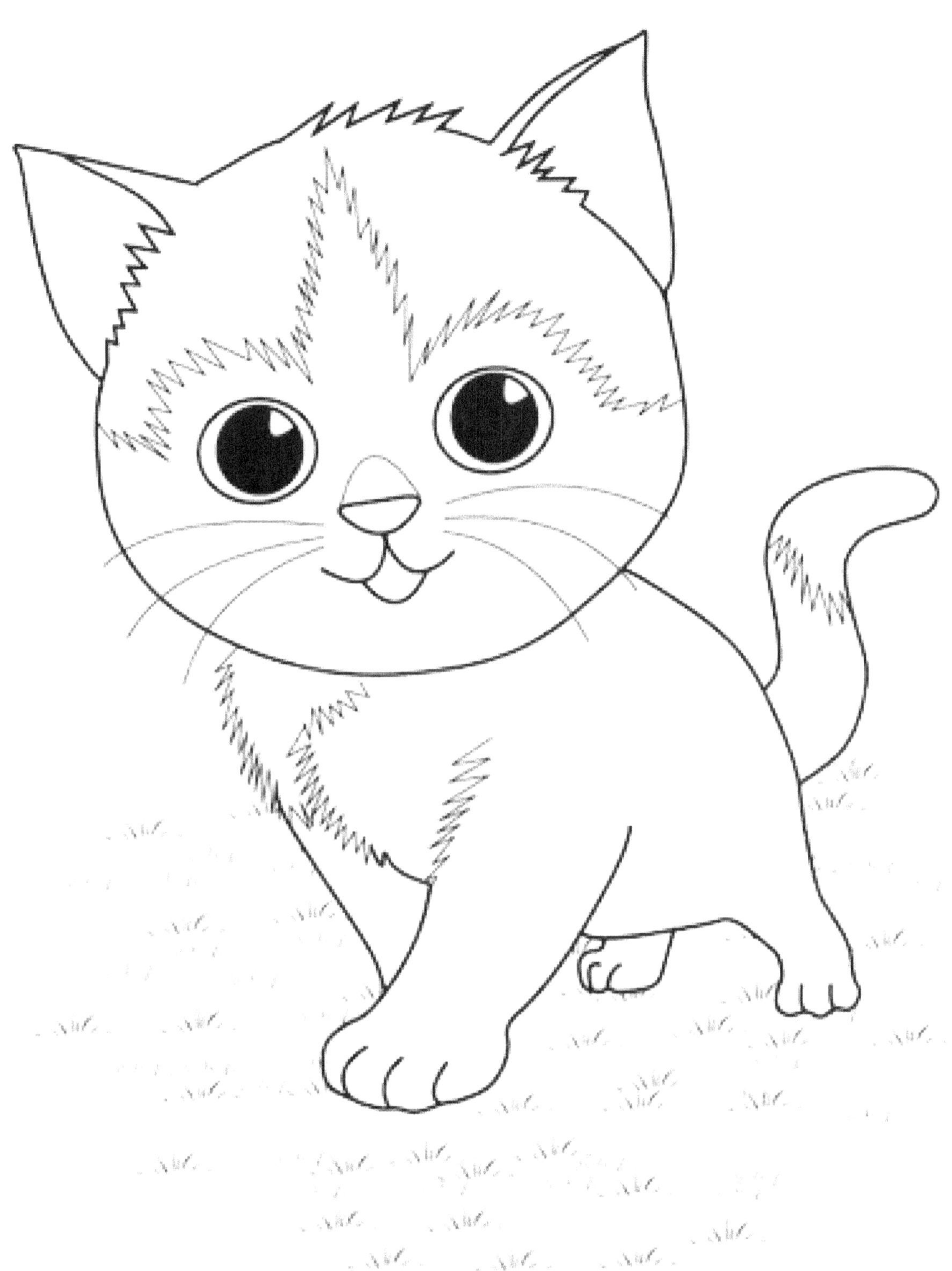

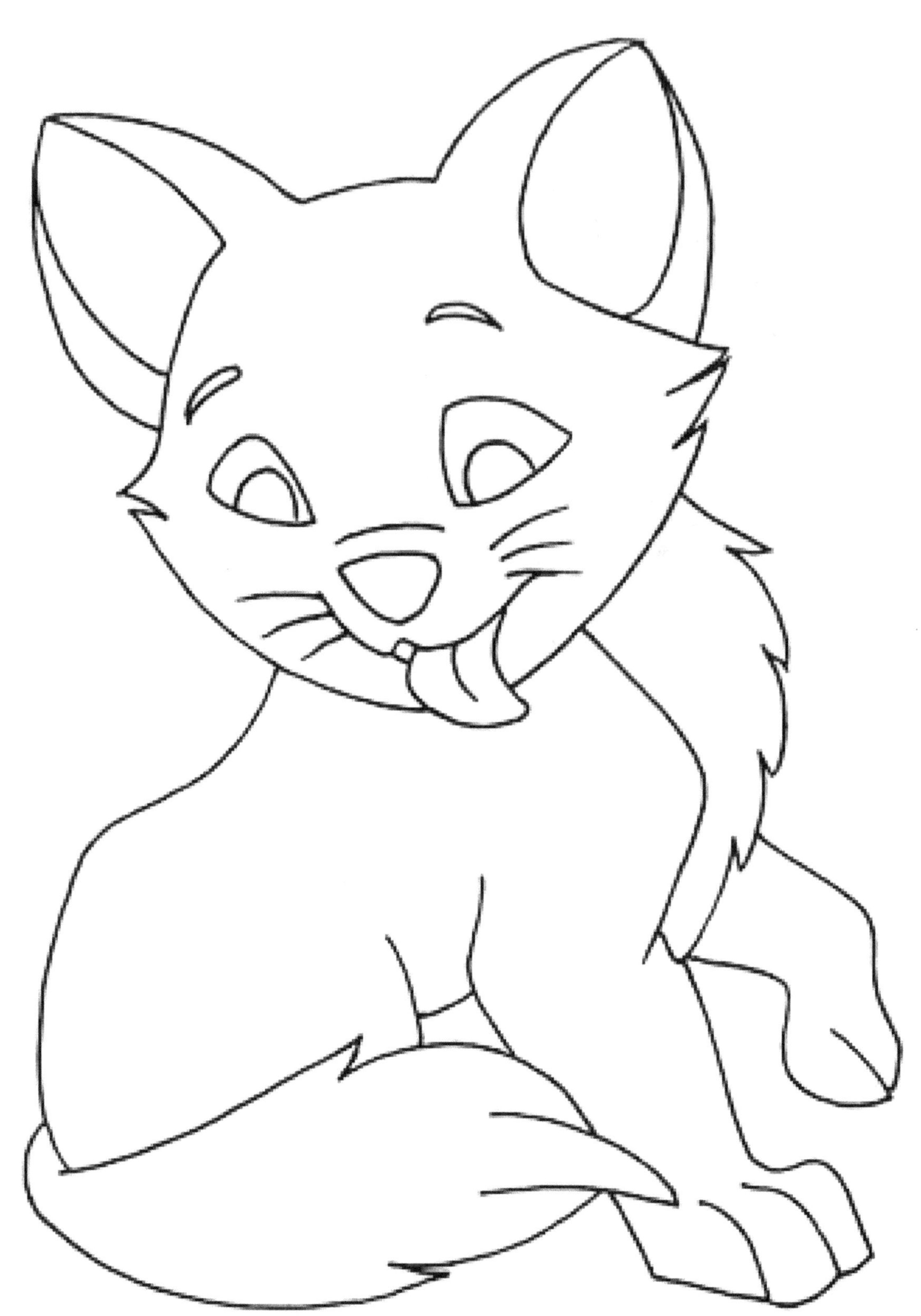